THE ART OF TEACHING SPANISH

THE ART OF TEACHING SPANISH

SECOND LANGUAGE ACQUISITION
FROM RESEARCH TO PRAXIS

RAFAEL SALABERRY &
BARBARA A. LAFFORD, Editors

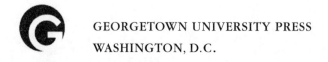

GEORGETOWN UNIVERSITY PRESS
WASHINGTON, D.C.

Georgetown University Press
Washington, D.C.

As of January 1, 2007, 13-digit ISBN numbers will replace the current 10-digit system.
Paperback: 978-1-58901-133-5

Georgetown University Press, Washington, D.C.

Library of Congress Cataloging-in-Publication Data

The art of teaching Spanish : second language acquisition from research to praxis / Rafael Salaberry and
Barbara A. Lafford, Editors.
    p. cm.
 Includes bibliographical references and index.
 ISBN 1-58901-133-3 (alk. paper)
 1. Spanish language—Study and teaching—Foreign speakers. 2. Second language acquisition.
I. Salaberry, M. Rafael. II. Lafford, Barbara Armstrong.
 PC4127.8.A825 2006
 468.0071—dc22

                                                                                          2006006685

13 12 11 10 09 08 07 06   9 8 7 6 5 4 3 2
First printing

Printed in the United States of America

To Julián, Lucas, and María José
—*Rafael Salaberry*

To the memory of Kathleen A. Glenn
(1923–2003),
beloved mother and friend

and to my husband, Peter,
for his unending love and support
—*Barbara A. Lafford*

CONTENTS

TABLES AND FIGURES

Tables

Figures

PREFACE

This book serves as a companion volume to *Spanish Second Language Acquisition: State of the Science*, coedited by Barbara Lafford and Rafael Salaberry and published in 2003 by Georgetown University Press. That work consisted of a critical review of the research done on the *products* and *processes* of Spanish second language acquisition (SLA). It was primarily intended as "a reference tool for second language acquisition researchers, graduate students in SLAT (second language acquisition and teaching) or linguistics programs, and practitioners and pedagogues who teach diverse second and foreign languages and want to keep up with current research trends in the field of SLA (with particular attention given to Spanish)."

This volume explores the extent to which the *art* of teaching L2 Spanish has been informed by the *scientific* (theoretical and empirical) research on SLA (and other relevant fields) referred to in the first volume. It also investigates the types of challenges that follow from initiatives to transfer findings from research to teaching and how to overcome practical problems associated with the implementation of new approaches to teaching.

This collection of contributions from respected SLA researchers and applied linguists is first and foremost a resource for foreign language practitioners and pedagogues wanting to benefit from the expertise of colleagues who have experience with the types of linguistic issues and applications treated by the authors—for example, FLAC (foreign language across the curriculum programs), various pedagogical approaches, the effect of study abroad versus classroom contexts on the learning process, testing issues, online learning, the incorporation of linguistic variation into the classroom, courses for heritage language learners, and the teaching of translation.

The increasing demographic visibility of Spanish speakers in the United States and the impact their presence has had on public policy have created a great demand for Spanish classes throughout our educational system, from primary-level bilingual programs to university-level and continuing education courses. In turn, this situation has generated a demand for courses for future teachers of Spanish at both the undergraduate and graduate levels on the application of Spanish SLA (and related) research to the classroom. This book, which brings together more different theoretically grounded perspectives on teaching Spanish than any other single published volume, could easily serve as a basic text in those courses.

As always, we owe a debt of gratitude to family, friends, and colleagues for their personal support and encouragement during this project. We would also like to express our gratitude to the reviewers (established publishing SLA scholars and applied linguists who must remain anonymous) of each of the chapters. Finally, we would like to acknowledge the assistance of Gail Grella of Georgetown University Press for her exceptional patience and wisdom regarding the preparation of this research project.

The State of the Art of Teaching Spanish
From Research to Praxis

Rafael Salaberry   *University of Texas–Austin*
Barbara Lafford   *Arizona State University*

This volume explores the extent to which the "art" of teaching of Spanish as a second language (L2) is informed by Spanish second language acquisition (SLA) research in particular and research on SLA and language-related fields (e.g., psycholinguistics, sociolinguistics) in general. It also investigates the types of challenges that accompany applied linguistics initiatives to transfer findings from research to teaching and how to overcome practical problems associated with the implementation of new approaches to teaching.

Some of the specific issues we asked the contributors to address in their chapters were the findings from Spanish SLA (and language-related) research that would be applicable to Spanish second language teaching (SLT), the theoretical frameworks that inform the research done and the extent to which the premises of those theories affect the application of the research findings to the teaching of Spanish, logistical factors that affect the way research findings can be applied to teach Spanish, and the extent to which findings from SLA research are explicitly represented in the Spanish curricula through objectives and goals (as evidenced in pedagogical materials such as textbooks and computer-assisted language learning, or CALL, software). Needless to say, no single chapter treats all of these questions in detail, but the reader does get answers to these questions from the combined contribution of the authors.

The reader will notice that a common theme running throughout all the chapters is the focus on bold pedagogical initiatives that can be substantiated by previous research but have not yet been incorporated into the majority of L2 Spanish curricula. Some of these proposals will have to withstand the test of time and additional research. We believe, however, that providing a venue for these ideas will further their discussion and positively affect the field of applied linguistics by engendering a more informed debate on Spanish SLA pedagogy. Our goal in this chapter is to provide a brief evaluative summary of the contents of all chapters in order to present an overall view of the state of the art of teaching Spanish as a reflection of second language acquisition and related research. To this end, in the following sections we present an evaluative summary of the content of each chapter. We invite the reader, however, to read each chapter individually to obtain a more comprehensive analysis of the topics addressed by chapter authors.

1.0 Chapter 2: A Content-Based Approach to Spanish Language Study

In their chapter, Klee and Barnes-Karol review the history, rationale, and pedagogical benefits of curricula that include Foreign Languages Across the Curriculum (FLAC), later termed Languages Across the Curriculum (LAC), courses. As the authors explain, FLAC courses provide learners with several benefits, among which they highlight the following: they enhance and expand specific disciplinary knowledge, they deepen the understanding of a given culture and its documents and artifacts, and they improve cross-cultural competence. According to Klee and Barnes-Karol, improvement in second language skills, while desired, is not necessarily a primary objective of FLAC courses.

The development of FLAC courses, the authors note, was prompted by several academic ventures, such as the writing across the curriculum movement of the 1970s and 1980s, the immersion school programs in Canada and the United States, and the implementation of Language for Special Purposes (LSP) programs. The advent of FLAC courses has been substantiated through important research strands in SLA studies. For instance, Klee and Barnes-Karol state that FLAC programs have been positively influenced by research findings from recent models of reading comprehension that emphasize the role of background knowledge and context on effective language use. Furthermore, current views on the multiple layers of competencies that make up a proficient speaker have also had an effect on developing knowledge about language-specific domains, including academic domains as they are represented in subject-matter courses. Finally, apart from specific research strands, the strategic effort of many universities to internationalize the curriculum has focused the attention of many faculty on the development of subject-specific language skills. Despite these favorable factors, however, FLAC courses face major strategic and institutional challenges. More important, Klee and Barnes-Karol believe that FLAC programs are unlikely to succeed over the long term unless they are embedded in a larger institutional context, they receive ongoing financial support, and they carefully match student L2 proficiency with program requirements and objectives.

It is possible that the underlying challenge of FLAC courses is that despite the avowed goal of giving students access to new perspectives on the subject matter, the courses are primarily focused on furthering the students' L2 development. In this respect, we underline the obvious: the traditional FLAC framework attempts to make a connection between two fairly distinct academic goals (i.e., language development and subject-matter development), but one of these goals may get the lion's share of attention and actual work. For instance, a subject in a FLAC course might be the history of colonial Caribbean nations with an emphasis on the Spanish colonies. In this hypothetical case, it is apparent that the connection between language development in Spanish and knowledge of the specific subject of history may be contrived—until the link between language and content area brings these areas more closely in line with each other.

We tentatively propose that a possible solution to this constraint would be to match up FLAC trailer sections with main subject areas that can be easily linked with language awareness and language use topics. For instance, most universities (large and small) offer several content-based courses that include language as one of their main topics of inquiry: sociolinguistics, first and second language learning, history of

Spanish, language planning and policies, and, obviously, courses in literature (although, for a FLAC course, not necessarily entirely in the second language). A second tier of courses also related to language inquiry, but less directly, include those on political philosophy, formal logic, general philosophy, and so on. Such courses would likely attract students interested in developing their language skills as well as their knowledge in the specific content area. In all the above-mentioned courses, language inquiry or the role of language in communication is the natural focus of analysis of the main course that is to be accompanied by a FLAC course. Odds are that students interested in language-related courses such as those mentioned above are the ones who would be likely to go the extra mile to tackle these two related but separate goals: second language development and subject matter understanding.

There is an additional strategic factor that may compromise the viability of a FLAC-enhanced curriculum. Despite the intended goal of expanding the focus of the subject matter in a second language, the apparent lack of continuity and support of FLAC courses described by Klee and Barnes-Karol brings up important questions: Is it possible that students perceive that their academic objectives can be more easily attained by avoiding FLAC courses and concentrating on the subject matter in English only? In other words, why would students sacrifice a more expeditious treatment and analysis of the subject matter in a language in which they are already proficient for a more laborious, time-consuming analysis of the same topic in a second language?

Finally, the focus on strictly language-oriented courses may be of interest to faculty as well. As noted by Klee and Barnes-Karol, FLAC courses are highly dependent on access to supplemental funding and adequate and extended curriculum support within and across departments. Unless instructors are compensated and/or substantially recognized in performance reviews for their extra effort devoted to these courses, the only other incentive that faculty will have to offer a FLAC course is to find some inherent pedagogical or research benefit in FLAC-oriented courses. Lack of continuous funding or course compensation clearly shows that FLAC courses can only be successful or, at a minimum, be offered to students as long as faculty find those courses relevant to their own teaching/research agendas. Therefore, the factor most likely to generate such interest among language faculty would be the focus of language development concurrently with subject matter development.

2.0 Chapter 3: Spanish SLA Research, Classroom Practice, and Curriculum Design

Collentine reviews and critiques three general lines of research that have had a major impact on how we design a second language curriculum through pedagogical tasks. The lines of research reviewed in his chapter are: (1) the general learning theory of constructivism, (2) psycholinguistics and cognition, and (3) social and sociocultural cognition. His view is that all these approaches have contributed important insights to the debates over the applications of SLA research to teaching.

Constructivist approaches emphasize the power of learner-centered inductive learning processes (e.g., from data to generalizations) that stand in contrast with the mostly deductive processes of teacher-centered approaches (e.g., rules are presented and then applied). Collentine argues that the main tenet of constructivism (i.e., learners must be active agents in the knowledge acquisition processing) is represented in many well-known pedagogical and institutional proposals, such as Krashen's *i*+1 hypothesis, the relevance of interpersonal communication in oral proficiency interviews, and, more important, the concept of task-based instruction.

Cognitive perspectives are not necessarily opposed to the constructivist view on acquisition, although their analysis focuses on an input-output metaphor of language development, that sometimes (although not always) leaves out the effect of social factors (beyond the simple give and take of strictly linguistic interactions). For instance, in contrast with one of the popular movements of the 1980s (i.e., Krashen's acquisition-learning hypothesis), Schmidt (1990) asserted that for input to become intake for the developing L2 grammar, the provision of input alone was not enough; learners needed to "notice" important formal properties of the L2. One of the important trends that grew out of this claim (or that paralleled it) is the notion of the focus on form (as opposed to forms), a notion that entails reactive interventions to breakdowns in comprehension that encourage the noticing of some linguistic feature such as verbal endings. Collentine points out that cognitive perspectives have contributed significantly to a better understanding of the development of a second language. For instance, there has emerged a general understanding that complex constructs are not acquired all at once in their entirety; rather, they emerge in stages (e.g., *ser/estar*, preterite/imperfect). Similarly, the recognition that some grammatical constructs require a multilayered description, as in the case of past tense marking in Spanish (i.e., semantic, discursive, etc.), has changed preterit/imperfect instruction, specially with regard to approaches to the teaching of how to tell stories.

On the other hand, there have been several critiques of strictly cognitive perspectives: (1) noticing and intake in communicative tasks foster morphosyntactic and grammatical development essentially by chance and are extremely time-consuming, (2) complex linguistic phenomena may require different methodological interventions from relatively simple linguistic phenomena, and (3) a strictly cognitive perspective may focus on a narrow conceptualization of language that omits not only strictly social factors but also discursive contextual factors. As Collentine argues, for example, the argument that language accuracy decreases as attention on meaning increases (e.g., VanPatten 1990) needs to be qualified, given both theoretical and empirical questions. More specifically, from a theoretical point of view, there are many grammatical items such as tense–aspect morphology that are very much dependent on the meaning of the discursive context (Andersen and Shirai 1994; Bardovi-Harlig 2000; Salaberry 2003). As such, their accuracy in narrative tasks may actually be higher when attention to meaning is as necessary as attention to form (Salaberry and López-Ortega 1998). Furthermore, while pointing out methodological shortcomings in previous studies, Dussias (2003) raises additional questions about a clear-cut distinction between the empirical effects of the competition of attention for form or meaning.

Finally, Collentine points out that within sociocultural theory, "language processing and production is not a reflection but rather a mediator of thought." As a consequence, the goal of instructed SLA should be to treat L2 learning as an additional cognitive tool (e.g., private speech) along with L1 (primary language) processing. More important, as argued by Collentine, "sociocultural theory privileges the role of output in that it rejects the premise that communication is reflected in the standard communication theory metaphor." Collentine argues that sociocultural theory "has not necessarily led to the design of sociocultural-specific teaching strategies and curricular design." On the other hand, it has validated (or reconceptualized) the role of well-known pedagogical activities such as language games, problem-solving tasks, and cooperative learning activities (for an example, see Negueruela and Lantolf, this volume). One important area of research within sociocultural theory, yet to be explored in detail, is the role of language development in the midst of intensive social interactions in an L2-speaking environment as represented in study-abroad programs (and, to some extent, on at-home immersion programs).

3.0 Chapter 4: Theoretical and Research Considerations Underlying Classroom Practice

VanPatten and Leeser investigate the role of input in the second language acquisition process and the theoretical and research considerations underlying classroom practice. The authors argue that SLA researchers (from universal grammar proponents to connectionists) generally accept the notion that input is the primary ingredient necessary for the construction of an underlying L2 grammatical system. However, input alone does not lead to acquisition. Learners must process the input in meaningful ways in order for it to be useful for the construction of the L2 system. The authors contend that pedagogues must ask how they can facilitate the learner's processing of input so that it is converted to intake and becomes integrated into the learner's interlanguage system. Therefore, the goal of effective language instruction would be to have the learner focus on form (attention is given to grammatical form within a communicative, meaningful context) in the input. In order to facilitate this noticing of new grammatical forms, instructors and materials authors must find ways to enhance the input. VanPatten and Leeser then discuss the pedagogical implications of the research on several different methods of textual enhancement: text enhancement, input flood, input/output cycles, structured input, and recasts.

Textual enhancement (TE) is defined as "typographical alterations of grammatical form or structures in a reading passage." VanPatten and Leeser point out that although TE is easy to implement, it only facilitates noticing of the new grammatical forms by the learner. It does not directly aid in the actual linguistic processing of those forms (the connecting of forms to a meaning or function). Input flood occurs when "instructors and/or materials developers provide lots of instances of a particular linguistic item in oral or written text." The authors report that although the research has shown that this technique may help learners understand what is possible in the language, it does not assist their comprehension of what is not possible, that is, the input flood provides positive evidence but not direct negative evidence for the construction of L2 grammatical systems. The third method, input/output cycle, is implemented when learners reading or listening to texts have to reconstruct or summarize them in some way. The authors briefly discuss the potential roles for output hypothesized by Swain (1995): the noticing/triggering function, the hypothesis testing function, and the metalinguistic function. Part of Swain's output hypothesis implies that learners who are forced to express themselves more accurately will be more likely to notice linguistic data in the input (the noticing/triggering hypothesis).

The concept of structured input (SI), favored by the authors, is based on the assumption that the "input can be manipulated in particular ways to push students to (1) replace incorrect processing strategies with correct (or better) strategies and (2) make better form-meaning connections in the input." Part of the pedagogical benefit claimed for the processing instruction hypothesis is that, as VanPatten and Leeser state, "assisting comprehension is consonant with the processes involved in acquisition, that is, comprehension is a precursor to acquisition." Unlike Krashen's view, however, the processing instruction hypothesis includes an explicit instructional effect given that students are "to be confronted with a mismatch between what they are observing and what they think they are hearing." Finally, the authors describe the benefits of recasts, a pedagogical technique in which the instructor spontaneously reformulates a student's incorrect utterance. Due to the fact that they occur in real time, recasts may not be uniformly applied and thus may not be as effective in regular classroom interactions as they have been found to be in laboratory research. Furthermore, complicating the effectiveness of recasts for eliciting learner self-correction is the fact that some learners fail to perceive recasts (interlocutor reformulations of their speech) as corrective feedback.

VanPatten and Leeser favor structured input activities over the other pedagogical techniques they review. For instance, they claim that "input/output cycles may suffer from the same problem as TE and input flood; they increase chances that learners may notice something but they do not guarantee it and they do not ensure that if learners notice something, they notice what the instructor intends for them to notice." In contrast, VanPatten and Leeser argue that structured input activities avoid this limitation because SI is based on the manipulation of the input presented to the learner and as such it requires "forced processing of the form" being targeted. Ironically, this proposed advantage of structured input activities (and processing instruction in general) over the other teaching techniques involves a significant trade-off: structured input activities are, by definition, teacher-centered activities, and as such they do not give students the benefits afforded by learner-centered tasks (the latter are discussed in more detail in Collentine, this volume). This is the major pedagogical conundrum faced by proponents of processing instruction. We hasten to add that the use of learner-centered activities *in addition to* SI activities in actual classroom practice, although justified from a pedagogical point of view, cannot be used to counteract the limitation of SI as a teacher-centered pedagogical technique.

That is, the additional set of learner-based activities introduces a new variable to the research design, thereby significantly modifying the theoretical construct under investigation.

There is also a significant theoretical gap in the proposed advantage of structured input activities. More important, we note that the role that VanPatten and Cadierno (1993) attributed to output processing (which they operationalized as traditional instruction) in their theoretical model is qualitatively different from the one they assigned to input processing. In their first study, VanPatten and Cadierno (1993) were faced with the fact (and dilemma for their analysis) that their traditional instruction group showed improvements in the production task but not the comprehension task, whereas their input processing group improved in both the comprehension and production tasks. VanPatten and Cadierno stated that "this is problematic in that to perform a language task, one must have some kind of knowledge" (238). Thus they argued for two different types of knowledge underlying the benefits shown by each one of their treatment groups: input processing leads to acquisition, whereas "traditional instruction results in a different knowledge system" that does "not provide intake for the developing system." More specifically, VanPatten and Cadierno argued that "explicit practice and negative evidence are not usable by the [language] module. Explicit practice and negative evidence can result in what she [Schwartz] calls learned linguistic knowledge" (238). As a consequence, VanPatten and Cadierno explicitly proposed that their study constitutes confirmatory evidence for the learning-acquisition distinction. The problem is that in all studies that have investigated processing instruction effects, the processing instruction group has always received negative evidence. In this respect, input- or output-based activities are no different from each other at least with reference to Schwartz's model. This theoretical inconsistency was voiced early on by Salaberry (1997) and Carroll (2001) but has yet to be addressed by VanPatten.

Processing instruction research has also suffered from important research methodological shortcomings. Salaberry (1997) argued that the methodological problem of the research design of the studies supporting processing instruction "is that their results show interaction effects between their proposed treatment variable—input or output practice—and one or more intervening factors." It is not difficult to see what some sources of additional variation are, considering that some researchers have been very candid about the limitations of their research design. For instance, Cadierno (1995), a study frequently cited as empirical evidence to support processing instruction, acknowledged two additional variables in her operationalization of the treatment conditions: (1) differential degrees of emphasis on meaning, and (2) the sequential versus the paradigmatic presentation of past tense verbal morphology. Cadierno justified this difference by pointing out that "this variation as to the types of activities is a direct reflection of what is commonly presented in Spanish textbooks" (190). Cadierno's characterization of traditional teaching practice may be accurate, but such statement does not invalidate the concern about possible confounding of treatment variables in the research design of her study. For similar critiques of other studies cited in favor of processing instruction research, we refer the reader to DeKeyser et al. (2002).

4.0 Chapter 5: Concept-Based Instruction and the Acquisition of L2 Spanish

The research on tense–aspect development in L2 acquisition in general and Spanish in particular and the basic theoretical claims of sociocultural theory were presented in detail in chapters 2 and 9 (respectively) of Lafford and Salaberry (2003). In this volume, Negueruela and Lantolf bring to bear the methodological framework of sociocultural theory for the analysis of the development of the concept of tense–aspect marking in L2 Spanish. The motivation to study tense aspect in Spanish is given by the fact that in Vygotskyan approaches to SLA, there is a "dialectical connection between instruction and development that coheres in conceptual knowledge." Negueruela and Lantolf are thus intrigued by the fact that "grammatical explanations found in the vast majority of current Spanish textbooks consist by and large of incomplete and unsystematic rules of thumb" that would hardly lead to a substantial redeployment of the conceptual apparatus already instantiated in the L1.

Negueruela and Lantolf contextualize their argument with data from a previous study from Negueruela. The data were collected among twelve students enrolled in an intermediate-advanced university course in Spanish grammar and composition (sixth semester of study). The focus of the study was the analysis of the evolution of the conceptual understanding of tense–aspect phenomena in Spanish. As Negueruela and Lantolf explain, the "key task for the learner is not so much to master the suffixes, but to understand the meaning potential made available by the concept of aspect and to learn to manipulate this in accordance with particular communicative intentions." For that to happen, the authors argue that the learner needs to understand how tense and aspect are marked in their native language and only then, eventually, the learner's task is to internalize "new or reorganizing already existing concepts." We note that an important methodological as well as pedagogical aspect of sociocultural approaches is the emphasis on the use of the students' native language as one nonexclusive medium that acts as a psychological tool during intrapersonal communication.

Negueruela and Lantolf argue further that L2 development is conceived as the reorganization of consciousness through instruction. They propose that the "key to the development of conceptual understanding of grammar is the construction of appropriate didactic models that learners can use to guide their performance and ultimately internalize as a means of regulating their meaning-making ability in the L2." One of the important findings of Negueruela's study was the fact that conceptual development of complex grammatical concepts takes a long time. This is important not only from the perspective of research methodology but also from a pedagogical point of view. For instance, instructors and program administrators often engage in wishful thinking when they assume that the titles of the courses they teach accurately reflect the knowledge that students have attained (e.g., beginning, intermediate, advanced).

We turn now to the discussion of three crucial points of debate in pedagogical applications of SLA theory that Negueruela and Lantolf's chapter successfully brings to the attention of the reader: the representational nature of knowledge about tense–aspect concepts, the contrast between learner-based pedagogical activities and teacher-based activities, and the psycholinguistic and developmental value of so-called "rules of thumb." Regarding the first point, we note that the theoretical description of the meaning of tense–aspect systems varies according to the specific construct favored by different researchers. For instance, strictly linguistic approches such as minimalism tend to discount pragmatic factors from the representation of tense–aspect knowledge (e.g., coercion), whereas others tend to take into account the discursive and nonlinguistic context as well (see Salaberry and Ayoun 2005 for a discussion). In this respect, it is not entirely clear that rules of thumb (whether or not accurate) are irrelevant or useless during the development of grammatical concepts such as aspect. In particular, we note that the majority of theoretical proposals (e.g., lexical aspect, constructionism, default past tense values) tend to favor a system that becomes increasingly more sophisticated by means of a constant refinement of the prevailing learner's hypothesis at any given moment (cf. rules of thumb) through a process of accretion of the L2 database.

With respect to the second point, learner-centered versus teacher-centered instruction, Negueruela and Lantolf argue that "CBI supports explicit instruction in grammar to promote learner's awareness and control over specific conceptual categories as they are linked to formal properties of the language." Although in their analysis the authors emphasize the need to counteract the misleading rules of thumb provided by textbook explanations through teacher-created didactic charts, we note that they also make the point that verbalizations (i.e., the mechanism through which internalization takes place) represent an inherently learner-centered pedagogical procedure that is very much in line with the tenets of constructivism (see Collentine, this volume). This is not surprising given that sociocultural theory tends to favor activities that are very much learner-centered approaches to learning. For instance, as Negueruela and Lantolf point out, socio-cultural theory assigns a central role to learners' verbalizations of the concepts as well as verbalizations of learners' explanations of their oral and written performances mediated by concept diagrams and other tools.

Finally, we would like to point out that there is a great deal of variation among both teachers and textbooks in terms of how the concept of aspect is presented to students. Notwithstanding the main point made by Negueruela and Lantolf, that "explanations that Spanish students receive are based on incomplete simplifications of grammatical rules derived from textbooks," we believe that second language teaching best practices may not be too far off the mark. Indeed, practicing second language methodologists have not been reluctant to point out socio- and psycholinguistically valid ways of teaching aspect (Blyth 1997, 2005), as in the case of discourse-based conceptualizations of aspect (e.g., foreground versus background). In fact, as Collentine argues in his chapter, a discourse-based presentation of aspectual morphology is not necessarily rare in textbooks more recent than the ones selected by Negueruela and Lantolf for their analysis. The outstanding question, as Collentine adds, is whether these new narrative-based approaches have had any impact on the learning of aspectual distinctions. As of today we have no empirical research data on which to form an opinion.

AH → At home contexts
SA → Study abroad

5.0 Chapter 6: The Effects of Study Abroad and Classroom Contexts on the Acquisition of Spanish as a Second Language

In their chapter, Lafford and Collentine review research that has been carried out on the acquisition of Spanish in study-abroad and classroom contexts. Their review has two main purposes. First, they comment on methodological factors that constrain the generalizability of the empirical findings of previous studies, and second, they discuss in detail possible programmatic and classroom applications emanating from their analysis of the previous research on this topic.

Lafford and Collentine show that, by and large, previous research confirms old assumptions about the benefit of study-abroad experiences on the SLA process. They point out, however, some unexpected results, especially with regard to the poor or limited improvement on measures of grammatical competence among study-abroad learners. With reference to data from Spanish in particular, research to date has shown advantages for study-abroad (SA) contexts on some measures, particularly on oral proficiency, fluency, pronunciation, lexical acquisition, and narrative and discursive abilities. On the other hand, learners in at-home (AH) contexts "are either equal or superior to their SA counterparts in other areas," especially in regard to grammatical abilities and, surprisingly, pragmatic abilities. In fact, Lafford and Collentine point out that in studies in which a AH control group was used, the positive effects of a SA context on grammatical development are called into question (e.g., DeKeyser 1991).

The authors argue that the most powerful advantage a study-abroad program affords students is in the area of fluency (e.g., words per syntactic unit, speed, segments without pauses/hesitations) by pointing to empirical evidence from various studies (e.g., DeKeyser 1986; Isabelli 2004; Segalowitz and Freed 2004). An additional important finding coming out of the available research is the existence of interaction effects of previous L2 academic experience and the SA experience. Lafford and Collentine tentatively propose "a kind of 'threshold hypothesis' for students studying abroad: those students with a well-developed cognitive, lexical, and grammatical base will be more able to process and produce grammatical forms more accurately after their experience in a SA context." An explanation advanced by Lafford and Collentine to account for the previous results is that "what was on the radar screen of the teacher/student in the typical classroom (e.g., grammatical accuracy) is not the same as what comes on the learner's radar screen when confronted with the interpersonal dynamics of the target culture (e.g., pragmatic constraints on the use of language)." For instance, the type of attention given to L2 word associations in the classroom rarely forms a part of foreign language classroom instruction (Lafford, Collentine, and Karp 2003). Lafford and Collentine, however, point out that "it is precisely the development of these L2 associations and pragmatic abilities that allow L2 learners to attain advanced levels of proficiency and to begin to think like native speakers of the target language."

As a corollary, Lafford and Collentine argue for the implementation of socially relevant communicative situations in classroom contexts to help learners attain similar levels of development in the areas where SA students seem to excel. Possible opportunities to achieve those goals are, for instance, internships and service-learning opportunities in the community at large (see Valdés, this volume) and controlled chatrooms in which English-speaking Spanish L2 speakers communicate with Spanish-speaking English L2 speakers living in target culture settings (see Blake and Delforge, this volume). On the other hand, given the paucity of research about the development of the components of language competence typically improved in SA contexts, Lafford and Collentine argue that any pedagogical intervention should be viewed as exploratory.

Lafford and Collentine point out that the findings in general show that the aspects of language learning that are traditionally the focus of research (e.g., lexical and grammatical development) are difficult to develop quickly in the study-abroad context (Collentine and Freed 2004). Not surprisingly, they suggest the creation of "more assessment instruments that really measure the kinds of gains made by learners in an SA context (e.g., pragmatic ability, vocabulary associations, fluency)." In addition, they suggest that more studies investigate the potential effects of other factors on SA success, such as individual factors (e.g., personality, demographic/background factors, field of study and career goals, type of previous instruction), the type of SA program in which he or she is participating, the type of host family with which he or she lives, as well as variation in performance among individuals (as opposed to groups) within both SA and AH contexts.

6.0 Chapter 7: Online Language Learning

Blake and Delforge explore some of the major recent technological innovations that have made online language learning potentially as effective as classroom learning. This has been made possible, in part, by new tools that allow for asynchronous and synchronous oral (as well as written) communication among students and instructors. The tools give students the opportunity to speak to one another in real time via their computers while at the same time augmenting their spoken communication with the additional support of written text as desired. In addition, these new communication tools suggest exciting pedagogical possibilities. For instance, students' metalinguistic analyses of transcripts of oral and written conversations can be related to the language awareness processes implemented through dictogloss activities and other consciousness-raising activities on output (e.g., Wajnryb 1990). However, due to the relatively recent advent of the use of CMC tools for oral communication, the research on the effectiveness of online learning on speaking abilities has only begun to be investigated (Payne and Whitney 2002) and needs more attention by researchers. In particular, we note that CMC and face-to-face communication should not necessarily be viewed as interactional formats that are in competition with each other. We believe that it is probably more accurate to look at these two different communication media as complementary ways of developing knowledge in the L2 (e.g., Salaberry 2000).

In their review of research to date on the effectiveness of distance learning language courses in hybrid and completely online formats, Blake and Delforge find no

[handwritten margin note top: SWW → Spanish without walls]

adverse effects of these formats on student outcomes. They also note that these studies found that certain abilities (aural/oral communication and reading/writing skills) may become more developed in the hybrid and online courses. However, the authors warn that methodological issues in some studies may limit the potential for generalizing these findings.

In their chapter, Blake and Delforge present the results of a study of the relative efficacy of a Spanish language course taught completely online through the University of California, Davis Extension (Spanish Without Walls) compared to regular face-to-face courses taught at UC Davis. They argue that the multimedia forms of CALL presently available are capable of providing not only interesting and authentic materials but also content-based activities that promote higher-order learning. More specifically, Blake and Delforge state that "CALL materials may have a positive effect on the language learning process because they stimulate metalinguistic awareness, allow for self-directed learning, . . . and can accommodate different learning styles." In addition, the computer-mediated communication (CMC) tools now available provide high levels of oral and written interactivity that allow for negotiation of meaning and maintain students' interest in learning Spanish in a virtual classroom setting.

[handwritten margin note: Multimedia related to Metalinguistic awareness / self direct learning]

The original study reported on by Blake and Delforge focuses on the evaluation of the effectiveness of an online course, Spanish Without Walls (SWW), a virtual first-year Spanish course that combines CD-ROM materials (Blake, Blasco, and Hernández 2001), Internet readings with online content-based activities, and sound/text CMC in both a synchronous and asynchronous format. Linguistic outcomes of students in this online course were compared to those of students enrolled in regular Spanish 1 and Spanish 2 courses. The SWW group received significantly higher scores in discrete-point language tests than the regular classroom groups. Since both the experimental and control groups were exposed to the same sequencing and amount of grammar, the authors state that these results might be attributable to the fact that SWW used primarily a textual medium (like the grammar tests) for self-study, while classroom students participated in more oral small-group practice in which they used their knowledge of grammar. Moreover, Blake and Delforge note that since the results of the grammar tests were incorporated into the SWW students' grades but did not affect the classroom students' grades, the former group was more motivated to score well on these tests. In addition, no significant differences were found between the writing samples of the two groups. Students in the online course (mostly working professionals) also praised the flexibility of the online format and the low-stress environment it provided. The qualitative and quantitative results of this study confirm the findings of prior research on these topics.

We note that although particular pedagogical features brought up by multimedia communication environments are not exclusive to such environments, they are nevertheless most easily, most efficiently, and least expensively implemented in online courses such as the one described by Blake and Delforge in their chapter. For example, Blake and Delforge point out that students in the online course they evaluated liked the ability to work at their own pace for two main reasons: They felt less anxious or pressured to perform and they were able to differentially distribute their attention and focus on areas where they felt they were weaker. Nevertheless, it is possible that these results are not solely attributable to the use of technology but to the pedagogical sequencing, time afforded for self-pacing, and so on allowed by the hybridized and online formats. However, this does not detract from the fact that technology-based courses may contain the optimal format for the provision of this benefit. Therefore, it does serve to point out that the pedagogical benefit of these formats may not reside in the technology per se but in the tools they utilize for language learning afford.

7.0 Chapter 8: Testing Spanish

In their chapter, Salaberry and Cohen present a broad overview of the research framework that informs second language testing at the tertiary level of education with a special emphasis on Spanish. Most Spanish courses, the authors state, use a wide variety of test types, such as fill-in-the-blank grammar tests, multiple-choice and open-ended reading comprehension questions, structured and open writing tasks, and structured or improvised oral interviews. Salaberry and Cohen argue, however, that the routine use of these instruments to assess language ability does not necessarily mean that such tests are reliable or valid. Hence, their analysis focuses mostly on the challenges faced by teachers as test designers, although they also review some practical principles that teachers as test designers can use.

Salaberry and Cohen preview their argument with a brief summary of some of the better known models of communicative competence and a description of some test types (e.g., task-based testing, real-life tests, and semidirect tests), emphasizing in their argument the relevance of using several complementary measures to assess second language performance. The bulk of their chapter focuses on the analysis of two challenges faced by test designers: the testing of a broad base of components of language competence and the inclusion of a well-attested developmental sequence in scales of proficiency.

For the first challenge, the authors focus on the testing of knowledge and competence about L2 pragmatics and L2 culture. Salaberry and Cohen state that even though both pragmatic and cultural knowledge represent two central components of the L2 in the majority of models of L2 competence, both the assessment of pragmatics and culture tend to be downplayed in most testing instruments. As for scales of proficiency, the authors briefly describe some of the limited knowledge researchers have about developmental sequences, thereby cautioning readers about the overreliance on received wisdom (traditional views) about sequences of acquisition. Their practical recommendations for the development of tests focus on overarching principles that represent an extension of the analysis of the two challenges they discuss in detail.

As Salaberry and Cohen attest, even though in recent years more attention has been paid to the teaching of pragmatic competence (Kasper 1997; Olshtain and Cohen 1991; García 1996, 2001), assessment instruments to gauge the acquisition of pragmatic competence are still lacking. For instance, until scholars, applied linguists, and pedagogues understand more about how Spanish-speaking individuals interpret and perform various speech acts, no native speaker pragmatic "models" can be created against which student progress would be measured. Moreover, another very important factor complicating the creation of evaluation instruments is the existence of interdialectal pragmatic variation (e.g., García 2004 showed that Peruvians and Venezuelans do not respond the same way to a reprimand). Unless learners understand that norms of politeness vary across the Spanish-speaking world, they risk offending a good number of native Spanish speakers whose ideas of linguistic politeness vary considerably from the monolithic models to which learners have been exposed.

Therefore, due to the incipient nature of Spanish L1 pragmatic research, at present, few rubrics for pragmatic evaluation of Spanish L2 learners can be created. As a first step, however, instructors familiar with the aforementioned research could use Olshtain and Cohen's model of teaching pragmatic competence to introduce models of speech acts being performed by the groups already studied (Peruvians, Venezuelans, and Argentineans). Students could then analyze how these different groups perform the same speech act and could create role plays to put their pragmatic understanding into practice.

This kind of focus on "local competencies" (how do Peruvian women apologize?) instead of on global competencies (how do Spanish speakers apologize?) is imperative if we do not want our students to fall into the "stereotype" trap. Not all Spanish speakers carry out speech acts in the same way, and failure to acknowledge this and teach localized pragmatic competence in the classroom can only lead to frustrating and sometimes humiliating experiences when our students get the chance to interact with native speakers of Spanish from various parts of the Hispanic world. The term *ugly American* was certainly not born of a failure to use the subjunctive correctly; rather, it was probably the result of our failure to behave or use language appropriately in different social situations abroad. More focus on the teaching and assessing of pragmatic and cultural competence is certainly in order for the Spanish language classrooms of today and tomorrow.

8.0   Chapter 9: Incorporating Linguistic Variation into the Classroom

Gutiérrez and Fairclough address fundamental questions faced by most teachers of Spanish in the U.S. setting: Should I teach students one specific variety of Spanish? Should I teach the dialect/variety I speak or the one presented in the textbook? Is it pedagogically feasible to teach students a comprehensive range of linguistic variation in Spanish? To answer these questions, Gutiérrez and Fairclough point out that the traditional Spanish classroom tends to favor the written norm of Spanish over features of the oral language. For instance, they show that the morphological future (as in *comeré*) is introduced early in Spanish textbooks, even though the synthetic form of the future is rare in spoken Spanish (not to mention that it is rapidly losing prevalence in the written language as well). As a matter of fact, the present form of the verb is used more frequently than the morphological future to functionally convey future tense meaning. This situation is even more disconcerting from a pedagogical point of view when we consider that the periphrastic form of the future is conceptually easy to learn due to the fact that English speakers already have a similar periphrastic future form in their native language. Moreover, from a computational point of view, the periphrastic form (e.g., *voy a ir* 'I will go,' *voy a comer* 'I will eat') is easier to learn than the inflectional form (e.g., *iré* 'I will go,' *comeré* 'I will eat') given that only the auxiliary verb is conjugated in the periphrastic alternative.

On the other hand, Gutiérrez and Fairclough review the evidence on linguistic variation and conclude that Spanish varieties spoken in the United States differ from other Spanish varieties mostly in terms of lexicon (vocabulary), the amount of code switching (very common when two languages are in contact), and, to a limited extent, in the grammatical system. Echoing Silva-Corvalán (1994, 2001), Gutiérrez and Fairclough point out that processes of linguistic change that are taking place in the language-contact situation of the United States are also present in monolingual varieties (although the bilingual situation in some cases seems to accelerate such changes). For instance, the authors describe the shift in use from *ser* to *estar* and the gradual erosion of subjunctive forms as examples of morphosyntactic change in several Spanish-speaking varieties (with or without close contact with English).

Furthermore, Gutiérrez and Fairclough argue that demographic data point to an increasingly large number of students entering college-level courses of Spanish as heritage learners (see Valdés, this volume). Heritage learners bring with them a Spanish knowledge continuum that goes from no knowledge to almost native-speaker proficiency in oral abilities, although in most cases heritage learners attending college-level language courses have limited or no literacy skills in Spanish.

Gutiérrez and Fairclough ask if we have to make available to students the full range of variation that occurs in the real world. If this is the right thing to do, how can we do it? From a sociolinguistic-sociopolitical point of view, introducing students to dialectal variations of Spanish is a useful endeavor for any liberal arts education program. On the other hand, it is fair to ask whether there are pragmatic pedagogical reasons to avoid teaching dialectal variation (e.g., not to confuse the student during beginning stages of acquisition). To some extent, this concern may be overstated, as long as the pedagogical goal is one of raising students' awareness of other dialects (as opposed to productive use of alternative dialects). Indeed, some recent textbooks have incorporated recurring sections throughout all chapters with an explicit focus on dialectal variation as a consciousness-raising activity (e.g., Salaberry et al. 2004).

Despite these outstanding pedagogical concerns, Gutiérrez and Fairclough conclude that "sociolinguistic variation should be incorporated into the classroom." In their view, this goal can be accomplished in two fundamental ways: by creating better-focused teacher education programs and by incorporating "key sociolinguistic concepts and samples of language variation . . . in all language textbooks, . . . even at the basic levels of instruction." Teacher training programs can be extremely effective in showing instructors how to avoid the typical teaching of what Gutiérrez and Fairclough call "sanitized standard" Spanish. This can be accomplished by making teachers aware of language variation and by helping debunk the mistaken belief that nonstandard forms of language are "incorrect." Similarly, the incorporation of even minimal information about dialectal and social variation in Spanish language textbooks will not only make students aware of language variation but also make students more accepting of valid nonstandard and regional forms of Spanish that, more often than not, are used by more Spanish speakers than the standard forms.

9.0 Chapter 10: Making Connections

In her chapter, Valdés focuses the reader's attention on definitional issues that should make us think carefully about, on the one hand, the wholesale adaptation of instructional techniques to teach heritage language speakers and, on the other hand, the basic theoretical aspects of the process of L2 acquisition. For instance, there are two difficulties with the definition of the term *heritage speaker:* linguistic versus nonlinguistic knowledge and range of linguistic proficiency. First, the definition tends to rely mostly on the historical and personal connection to the language rather than on the person's actual proficiency. Second, as Valdés points out, the term *L2 user* (as opposed to the term *monolingual speaker*) is not entirely appropriate for the description of heritage language learners. Pointing out that the term *L2 user* still tends to emphasize and focus attention primarily on the L2, she proposes the term *L1/L2 user* to describe heritage learners, many of whom acquire the L2 in a combination of naturalistic and instructed settings and continue to use the L1 to some degree in their everyday lives. More important, while absolutely equivalent abilities in two languages are theoretically possible, except for rare geographical and familial accidents, individuals seldom have access to two languages in exactly the same contexts in every domain of interaction.

In her historical survey of teaching Spanish to heritage speakers, Valdés notes that during the 1960s and 1970s the teaching profession used a remedial approach for the teaching of Spanish to heritage speakers. By the late 1980s and early 1990s there was a new wave of research that criticized many unquestioned assumptions about the teaching of heritage languages (e.g., the role of oral proficiency interviews with bilingual students and the question of dialect and standard). Valdés points out, however, that despite the recent increased awareness about the reality of bilingualism, at the moment we still have "almost no empirical research on the effects of different types of instruction in developing heritage languages nor about what might be reasonable goals and objectives." For instance, few studies of bilingual language acquisition have been carried out in Type 6 contexts (cf. Romaine's classification).

Thus we have little information about children who are born and raised in heritage language communities among both monolingual speakers of the heritage language *and* bilingual speakers of the dominant and the heritage language. Most important, Valdés argues that to understand the role of formal instruction in developing or maintaining heritage languages, one needs to know whether we are dealing with

(1) the acquisition of incompletely acquired features of a native language, (2) the (re)acquisition of attrited features, (3) the acquisition of a second dialect (D2 acquisition), or (4) the expansion of the range of registers and styles (R2 acquisition).

Along the lines of Gutiérrez and Fairclough's argument, Valdés claims that the arrival of more heritage speakers to the typical college-level classroom brings up important questions for both theory and pedagogy. For instance, she notes that "without evidence to the contrary, one could not conclude that direct forms- or form-focused instruction or other typical pedagogies used in L2 instruction would be particularly beneficial in the process of (re)acquisition or reversal of attrition." Furthermore, Valdés makes the point that teaching Spanish to heritage learners brings up the debate about the relationship between receptive and productive grammars, how these systems develop, and how they affect each other during academic instruction. In sum, "national investments in the simple adaptation of pedagogies currently used with L2 learners" may be unsuccessful or simply inefficient. Considering the situation, Valdés outlines a research agenda on heritage language learning that includes the development of language assessment procedures, the analysis of L2 implicit systems of different types of heritage learners, the study of second dialect (D2) acquisition, and an investigation of the role of different types of instruction in heritage language reacquisition/restructuring,

As a major corollary of her argument, Valdés calls for the building of connections between Spanish SLA and the heritage language teaching profession. As she argues, this partnership can contribute to both theory development in the area of heritage language instruction and the broadening and reconceptualization of SLA research, particularly in the area of the concept of multicompetence. Valdés discusses in detail six main goals she believes heritage language instruction may include: (1) the acquisition of a standard dialect, (2) the transfer of reading and writing abilities across languages, (3) the expansion of the bilingual range, (4) the maintenance of the heritage language, (5) the development of academic skills, and (6) the increase of students' pride and self-esteem.

10.0 Chapter 11: Spanish Second Language Acquisition

Colina's chapter proposes that "the application of SLA findings to the teaching of translation and interpretation is very much in its infancy." Part of the problem, she argues, is that there exist in the profession obdurate "prescriptivist, oversimplified notions regarding the role of language proficiency in the education of translators and interpreters." In particular, she isolates the negative effect of "methodologies based on behaviorist and formalist theories of language acquisition." The latter have envisioned translation as an interlingual transcoding process that has perpetuated the stranglehold of transmissionist teaching approaches in translator education. Colina thus endeavors to show how the findings of second language acquisition research may inform the teaching and the practice of professional translation and interpretation of Spanish in the United States.

As part of the main thrust of her argument, Colina proposes that second language acquisition research has relevance for the teaching of translation and interpretation for two major reasons. First, recent demographic factors stand in stark contrast with the major theoretical tenet that proposes that translators should always translate into their native language. This is not necessarily true for Spanish as the target language in the United States, given that many translators translate into their heritage language (Valdés, this volume). The problem in this case is that the heritage language may no longer be the dominant language (even for first-generation Spanish speakers). This means that "translation into the heritage language is translation into the second-language." As a consequence of this major demographic shift, Colina argues that "considerable amounts of language acquisition take place during and after translation and interpretation training and that, therefore, SLA research must fall within the purview of descriptive translation studies and more specifically the teaching of translation and interpretation."

The second reason that SLA research is relevant for the teaching of translation and interpretation is that recent accounts of language acquisition and bilingualism bring up a host of factors that should make us wary of the idealized notion of native speaker. For instance, Colina rightfully argues that "the notion of native speaker as applied to translation also assumes that language acquisition is static, leaving no room for attrition." Current research on bilingualism makes this notion spurious— or at a minimum an oversimplification. Colina further reviews the relevance of several areas of SLA research for the teaching of translation. For instance, she highlights the importance of reading comprehension research on schemata and background knowledge. More important, she highlights the fact that even "gaps in cultural and textual knowledge regarding the source text" may generate serious misunderstandings. We note that Colina's review of pertinent research findings highlights the lack of sufficient research on the acquisition of pragmatic knowledge and rhetorical structure. This lacuna was also pointed out in chapters 3 and 8 of this volume (on SLA teaching and testing, respectively). In the area of translation, however, as Colina points out, there are some studies that have focused on contrastive rhetorical analysis.

Finally, Colina provides practical suggestions for the eventual integration of translation programs into rapidly evolving second language programs. Hence, she argues that translation and interpretation research and pedagogy could be embedded in established programs of study. One of the benefits of embedding translation programs within other programs is that it is faster and more likely to succeed than the design of new, specialized programs in translation studies. Colina argues further that, whether taught as an independent course or as a module in a language methods course, translation pedagogy can be useful not only to linguistics students but also, for instance, to literature majors who teach language courses. An additional benefit is that, consonant with the review of research outlined in her chapter, Colina argues that "the inclusion approach would foster understanding, dissemination and research in related disciplines, thus facilitating the opening of the 'closed circle' and the enrichment of translation teaching by incorporating the research findings of relevant fields."

11.0 Conclusion

In our review of the chapters that comprise this volume we made references to several overarching themes that are likely to shape both future research on Spanish SLA and the applications of research to teaching Spanish. Due to space considerations, we will highlight five main themes we believe are shared by the majority of the contributors to this volume.

First, most of the chapters in the volume point out that the notion of a monolithic language competence is inherently flawed from a theoretical point of view (e.g., the native-speaker concept in Valdés) and is a pedagogical challenge at the same time, given the multifaceted nature of language competence among Spanish speakers (e.g., selection of the standard language to be taught in Guitiérrez and Fairclough). For instance, raising awareness of interdialectal variation in the use of courtesy formulas (e.g., pronouns of address) or certain politeness strategies in the Spanish-speaking world is crucial to the development of the learner's interlanguage pragmatic compe- *[handwritten: Avoiding language stereotypes]* tence (Salaberry and Cohen) and in helping learners to avoid creating global stereo- types regarding all members of target culture communities. However, it cannot be assumed that the norms of politeness among dialects of Spanish will be more similar to each other than those of any two dialects of English or Spanish when compared to each other. For instance, the linguistic strategies used by Peruvian Spanish speakers, who place great emphasis on complex courtesy formulas when making requests, may be more similar to those used by older English speakers in the American South or by speakers of British English than to those utilized by Venezuelan or peninsular Spanish speakers. The latter's use of more direct strategies may more closely resemble those used by speakers of New York English than those of Spanish speakers from Peru. Such emphasis on the diversity of cultural and linguistic practices within the target lan- guage culture(s) will assist learners to understand the complexities of the interaction *[handwritten: understanding of perspectives and practices]* of various perspectives, practices, and products within sociocultural contexts and will help students avoid overgeneralizing assumptions about behavioral practices in places where the target language is spoken.

Second, in line with the previous theme, several chapters have argued for the need of going beyond the traditional decontextualized definition of language knowledge. For instance, the traditional view of second language culture as a combination of dis- crete products and practices (and taught outside of the normal grammar-based lan- guage curriculum) sets up cultural competence to be viewed as an "expendable fifth skill." We point out that this is not a new concept. Kramsch (1993), for instance, *[handwritten: language as social practice C's Standards]* objected to this view of culture and noted that "if language is seen as social practice, culture becomes the very core of language teaching." Her view of "language as social practice" is also reflected in the National Standards (1996) movement, in which cul- ture is integrated with the other C's (communication, connections, comparisons, communities) in the language learning process. Most authors in this volume reaffirm such a broadened view of "language as social practice" and emphasize that the teach- ing of sociocultural competence becomes part and parcel of the foundation of all sec- ond language curricula and no longer needs to be seen as an ancillary skill outside the purview of core language instruction (Guitiérrez and Fairclough, Lafford and Collentine, Salaberry and Cohen, Valdés).

Third, we note that several chapters have advanced a (re)conceptualization of second language learning as a psycholinguistic construct with direct reference to the learning of grammatical concepts (e.g., Negueruela and Lantolf) and language learning processes in general (e.g., Collentine, VanPatten and Leeser). Some authors have speculated about the existence of a cognitive and linguistic "threshold" that may have to be attained before certain other competences can be acquired in various learning contexts (Lafford and Collentine, Salaberry and Cohen). Moreover, in SLA and applied linguistics research there is a notable lack of attention paid to the teaching and assessment of the components of language (other than grammar) that still form part of a psycholinguistic construct (e.g., pragmatic and sociolinguistic competence) (Lafford and Collentine, Klee and Barnes-Karol, Salaberry and Cohen, Colina, Valdés). The need for this kind of research is supported by the notion that the recognition of both social and cognitive factors in SLA (Firth and Wagner 1997) is a necessary step toward understanding the complexities involved in the acquisition of a second language.

Fourth, several chapters have emphasized the need to find and explore language learning opportunities beyond the traditional classroom. New opportunities can be found in connections made with other disciplines that are intent on developing a critical liberal arts curriculum (FLAC courses as discussed by Klee and Barnes-Karol), uses of technology (as summarized by Blake and Delforge), and the widely available opportunities for nonacademic social or work-related exchanges with target language communities (as highlighted by Lafford and Collentine and Valdés). On the other hand, several of the chapters in this volume (e.g., Klee and Barnes-Karol) also note barriers that exist to second language pedagogical innovations. For instance, the lack of administrative support (in the form of monetary or merit incentives) for faculty to try new things has discouraged instructors from spending time and energy on creating research-based activities that may enhance the second language learning process (e.g., FLAC courses, CALL activities). As a result, the publishers of pedagogical materials (books and CALL software) do not always have the benefit of the input of established SLA scholars.

This brings up the final point: the need for more communication and cross-fertilization of ideas among SLA researchers, scholars from fields related to SLA (e.g., sociolinguistics, psycholinguistics, and educational psychologists), members of the target language community, the applied linguists who create pedagogical materials, and the instructors who utilize them and assess student performance in the classroom. This point has been made in one way or the other by almost all of the authors in this volume and has been given lip service for years in our profession. What is needed now is for teams consisting of members from each of those communities to sit down together and set goals for student L2 learning outcomes for a given language course, stressing learner autonomy, task-based activities to achieve goals, assessment measures of the attainment of those goals, and a plan for constant reassessment and evaluation of the original pedagogical course. Truly innovative planning of language learning curricula from an interdisciplinary viewpoint should be devised to attract the attention of administrators and bring in grant funding. This would allow members of the team the time to carry out these objectives and would give them positive recognition of their efforts to apply the findings of SLA and related research to the teaching of second languages.

References

Andersen, R., and Y. Shirai. 1994. Discourse motivations for some cognitive acquisition principles. *Studies in Second Language Acquisition* 16:133–56.

Bardovi-Harlig, K. 2000. *Tense and aspect in second language acquisition: Form, meaning and use.* Malden, MA: Blackwell.

Blake, R., J. Blasco, and C. Hernández. 2001. *Tesoros CD-ROM: A multi-media-based course.* Boecillo: Boecillo Editorial Multimedia (BeM); New York: McGraw-Hill.

Blyth, C. 1997. A constructivist approach to grammar: Teaching teachers to teach aspect. *Modern Language Journal* 81 (1): 50–66.

———. 2005. From empirical findings to the teaching of aspectual distinctions. In *Tense and aspect in Romance languages: Theoretical and applied perspectives,* ed. D. Ayoun and R. Salaberry, 211–52. Amsterdam: John Benjamins.

Cadierno, T. 1995. Formal instruction in processing perspective: An investigation into the Spanish past tense. *Modern Language Journal* 79:179–94.

Carroll, S. 2001. *Input and evidence: The raw material of second language acquisition.* Amersterdam: John Benjamins.

Collentine, J., and B. Freed. 2004. Learning context and its effects on second language acquisition: Introduction. *Studies in Second Language Acquisition* 26 (2): 153–72.

DeKeyser, R. 1986. From learning to acquisition? Foreign language development in a U.S. classroom and during a semester abroad. Ph.D. diss., Stanford University.

———. 1991. Foreign language development during a semester abroad. In *Foreign language acquisition research and the classroom,* ed. B. Freed, 104–19. Lexington, MA: D. C. Heath.

DeKeyser, R., R. Salaberry, P. Robinson, and M. Harrington. 2002. What gets processed in processing instruction: A response to Bill VanPatten's "Update." *Language Learning* 52 (4): 805–23.

Dussias, P. 2003. Cognitive perspectives on the acquisition of Spanish as a second language. In *Studies in Spanish second language acquistion: State of the science,* ed. B. Lafford and R. Salaberry, 233–61. Washington, DC: Georgetown University Press.

Firth, A., and J. Wagner. 1997. On discourse, communication and (some) fundamental concepts in SLA research. *Modern Language Journal* 81:285–300.

García, C. 1996. Reprimanding and responding to a reprimand: A case study of Peruvian Spanish speakers. *Journal of Pragmatics* 26:663–97.

———. 2001. Perspectives in practices: Teaching culture through speech acts. In *Teaching the cultures of the Hispanic world: Products and practices in perspective,* ed. V. Galloway, 95–112. Cincinnati: Thomson Learning.

———. 2004. Reprendiendo y respondiendo a una reprimenda. Similitudes y diferencias entre peruanos y venezolanos. *Spanish in Context* 1 (1): 113–47.

Isabelli, C. A. 2004. The acquisition of null subject parameter properties in SLA: Some effects of positive evidence in a natural learning context. *Hispania* 87 (1): 150–62.

Kasper, G. 1997. Can pragmatic competence be taught? Second Language Teaching and Curriculum Center. National Foreign Language Research Center website. www.lll.hawaii.edu/nflrc/NetWorks/NW6/NW6references.html (accessed June 20, 2006).

Kramsch, C. 1993. *Context and culture in language teaching.* Oxford: Oxford University Press.

Lafford, B., J. Collentine, and A. Karp 2003. The acquisition of lexical meaning by second language learners: An analysis of general research trends with evidence from Spanish. In *Studies in Spanish second language acquisition: State of the science,* ed. B. Lafford and R. Salaberry, 233–61. Washington, D.C.: Georgetown University Press.

Lafford, B., and R. Salaberry. 2003. *Studies in Spanish second language acquisition: State of the science.* Washington, DC: Georgetown University Press.

National Standards in Foreign Language Education Project. 1996. *National standards for foreign language learning: Preparing for the 21st century.* Lawrence, KS: Allen Press.

Olshtain, E., and A. D. Cohen. 1991. Teaching speech act behavior to nonnative speakers. In *Teaching English as a second or foreign language,* ed. M. Celce-Murcia, 154–65. New York: Newbury House.

Payne, S., and P. J. Whitney. 2002. Developing L2 oral proficiency through synchronous CMC: Output, working memory and interlanguage development. *CALICO Journal* 20 (1): 7–32.

Salaberry, R. 1997. The role of input and output practice in second language acquisition. *Canadian Modern Language Review/Revue canadienne des langues vivantes* 53 (2): 422–51.

———. 2000. Pedagogical design of computer mediated communication tasks: Learning objectives and technological capabilities. *Modern Language Journal* 84 (1): 28–37.

———. 2003. An analysis of the selection of past tense endings in personal and fictional narrative in L2 Spanish. *Hispania* 86 (3): 559–73.

Salaberry, R., and D. Ayoun. 2005. The development of L2 tense–aspect in the Romance languages. In *Tense and aspect in Romance languages: Theoretical and applied perspectives,* ed. D. Ayoun and R. Salaberry, 1–33. Amsterdam: John Benjamins.

Salaberry, R., C. Barrette, M. Fernández-García, and P. Elliot. 2004. *Impresiones.* Upper Saddle River, NJ: Pearson–Prentice Hall.

Salaberry, R., and N. López-Ortega. 1998. Accurate L2 production across language tasks: Focus on form, focus on meaning communicative control. *Modern Language Journal* 82 (4): 514–32.

Schmidt, R. 1990. The role of consciousness in second language learning. *Applied Linguistics* 11 (2): 127–58.

Segalowitz, N., and B. Freed. 2004. Context, contact, and cognition in oral fluency acquisition: Learning Spanish in at home and study abroad contexts. *Studies in Second Language Acquisition* 26 (2): 173–99.

Silva-Corvalán, C. 1994. *Language contact and change: Spanish in Los Angeles.* Oxford: Clarendon Press.

———. 2001. *Sociolingüística y pragmática del español.* Washington, DC: Georgetown University Press.

Swain, M. 1995. Three functions of output in second language learning. In *Principles and practice in applied linguistics: Studies in honor of H. Widdowson,* ed. G. Cook and B. Seidldhofer, 125–44. Oxford: Oxford University Press.

VanPatten, B. 1990. Attending to form and content in the input. *Studies in Second Language Acquisition* 12 (3): 287–301.

VanPatten, B., and T. Cadierno. 1993. Explicit instruction and input processing. *Studies in Second Language Acquisition* 15 (2): 225–44.

Wajnryb, R. 1990. *Grammar dictation.* Oxford: Oxford University Press.

A Content-Based Approach to Spanish Language Study
Foreign Languages Across the Curriculum

Carol A. Klee   *University of Minnesota*
Gwendolyn Barnes-Karol   *St. Olaf College*

Beginning in the 1980s with efforts to internationalize North American universities, a new initiative, Foreign Languages Across the Curriculum (FLAC) (later termed Languages Across the Curriculum, or LAC), gained momentum. FLAC courses were developed at a variety of postsecondary institutions with support from the National Endowment for the Humanities (NEH), the Fund for the Improvement of Postsecondary Education (FIPSE), the Center for International Education at the Department of Education, and several private foundations, such as the American Council on Education (ACE). The primary purpose of these programs is to provide opportunities to students who have already achieved a minimum proficiency in a foreign language to use their language skills in selected courses outside language and literature departments. The rationale for FLAC, as stated by the Consortium for Language Across the Curriculum (1996), is as follows:

1. Understanding of a given culture and its documents and artifacts is greatly enhanced through a knowledge of its language.

2. A curriculum that includes materials in multiple languages provides access to a wider range of perspectives, encourages greater depth of exploration, and opens the door to greater understanding.

3. The use of materials in multiple languages significantly enhances any and all disciplinary inquiry.

4. Languages Across the Curriculum enhances cross-cultural competence and the ability of students to function in an increasingly multicultural society and a globalized economy.

The primary focus of most FLAC programs is on the content of the discipline-based courses. As can be noted in the statement above, improvement in second language skills, while desired, is usually not a primary objective.

FLAC initiatives began as a result of several concurrent influences, some from the field of second language acquisition and teaching and others emanating from disciplines outside of languages and literatures. In the first section of this chapter we will review the SLA research findings that provide the rationale for the development of these programs. We will then examine the primary Spanish FLAC models that have been implemented in institutions across the United States and describe the factors that have promoted the continued viability and/or created obstacles for the continued survival of a given model. In the last section we will highlight lessons learned from the FLAC experience.

1.0 SLA Rationale for FLAC Programs

From their initiation, FLAC programs have generally involved faculty in literature and language departments who have at least some familiarity with the field of foreign language pedagogy and are aware of recent applications of SLA research and teaching. Early influences on FLAC and other types of postsecondary content-based instruction (CBI) included three foundational approaches to CBI: the writing across the curriculum movement of the 1970s and 1980s, which sought to integrate writing in the L1 (English) with academic learning in a variety of disciplines; immersion school programs in Canada and the United States, which were viewed as the most successful programs for developing the proficiency of majority language speakers; and Language for Special Purposes (LSP) programs (Brinton, Snow, and Wesche 2003, 241). As Brinton, Snow, and Wesche (2003) point out, these programs developed in response to the perceived failure of traditional language teaching methods to produce competent users of the L2. They define the primary rationale for a CBI curriculum as providing learners with "the necessary conditions for second language learning by exposing them to meaningful language in use" (241). However, they also mention several other reasons for implementing a CBI curriculum, including that CBI

1. builds on the learner's previous learning experiences in the subject matter, the target language, and in formal educational settings;

2. takes into account the interests and needs of the learners through their engagement with the academic subject matter and discourse patterns that they need to master;

3. allows a focus on (communicative language) use as well as on (accurate) usage; and

4. incorporates the eventual uses the learner will make of the language through engagement with relevant content and L2 discourse with a purpose other than language teaching. (241–42)

The pioneering work by Brinton, Snow, and Wesche (1989) on CBI had an immense impact on the development of FLAC programs, as it provided a variety of models for CBI as well as guidelines for the implementation of a content-based program, concrete suggestions for content-based materials development and adaptation, and a review of evaluation in content-based courses. Another major influence on the development of CBI and FLAC programs was Krashen's (1982) monitor theory, which emphasized the importance of comprehensible input for second language acquisition. Although Krashen's monitor model has been criticized by a number of SLA researchers (cf. Spolsky 1985; Swain 1985; Gregg 1986; McLaughlin 1987), there is a consensus in second language circles that "access to meaningful input is somehow a critical factor in successful language development" (VanPatten 1987, 157).

Systematic attention has been paid in most programs to making the primary documents students are asked to read comprehensible. To do this, several theoretical models of reading have provided guidance, among them schema theory. According to this theory (Carrell and Eisterhold 1983), comprehension of a text occurs through an interactive process that involves both the reader's background knowledge, including previously acquired knowledge structures or schemata, and the text itself. Readers engage in two types of information processing as they read, *bottom up*, or data-driven, processing and *top down*, or conceptually driven, processing. Top down processing is facilitated through familiarity with formal schemata (i.e., the rhetorical organizational structures of different types of texts) as well as content schemata (i.e., knowledge of the content area of a text). It is thought that such background knowledge may allow students to compensate for some syntactic deficiencies (Coady 1979).

More recent models of reading comprehension (Kern 2000) have also influenced the development of prereading activities and reading tasks for FLAC courses. Kern (2000, 38) describes his view of literacy as combining "a focus on language use in social constructs (essential to communicative approaches) with an additional component of active reflection on how meanings are constructed and negotiated in particular acts of communication." Students are guided in developing metacommunicative awareness of "how discourse is derived from relations between language use, contexts of interaction, and larger sociocultural contexts" (Kern 2000, 303). Kern recommends that the design processes of interpretation, collaboration, problem solving, and reflection be operationalized through various types of instructional activities that can be adapted for use in FLAC courses and that foster awareness of how meaning is produced through the interaction of forms and contexts.

In addition to the research on reading, Adamson's (1993) work on academic competencies and his recommendations on how to prepare students for content courses have proven useful to FLAC instructors and to language program instructors who are preparing students for FLAC courses. Adamson notes that in addition to general language proficiency, students need both background knowledge of the content material and effective study skills to succeed in content courses. He describes in detail activities to help students understand academic subjects taught in an L2 course, such as how to prepare a study guide for reading or listening/note-taking activities in response to lectures. Nunan (1989) also has provided guidelines on how to structure learning tasks to help students at various levels of proficiency develop academic competencies.

All of these influences have helped shaped FLAC instruction by demonstrating how academic content can be made accessible to students with varying degrees of language competence through the careful selection, organization, and presentation of course materials and the design of tasks that correspond to the level of the learner. In some courses, for example, faculty assign background readings in English before texts are assigned in the L2. In this way they can provide students with adequate background knowledge to aid their comprehension of the L2 text. In addition, many faculty prepare reading guides, which include prereading tasks to help students activate appropriate schemata for the assigned L2 reading and define clear purposes or tasks for reading the text. When students are given too much reading or are not given sufficient guidance for reading an L2 text, they can become very frustrated, thus rendering FLAC instruction less effective.

In addition to the impact of SLA research, these FLAC programs received impetus from historians, social scientists, and other faculty outside the departments of language and literature who were interested in internationalizing the curriculum and felt that students could use their language skills to enhance their course work outside language and literature departments. Most often, faculty who advocated FLAC programs were already proficient in one or more languages themselves and used their L2 to conduct research. They sought to encourage students to deepen their knowledge of specific subject matter through the use of the L2. Often they worked in consultation with language and literature faculty to develop FLAC courses.

The wealth of influences on the development of FLAC programs have resulted in the creation of a variety of models that correspond to different institutional contexts and to differing levels of competence in the L2.

2.0 Principal FLAC Models

There are three major models for FLAC courses that have developed since the 1980s as documented in volumes edited by Krueger and Ryan (1993), Straight (1994), Stryker and Leaver (1997), and Kecht and von Hammerstein (2000), all of which include broad descriptions of content-based language and FLAC programs at colleges and universities across the United States and Canada. The first model requires the lowest level of L2 proficiency and simply introduces some work in the L2 in a course that is otherwise delivered in English. The second model, the discussion section, requires somewhat higher levels of L2 competence as students are asked to read materials in the L2 throughout the academic term and meet to discuss them once a week in Spanish. The discussion section is tied to a course taught completely in English so that students can draw on background knowledge attained in that class to interpret the L2 texts. The final model is the one that requires the highest level of L2 competence and involves courses taught entirely in Spanish outside the Spanish program.

2.1 Some Use of Spanish in English Language Courses

The first of the three major FLAC models is that of the course in which texts in Spanish replace a percentage of the English language readings assigned for a course. This model developed out of pioneering work done at Earlham College in the early 1980s involving faculty who taught courses that featured texts in translation and had reading knowledge of the original language of those texts. These faculty members, referred to as "facilitators," integrated foreign languages into designated courses in a more systematic fashion through introducing relevant terminology in the language into course lectures, helping students read a significant portion of one course assignment in the original language or encouraging students with appropriate levels of proficiency to read entire texts in the foreign language or use foreign language resources for research projects. For example, the instructor of a Latin American politics course made key Spanish terms such as *latifundio* and *caudillo* part of the course terminology, allowed students to choose between an English language text and a Spanish alternative for one of the reading assignments, and asked students of Spanish to consult at least one Spanish source for an annotated bibliography assignment (Jurasek 1988, 53–55). This model appeals to faculty and students because of the modest demands it makes on both: faculty need not have speaking ability in the language to participate, and students can choose a level of participation that fits their language abilities (Jurasek 1988, 54). Yet it promotes a broad-based infusion of foreign languages into the curriculum as a whole rather than restricting it to a few selected courses as in other models and easily allows for incremental adjustments upward in the amount of language used in courses. At the same time, the design itself limits the intensiveness of students' engagement with Spanish in any one course and, consequently, limits both content and language learning. Because it does not alter teaching loads, however, it is a low-cost approach to FLAC and, thus, more sustainable over time than other models.

2.2 One-Credit Discussion Sections in Spanish

The most widely used FLAC model is that of the one-credit discussion section in Spanish attached to a full-credit English language core course in a variety of disciplines. For example, students enrolled in a regular three- or four-credit international relations course who have reached a predetermined level of Spanish have the option to enroll concurrently in a one-credit weekly discussion section in Spanish coordinated with the English language course. This model, first developed and popularized by St. Olaf College under the rubric of the "applied foreign language component," has many variants that have emerged in response to the specific institutional contexts of the colleges and universities that have adapted it to their needs. These discussion sessions are referred to by many terms, such as "trailer sections" at the University of Minnesota or Webster University or "enhancement sections" at Oregon State University or the University of Florida at Gainesville.

At some institutions, such as St. Olaf, the applied foreign language component continues to follow a "paired instructor" model, consisting of a two-person team: the instructor of the core English language course, who has both reading and speaking proficiency in Spanish, and a Spanish instructor, both tenured and tenure-track faculty. With the support of course development funds, the two instructors work prior to the first offering of the course to modify the original English language syllabus to integrate the weekly Spanish discussion section and to determine what types of Spanish language texts would be appropriate substitutes for or complements to core-course English language readings. Both instructors consult as they select Spanish language texts, and the Spanish instructor didacticizes the texts for discussion sessions. Normally, the Spanish instructor attends the English language course daily during its first offering as a FLAC course but may or not continue to do so in subsequent offerings. Both instructors are always present at the weekly Spanish language discussion sessions.

Other institutions, such as St. Michael's College, have contemplated offering multiple foreign language discussion sections for a single English language core course. The inverse approach was recently a feature of a Webster University initiative in which a Spanish language trailer course, "Encounters, Changes, and Exchanges: 1492 and Its Consequences," was developed to complement a cluster of five different history, political science, and international relations courses. Both projects met with logistical hurdles that prevented full implementation of the plans.

At the heart of the discussion section model lies the Spanish language text, an authentic text produced for and by native speakers/readers of Spanish and chosen by FLAC instructors to illustrate, amplify, dialogue with, provide an alternative viewpoint to, or even subvert a topic or reading introduced in the core English language course. With regard to text selection, FLAC instructors place primary importance on the subject-matter relevance of the text to the intellectual goals of the FLAC course as a whole, encompassing the package of the English language core course and the accompanying Spanish language discussion session. While a text's linguistic features may have an impact on how a Spanish instructor didacticizes it through various techniques of pedagogical scaffolding so that students can process it effectively (Jurasek 2000, 187–89), they are not the primary determinants of a text's appropriateness.

Most texts chosen for FLAC courses are primary documents not available in English translation and from genres not usually used in the regular English language classroom. For a unit on liberation theology in a Modern Latin American History Survey course at St. Olaf College, for example, students read background information on the radical Catholic movement in a course textbook as well as selected portions of Gustavo Gutiérrez's *Theology of Liberation* (1988), a major theological treatise, in English translation. To gain access to another dimension of the movement, Spanish FLAC students read documents that illustrate liberation theology for and from the layperson's perspective: *Puebla en dibujos* (1980), instructional material in a comic-book format that explains the basic tenets of liberation theology to an intended audience of semiliterate factory workers and farmers or selections from *El evangelio en Solentiname* (Cardenal n.d.), transcripts of Bible study sessions in which Nicaraguan peasants struggled with interpreting the Gospels as revolutionary texts.

Even though the English language course itself provides ample content background to make the ideas in a given Spanish language text familiar to students, most Spanish instructors didacticize the texts to facilitate more productive discussion sessions. Study guides may provide prereading activities to help build a bridge between English language work and the text at hand, to activate students' knowledge of the conventions of a particular genre, or to focus students' attention on the advance organizers of the text; vocabulary activities to introduce lexical items not readily found in conventional bilingual dictionaries; and/or study questions to guide students' processing of the text in preparation for discussion sessions. In this way, writing activities serve as support for subsequent speaking activities. Weekly discussion sessions in Spanish, then, focus on further processing the text through a variety of postreading speaking activities, such as pair, small group, or large group discussions, debates, round tables, or individual or group oral presentations. The ultimate goal of these sessions is to link the content of the Spanish language discussion sessions back to the perspectives in the English language core course in a significant way.

The discussion course model simultaneously enhances learning of content and language learning through the systematic integration of Spanish language texts processed through writing and speaking activities. In the two-instructor model, which pairs faculty from Spanish with colleagues from another discipline and creates teams of permanent faculty that work together on an ongoing basis, participants benefit from a highly integrated experience that is the product of interdisciplinary collaboration. Students wrestling with a Spanish language text do so with the simultaneous support of an instructor well versed in second language acquisition and of another with disciplinary expertise in the topic at hand. Furthermore, they see firsthand how different disciplines treat the same text and they engage in dialogue with one another.

In the aforementioned Modern Latin American History course, for example, while students were discussing Jacobo Timerman's (1981) testimony, *Preso sin nombre, celda sin número,* a heated disagreement broke out as to whether the text was considered literature or a historical document. Students demanded consensus regarding its classification. The exchange between the history instructor and the Spanish instructor allowed for a nuanced discussion of history and literature as two different types of narrative construct that led students away from their demand that the text be labeled exclusively one or the other.

Finally, the instructor of the English language core course serves for the students as a role model of a professional who uses (and sometimes struggles with) Spanish in a significant way in the real world in ways not always imaginable in the conventional foreign language classroom.

The obstacles to the continued survival of this model derive from the same feature that makes it such a powerful academic experience: its labor intensiveness and cost. In addition to the time involved in initial course and materials development, always time-consuming but doubly so when faculty members must coordinate as a team, the discussion section is often taught on an overload basis for both faculty. The institutions that have been successful in maintaining this model over time after grant funding has ended are those that have been able to provide compensation to faculty in the program, either in the form of overload stipends (St. Olaf College) or by allowing instructors to "bank" overload credits toward an eventual course release (Agnes Scott College n.d.).

Several variations on this model are in place at institutions across the United States. At research institutions with graduate programs, such as the Universities of Florida (Gainesville), Kansas, and Minnesota, the team approach often pairs a tenured faculty member in charge of the English language core course with a graduate teaching assistant (TA) from a Spanish department or a native speaker of Spanish who is a teaching assistant in the home disciplinary department of the core course. The degree and frequency of interaction between faculty member and teaching assistant and the amount of participation of the faculty member in the weekly Spanish discussion session is usu-ally a function of the particular team rather than an institutional mandate. The State University of New York at Binghamton has developed yet another version of the two-instructor model in their LxC (Languages Across the Curriculum) Program. The fac-ulty member teaching the core English language course may or may not be proficient in Spanish but identifies the language experience of students at the beginning of the course. Given sufficient interest, Spanish study group meetings with the students are organized and conducted by graduate teaching assistants proficient in Spanish, usual-ly international graduate students, referred to as language resource specialists (Straight, Rose, and Badger 1994, 8).

These variations of the two-instructor model can be highly cost-effective, as grad-uate student stipends are less than faculty compensation. Moreover, they afford grad-uate students unique preprofessional experience. At the same time, the transient nature of graduate student populations may be an impediment to continuity of pro-grams over time. Finally, unless there is significant ongoing faculty-graduate student collaboration, the full integration of content learning and language learning in the Spanish discussion session may be at risk. TAs from Spanish may excel in helping through texts linguistically but may lack sufficient background knowledge in the dis-cipline to exploit their content fully; conversely, native-speaking TAs from other dis-ciplines may be subject area specialists but may not have experience in how to help language learners process texts effectively in Spanish.

At St. Olaf College, some discussion section courses are now taught as designated "single instructor" courses, in which the same faculty member offers both the English language core course and the weekly discussion session. This has been done when the core course instructor is already proficient in the foreign language and there are per-sonnel constraints (lack of a foreign language partner due to sabbatical or other leaves or because of other staffing needs) or when a foreign language instructor is already the core course instructor, as in the case, for example, of an interdisciplinary Hispanic studies seminar on contemporary Latin American issues. The "single instructor" model is more cost-effective than the two-instructor model, but it sacrifices the inter-disciplinary collaboration of the two-person team.

2.3 Courses in Spanish

The final model involves teaching a course outside the Spanish program completely in Spanish and, at some institutions, combining it with other course work to form a Spanish immersion semester. Temple University, for example, has offered a success-ful Latin American Studies Semester (LASS), a fifteen-credit total immersion, inter-disciplinary program, each spring since 1973. Students meet daily from 9:00 a.m. to 3:00 p.m., attending Spanish language courses in the morning and courses in Spanish focusing on the study of Latin America through social science, literature, and film in the afternoon. During spring break the entire class travels to Mexico for two weeks of on-site instruction.

Since 1993 the University of Minnesota has offered a Foreign Language Immersion Program that allows students who have completed a minimum of five semesters of university-level Spanish to take an entire semester of course work in Spanish. Students choose from a variety of courses offered in the Department of Spanish and Portuguese Studies as well as one or two social science courses. While many students have benefited from the program, it is clear from previous research (Klee and Tedick 1997; Lynch, Klee, and Tedick 2001) that those who enter the program with the minimum number of courses and/or are not at the Intermediate High level of proficiency on the American Council on the Teaching of Foreign Languages scale find the program to be too rigorous, and often their proficiency level does not improve over the course of the semester. Students whose Spanish proficiency is at the threshold level do tend to improve, and they report that their comfort level with Spanish increases (cf. Klee and Tedick 1997).

This model has faced considerable challenges. Some of the social science instructors have resisted employing sheltering strategies because they believe that the course content will be watered down; the consequences are devastating for students who are overwhelmed by the difficulty of the readings and lectures in Spanish. Ideally, the social science instructors who are comfortable delivering content in Spanish would teach a course in the program each spring. Unfortunately, due to budget constraints and the fact that, for example, a Latin American Politics class can be taught in English to seventy-five students as opposed to twenty-five students when taught in Spanish, it has not been possible to have faculty teach on a regular basis. As a result, advanced graduate students normally teach the courses. Many of them have taught Spanish language courses and are sensitive to the challenges inherent to content-based instruction, but training must be ongoing. It is hoped that they will be able to transport their experience with advanced CBI to another institution when they complete their doctoral degree.

3.0 Lessons Learned

The 1990s saw the birth and demise of many innovative Spanish FLAC programs nationwide. An infusion of grant money and support from public and private sources encouraged a number of institutions to create programs in addition to those already mentioned in this chapter, including Birmingham-Southern College, Brown University, Colgate University, Dickinson College, Duke University, Grinnell College, Hartwick College, Kalamazoo College, Michigan State University, Pacific Lutheran College, Skidmore College, SUNY-Oswego, SUNY-Potsdam, Syracuse University, Transylvania University, Trinity University, University of California–Santa Cruz, University of Connecticut, University of Michigan, University of North Carolina, and University of Rhode Island.

Initially, FLAC seemed to respond to a number of intersecting academic objectives: the nationwide interest in internationalizing institutions of all sizes, innovations in foreign language curricula that looked beyond the study of literature as the only end point of language instruction, the decentralization of other aspects of postsecondary education (such as writing-across-the-curriculum programs), and so forth. The enthusiasm and success of FLAC programs heralded changes with the capacity to transform institutions. Emily Spinelli summed up the possibilities of FLAC in the mid-1990s: "In many cases the entire ethos of the institution changes as faculty members and students alike see the advantages of using foreign languages to acquire multicultural perspectives within a variety of disciplines" (Spinelli 1995 n.p.).

But while some programs continue to flourish, albeit with a more limited array of course options than in place during grant-funded stages of development, others exist only as memories of past projects on websites or as intermittent offerings by a few committed individuals who struggle on with minimal or no institutional support. Analyses of current programs yield a few patterns.

3.1 Embeddedness in a Larger Curricular or Programmatic Context

One of the major challenges facing FLAC programs is that they are often perceived as "dilettante add-ons to the regular curriculum" because of the ad hoc way in which they originally drew upon the talents and enthusiasm of a collection of instructors from a variety of disciplines. Instability in staffing makes them subject to the professional and personal situations of individuals or may prevent intellectual integration into broader programs (James 2000, 48). James points out that serious FLAC programs need to recognize the differences between various FLAC initiatives and examine their curricular appropriateness in terms of by whom, for whom, and at what level they should be taught (James 2000, 49).

Evidence of successful ongoing programs is their embeddedness in a larger curricular or programmatic context. For example, over twenty years of work with FLAC at Earlham College has permitted the development of what James refers to as a pervasive "culture of support" on that campus that permeates the institution (James 2000, 52). In the case of the University of Rhode Island, FLAC is fully integrated into the university's International Engineering Program (IEP), which awards students a dual degree (bachelor of science degree in an engineering field with a bachelor of arts degree in a foreign language). Students enrolled in the Spanish IEP complement on-campus work in Spanish and engineering by participating in study-abroad programs in Spain or Latin America and internships in Spanish-speaking countries.

"FLAC at FLA," the University of Florida–Gainesville's program, is a joint project of the Department of Romance Languages and Literatures and the Center for Latin American Studies. The program's stated goal is to "integrate the study of Latin American or European topics with the practice of Romance languages" (University of Florida n.d.). All FLAC sections are taught by graduate students from Romance Languages and Literatures, and training in content-based teaching is provided, with a salary supplement (University of Florida n.d.). At Agnes Scott College, the program is administered by a director who is assisted by an advisory committee. Credits from Spanish LAC courses count toward either the Spanish major or minor (Agnes Scott College n.d.).

St. Olaf College's FLAC program is a recognized interdisciplinary program within the Faculty of Humanities and has a director appointed for a three-year term and a permanent steering committee made up of faculty from foreign languages and other disciplines. Students who complete two FLAC courses receive an "applied foreign language competency" designation on their transcript. Embedding FLAC programs not only gives them intellectual institutional homes but also facilitates maintaining other components important for continued success: ongoing program administration, stable staffing and course rotations, institutionalization of incentives and recognition for participation for both faculty and students, and access to ongoing financial support and some degree of protection in times of institutional budget cutting.

3.2 Ongoing Financial Support

Academic embeddedness alone, however, cannot ensure survival of a program over time. For programs to thrive, they must have guaranteed financial support to provide compensation for program administration, course development, instructor or TA training, and teaching stipends. Institutions with Title VI–funded area studies programs, such as the University of Florida, can count on a steady stream of outside funding. Many other successful programs have internal sources of funding. KULAC, Kansas University Languages Across the Curriculum, for example, enjoys continued funding from the College of Liberal Arts and Sciences (Merydith-Wolf 2002, 3). St. Olaf College has a permanent endowment that provides compensation for the program director, course development money for faculty creating new FLAC courses, and stipends for overload teaching. Faculty at Agnes Scott College have access to course development funds and can "bank" credits earned in teaching discussion sections as overloads toward an eventual course release (three FLAC sections would earn one three-credit course release). The University of Rhode Islands's International Engineering Program benefits from support from international companies as well as from private donors (University of Rhode Island 2003).

3.3 Careful Match between Student Language Proficiency and Program Requirements

Criticisms of FLAC have focused on the insufficient linguistic preparation of students, especially in terms of foreign language reading skills, for them to be to able to participate in a "substantive" rather than "illustrative" program (Sudermann and Cisar 1992). In response to these criticisms, James has pointed out that the potential mismatch between student proficiency and course expectations with regard to reading is not in itself limited to FLAC courses but is endemic in upper-division literature courses (James 2000, 57). Others admonish FLAC practitioners from seeming to divorce FLAC's emphasis on content learning from its language learning context (Byrnes 2000, 159–60). Byrnes in particular exhorts instructors involved in content-based initiatives to base their work on "refined reflection on language as the medium for content, knowledge, and meaning *within and through a discourse context* that is both linguistic and extralinguistic" (171). Doing so, in her judgment, implies envisioning FLAC as part of a coherent language learning curriculum that focuses on continuous language development overall rather than a series of add-ons to highlight links with specific content areas.

Although most Spanish FLAC programs are not yet as intimately integrated into their local curricula as Byrnes recommends, the most successful programs have identified clearly the level of proficiency necessary for entry into the program (usually the completion of a four-semester language requirement, the point of entry into Spanish major-level courses), have coordinated reading expectations of FLAC instructors with the actual reading proficiency of students enrolled in the program, and provide ongoing support for FLAC students as language learners. Development of a FLAC program can also have a positive influence on the Spanish curriculum. At St. Olaf College, for example, the involvement of a high number of permanent Spanish faculty in the FLAC program has had a major impact on all levels of instruction in Spanish, including (1) the development of a content-based second-year Spanish sequence, (2) the transformation of nonliterature classes, such as Spanish and Latin American culture and civilization and advanced oral and written expression, to include a greater variety of primary sources, both literary and nonliterary, and (3) a focus on enhanced contextualization of literary texts in upper-level courses.

Although all three types of changes were under way simultaneously, the first to be systematically implemented was the creation of a content-based second-year curriculum. Careful observation of students' challenges and successes reading a variety of nonliterary texts in Spanish FLAC sections, ranging from carefully selected constitutions and speeches to illustrated accounts of the Spanish conquest of the Americas, testimonies, and turn-of-the-century essays on the dangers of miscegenation, showed both what students can achieve in terms of content learning when Spanish language texts are read against the backdrop of in-depth topic familiarity (provided, in these cases, by the English language core courses) and the limitations of the previous grammar-based second-year syllabus. The second-year language program was restructured around a content focus (the material and human diversity of the Spanish-speaking world in the third semester and the culture of U.S. Hispanics in the fourth semester) with carefully integrated language-learning goals.

Ongoing instruction in reading strategies became an essential part of the entire sequence. Authentic texts, primarily from the periodical press in third-semester Spanish, and a wide range of text types, including an autobiography, in fourth-semester Spanish, were chosen to expose students to different types of language: demographic, economic, sociological, political, and so forth. Drawing on work didacticizing texts for the Spanish FLAC components with prereading, reading, and postreading activities, reading guides were developed for all texts used in the second-year program. Furthermore, language practice and use activities were wrapped around the authentic texts, coordinating specific language learning objectives with features of the texts themselves and then recycling them throughout the sequence. For example, the third-semester course starts with readings from Spanish language atlases that describe the United States and all Spanish-speaking counties. The language in the atlas pages is primarily descriptive, thus providing an opening for language use activities that highlight use of *ser* versus *estar* and descriptive adjectives. Yet these texts, apparently objective at first glance, also contain some highly debatable conclusions about the countries portrayed. Students bristle at some of the representations of the United States and immediately want to respond to them, creating a natural opening for practicing agreeing and disagreeing with other opinions (and for the use of the subjunctive with verbs of doubt). Evaluation of student learning in these courses through speaking and writing activities interweaves the learning of new course content, acquisition of appropriate topic-specific vocabulary, and use of linguistic and discursive elements necessary for communicative tasks (the subjunctive for recommendations, for instance).

Furthermore, faculty started to intentionally point out links between the readings or themes explored in Spanish classes to materials or topics or courses outside the department. Thus readings on the history of the tension between economic development through tourism and environmental preservation in the Galápagos Islands led faculty to bring to students' attention a biology course taught as part of the January interim offerings. Soon students began to do the same. A student enrolled in a women's studies course one semester, for example, explained relevant information from her English language course to her classmates in Spanish on a daily basis while the class was studying changing family structures in the Spanish-speaking world.

The second major change in the Spanish curriculum was the systematic use of a variety of primary documents and texts in upper-level nonliterature courses. For example, the course syllabi for culture and civilization courses used to be organized around a conventional culture and civilization textbook and some supplemental literary works (including poems, short stories, and/or plays). After seeing students successfully read and discuss primary sources in Spanish FLAC courses, faculty imported the practice of using selected primary documents to complement key themes in the textbook. Thus students in the Culture and Civilization of Spain course studying the growing religious intolerance in fifteenth- and sixteenth-century Spain read the actual 1492 Edit of Expulsion issued by Ferdinand and Isabella and King Charles V's promise to vanquish Northern European Protestants after the 1521 Diet of Worms in the original Spanish instead of only reading about these events.

Finally, the value of contextualizing texts in order to help students read them effectively became very apparent in the Spanish FLAC components. Once faculty saw the degree to which the intellectual framework of the English language core course prepared students to read what would have originally perceived to be very difficult Spanish language texts by giving them important topic-relevant or sociocultural background, faculty realized that students in literature courses would read literary texts more effectively if they had similarly appropriate background knowledge in advance. After all, as Kern (2000) reminds us, foreign language readers are by nature unintended readers of texts and, thus, are often lacking in knowledge of the sociohistorical or cultural circumstances underlying texts. Yet he warns also that providing excessive background information can be counterproductive, as it may limit students' ability to learn from their reading and thus reduce their motivation, for "we rarely bother to read texts that tell us what we already know" (2000, 98). The challenge, then, became how to contextualize literary texts sufficiently to aid students in reading them as cultural outsiders without destroying their enthusiasm for reading. Colleagues using Angeles Mastretta's *Mal de amores* (1996), for example, have designed activities to introduce students to key aspects of the Mexican Revolution to help them connect the discourse of the novel to its sociocultural frame.

Finally, across all levels of the curriculum, faculty have become more attuned to the need to clearly define reading tasks for the benefit of students and instructors alike and to continue to consider how to best do so. In this regard, Byrnes's (2000) emphasis on task complexity (the particular cognitive load of a given task), task difficulty (related to factors internal to the individual learner), and task conditions that can have an impact on performance provides guidelines that can orient instructors (170).

4.0 Conclusion

FLAC programs were initiated with great enthusiasm at a wide variety of postsecondary institutions in the 1980s and 1990s as interest rose in internationalizing the curriculum and as funding agencies provided support. Unfortunately, once external funding ended, many programs suffered reductions in the number and types of courses they could offer, and some programs have ceased operating. Unless FLAC programs are embedded in a larger institutional context, receive ongoing financial support, and carefully match student L2 proficiency with program requirements and objectives, they are unlikely to succeed over the long term. When these basic requirements are in place, however, FLAC programs can provide students with opportunities to use and perhaps further develop their language skills through a wider variety of disciplines than is offered through most Spanish programs. In addition, FLAC programs can have a positive impact on curriculum development in Spanish programs, as is evident in the St. Olaf experience described above.

Standards for Foreign Language Learning (1996) has provided support for FLAC by including a primary goal that calls for students to further their knowledge of other disciplines through their L2 and acquire information and recognize distinctive viewpoints only available through the L2. While FLAC courses are still relatively rare for non-immersion K–12 students, their use may expand in the future.

It is widely believed that FLAC programs provide benefits to students both in terms of furthering their L2 development, particularly in reading, and by providing them with access to new perspectives through their L2. Effective programs tend to be context-specific; what functions well in one institution may not work well in another. Certainly, more qualitative and quantitative research is needed to determine the degree to which FLAC programs are contributing to students' language and content development as well as to their continued use of the L2 once they graduate.

References

Adamson, H. D. 1993. *Academic competence: Theory and classroom practice: Preparing ESL students for content courses.* White Plains, NY: Longman.

Agnes Scott College. N.d. Spanish program requirements. www.agnesscott.edu/academics/
   p_programrequirements.asp?type=d&id=34 (accessed June 10, 2006).

Brinton, D. M., M. A. Snow, and M. Wesche. 1989. *Content-based second language instruction.*
   Rowley, MA: Newbury House.

———. 2003. *Content-based second language instruction.* 1989, Reprint, with an epilogue of
   new developments, Ann Arbor: University of Michigan Press.

Byrnes, H. 2000. Languages across the curriculum—Intradepartmental curriculum construction. In *Languages across the curriculum: Interdisciplinary structures and internationalized
   education,* ed. M.-R. Kecht and K. von Hammerstein, 151–75. Columbus, OH: National
   East Asian Languages Resource Center.

Cardenal, E., ed. N.d. *El evangelio en Solentiname.* Managua: Departamento Ecuménico de
   Investigaciones.

Carrell, P. L., and Joan Eisterhold. 1983. Schema theory and ESL reading pedagogy. *TESOL
   Quarterly* 14:553–73.

Coady, J. 1979. A psycholinguistic model of the ESL reader. In *Reading in a second language,*
   ed. R. Mackay, B. Barkman, and R. R. Jordan, 5–12. Rowley, MA: Newbury House.

Consortium for Languages Across the Curriculum. 1996. Languages across the curriculum
   website. www.language.brown.edu/LAC/ (accessed June 10, 2006).

Gregg, Kevin R. 1986. The input hypothesis: Issues and implications. *TESOL Quarterly*
   20:116–22.

Gutiérrez, G. 1988. *A theology of liberation.* Maryknoll, NY: Orbis Books.

James, D. 2000. Into the institutional mainstream: The professionalization of LAC. In
   *Languages across the curriculum: Interdisciplinary structures and internationalized educa-
   tion,* ed. M.-R. Kecht and K. von Hammerstein, 39–60. Columbus, OH: National East
   Asian Languages Resource Center.

Jurasek, R. 1988. Integrating foreign languages into the college curriculum. *Modern Language
   Journal* 72 (1): 52–58.

———. 2000. Languages across the curriculum as meaning making: Triangulating the ways
   we understand field reading, classroom pedagogy, and learning outcomes. In *Languages
   across the curriculum: Interdisciplinary structures and internationalized education,* ed.
   M.-R. Kecht and K. von Hammerstein, 177–99. Columbus, OH: National East Asian
   Languages Resource Center.

Kecht, M-R., and K. von Hammerstein, eds. 2000. *Languages across the curriculum:
   Interdisciplinary structures and internationalized education.* Columbus, OH: National East
   Asian Languages Resource Center.

Kern, R. 2000. *Literacy and language teaching.* Oxford: Oxford University Press.

Klee, C. A., and D. J. Tedick. 1997. The undergraduate foreign language immersion program
   in Spanish at the University of Minnesota. In *Content-based instruction in the foreign language classroom,* ed. S. Stryker and B. L. Leaver, 140–73. Washington, D.C.: Georgetown
   University Press.

Krashen, S. 1982. *Principles and practice in second language acquisition.* New York: Pergamon
   Press.

Krueger, M., and F. Ryan, eds. 1993. *Language and content: Discipline- and content-based
   approaches to language study.* Lexington, MA: D.C. Heath.

Lynch, A., C. A. Klee, and D. J. Tedick. 2001. Social factors and Spanish language proficiency
   in postsecondary Spanish immersion: Issues and implications. *Hispania* 84:265–79.

Mastretta, A. 1996. *Mal de amores.* Madrid: Alfaguara.

McLaughlin, B. 1987. *Theories of second language learning.* London: Edward Arnold.

Merydith-Wolf, A., ed. 2002. *Annual report, 2001–02: Office of International Programs, the
   University of Kansas.* Lawrence: Office of International Programs, University of Kansas.

Nunan, D. 1989. *Designing tasks for the communicative classroom.* Cambridge: Cambridge University Press.

Puebla en dibujos. 1980. Bogotá: Corporación Integral para el Desarrollo Cultural y Social.

Spinelli, E. 1995. Languages across the curriculum: A postsecondary initiative. ACTFL white paper. *ACTFL Newsletter,* fall, n.p.

Spolsky, B. 1985. Formulating a theory of second language acquisition. *Studies in Second Language Acquisition* 7:269–88.

Standards for foreign language learning: Preparing for the 21st century. Yonkers, NY: National Standards in Foreign Language Education Project, 1996.

Straight, H. S., Ed. 1994. *Languages across the curriculum: Invited essays on the use of foreign languages throughout the postsecondary curriculum.* Binghamton, NY: Center for Research in Translation.

Straight, H. S., M. G. Rose, and E. H. Badger. 1994. International students as resource specialists: Binghamton's languages across the curriculum program. In *Language across the curriculum: Translation perspectives VII,* ed. H. S. Straight, 7–34. Binghamton, NY: Center for Research in Translation.

Stryker, S. B., and B. L. Leaver, eds. 1997. *Content-based instruction in foreign language education.* Washington, DC: Georgetown University Press.

Sudermann, D. P., and M. A. Cisar. 1992. Foreign language across the curriculum: A critical appraisal. *Modern Language Journal* 76 (3): 295–308.

Swain, M. 1985. Communicative competence: Some roles of comprehensible input and comprehensible output in its development. In *Input in second language acquisition,* ed. S. M. Gass and C. G. Madden, 235–53. Rowley, MA: Newbury House.

Timerman, J. 1981. *Preso sin nombre, celda sin número.* New York: Random.

University of Florida. Department of Romance Languages and Literatures. N.d. FLAC courses. http://web.rll.ufl.edu/FLAC/about—courses.html (accessed June 10, 2006).

University of Rhode Island. 2003. International Engineering Program website. Spanish IEP Questions & Answers. www.uri.edu/iep/spanish/overview/faqs.htm (accessed June 10, 2006).

VanPatten, B. 1987. On babies and bathwater: Input and second language learning. *Modern Language Journal* 71:156–64.

Spanish SLA Research, Classroom Practice, and Curriculum Design

Joseph Collentine *Northern Arizona University*

The study of second language acquisition (SLA) and its pedagogical practices for fostering learner development are underscored by theoretical premises that reflect both general learning theory and SLA-specific theories. While there is overlap in terms of the basic premises of the theories and their implications for Spanish educators (e.g., constructivism and sociocultural theory), each has uniquely contributed to investigative and instructional practices. In considering the lines of theoretical and applied research that prevail in SLA (and related fields), three general strands impact how we design both our curriculum from the beginning to more advanced levels and individual sequences/tasks. The consideration of curriculum design issues along with (particular) task design issues necessitates an understanding of not only how Spanish educators establish the linguistic and sociolinguistic foundations of communicative competence but also how we promote advanced communicative abilities. The lines of research are (1) the general learning theory of constructivism, (2) psycholinguistics and cognition, and (3) social and sociocultural cognition.

1.0 Constructivism

Up until the late 1970s, the traditional learning theory that informed curricular and classroom practices was objectivism, which assumes that the essential elements of instruction are communication and deduction. The objectivist approach to education supposes that new knowledge is delivered to learners. Once a construct has been (properly) explained to learners, they are to infer its application to both concrete and abstract phenomena. In many educational settings this approach to instruction is termed teacher-centered education (cf. Shane 1986). The cognitive code method is one of the best examples of the manifestation of objectivist principles of learning in the second and foreign language classroom. This method normally encourages teachers to present grammar rules to students in the clearest fashion and allow for ample, controlled practice; the premise is that once this information becomes catalogued in learners' minds, they—helped by their powerful, innate language-processing abilities (Boey 1975)—will be able to extrapolate the applications of those rules (Chastain 1969). Textbooks contained exhaustive descriptions of, say, the uses of *por* and *para*, which were followed by largely decontextualized practice items in which students were to infer which preposition was most appropriate.

In the 1980s constructivism—the theoretical antithesis of objectivism—became increasingly important in dialogues on educational practice, as researchers brought forth studies showing the benefits of taking into account a learner's background knowledge (Ausubel 1968) and the importance of linguistic negotiations (be it with peers in group activities or instructors in Socratic discussions/lessons; Bruner 1996) on knowledge development. This paradigm shift proposed that learners must be active agents in the knowledge acquisition processing, building new stores on top of and in relationship to their linguistic, encyclopedic, and experiential knowledge stores to acquire new knowledge (McGroarty 1998; Spivey 1997). As agents they must explore new concepts from multiple perspectives to increase the likelihood that their previous knowledge stores interface with how they uncover new concepts. Reading tasks began to incorporate advanced organizers to maximize comprehension and facilitate the acquisition of vocabulary. Problem-solving tasks began to emerge in lesson plans, in which, for instance, learners were to design and present a synthesis of the week's important news items in Spanish.

If one broadly interprets the constructivist movement as a shift to viewing the learner as an agent rather than a recipient of knowledge, we see the context in which Krashen essentially translates a constructivist model of reading to the FL classroom, postulating that acquisition will result from listening-comprehension and reading activities that are interesting to learners (i.e., for which they have background knowledge) and are a bit beyond their current level of development (i.e., i + 1 input with which the learner can add to what he or she already knows). Additionally, proficiency-based approaches to instruction (stemming from the assessment role of the Oral Proficiency Interview, or OPI) stressed the importance of interpersonal communication. It became less important that a student could describe a grammatical construct; rather, the recognition that acquisition stems from agency coincided with the widespread incorporation of assessment measures (such as the OPI and the popularity of role-play "oral exams") that gauged whether a learner could employ that (or like) constructs (Kramsch 1986). At this time, role-play activities began to replace oral tasks that only entailed a question-answer format.

Constructivist tenets of knowledge development probably continue to be so pervasive in second language education because, even in general learning theory, language skills (i.e., syntactic, morphological, phonological, discourse, pragmatic) are the primary means by which the learner takes control of his own development (Bruner 1983). Approaches to instruction that involve apprenticeships, problem-based learning, and student collaboration are direct manifestations of the constructivist philosophy (Brown and King 2000). Indeed, as will be seen below, these instructional strategies are built into the fabric of output-oriented approaches to SLA and task-based instruction.

Nevertheless, while constructivism signals a broad, general paradigm shift in education, its most frequently studied construct is situated learning, which occurs when learners experience how a particular knowledge construct is useful in problem solving that is often real-world in nature (Brown, Collins, and Duguid 1989; see also Salaberry 1996). SLA pedagogues have spoken of the need to involve learners in task-based activities or assignments where they not only employ the target language but also work toward some nonlinguistic goal (Crookes and Gass 1993; Long 1997; Nunan 1989). Task-based activities impose real-world goals on learners; they must use the target language to relate meaning, and successful task completion is measured against outcomes-based criteria rather that linguistic criteria (Skehan 1998). The types of tasks that have worked their way into the curriculum range from informa- tion gaps, where learners individually depend on their own background knowledge to help each other solve a problem (e.g., jigsaw), to shared tasks, where students assist each other in bridging some learning problem (Pica, Kanagy, and Falodun 1993). Those tasks that allow learners to converge on how to achieve a task (and therefore converge on the immediate knowledge that they use and the conclusions on which they draw to achieve task completion) yield more negotiation of meaning than diver- gent tasks such as a debate (Doughty and Pica 1986). In a convergent task-based activity, groups of learners might converse in Spanish to, say, design a menu for a theme restaurant they own.

The focus of the research on the efficacy of task-based instruction has been on its ability to foster the development of learners' morphosyntactic knowledge. The research to date clearly suggests that task-based activities will only promote the devel- opment of specific constructs in tasks where learners' attention is specifically drawn beforehand to the presence and/or function of the construct (e.g., through some consciousness-raising precursor). After that is established, the focus of the task for the learner can be on its nonlinguistic goal (Ellis 2000). Rosa and Leow (2004) present research indicating that a task that requires the use of the *si* conditional construct is better at promoting the construct's noticing when learners receive explicit pretask instruction about the *si* conditional. Pellettieri (2000) examines the types of negoti- ations that occur in different Spanish CMC activities, finding that those that require more attention to form and coherence lead to more negotiations that require the repackaging of messages with different morphosyntactic configurations; conversely, open-ended tasks lead to negotiations that involve alterations in lexical choice.

Task-based activities will more likely promote fluent speech if they are highly structured (e.g., where the steps that the learner takes are essentially sequenced over time, such as in a cooking activity); they are more likely to promote accuracy and complexity if learners have a chance to plan their output under structured conditions (Foster and Skehan 1999). What is most interesting about the research that has exam- ined the effects of goal-oriented activities on learner performance is that, contrary to the prediction that accuracy will decrease when attentional resources are directed at meaning (as learners cannot divide their attention between accuracy and relating meaning; cf. VanPatten 1990), tasks requiring learners to attend to relating a coher- ent message (such as a narrative) may well lead to more accurate performance (Salaberry and López-Ortega 1998).

A special note is necessary here about the influence of constructivist tenets on the design of computer-assisted language learner (CALL) activities. The growth of com- puter and web-based instruction in the 1990s led many educators to question the effi- cacy of objectivist models of instruction on learning in general, and considerations of constructivist principles of learning have become especially popular in attempts to devise successful computer learning environments. Educators affirm that electronic collaboration may force learners to interact and problem solve in ways that are compatible with the constructivist principles of two or more learners strategizing, sharing knowledge and experiences, linking new to old knowledge, and contextualizing learning (Bonk and King 1998; Bonk and Cunningham 1998). The premise is that electronic environments require learners to take an active role and be agents in their own learning (de Verneil and Berge 2000). Salaberry (1996) challenges CALL educators to abandon drill-and-practice tasks and to consider the benefits of FL software that encourages situated cognition. De la Fuente (2003) presents evidence indicating that CALL environments are equally effective at promoting the acquisition of receptive knowledge of new Spanish vocabulary as face-to-face task-based (quasi-roleplay) activities. Lafford and Lafford (2005) outline task-based activities that lend themselves to participation and interaction in a CMC (computer-mediated communication; e.g., text-based network chats) environment using a combination of wired and wireless technologies.

Nunan (2004) outlines a framework for the development of a syllabus that is designed around task-based principles and activities. To promote SLA, these activities involve evoking students' relevant schemata for a linguistic construct, giving students controlled practice with the construct, exposing them to the construct in some input activity, consciousness-raising activities, role play, and convergent decision making and consensus building. Salaberry et al.'s (2004) textbook *Impresiones* is one of the first serious attempts to infuse the Spanish language market with a curriculum and materials that encourage learners to engage in task-based activities. "One of the foundational principles for the design of *Impresiones* activities," the authors state, "is the assumption that to achieve functional communicative abilities in a second language, communication requirements must be established first" (xi).

Clearly the constructivist influence on education has been widely felt. To be sure, upon examination of its core principles of learner agency and interactivity, it becomes evident that interactionist theory and sociocultural theory are highly compatible with constructivist tenets. Interactionist theory, nonetheless, is more of a reaction to strong claims about the efficacy of input-oriented approaches to instruction that rely heavily on cognitive psychology, and so I treat its role and influence on instruction in the next section. Sociocultural theory stems directly from Vygotsky's influence on learning theory in general, which I explore in a separate section.

2.0 Psycholinguistics and Cognition

Psycholinguistic and cognitive perspectives on how to promote acquisition have focused on the development of the L2 cognitive machine and the ways that external data (from reading and aural sources as well as from interlocutors) interact with such growth. During the 1980s the importance and popularity of Krashen's monitor model of acquisition and the natural approach (Krashen and Terrell 1983) led to a marked rejection of the cognitive code method. Many Spanish curricula were employing *Dos mundos* (Terrell et al. 2002). This focus on meaning (FonM) approach exposed students to vast amounts of aural and textual input while largely abandoning a focus on forms (FonFs) syllabus (i.e., one that organizes the curriculum around the segmentation of various grammatical structures; Long and Crookes 1992) that expects learners to synthesize (extrapolate in the objective terms) their communicative uses. *Dos mundos,* which is still popular in university curricula, required learners to read many articles and short stories and listen to lengthy listening comprehension segments and narratives. The first edition contained few grammatical explanations and did not provide exhaustive descriptions of any given verb paradigm (e.g., providing information and practice with only the first-, second-, and third-person singular preterit forms).

FonM approaches were not providing suitable results. Canadian immersion programs were reporting that learners' grammars were deficient (see Sanz 2000). Even Terrell (1991) acknowledged that comprehensible input was not sufficient for the acquisition of many structures. Psycholinguistically speaking, it was generally agreed that learners could not, on a consistent basis, simultaneously attend to the messages they were reading/listening to and that input's formal features (VanPatten 1990).[1] Schmidt (1990) asserted that input alone was not adequate and that learners needed to "notice" important formal properties in input so that they might become intake, that is, so that these forms could be incorporated into the learner's underlying competence. The theoretical proposal that ensued emphasized that noticing forms in input leads to their intake, which in turn leads to their acquisition. Out of this grew the Focus on Form (FonF) movement, entailing reactive interventions to breakdowns in comprehension that encourage the noticing of some linguistic feature such as an inflection or a functor (Long and Crookes 1992). The FonF approach is a subset of the FonM approach to the extent that it occurs when learners are focused on communication; it distinguishes itself in that it is transitory (e.g., asides in a communicative lesson), not directed at any particular grammatical element, and overall unplanned and reactive (Ellis, Basturkmen, and Loewen 2001). Nonetheless, in a meta-analysis on FonF research Norris and Ortega (2001) conclude that FonF is only as effective as the traditional FonFS approach in promoting linguistic development. It is generally accepted that FonF can only be effective if planned interventions are built into the task.

Various approaches to improving FonF exist today. Interactionist research (e.g., Long 1996) specifically set out to understand the types of linguistic strategies that one interlocutor can use with a learner so that the student becomes aware of (i.e., notices) particular shortcomings in his or her own competence. This line of investigation uncovered the benefits of tasks requiring students to "negotiate for meaning" Swain (1993), and Swain and Lapkin (1995) conclude that pushing students to generate output in communicative activities encourages them to notice gaps in their competence, and that pushed output is particularly effective at promoting the acquisition of complex syntactic structures. The ramifications for this perspective are that, while input-oriented tasks may well be appropriate for the initial stages of development, they will, at best, need to live side by side with tasks requiring output.[2] The research on Spanish—apart from the CMC investigations reported above—indicates that negotiations of meaning involving jigsaw activities are effective at promoting the negotiation of meaning (Brooks 1992) but that instructors must carefully plan such tasks since breakdowns into the L1 may be common (Brooks 1991). In general, the Spanish curriculum has continued to embrace production tasks alongside input-oriented ones like those espoused by Krashen. Students are asked to engage in role-play activities in Spanish and information-gap exercises in which one student sees graphic representations of half of a narrative and the fellow student sees graphics for the other half of a narrative, which they co-construct orally.

Nonetheless, many researchers surmise that noticing and intake in communicative tasks involving the negotiation of meaning foster morphosyntactic and grammatical development essentially by chance (i.e., because they are essentially reactive and transitory), and so they are not the best ways to spend class time. Several responses to this criticism have arisen. Consciousness-raising tasks increase learners' awareness of a targeted structure before using or confronting it in some authentic input or output activity (Fotos 1994). Doughty and Williams (1998) advocate planned lessons directed at specific linguistic constructs that will subsequently be necessary in some communicative activity. The most popular approach within the Spanish curriculum is an entirely input-oriented approach developed by VanPatten, who has developed a model of acquisition and a methodology informed by the model whose strategies and activities take into account how learners process grammatical information in input (Lee and VanPatten 1995; VanPatten 1993).[3]

VanPatten's processing instruction (PI) considers that (1) learners prioritize the few attentional resources they possess depending on whether their current language task is to derive meaning or notice formal properties, and (2) learners have biases, largely based on their L1, about where they look for information in a sentence and in particular words (e.g., automatically interpreting the first noun of any Spanish sentence as its subject). Accordingly, PI seeks to train learners to process input differently so that they will notice more morphosyntactic information when listening to or reading Spanish.[4] For example, VanPatten and Cadierno (1993) note that English speakers process most first nouns of sentences as subjects (due to the inflexible English predicate structure of subject + verb). They often interpret a sentence such as *Lo come*

Figure 3.1 The relationship between focus-on-form, processing instruction, and grammatical development (adapted from VanPatten and Cadierno 1993)

Focus on Form: draw attention to forms causing comprehension breakdowns

input ———→ intake ———→ developing system ———→ output

Processing Instruction: focused practice to alter processing mechanisms

'You/he/she eat(s)' as "He eats." PI trains students to process first nouns differently, allowing them to be either subjects or objects.

PI research has generated dynamic dialogue—with differing interpretations of data, construct validity, and ecological validity—over the past ten years. Nevertheless, it has also been practical in nature. This research enterprise has outlined cognitive principles to which teachers should adhere and has developed teaching practices that promote the acquisition by L2 learners of Spanish of such constructs as object pronouns (Salaberry 1997; VanPatten and Cadierno 1993), the preterit (Cadierno 1995), the subjunctive (Collentine 1998, 2002; Collentine et al. 2002; Farley 2001), ser/estar (Cheng 2002), and conditional verb forms (DeKeyser and Sokalski 1996). VanPatten, Lee, and Ballman's (1996) ¿Sabías Que . . . ? is a textbook that considers the cognitive processing principles identified by VanPatten and his students and incorporates numerous PI activities with copious amounts of input.

A point that has gone relatively unexplored in the acquisitional and instructional literature is that even these FonF approaches that reactively or intentionally (prior to some communicative task) help learners to notice formal properties in input may not be effective with all types of structures. Robinson (1996, 1997) posits that complex linguistic phenomena require different methodological interventions than relatively simple linguistic phenomena. Specifically, learners are more likely to develop knowledge for complex rules under "enhanced learning" conditions (Robinson 1997). Enhanced learning involves tasks where a learner is instructed to get meaning from some type of input while some heuristic modification to that input attempts to draw the learner's attention to a targeted grammatical phenomenon (e.g., underlining or colorizing a subordinating conjunction). Collentine et al. (2002) present evidence that such an approach—coupled with PI techniques in a CALL environment—can positively affect the syntactic environments where they employ the subjunctive. They used various coloring and aural techniques to help students learn the logical relationships encoded by various conjunctions (e.g., cuando, que, si) and to associate the subjunctive with que.

As psycholinguistic perspectives of morphosyntactic processing have continued to inform both research and pedagogy, general psychological theories of memory have had important impacts on the Spanish curriculum, especially as it relates to the preterit/imperfect distinction. Activities that involve learners' episodic memory and cognitive "scripts" (e.g., advanced organizers) facilitate the acquisition process because they add new memories to related, rather than isolated, bits of information (McLaughlin 1987). Additionally, linguists have dedicated a great deal of their efforts to understanding the role of lexical aspect (Comrie 1976; Vendler 1957) and discourse theories (Dahl 1985; Hopper 1982) in the distribution and functions of the preterit and the imperfect in narratives. According to Montrul and Salaberry (2003), the research indicates that at the beginning stages of acquisition learners of Spanish generalize the preterit to all instances of the past, and that as learners progress in their development there is a general tendency to depend on lexical aspect rather than discourse function when determining which tense to employ (e.g., using the imperfect for all instances of stative verbs; the preterit for all achievements).

Interestingly, while the linguistic research on the "grammar of the narrative" indicates that the preterit's function is largely one of marking foreground events and the imperfect backgrounds events, there is no evidence in Spanish suggesting that students can develop their preterit/imperfect abilities if they learn these discourse functions. Nonetheless, textbooks such as *Puntos de Partida* (Knorre et al. 2005) now include allusions to these theories in their student presentations (e.g., completed events versus background). Most important, the general acceptance by Spanish educators that these two paradigms do more than comment on the past and that they are the primary tools for telling stories has changed preterit/imperfect instruction: for the most part, preterit/imperfect activities ask learners to complete a narrative or produce one, especially in oral interviews.

At the same time that researchers have been incorporating psycholinguistic principles into curricular and task design, there has emerged a general understanding that complex constructs are not acquired in their entirety; rather, many constructs that are explainable within a single lesson evidence themselves in learner performance in various steps (Ellis 1990; Hatch 1978). Indeed, Pienneman (1998) has studied in depth the notion of "learnability," which assumes that certain linguistic phenomena can only be acquired when the developing system is ready (e.g., learners will only begin to master the L2's subordination strategies once they mastered its coordination strategies). Currently, Pienneman terms this hypothesis *processability theory* to reflect the fact that learners gradually develop the ability to process—given their limited attentional resources—morphosyntactic information over long distances, which explains why, for instance, learners do not denote interclausal relationships well (e.g., distinguishing between the indicative and the subjunctive in subordinate clauses) until they have relatively mastered the syntax of simple clauses. We now have ample evidence that constructs such as *ser/estar* (Geeslin 2002a, 2002b, 2003; Guntermann 1992b; Ryan and Lafford 1992; VanPatten 1987) and *por/para* (Guntermann 1992a; Lafford and Ryan 1995) emerge in stages (over the course of several years, the semantic and pragmatic functions of these phenomena become increasingly diverse). Research has shown that the subjunctive is not simply acquirable; rather, learners must previously have developed a certain broad linguistic base in Spanish as well as certain requisite syntactic knowledge (Collentine 1995). It is not uncommon for Spanish textbooks today to sequence the presentation of these constructs over the course of a year's worth of curriculum (cf. Terrell et al.'s *Dos Mundos* [2002] and Knorre et al.'s *Puntos de Partida* [2005]).

The last relationship between psycholinguistic/cognitive research and instructional practices does not arguably result from any developmental theory. Instead, it is an offshoot (if not a logical progression) of the interactionist investigations, namely, the research into communication strategies and pragmatics, since negotiating meaning entails not only lexico-grammatical knowledge but also paraphrasing, lexical avoidance, and self-repairs, as well as appropriately requesting information from one's interlocutor.[5] Regarding communication strategies, Liskin-Gasparro (1996) argues that they appear in learner interactions during a narrow range of development, namely, after the initial stages of acquisition (when the learner does not have a productive repertoire) up to more advanced stages (when they are unnecessary). However, it may be that students will need a repertoire of communication strategies to interact in synchronous, non-face-to-face communication. Lee (2001) examined the use of communication strategies by foreign language learners of Spanish in a CMC environment, producing evidence that across proficiency levels students use a variety of strategies (e.g., comprehension checks, clarification checks, requests, and self-repairs). Interestingly, this research has not been limited to the traditional, at-home classroom but has also been extended to consider study abroad contexts. Lafford's (2004) research shows that study-abroad learners tend to use fewer communication strategies when they have much interaction with native speakers of Spanish and their host families. As the learner progresses in his or her development grammatically and lexically, the ability to problem solve increasingly complex linguistic and social negotiations is as valuable as the linguistic rules that a learner has in his or her own armament. The effect of this research is readily felt in materials available today. Current textbooks contain sections that provide activities that promote the development of a lexical repertoire for employing communication strategies and pragmatically appropriate speech.

3.0 Social and Sociocultural Cognition

Sociocultural theory asserts that language is the primary cognitive tool for achieving complex cognitive calculations and abstract thought (Vygotsky 1978). Language processing and production is not a reflection but rather a mediator of thought (i.e., a type of cognition as important or more important than, say, processing procedural knowledge), and raising the L2 to such a status should be the goal of instructed SLA (Lantolf 2000). Indeed, sociocultural theory privileges the role of output in that it rejects the premise that communication is reflected in the standard communication theory metaphor of *encoding* → *output* → *input* → *decoding* (see Firth and Wagner 1997). Interlocutors communicate by creating and converging on new meanings (sometimes referred to as "understandings," in layman's terms), implying that sociocultural theory supports activities where learners negotiate for meaning.

There are various factors that will convert the learner's L2 into a mediator of thought, which will in turn lead to greater levels of proficiency. Like constructivism, sociocultural theory predicts that apprenticeship fosters L2 acquisition.[6] According to Vygotsky (1978), learners operate in a "Zone of Proximal Development" (ZPD), where slightly more advanced peers with whom a learner interacts have an important, necessary role in the development process. Two peers can often achieve greater convergence since they share more background knowledge for any physical, cognitive, or linguistic task than do the learner and the teacher. This does not imply that the teacher has no role (indeed, the teacher is a necessary magister in the development process); instead, group work is predicted to be necessary for fostering development.

The use of private speech, or self-directed oral or written expressions in the L2, also fosters acquisition (Frawley and Lantolf 1985). Consistent with the notion that language mediates thought, a learner employs private speech to regulate learning and intake. Private speech is, however, anarchic, in that it contains a multitude of grammatical tenses rather than a coherent discourse in the present or past, and elliptic, that is, incomplete (e.g., *Yo voy a . . . tengo que . . . ah bueno . . . ésa es la cosa*) (Roebuck 1998). Private speech may also entail language games such as producing neologisms (e.g., *Voy a la librería y a la *comidería [sic = supermercado] . . . ¡Ja ja!*) and repeating key phrases to oneself (Lantolf 2000). Interestingly, the sociocultural perspective does not see L1 usage in activities as counterproductive (e.g., Brooks and Donato 1994).

The sociocultural understanding of SLA has not necessarily led to the design of sociocultural-specific teaching strategies and curricular design. Instead, it has largely validated the inclusion of task-based activities in the classroom (see above). Language games, problem-solving tasks, and cooperative learning activities are highly compatible with this theory's tenets. Antón, Dicamilla, and Lantolf (2003) suggest that the L2 is more likely to become a mediator of thought if the learner uses the L2 with authentic participants or authentic contexts, such as in a study-abroad or an immersion setting. Since sociocultural theory believes that thought emanates from interpersonal communication, language cannot be divorced from its social properties and functions. Grabois (1999) examines lexical development from a Vygotskian perspective, presenting some evidence that the denotations (i.e., the meanings) that study-abroad learners assign certain emotive words (e.g., *felicidad, amor, muerte, tener miedo*) are much more commensurate with native speakers than are the denotations that classroom learners assign such words.

Even researchers who take a decidedly psycholinguistic approach to SLA recognize the importance of considering the external conditions where acquisition occurs. Chaudron (2001) observes: "The increasing effort seen in the 1990s to document the details of classroom interaction with respect to linguistic and social features is encouraging, but it will have to be coupled with a well developed social and pedagogical theory" (65). Researchers are taking a renewed interest in understanding the particular role that study abroad has on acquisition (Collentine 2004a; Collentine and Freed 2004; Lafford 2004).

4.0 Conclusion

The shift to learner-centered teaching practices that constructivist principles encouraged had a broad impact on Spanish SLA research and pedagogical practices. It is not an exaggeration to claim that the initial issue with which Spanish educators struggled was whether to adopt an input-rich environment, which was premised on Krashen's theory of L2 acquisition, or foster proficiency, which was essentially a description of observable behaviors learners should exhibit at various stages of their development. When the input-oriented approach did not produce the desired results, researchers advocated the development of more principled input and output oriented approaches to learner development. The virtues of both approaches continue to be debated today, which will be ultimately healthy for instruction since both input and output approaches are highly scrutinized in the SLA research. Alongside this dynamic, the consideration of the sociocultural conditions where acquisition occurs has become a valid focus of research and materials development.

Spanish L2 instruction has changed dramatically in the past twenty-five years. We understand much better what to introduce and when. We also have a greater appreciation of what it means to acquire an L2, which is not exclusively a mapping of lexical items onto grammar. That said, comparatively speaking, there is very little research available today on the acquisition of vocabulary. Even less effort has been invested in improving the types of activities that foster lexical development, and it will surely be a focus of future research. Additionally, language does not live separately from its surrounding society. This becomes surprisingly evident upon consideration of what learners do and do not acquire in a study-abroad context. The effects of the context of learning on development will undoubtedly need more attention in a (post–September 11) world in which international borders are breaking down digitally and physically.

Notes

1. See Salaberry and López-Ortega (1998) for an alternative perspective.
2. The interactionist approach is also in line with nativist perspectives on SLA to the extent that it presumes that negative feedback—in the form of feedback, recasts, clarification requests, and so on—is often necessary to disprove erroneous learner hypotheses about the nature of the L2 (Mackey 1999).
3. Most of the research stemming from Schmidt's noticing hypothesis spotlights grammatical development. The scope of the research completed on vocabulary development is vast; nonetheless, it has had no appreciable impact on the shape of the Spanish curriculum, on the design of vocabulary activities, or on textbook design. A cognitive theory that is increasingly referenced in research on lexical development is connectionism, which combines key premises of neurology and semiotics to predict how vocabulary will be acquired and incorporated into the learner's competence. See Lafford, Collentine, and Karp (2003) for a comprehensive view of vocabulary research in the context of Spanish SLA.
4. Collentine (2004b) conducted a meta-analysis of the PI research. His data indicate that the PI research produces effect sizes that are high for both PI and so-called traditional approaches to grammar instruction, effect sizes that are much larger than those found for FonF and FonFS research in general reported by Norris and Ortega (2001). That is, similar to the findings of Norris and Ortega, the data-collection instruments used in PI research have essentially shown that both PI and traditional approaches can yield positive results in promoting grammatical development.
5. See Koike, Pearson, and Witten (2003) for a comprehensive review of Spanish SLA research and pedagogy relating to pragmatics.
6. See Antón, Dicamilla, and Lantolf (2003) for a comprehensive review of sociocultural theory and Spanish SLA.

References

Antón, M, F. Dicamilla, and J. Lantolf. 2003. Sociocultural theory and the acquisition of Spanish as a second language. In *Studies in Spanish second language acquisition: The state of the science,* ed. B. Lafford and R. Salaberry, 262–84. Washington, DC: Georgetown University Press.

Ausubel, D. 1968. *Educational psychology: A cognitive view.* New York: Holt, Rinehart & Winston.

Boey, L. K.. 1975. *An introduction to linguistics for the language teacher.* Singapore: Singapore University Press.

Bonk, C., and D. J. Cunningham. 1998. Searching for learner-centered, constructivist, and sociocultural components of collaborative educational learning tools. In *Electronic collaborators: Learner-centered technologies for literacy, apprenticeship, and discourse,* ed. C. Bonk and K. King , 25–50. Mahwah, NJ: Lawrence Erlbaum Associates.

Bonk, C., and K. King. 1998. Computer conferencing and collaborative writing tools: Starting a dialogue about student dialogue. In *Electronic collaborators: Learner-centered technologies for literacy, apprenticeship, and discourse,* ed. C. Bonk and K. King, 3–24. Mahwah, NJ: Lawrence Erlbaum Associates.

Brooks, F. B. 1991. Talking and learning to talk in the Spanish conversation course. *Hispania* 74 (4): 1115–23.

———. 1992. Spanish III learners talking to one another through a jigsaw task. *Canadian Modern Language Review/Revue canadienne des langues vivantes* 48 (4): 696–717.

Brooks, F. B., and R. Donato. 1994. Vygotskyan approaches to understanding foreign language learner discourse during communicative tasks. *Hispania* 77 (2): 262–74.

Brown, J. S., A. Collins, and S. Duguid. 1989. Situated cognition and the culture of learning. *Educational Researcher* 18 (1): 32–42.

Brown, S. W., and F. B. King. 2000. Constructivist pedagogy and how we learn: Educational psychology meets international studies. *International Studies Journal* 1:245–54.

Bruner, J. S. 1983. *Child's talk: Learning to use language.* New York: Norton.

———. 1996. *The culture of education.* Cambridge: Harvard University Press.

Cadierno, T. 1995. Formal instruction from a processing perspective: An investigation into the Spanish past tense. *Modern Language Journal* 79 (2): 179–93.

Chastain, K. 1969. The audiolingual habit theory versus the cognitive-code learning theory: Some theoretical considerations. *International Review of Applied Linguistics in Language Teaching* 7 (2): 97–106.

Chaudron, C. 2001. Progress in language classroom research: Evidence from the *Modern Language Journal,* 1916–2000. *Modern Language Journal* 85:57–76.

Cheng, A. C. 2002. The effects of processing instruction on the acquisition of *ser* and *estar.* *Hispania* 85 (3): 308–23.

Collentine, J. 1995. The development of complex syntax and mood-selection abilities by intermediate-level learners of Spanish. *Hispania* 78 (1): 122–35.

———. 1998. Processing instruction and the subjunctive. *Hispania* 81 (3): 576–87.

———. 2002. On the acquisition of the subjunctive and authentic processing instruction: A response to Farley. *Hispania* 85 (4): 879–88.

———. 2004a. The effects of learning contexts on morphosyntactic and lexical development. *Studies in Second Language Acquisition* 26 (2): 227–48.

———. 2004b. Commentary: Where processing research has been and where it should be going. In *Applications of input processing: Research on processing instruction,* ed. B. VanPatten, 169–82. Mahwah, NJ: Lawrence Erlbaum Associates.

Collentine, J., K. Collentine, V. Clark, and E. Friginal. 2002. Subjunctive instruction enhanced with syntactic instruction. In *Structure, meaning, and acquisition in Spanish: Papers from the 4th Hispanic linguistics symposium,* ed. J. F. Lee, , K. L.Geeslin, , and J. C. Clements, 32–45. Somerville, MA: Cascadilla.

Collentine, J., and B. F. Freed. 2004. Learning context and its effects on second language acquisition: Introduction. *Studies in Second Language Acquisition* 26 (2): 153–71.

Comrie, B. 1976. *Aspect.* Cambridge: Cambridge University Press.

Crookes, G., and S. Gass. 1993. *Tasks in a pedagogical context: Integrating theory and practice.* Clevedon, U.K.: Multilingual Matters.

Dahl, O. 1985. *Tense and aspect systems.* Oxford: Basil Blackwell.

DeKeyser, R., and K. Sokalski. 1996. The differential role of comprehension and production practice. *Language Learning* 46 (4): 613–42.

de la Fuente, M. J. 2003. Is SLA interactionist theory relevant to CALL? A study on the effects of computer-mediated interaction in L2 vocabulary acquisition. *Computer Assisted Language Learning* 16 (1): 47–81.

de Verneil, M., and Z. Berge. 2000. Going online: Guidelines for faculty in higher education. *International Journal of Educational Telecommunications* 6 (3): 227–42.

Doughty, C., and T. Pica. 1986. "Information gap" tasks: Do they facilitate second language acquisition? *TESOL Quarterly* 20 (2): 305–25.

Doughty, C., and J. Williams. 1998. *Focus on form in classroom second language acquisition.* Cambridge: Cambridge University Press.

Ellis, R. 1990. *Instructed second language acquisition.* Oxford: Basil Blackwell.

———. 2000. Task-based research and language pedagogy. *Language Teaching Research* 4 (3): 193–220.

Ellis, R., H. Basturkmen, and S. Loewen. 2001. Learner uptake in communicative ESL lessons. *Language Learning* 51 (2): 281–318.

Farley, A. P. 2001. Authentic processing instruction and the Spanish subjunctive. *Hispania* 84 (2): 289–99.

Firth, A, and J.Wagner. 1997. On discourse, communication, and (some) fundamental concepts in SLA research. *Modern Language Journal* 81:285–300.

Foster, P., and P. Skehan. 1999. The influence of source of planning and focus of planning on task-based performance. *Language Teaching Research* 3 (3): 215–47.

Fotos, S. 1994. Integrating grammar instruction and communicative language use through grammar consciousness-raising tasks. *TESOL Quarterly* 28 (2): 323–51.

Frawley, W., and J. Lantolf. 1985. Second language discourse: A Vygotskyan perspective. *Applied Linguistics* 6 (1): 19–44.

Geeslin, K. L. 2002a. Semantic transparency as a predictor of copula choice in second-language acquisition. *Linguistics* 2 (378): 439–68.

———. 2002b. The acquisition of Spanish copula choice and its relationship to language change. *Studies in Second Language Acquisition* 24 (3): 419–50.

———. 2003. A comparison of copula choice: Native Spanish speakers and advanced learners. *Language Learning* 53 (4): 703–64.

Grabois, H. 1999. The convergence of sociocultural theory and cognitive linguistics. Lexical semantics and the L2 acquisition of love, fear and happiness. In *Cultural constructions of emotional substrates,* ed. G. B. Palmer and D. J. Occhi, 201–33. Amsterdam: John Benjamins.

Guntermann, G. 1992a. An analysis of interlanguage development over time: Part I, *por* and *para. Hispania* 75 (1): 177–87.

———. 1992b. An analysis of interlanguage development over time: Part II, *ser* and *estar. Hispania* 75 (5): 1294–1303.

Hatch, Evelyn, ed. 1978. *Second language acquisition.* Rowley, MA: Newbury House.

Hopper, Paul. 1982. *tense–aspect: Between semantics and pragmatics.* Amsterdam: John Benjamins.

Knorre, M., T. Dorwick, A. Pérez-Gironés, B. Glassand, and B. Villarreal 2005. *Puntos de partida.* 7th ed. New York: McGraw-Hill.

Koike, D., L. Pearson, and C. Witten 2003. Pragmatics and discourse analysis in Spanish second language acquisition research and pedagogy. In *Studies in Spanish second language acquisition: The state of the science,* ed. B. Lafford and R. Salaberry, 160–88. Washington, DC: Georgetown University Press.

Kramsch, C. 1986. Proficiency versus achievement: Reflections on the proficiency movement. *ADFL Bulletin* 18 (1): 22–24.

Krashen, S. D., and T. D. Terrell. 1983. *The natural approach: Language acquisition in the classroom.* London: Prentice Hall Europe.

Lafford, B. A. 2004. The effect of the context of learning on the use of communication strategies by learners of Spanish as a second language. *Studies in Second Language Acquisition* 26 (2): 201–25.

Lafford, B., J. G. Collentine, and A. Karp. 2003. The acquisition of lexical meaning by second language learners: An analysis of general research trends with evidence from Spanish. In *Studies in Spanish second language acquisition: The state of the science,* ed. B. Lafford and R. Salaberry, 130–59. Washington, DC: Georgetown University Press.

Lafford, B. A., J. M. Ryan. 1995. The acquisition of lexical meaning in a study abroad context: The Spanish prepositions *por* and *para. Hispania* 78 (3): 528–47.

Lafford, P., and B. Lafford. 2005. CMC Technologies for teaching foreign languages: What's on the horizon? *CALICO Journal* 22:679–709.

Lantolf, J. P. 2000. *Sociocultural theory and second language learning.* Oxford: Oxford University Press.

Lee, J., and B. VanPatten. 1995. *Making communicative language teaching happen.* New York: McGraw-Hill.

Lee, L. 2001. Online interaction: Negotiation of meaning and strategies used among learners of Spanish. *ReCALL* 13 (2): 232–44.

Liskin-Gasparro, J. E. 1996. Circumlocution, communication strategies, and the ACTFL proficiency guidelines: An analysis of student discourse. *Foreign Language Annals* 29 (3): 317–30.

Long, M. H. 1996. The role of linguistic environment in second language acquisition. In *Handbook of second language acquisition,* ed. W. C. Ritchie and T. K. Bhatia, 413–68. San Diego: Academic Press.

———. 1997. Focus on form in task-based language teaching. www.mhhe.com/socscience/foreignlang/conf/first.htm (accessed November 15, 2001).

Long, M., and G. Crooks.1992. Three approaches to task-based syllabus design. *TESOL Quarterly* 26 (1): 27–55.

Mackey, A. 1999. Input, interaction, and second language development: An empirical study of question formation in ESL. *Studies in Second Language Acquisition* 21 (4): 557–87.

McGroarty, M. 1998. Constructive and constructivist challenges for applied linguistics. *Language Learning* 48 (4): 591–622.

McLaughlin, B. 1987. *Theories of second language learning.* London: Edward Arnold.

Montrul, S., and R. Salaberry. 2003. The development of tense–aspect morphology in L2 Spanish. In *Studies in Spanish second language acquisition: State of the science,* ed. B. Lafford and R. Salaberry, 47–73. Washington, DC: Georgetown University Press.

Norris, J. M., and L. Ortega. 2001. Does type of instruction make a difference? Substantive findings from a meta-analytic review. *Language Learning* 51 (supplement 1): 157–213.

Nunan, D. 1989. *Designing tasks for the communicative classroom.* Cambridge: Cambridge University Press.

———. 2004. *Task-based language teaching.* Cambridge: Cambridge University Press.

Pellettieri, J. 2000. Negotiation in cyberspace: The role of chatting in the development of grammatical competence. In *Network-based language teaching: Concepts and practice,* ed. M. Warschauer and R. Kern, 59–86. New York: Cambridge University Press.

Pica, T., R. Kanagy, and J. Falodun. 1993. Choosing and using communication tasks for second language instruction. In *Tasks and language learning: Integrating theory and practice,* ed. G. Crookes and S. Gass, 9–34. Clevedon, U.K.: Multilingual Matters.

Pienemann, M. 1998. *Language processing and second language development: Processability theory.* Amsterdam: John Benjamins.

Robinson, P. 1996. Learning simple and complex second language rules under implicit, incidental, rule-search, and instructed conditions. *Studies in Second Language Acquisition* 18 (1): 27–67.

———. 1997. Generalizability and automaticity of second language learning under implicit, incidental, enhanced, and instructed conditions. *Studies in Second Language Acquisition* 19 (2): 223–47.

Roebuck, R. 1998. *Reading and recall in L1 and L2: A sociocultural approach.* Stamford, CT: Ablex.

Rosa, E. M., and R. P. Leow. 2004. Computerized task-based exposure, explicitness, type of feedback, and Spanish L2 development. *Modern Language Journal* 88 (2): 192–216.

Ryan, J. M., and B. A. Lafford. 1992. Acquisition of lexical meaning in a study abroad environment: *Ser* and *estar* and the Granada experience. *Hispania* 75 (3): 714–22.

Salaberry, R. 1997. The role of input and output practice in second language acquisition. *Canadian Modern Language Review/Revue canadienne des langues vivantes* 53 (2): 422–51.

Salaberry, R. 1996. A theoretical foundation for the development of pedagogical tasks in computer mediated communication. *CALICO Journal* 14 (1): 5–36.

Salaberry, R., C. Barrette, M. Fernández-García, and P. Elliot. 2004. *Impresiones.* Upper Saddle River, NJ: Pearson–Prentice Hall.

Salaberry, R., and N. López-Ortega. 1998. Accurate L2 production across language tasks: Focus on form, focus on meaning and communicative control. *Modern Language Journal* 82 (4): 514–32.

Sanz, C. 2000. What form to focus on? Linguistics, language awareness, and education of L2 teachers. In *Form and meaning: Multiple perspectives,* ed. J. Lee and A. Valdman, 3–24. Boston: Heinle & Heinle.

Schmidt, R. 1990. The role of consciousness in second language learning. *Applied Linguistics* 11 (2): 127–58.

Shane, A. 1986. Individualized, self-paced instruction: Alternative to the traditional classroom? *ADFL Bulletin* 12 (4): 28–32.

Skehan, P. 1998. Task-based instruction. *Annual Review of Applied Linguistics* 18:268–86.

Spivey, N. N. 1997. *The constructivist metaphor: Reading, writing, and the making of meaning.* San Diego: Academic Press.

Swain, M. 1993. The output hypothesis: Just speaking and writing aren't enough. *Canadian Modern Language Review/Revue canadienne des langues vivantes* 50 (1): 158–64.

Swain, M., and S. Lapkin. 1995. Problems in output and the cognitive processes they generate: A step towards second language learning. *Applied Linguistics* 16 (3): 371–91.

Terrell, T. 1991. The role of grammar instruction in a communicative approach. *Modern Language Journal* 75 (1): 52–63.

Terrell, T., .M. Andrade, J. Egasse, and E. Miguel Muñoz. 2002. *Dos mundos.* 5th ed. McGraw-Hill: New York.

VanPatten, B. 1987. Classroom learners' acquisition of *ser* and *estar:* Accounting for developmental patterns. In *Foreign language learning: A research perspective,* ed. B. VanPatten, T. Dvorak, and J. Lee, 61–76. Cambridge: Cambridge University Press.

———. 1990. Attending to form and content in the input. *Studies in Second Language Acquisition* 12 (3): 287–301.

———. 1993. Grammar teaching for the acquisition rich classroom. *Foreign Language Annals* 26 (4): 435–50.

VanPatten, B., and T. Cadierno. 1993. Explicit instruction and input processing. *Studies in Second Language Acquisition* 15 (2): 225–44.

VanPatten, B., J. F. Lee, and T. L. Ballman. 1996. *¿Sabías que . . . ?* 2nd. ed. New York: McGraw-Hill.

Vendler, Z. 1957. Verbs and Times. *Philosophical Review* 66:143–60.

Vygotsky, L. S. 1978. *Mind in society.* Cambridge: Harvard University Press.

Theoretical and Research Considerations Underlying Classroom Practice
The Fundamental Role of Input

Bill VanPatten   *University of Illinois–Chicago*
Michael Leeser   *Florida State University*

How do second language learners construct linguistic systems? This question has been the central concern of L2 research since its contemporary inception (e.g., Corder 1969; Dulay and Burt 1974). For almost forty years we have seen a number of theories address this question. In the early days, creative construction (Dulay, Burt, and Krashen 1982) and the monitor model (e.g., Krashen 1982) dominated discussion. In the 1980s and 1990s an interest in theory construction emerged that stemmed from theories of language such as the universal grammar (UG) approach (e.g., White 1989, 2003), functional approaches (e.g., Pfaff 1987), fusions of linguistic theories with processing theories (e.g., Carroll 2001; Pienemann 1998), and general nativism (e.g., O'Grady 2003). In contradistinction, some theories have taken nonlinguistic approaches that rely more on constructs and theories from psychology such as connectionism (e.g., Ellis 2003) and general skill learning (DeKeyser 1998).[1] Other theories are more hybrid in nature, borrowing from psychology, linguistics, and language processing, including work on input processing (e.g., VanPatten 1996, 2004a) and interaction (e.g., Gass 1997). Still other theories fall outside of the scope of inquiry of most of these other theories, focusing instead on processes external to the learner, such as sociocultural theory (e.g., Lantolf 2000). Each theory has proponents and critics, each theory has particular domains of inquiry and (in)appropriate evidence for its domain (see, for example, some of the chapters in Lafford and Salaberry 2003, as well as VanPatten and Williams 2006). It is likely that these various approaches will continue to compete for explanatory adequacy in answering the central question: How do learners construct linguistic systems?

To address practical considerations derived from SLA theory and research, then, is a daunting task. One is immediately confronted with, What theory for what purpose? Because theories treat SLA like the Brahmin treated the elephant—each grabbing a different piece of the puzzle and unable to encompass the whole—to latch onto one theory in particular to address instructional issues may or may not be tenable or may lead to different instructional conclusions, depending on the theory. We believe, however, that there is another route to take by asking the following question: Is there something in common to all or most of the theories and research paradigms in SLA? If there is, are there implications for classroom praxis from such a commonality? We believe there is, and that commonality is the fundamental role that input plays in the creation of a linguistic system.

In this chapter, we will review the role of input in SLA and discuss its implications for classroom praxis. We would like to say at the outset that a focus on input for extracting implications for the classroom does not mean there is no role for, say, output and interaction. Indeed, we have argued elsewhere that there is (Leeser 2004; VanPatten 2003). We limit ourselves to input in this chapter due to space considerations and our own research agenda, which has largely been related to input and its role in instructed SLA as well as acquisition in general. We believe that the roles of output and interaction deserve their own treatment.

1.0   Staking Out the Territory: The "What" of Acquisition

Confusion and debate over approaches and their implications for instruction are sometimes due to conceptualizations of language or, more explicitly, the nature of a linguistic system. Because we cannot address either acquisition or implications of theory and research for instruction without some definition of language, and because we hope the reader will interpret the implications for instruction within the particulars we set forth, we turn our attention to the "what" of acquisition.

We take language to be a human-specific attribute (e.g., Pinker 1994). As such, it is viewed not so much as a means of communication (because animals certainly communicate in various ways, e.g., crickets do not rub their legs together to keep warm and bees do not dance because of the latest craze) as a mental representation. That is, each and every human possesses some kind of *underlying competence that is specifically linguistic in nature and is implicit*. It is implicit because it lies outside of awareness; we may know we have this competence in our minds, but as everyday people we do not really know what it is or what is in it. This competence is clearly different from what many call *skill*, that is, the ability to use the competence in some kind of performance (e.g., speaking).

Generally, this underlying competence is abstract and difficult to verbalize when we do become aware of it. For example, we may be able to judge the following sentence as ungrammatical but not know why: *Juan ha hecho su trabajo y María ha también*. We are relying on implicit knowledge to render this judgment, and the reasons the sentence is ungrammatical are simply too abstract and complex to articulate in a simple manner. Simply saying, "You cannot drop lexical verbs and leave auxiliaries alone in Spanish" provides a description but not the reason why the sentence is ungrammatical. Likewise, when given the pair *Se comió bien allí* and *Se comía bien allí*, we are able to correctly indicate that the former refers to a specific event that can involve the speaker (as in "We ate well there") while the latter rules that possibility out and can only be used in a generic sense ("One used to eat well there"), but we do not know why. Again, we are relying on abstract and complex implicit knowledge for these determinations. This implicit competence is distinct from explicit knowledge about language; with explicit knowledge we know we have it and we can call it forth and describe it in some way. If we say something like "*Manzana* is feminine so you have to use a *la* with it," we are tapping explicit knowledge to make this particular statement. Generally, explicit knowledge of rules does not represent the way the language is actually structured in the mind/brain and at best is a catalogue of rules of thumb to describe something that is pretty much indescribable in lay terms.[2]

So just what exists inside this implicit mental representation that all knowers of a language have? Minimally, it consists of the following:

- *A lexicon:* words and how words are formed (for example, why we say *honesto* and *deshonesto* but not *americano* and **desamericano*); syntactic information carried by words, such as the verb *poner* requiring a theme (something that is put) and an agent (something that does the putting), which are obligatorily realized in sentences as the object and subject, respectively, even when the verb is not used in its everyday sense (e.g., *Se puso a correr*)
- *Morphological form:* inflections on nouns, verbs, and other word classes; the rules that govern these inflections; particles
- *Syntax:* constraints on the nature of sentence structure that are both universal and language specific
- *Semantics:* information about meanings and information structure that places constraints on certain aspects of syntax and sentence possibility; closely tied to the lexicon in that lexical items store semantic information, and thus the verb *echar* requires animacy, which explains why *El niño se echó a correr* is fine but **La piedra se echó a brillar* sounds weird at best (even though syntactically the sentence is fine)
- *Phonological form:* the sound system and the rules and constraints contained in it such as constraints on syllable structure
- *Pragmatics:* knowledge of speaker intent and the nature of speech acts
- *Discourse and sociolinguistics:* knowledge of cohesion and appropriate language use

Any discussion of theoretical and research considerations underlying classroom practice must clearly state what that practice attempts to effect as well as affect. Although we believe that all components of language are acquired via the same core processes used in learning, because no single chapter can do justice to addressing all components of a linguistic system, we will focus on classroom practice that includes morphological form, grammatical properties of words, and syntactic constraints.

It should be clear from this discussion that we are not addressing matters such as skill, the development of fluency and accuracy, communicative competence, and communicative language ability, among other aspects of language use. The reason we limit ourselves is not because these areas of language behavior and development are unimportant but because they are important and, as we mention for the case of output and interaction in our introduction, deserve their own treatment elsewhere.

2.0 The Role of Input

It is commonly accepted in SLA theory and research that at some level input is the primary initial ingredient for the development of an underlying grammatical competence.[3] Input cannot be just any old input, however. Input in the context of creating a second language linguistic system means any sample of language that is used to communicate a message or language that is somehow processed by the learner for its meaning. This input-dependent nature of acquisition is true regardless of any particular theoretical framework for which the main focus of inquiry is how learners develop a linguistic system.[4] That is, mentalist and nonmentalist, linguistic and nonlinguistic theories alike posit a fundamental role for input; namely, as initial data for acquisition.

For example, let us examine the assumed role of input in two radically different theories: universal grammar and connectionism. Within a UG framework, an innate knowledge system whose job is to constrain the shape of possible human grammars is said to guide language acquisition (Schwartz 1998; White 2003). Two questions drive the UG approach to acquisition: What do learner grammars allow and disallow? And how can learners come to know what they know about language with the data they are exposed to? In a connectionist framework, there is no innate knowledge structure or special component of the mind that guides language acquisition. If there is a language-specific system, it emerges over time; it is not there from the outset (Ellis 1998; Elman et al. 1996). Within this framework, learners construct a neural network of information nodes with links between them. These links are either strengthened or weakened via activation and nonactivation. For example, once a link is established between a particular form and its meaning, that link is increasingly strengthened each time the connection between form and meaning is made. Thus frequency in the input has an impact on the strength of connections and the mind/brain is predisposed to look for regularities in the input and to create links between associations (Ellis 2002).

As sketchy as these descriptions of a UG-based account and a connectionist account are here, we can use them to illustrate that even theories as divergent as UG and connectionism rely on or imply a fundamental role for input in the creation of a linguistic system. For UG, some of the data needed for grammar construction are to be found in the input (the rest are in the principles of UG itself). For connectionism, data for the creation of nodes and associations between them are to be found in the input. Both theories posit a role for input, but they posit completely different mind/brain mechanisms that make use of that input.[5] In short, whether one ascribes to UG or to connectionist processes (or some other theory), one also ascribes to a fundamental role for input.[6]

In spite of a universally accepted role for input in SLA, it is clear that learners do not immediately acquire from mere exposure to input. What is clear to theorists and researchers is that learners possess processors or some kind of processing mechanism that acts on input. That is, as learners attempt to comprehend a contextualized utterance, their internal processing mechanisms do something to that input. What this processing mechanism is and what actually happens to input during comprehension is not clear, and there are several models and theories addressing the matter (e.g., Carroll 2001; Towell and Hawkins 1994; Truscott and Sharwood-Smith 2004; VanPatten 1996, 2004a). Nonetheless, research on instructed SLA has attempted to address the following question: Can we help learners with input in some way?

tions for Classroom Practice

ise that when people hear someone talk about the role of input in class-
mediately make the connection to Krashen and comprehensible input
982). Krashen has long been a champion of the maxim that goes some-
If learners get enough good, comprehensible input in a stress-free environment, acquisition will happen. Regardless of whether researchers agree with various aspects of the theory on which this claim is based, Krashen's point is well taken in
terms of teaching practices, and that point is basically this: Without input, there is no
acquisition, no matter what we do. Something else may result—what Krashen calls
"learning" or what Schwartz (1993) calls "learned linguistic knowledge"—but it is not
acquisition as defined in this chapter and elsewhere in the literature on SLA: the creation of an implicit mental representation of language (see Doughty 2003 for extensive discussion).

But is comprehensible input enough? It might be in the long run, but the business
of language teaching is to help acquisition in any way it can. Given this aim, we might
ask the following question: In what way can instruction help so that comprehensible
input is indeed accessible and learners can maximize what they do with it? In asking
this question, we are clearly going beyond the use of Total Physical Response (TPR),
the use of visuals, the natural approach, content language learning, and other communicative techniques and approaches in which any focus on grammatical form may
be absent. We are also going beyond the idea of providing comprehensible input by
itself. We are, in effect, suggesting that we need to augment comprehensible input.
The questions that confront us are these: Can we manipulate input in some way to
maximize acquisition? Can we get learners to do particular things with input to maximize acquisition?

Sharwood-Smith (1993) coined the term *input enhancement* (IE), which is any
attempt to direct learners' attention to a relevant grammatical form while their attention is also on processing meaning. This is important, because as Sharwood-Smith
and pretty much everyone else in instructed SLA theory and research would argue,
attention to grammatical form without meaning does not lead to acquisition. Many
instructors still cling to form-only activities, such as mechanical drills and fill-in-the-
blanks, which most of the time do not require learners to attend to meaning. Thus IE
must involve attention to both meaning and form in order to aid acquisition.

Five examples illustrate what IE is: text enhancement, input flood, input/output
cycles, structured input, and recasts. We will illustrate each, although in our presentation we are going to be necessarily brief. The reader is referred to Wong (2005) for
detailed presentation and discussion of various types of input enhancement.

3.1 Text Enhancement
3.1.1 Description

Because written texts qualify as input (i.e., they contain language the learner reads for
meaning), some researchers have examined the effects of text enhancement. Text
enhancement (TE) refers to typographical alterations of grammatical form or structures

in a reading passage. The alterations serve to get learners to notice the form and to process it in some way. As an example, we could take a story about something that happened in the past and highlight the preterit and imperfect endings in Spanish to make them stand out for the learner:

> Y luego la chica salió de la casa en busca de su perro. Tan ocupada que est*aba* con la idea de encontrar a su perro que se le olvidó llevarse un paraguas. El cielo est*aba* oscuro y parec*ía* que en cualquier momento pudiera abrirse para inundar el campo. Pero la chica no hac*ía* caso. Una idea singular la gui*aba*: ¿Dónde está Osito? Y así *fue* que la chica se lanzó a una aventura inesperada.

With TE, learners are primarily engaged in getting meaning and are responsible for the content of the text somehow (by quiz, classroom discussion, application of information to a different task, and so on). That is, although the instructor may or may not discuss the highlighted forms/structures, the instruction will always lead students through activities regarding the informational content of the text.

3.1.2 Research

The research on text enhancement has yielded mixed effects: Sometimes it is effective, sometimes it is not, and sometimes it seems partially effective. For example, in J. White (1998), French-speaking learners of English were "instructed" on his/her possessives (e.g., his dog, her goat). This particular form presents a problem for French (and Spanish) speakers because there is no gender distinction in possessives (e.g., *son chien/son chevre* could mean "his/her dog" and "his/her goat," respectively). White divided her participants into three groups: an E group, which received written texts with possessives highlighted; a U group, which received the same tests with no highlighting; and a third group, E+, which received the same highlighted texts as E but also had additional readings in which possessives appeared naturally, without highlighting. There was no explicit rule presentation prior to or during interaction with the texts. Pre- and posttesting involved picture description tasks. White's analyses revealed that after treatment, all groups (1) attempted to use more possessives and (2) improved in their use of them. There was a significant difference between the E+ and the other two groups on the immediate posttest and no difference between E and U. However, all differences disappeared by the second posttest, administered two weeks later.

Sometimes the effects of TE are noticeable only when there is prior explicit information presented to the learners, as in the case of Robinson (1995) and Alanen (1995). In these two studies, learners in the groups that received explicit instruction on the rules/forms highlighted in the texts outperformed groups in other conditions. These findings led these researchers to argue for explicit instruction as either necessary or beneficial for learning from input (or more strictly speaking, TE). However, it is also likely that the effects are due to monitoring; that is, the assessment tests biased for learners who could apply explicit rules during performance on tests.

In other studies, positive results of TE seem to be influenced by cognitive load. Wong (in press), for example, examined this issue by having English-speaking learners of French read texts in which two variables were manipulated: highlighting of the French subjunctive and discourse/sentence level reading. Group A received highlighted text in discourse form. Group B received the same text without highlighting. Group C received the highlighted text but in sentence form; that is, each sentence of the text was displayed on its own line. Group D received the sentence treatment as in C but without highlighting. What Wong found was that although highlighting alone made some difference, there were significant differences in performance on posttest with Group C; that is, they made greater gains compared to Group A. In short, processing sentences is easier than processing connected sentences in a discourse.

3.1.3 Pros and Cons

In terms of ease of use, TE is a simple technique for instructors to implement. Texts can be manipulated to contain multiple instances of a particular grammatical feature and the instructor can highlight those instances, as in the preterit/imperfect example earlier in this section. TE has one major drawback: efficacy. As our brief review of the research suggests, TE is not always effective unless accompanied by explicit instruction on the grammatical feature. This is most likely due to the fact that TE is predicated not on any theory of how learners perceive and/or process input but on the simple phenomenon of noticing. The idea, as we discussed previously, is that if text is enhanced in some way, learners are more likely to notice the form in the input. But noticing does not equate with processing and acquisition. For acquisition to occur, learners must not only notice but also process the form by connecting it to meaning and/or function (Izumi 2002; VanPatten, Williams, and Rott 2004). In other words, learners may indeed notice the form in TE treatment but they may not process it in a way useable by the processing mechanisms for acquisition. In addition, there is probably a complex interaction among the degree of comprehensibility/difficulty of the text, the type of linguistic structure employed, and the actual sentential contexts in which the form or structure appears (Hulstijn 1995). These factors will need to be sorted out for us to truly see under what conditions TE is effective and useful for instructed SLA. In the meantime, it is clear that TE at least provides input to learners, and that in and of itself is not a bad thing.

3.2 Input Flood

3.2.1 Description

As the name suggests, input flood is a technique in which instructors and/or materials developers provide lots of instances of a particular linguistic item in oral or written text. The idea behind this "flooding" is that learners will be more likely to notice and process linguistic items that frequently occur in the input (e.g., Gass 1997). For example, if instructors are attempting to facilitate learners' noticing of adjective agreement in Spanish, they might use several instances of masculine and feminine adjectives when describing two people:

> María Sánchez es una mujer ambiciosa, enérgica, extrovertida, y trabajadora. Su amigo Jaime Talavera tiene muchas de las mismas características: es ambicioso, enérgico, extrovertido, y muy trabajador también.

Regardless of whether instructors provide explicit information about how adjective agreement works in Spanish, learners' primary goal is to extract meaning in some way from the flooded input, and they may be held responsible for the content via some kind of comprehension check or quiz.

3.2.2 Research

In one study, Trahey and White (1993) investigated whether input flood could trigger the appropriate English setting of the verb movement parameter for Francophone Quebec children. In French (and Spanish) verbs "raise" past the adverb, allowing for SVAO word order (*Jean regard souvent la téle*), but in English they do not (*"John watches often TV"). In addition, French does not allow SAVO, but English does. In their study, these English as a second language (ESL) children were exposed to input floods containing hundreds of instances of English SAVO sentences over a two-week period but were not given any explicit instruction or negative evidence on adverb placement. Immediate and delayed posttests revealed that although these ESL learners accepted correct SAVO English sentences, which are not possible in French, they continued to accept incorrect SVAO sentences, which are possible in French. The findings of this study suggest that although input flood may help learners discover what is possible in the L2, it may not be enough for them to arrive at a knowledge of what is not possible, at least in the short term. Spada and Lightbown (1999) report similar findings regarding input flood and English question formation.

The results of Trahey and White (1993) and Spada and Lightbown (1999) might suggest that input flood needs to be coupled with explicit information and/or negative evidence in order to be effective. However, Williams and Evans (1998) found that the need for explicit rules and feedback along with input flood might depend upon the target structure. The researchers examined the effects of input flood with or without explicit rules and feedback on ESL learners' development of participle adjectives of emotive verbs (e.g., "He is interested/interesting") and the English passive construction (e.g., "The data were analyzed"). Although their study contained a small sample size, the results revealed an interaction between instructional treatment and structure. That is, for the participle adjectives, learners who received input flood alone and those who received it in combination with explicit rules and feedback improved from pretest to posttest; those that received explicit instruction improved more. However, for the passive construction, both groups made significant improvements and there was no advantage for the group that received explicit instruction. These findings suggest that explicit information might be useful in combination with input flood for some forms, but for others, input flood may be enough.

3.2.3 Pros and Cons

An obvious advantage to input flood is that it provides learners with an abundance of meaning–bearing input, which, as we noted at the beginning of this chapter, is the primary ingredient for the development of an implicit system, regardless of one's theoretical framework. Furthermore, given that input flood does not require explicit linguistic information, this technique does not disrupt the flow of communication or learners' attention to focusing on meaning (Doughty and Williams 1998). Another advantage is that it is relatively easy to implement. Instructors can provide many contexts in which they can flood their speech or written texts with adjective agreement, reflexive pronouns, verb tenses, and so on, thereby providing learners with lots of exposure to targeted forms. Yet there is no guarantee that flooding the input will actually cause learners to notice or process these forms or develop knowledge about what is not possible in the L2. The rationale behind input flood is that learners are more likely to notice forms that frequently occur in the input, but that does not mean they will (see Wong 2005 for further discussion). In other words, the potential efficacy of input flood is based on a hypothesized relationship between frequency and noticing, not on any theory of how learners process input. As with text enhancement, there are probably a number of factors that impact on the efficacy of input flood, and we have already seen that type of linguistic structure is one. While we wait for further studies to elucidate how and when input flood can be effective, it is one way in which learners can be exposed to linguistic data in meaning–bearing input.

3.3 Input/Output Cycles
3.3.1 Description
Although a fundamental role for input is undisputed in the development of a learner's mental representation of language, less clear is the role of output. One position has been championed by Merrill Swain, with some research offering insights into the relationship between output and input. Based on the findings of French immersion students, Swain proposed that during comprehension, learners are engaged in "semantic processing," relying on semantic and pragmatic information in order to construct meaning. She claimed that this type of processing may circumvent morphosyntactic information. However, by being pushed to be precise in their production, learners may engage in "syntactic processing," which entails coming up with morphosyntactic forms needed to convey meaning. In her now famous output hypothesis (Swain 1985, 1995, 1998), Swain hypothesized three potential functions of output in SLA: noticing/triggering, hypothesis testing, and metatalk (i.e., talking about language and showing metalinguistic awareness). Of interest here is Swain's claim that by needing to express themselves more accurately, learners will notice linguistic data in the input more than if they were not required to express themselves (i.e., noticing/triggering). This led to research on what might be called "input/output cycles."

Input/output cycles basically consist of learners reading or listening to texts and then having to reconstruct or summarize them in some way. These texts contain target structures, much the same way structures are embedded in an input flood or in text enhancement activities. Once learners complete their reconstructions, they are given another text with more examples of the target structure embedded and are once again asked to reconstruct or summarize the information. These successive cycles of input/output can be repeated as often as it makes sense for the time constraints and needs of a particular lesson. Let's suppose the target structure is impersonal *se* in Spanish. The lesson might look like this:

> Phase 1. Learners receive a passage about things to do and see in New York and things to avoid. Impersonal *se* is used repeatedly (e.g., *se debe, si se quiere, se puede*).

> Phase 2. After the passage is read, it is put away, and in groups of two, students attempt to reconstruct the passage. This is followed by whole class discussion about what they remembered from the text, who remembered the most, and so on. The instructor may use an overhead or the blackboard to write out important ideas.

> Phase 3. Learners receive a different passage about things to do and see in Mexico City and things to avoid. Impersonal *se* is used repeatedly as before.

> Phase 4. Same as phase 2, but afterward the instructor may now lead students into a comparison and contrast of what to do and see in New York versus Mexico City.

3.3.2 Research

In one of the best and perhaps most informative studies on input/output cycles, Izumi (2002) examined how output and textual enhancement (separately and in combination) would prompt ESL learners to notice and learn English relative clauses if (written) input was subsequently provided following learners' output (reconstruction of written texts). He divided participants into four groups: one that received input texts only, another that received input texts that were enhanced (i.e., TE), a third group that received input texts and was asked to reconstruct the texts, and a group that received enhanced input texts and was asked to reconstruct the texts. The target structure was relative clauses. He found that although all groups noticed more target forms upon subsequent exposure to input (as measured by note scores), and although all groups improved from pre- to posttests, learners who produced output improved more than the input-only groups on various measures of relative clause knowledge. Izumi concluded from these findings that upon "exposure to relevant input immediately after their production experience, the heightened sense of problematicity would lead [learners] to pay closer attention to what was identified to be a problematic area in their IL. In short, pushed output can induce the learners to process the input effectively for their greater IL development" (566). It is important to point out that because the enhanced input groups also made significant gains in both noticing and learning target forms, it cannot be concluded that output is necessary for acquisition in the same way that input is necessary. However, the findings of Izumi's study suggest that output may facilitate both noticing and learning, thereby speeding up the acquisition process.

In a different study, Izumi et al. (1999) researched the following phases of input/output cycles: output, input text, and output again. In this study, the target was if/then constructions and there was an experimental group and a control group (text enhancement was not a variable in this study). The difference between the two groups was that the experimental group was required to produce language but the control group instead answered comprehension questions. What Izumi et al. found was that the experimental group was not particularly better at either noticing or acquiring the target form. It turns out that the control group was as successful as the experimental group (overall) on the two measures—a measurement for noticing (i.e., how often participants underlined things in the text they read) and a measurement for acquisition (i.e., grammaticality judgment task and a picture cued production task). Izumi et al. concluded that the comprehension questions alone were sufficient to redirect learner attention during the input phase. That is, if the question required participants to judge the truth value of "Christopher Reeve continues to ride horses," they had to have processed "If he [Reeve] had stayed healthy, he would have continued riding horses" correctly in the text. So in this particular study, it is not only output but also certain kinds of comprehension questions that can push learners to process input in particular ways.

3.3.3 Pros and Cons

Like input flood and TE, input/output cycles are not difficult to construct for classroom practice. Instructors can easily put together texts and then have learners attempt to reconstruct them so that they would be forced to rely on particular structures to do so. Although the results from the Izumi studies are encouraging, there is one aspect of them that deserves mention: variability in performance. In Izumi et al. (1999), for example, the researchers found that individual learners varied greatly at what they paid attention to when reading the texts. They state that "at least some participants paid attention to [the grammatical structure] after output. Others, however, seemed to pay little attention to the grammatical aspects of the passage even after output. These participants appeared to have been more preoccupied with generating or organizing their ideas than with finding inadequacy in the IL grammar during output. It appears, then, that these participants' awareness of the grammatical form was not particularly heightened even after output" (446). This particular insight suggests that input/output cycles may suffer from the same problem as TE and input flood; they increase chances that learners may notice something, but they do not guarantee it and they do not ensure that if learners notice something, they notice what the instructor intends for them to notice. However, given Izumi et al.'s (1999) findings regarding how comprehension questions may force learners to process certain target forms, we believe that input/comprehension-question cycles may be just as useful if not more so than input/output cycles for enriching learner intake and deserve further research.

3.4 Structured Input

3.4.1 Description

Structured input (SI), a term coined by VanPatten (1993; see also Lee and VanPatten 1995, 2003; Wong 2004a), is part of what has come to be known as *processing instruction* (PI).[7] The idea behind SI is that once particular input processing problems are identified in acquisition, the input can be manipulated in particular ways to push students to (1) replace incorrect processing strategies with correct (or better) strategies and (2) make better form-meaning connections in the input. Let us take Spanish word order and clitic object pronouns as an example. Input processing research has identified the problem of a first-noun strategy that learners of English take to the acquisition of Spanish: they tend to assign the first (pro)noun they hear as the subject of the sentence (see VanPatten 2004a and in press for details). Although this is not a problem if the sentence is *Juan quiere verla* or even *Juan la ve*, it is a problem if the sentence is *La ve Juan* or simply *La ve*. Learners tend to tag the pronoun as a subject, and the pronoun system (as well as how word order works in Spanish) becomes a jumble in their mental representations. Given that OVS and OV structures are not uncommon in Spanish (e.g., *A Juan le gusta Maria, Me dijo que lo vio María, Se levantó*), the first-noun strategy can have quite a (negative) impact on processing and subsequent acquisition of syntax in Spanish.

One way in which structured input would handle this is by having learners hear mixtures of SVO, SOV, and OVS sentences and then match them to appropriate pictures. For example:

Activity A. Listen to each sentence and match it to the correct picture.
1. [Student hears]   Lo busca la niña.
   [Student chooses] a. A picture of a boy looking for a girl.
                     b. A picture of a girl looking for a boy.

2. [Student hears]   La mamá lo abraza.
   [Student chooses] a. A picture of a mother with her arms around a boy.
                     b. A picture of a boy with his arms around his mother.

3. [Student hears]   Los saluda el chico.
   [Student chooses] a. A picture of two guys saying "hi" to another guy.
                     b. A picture of a guy saying "hi" to two other guys.

Again, sentences vary so as to scramble word order and force students to pay attention to the formal properties of the sentences to get meaning. Students are told whether their answers are right or wrong. Depending upon instructor preference, explicit information may or may not be provided. These are called referential activities because they have right or wrong answers. After three or four such referential activities, which begin to push learners away from incorrect processing, activities that are more affective and learner focused follow. In these activities, OVS and OV are the preferred word orders to continue pushing the new processing strategy:

Activity D. Select a female relative and write her name and relationship below. Then indicate which statements are true about her and you.

Nombre: _____ Relación: _____

1. La respeto.

2. La detesto.

3. La admiro.

4. La conozco bien.

5. La veo/llamo por teléfono con frecuencia.

6. Trato de imitarla.

7. La _____ .[8]

Now think of a male relative and do the same as you did above.

Nombre: _____ Relación: _____

1. Lo respeto.

2. Lo detesto.

3. Lo admiro.

4. Lo conozco bien.

5. Lo veo/llamo por teléfono con frecuencia.

6. Trato de imitarlo.

7. Lo _____ .

Based on what you've answered, with whom to you have a better relationship? Do you favor one person over the other?

There is more to processing input that the first-noun strategy. In one model of input processing, one claim is that learners use lexical devices to bootstrap themselves into meaning and may not attend to redundant grammatical forms for some time. This may be especially true for the less frequent or less transparent forms. Activities are thus created to force learners to process the grammatical form for its meaning/function. In the case of tense markers, adverbials of time are omitted from sentences and learners must get temporal reference from verb forms:

Activity G. Listen to each sentence and then indicate the time frame for the event expressed in the sentence.

1. [Students hear]   Me llamó mi hermana.
   [Students choose] a. past
                     b. present
                     c. future

2. [Students hear]   No estudia mucho.
   [Students choose] a. past
                     b. present
                     c. future

In an alternative version, students select the word that best fits with each sentence, for example, (*a*) anoche, (*b*) estos días, (*c*) en diez años. As in the case for word order, sentences are scrambled so that even if the focus is on, say, past tense forms, both present and future are included so that learners are forced to pay attention to form for meaning. Such referential activities would be followed by affective activities such as, "Below are ten statements about what your instructor did last night. Which are true? First, select the ones you believe are true and then put them in the order in which he/she did them." These instructions would be followed by ten sentences with the adverbial *anoche* removed, for example, *Preparó la cena, Vio televisión, Salió con amigos, Tomó un cóctel.* (For more detailed information on guidelines for creating SI activities, see Wong 2004a).

3.4.2 *Research*

SI and processing instruction in general have enjoyed a rigorous research agenda, with the result that PI and SI are, at worst, as good as any other approach. In all cases when PI and SI are compared to traditional approaches that include mechanical activities and a move from form-only to form-plus-meaning exercises, PI and SI are superior on a variety of measures (e.g., Cadierno 1995; VanPatten and Cadierno 1993; VanPatten and Wong 2004). When PI and SI are compared to meaning-based output approaches, PI is sometimes better but never worse (e.g., Benati 2005; Farley 2004). In addition, unlike other instructional interventions researched to date, only PI has yielded long-term results. In VanPatten and Fernández (2004), learners' performance continued to be significantly better after eight months (compared to pretest performance), albeit with some decline from the immediate posttest.

The research on PI and SI has been conducted with English, French, Italian, and Spanish as second languages and on a variety of structures: verb forms, lexical-semantic features, sentence structure and word order, mood, adjective agreement, use of articles, and others. This research is summarized in VanPatten (1996, 2002a), and additional research appears in VanPatten (2004a) and Benati (2005).[9] One of the reasons that PI and SI appear to be effective is that they are predicated on identified non-optimal processing strategies that underlie acquisition and activities are created to push learners away from those strategies. Unlike TE and input flood, which involve mere noticing, SI involves both noticing and forced processing of the form or structure for its meaning and function.[10]

3.4.3 *Pros and Cons*

In spite of the promising results of PI and SI research, SI is not without its critics, and criticism has been leveled on two grounds. The first is that the instruction is derived from a problematic theory. In DeKeyser et al. (2002), for example, VanPatten's model of input processing is critiqued for its conceptualization of attention (as a cognitive construct) and because the sentence processing is "meaning based" (as opposed to structurally dependent, as in L1 parsing models). (These criticisms are continued in Harrington 2004.) The second grounds for criticism involve constructs of research design and internal validity for the various PI studies. Although these criticisms have been addressed by VanPatten (2002b; see especially 2004c) and are addressed in various ways by Wong (2004a), Doughty (2003), and Carroll (2004), we will briefly review one of them here.

One of the major criticisms offered by DeKeyser et al. (2002) and Salaberry (1997, 1998) is that PI contains an inherent contradiction in that it purports to promote acquisition and yet contains both explicit instruction (i.e., explanation) and negative evidence. Acquisition, by definition, is not amenable to explicit instruction or negative evidence, only learning is (in a Krashenian sense). In VanPatten and Oikennon (1996), Wong (2004b), Farley (2004), Sanz and Morgan-Short (2004), and Fernández (2005), it has been shown that explicit information/instruction is not a necessary component of PI nor a causative factor; SI activities alone are sufficient, although it seems that explicit information can help learners bootstrap themselves into processing quicker than if it is absent, for some structures, at least, though not for all (Fernández 2005). That explicit information/instruction is beneficial and not necessary is completely consistent with the definition of acquisition, that is, acquisition being a byproduct of comprehension. In PI, what explicit information actually does is push comprehension along. If learners are told how to interpret a sentence and are given information about what parts of sentences mean, this promotes comprehension. Promoting comprehension in turn promotes acquisition.

As for negative evidence, there are two issues here. The first concerns what negative evidence is. Negative evidence that cannot work is explicit correction, telling learners not to say it one way but to say it another, and so on. This is called direct negative evidence. There is also indirect negative evidence, evidence about doing something wrong that comes in the way of a confirmation check, a recast, or some negotiated meaning. It is generally accepted in all theories that such indirect evidence can indeed be useful to acquisition but that it cannot be necessary because it is inconsistently offered and is sometimes contradictory. So indirect negative evidence in and of itself is not the problem; the issue deals with robustness of its provision. The second issue regarding negative evidence has to do with input and output. We would like to point out that negative evidence in the general literature refers to evidence triggered by learner output. In PI, negative evidence is a response to learner processing of input. If learners select picture A to match with an utterance when only picture B illustrates what the utterance means, they are told that their selection is wrong. In this scenario, learners are not getting negative evidence about their output. They are getting information that their comprehension is wrong. Again, assisting comprehension is consonant with the processes involved in acquisition, that is, comprehension is a precursor to acquisition. The kind of negative evidence in PI/SI is precisely what learners would need in the natural world to correct processing problems and enhance comprehension. That is, they would need to be confronted with a mismatch between what they are observing and what they think they are hearing (e.g., White 1987). This type of mismatch forces the processors to readjust themselves and add or delete processing strategies. In PI, rather than wait for this to happen accidentally as it would in the real world, the issue is simply forced early on. What is more, in SI, the feedback is consistent and constant; it is not haphazard as it might be in the real world.

Although the research on PI and SI is very promising in that there are consistent and robust results found in all of the studies, there is a downside to SI; namely, SI activities are not easy for instructors to create and implement on their own. Because they entail a thorough understanding of the input processing model upon which they are derived as well as a thorough understanding of the principles for their construction (e.g., Lee and VanPatten 2003; Wong 2004a), SI activities are not easy to create and instructors encounter a number of pitfalls when attempting to develop them. (See Farley 2005 as well as Sanz and VanPatten 1998; VanPatten and Wong 2004; and Wong's 2004a review of various PI "replication" studies for more information.) In short, SI activities are time-intensive and require considerable instructor training before they can be developed and implemented.

3.5 Recasts
3.5.1 Description

Unlike the other techniques for input enhancement we have discussed, recasts are not really activities that can be planned and implemented in the classroom, as is the case with input flood, text enhancement, input/output cycles, and structured input. Instead, recasts are real-time, in-the-moment responses to learner output that do not disrupt the flow of communication. As a type of oral feedback, recasts are reformulations of a learner's incorrect utterance in correct form. For example, a learner might say, *En la mesa hay una taza rojo,* and the response might be *Sí, una taza roja. ¿Y qué más?* in an attempt to draw the learner's attention to adjective agreement. If a learner says, *Elena toma café a veces,* the response might be *Elena toma a veces café, sí, uhuhm,* with the intent of getting the learner to notice the particular effects of verb movement, in this case adverb placement. Even though recasts are normally classified as implicit negative evidence, because they involve a targetlike reformulation of the learners' original utterance, recasts also provide positive evidence (Leeman 2003). Some researchers have suggested that because recasts maintain the meaning of the original utterance, they allow learners to utilize their cognitive resources to focus on form and "notice the gap" between their non-targetlike output and the subsequent input (Doughty 2001; Long and Robinson 1998).

3.5.2 Research

The research on recasts suggests that they are effective, at least for some structures and when compared with learners who receive no feedback (Lyster 2004). For example, Long, Inagaki and Ortega (1998) found that recasts were more effective than models (i.e., positive evidence alone) during experimentally controlled interaction to move L2 Spanish learners to more targetlike production of Spanish SVAO word order. Similarly, Mackey and Philp (1998) found that "intensive recasts" provided to developmentally ready learners during interactive tasks on English question formation were more effective than interaction that did not contain recasts. In another experimental study (Leeman 2003), results indicated that beginning L2 Spanish learners who received recasts on noun adjective agreement during picture difference task interaction with the researcher made significant gains on posttreatment measures, whereas learners who received negative evidence only or were part of a control group did not. In a classroom-based study, Doughty and Varela (1998) reported that "corrective recasts" (e.g., a repetition of a learner's non-targetlike utterance followed by a recast) were more effective than no feedback on middle school ESL learners' development of the past and past conditional.

Although the studies briefly discussed here suggest that recasts are more beneficial to learners than no feedback at all, Lyster (2004) examined the efficacy of form-focused instruction (FFI) in combination with different types of feedback on L2 French children's assignment of grammatical gender. Learners in his study received FFI in combination with (1) no feedback, (2) recasts, or (3) prompts (i.e., feedback consisting of clarification requests, repetitions, metalinguistic cues, or elicitation, all of which push learners to be more accurate in their output). Another group served as a control and received no form-focused instruction. Results of delayed posttest measures (two months after treatment) revealed that only the FFI-prompt group outperformed the control on all written and oral measures, whereas the FFI-recast group outperformed the control on the oral measures only. These findings suggest that although recasts may be one effective means of providing learners with feedback, they may not be the most effective.

In addition to investigating the effectiveness of recasts in L2 development, research has also examined how learners perceive recasts, given that they are implicit and it is up to the learner to notice the difference between their original utterance and the recast. For example, Mackey, Gass, and McDonough (2000) found that during experimentally controlled interactive tasks, learners were least likely to perceive feedback if it related to morphosyntax. Interestingly, the most common type of feedback provided to non-targetlike morphosyntax was recasts. Although their study did not set out to examine the effects of recasts per se, the researchers suggest that the provision of recasts to morphosyntactic errors may be "suboptimal, at least in terms of learners' perceptions about feedback" (493). In another study, Morris and Tarone (2003) reported that when interpersonal conflict arose within dyads, learners perceived recasts as a negative form of imitation or even mockery and not as corrective feedback. Subsequently, these learners continued to produce these non-targetlike forms on posttests.

3.5.3 Pros and Cons

Because recasts are in-the-moment responses to learner errors, they do not require the planning that input flood, text enhancement, and, especially, structured input activities do. They provide both implicit negative and positive evidence to learners and generally do not interrupt the flow of communication (Doughty and Varela 1998). However, because they occur in real time, recasts are likely to be haphazard and unevenly applied, potentially diminishing the effect that is found in laboratory research. Nonetheless, the limited research on recasts in classrooms suggests that they may be beneficial, particularly when they are focused on a limited number of target forms and occur within a communicative context.

4.0 Conclusion

In this chapter, we have reviewed various approaches to input enhancement that have been the foci of research in instructed SLA. We have suggested that some techniques are more consistently effective than others and that the effectiveness of some may depend on the interaction of other variables (e.g., the provision of explicit information, structure type). As research on instructed SLA continues, any current perspectives on the effectiveness of various input enhancement techniques will need updating. One area in need of study is long-term effects. Only PI has been researched to see if the effects of instruction last over time. No such research has been conducted to date on the other input enhancement techniques described in this chapter.

As we stated earlier, a focus on input does not exclude roles for other factors such as output and interaction. Indeed, we did review one particular role for output—as a potentially important noticing device—in the section on input/output cycles. And a focus on the acquisition of mental representation of language does not deny the importance of factors related to language use (e.g., communicative ability, skill, and fluency). What is important to say here is at this time it is not clear to what extent these other factors, including language use, affect or interact with the processes the mind uses to construct a mental representation of language, and such discussion warrants its own treatment (e.g., Gass 1997; VanPatten 2004b). It is clear, however, in terms of preparing materials for promoting the acquisition of a grammar, instructors have a variety of input-based options to examine. Some of these options are easier to implement than others, and theory and research may support some techniques more than others. But in the end, issues of curriculum development and the practicality of materials preparation will undoubtedly influence instructors' selection process.

Notes

1. Strictly speaking, not all psychological theories ascribe to the existence of a linguistic system and instead focus on behaviors and emergent properties that look like what linguists call language.

2. In the case of determiner agreement with nouns, the construct "feminine" is not a real mental construct in a linguistic system but a shorthand way for us to talk about the phenomenon. Most agreement with nouns is a result of the intersection of abstract phonological and syntactic principles.

3. Due to space constraints, we cannot give a detailed argument here on the role of input. See R. Ellis (1994), Gass (1997), Larsen-Freeman and Long (1991), VanPatten (2003, 2004a), and some of the other references cited within our discussion. Of course, this work is traceable to Krashen (1982 and elsewhere).

4. To be sure, some theories pay greater or lesser attention to input while still acknowledging its role. Some theories are simply mute on the role of input.

5. It is sometimes said that within UG the role of input is downplayed, that if learners come to know more than what they are exposed to, it is because of the principles contained in UG, not because of something in the input. What we mean to suggest here is that in the totality

of acquisition, input is necessary. According to White (2003, 2), "The primary linguistic data (PLD) are critical in helping the child to determine the precise form that the grammar must take." Later she says, "In L2 acquisition, learners are faced with a similar task to that of L1 acquirers, namely the need to arrive at a system accounting for the L2 input" (22).

6. Even perspectives on acquisition that do not adhere to a particular theory place input in a central role in acquisition. Schmidt (1995) asked the question, "Can language be learned without some kind of awareness of what one is learning?" Although this question can be researched in a variety of ways, it is important to note that Schmidt refers to awareness during input processing. What is more, his list of tips for language learners includes statements such as "Pay attention to input" and "Pay particular attention to whatever aspects of the input that you are concerned to learn" (Schmidt 1995, 45). Although he did not take a stance on theoretical models such as UG or connectionism, Schmidt was clear in his position on the role of input in the development of a linguistic system by L2 learners.

7. In Erlam (2003) the term is used with a different meaning and should not be confused with its original conceptualization.

8. Students think up their own verb to include.

9. Research is currently under way in other languages such as Russian.

10. See also Wong's discussion of various studies that purport to research SI (or PI) but fail to do so (Wong 2004a).

References

Alanen, R. 1995. Input enhancement and rule presentation in second language acquisition. In *Attention and awareness in foreign language acquisition,* ed. R. Schmidt, 259–302. Honolulu: University of Hawai'i Press.

Benati, A. 2005. The effects of processing instruction, traditional instruction and meaning-output instruction on the acquisition of the English past simple tense. *Language Teaching Research* 9 (1): 67–93.

Cadierno, T. 1995. Formal instruction in processing perspective: An investigation into the Spanish past tense. *Modern Language Journal* 79 (2): 179–94.

Carroll, S. 2001. *Input and evidence: The raw material of second language acquisition.* Amersterdam: John Benjamins.

———. 2004. Some comments on input processing and processing instruction. In *Processing instruction: Theory, research, and commentary,* ed. B. VanPatten, 293–310. Mahwah, NJ: Lawrence Erlbaum Associates.

Corder, S. P. 1969. The significance of learners' errors. *International Review of Applied Linguistics* 5:161–70.

DeKeyser, R. 1998. Beyond focus on form: Cognitive perspectives on learning and practicing second language grammar. In *Focus on form in classroom second language acquisition,* ed. C. Doughty and J. Williams, 42–63. Cambridge: Cambridge University Press.

DeKeyser, R., R. Salaberry, P. Robinson, and M. Harrington. 2002. What gets processed in processing instruction: A response to Bill VanPatten's "Update." *Language Learning* 52 (4): 805–23.

Doughty, C. 2001. Cognitive underpinnings of focus on form. In *Cognition and second language instruction,* ed. P. Robinson, 206–57. Cambridge: Cambridge University Press.

———. 2003. Instructed SLA: Constraints, compensation, and enhancement. In *Handbook of second language acquisition,* ed. C. Doughty and M. Long, 256–310. Malden, MA: Blackwell.

Doughty, C., and E. Varela. 1998. Communicative focus on form. In *Focus on form in classroom second language acquisition,* ed. C. Doughty and J. Williams, 114–38. Cambridge: Cambridge University Press.

Doughty, C., and J. Williams, eds. 1998. *Focus on form in classroom second language acquisition.* Cambridge: Cambridge University Press.

Dulay, H., and M. Burt. 1974. Natural sequences in child second language acquisition. *Language Learning* 23 (2): 245–58.

Dulay, H., M. Burt, and S. Krashen. 1982. *Language two.* Oxford: Oxford University Press.

Ellis, N. C. 1998. Emergentism, connectionism and language learning. *Language Learning* 48 (4): 631–64.

———. 2002. Frequency effects in language acquisition: A review with implications for theories of implicit and explicit language acquisition. *Studies in Second Language Acquisition* 24 (2): 143–48.

———. 2003. Constructions, chunking, and connectionism: The emergence of second language structure. In *Handbook of second language acquisition,* ed. C. Doughty and M. Long, 63–103. Malden, MA: Blackwell.

Ellis, R. 1994. *The study of second language acquisition.* Oxford: Oxford University Press.

Elman, J. L., E. A. Bates, M. H. Johnson, A. Karmiloff-Smith, and K. Plunkett. 1996. *Rethinking innateness: A connectionist perspective on development.* Cambridge, MA: MIT Press.

Erlam, R. 2003. Evaluating the relative effectiveness of structured-input and output-based instruction in foreign language learning: Results from an experimental study. *Studies in Second Language Acquisition* 25 (4): 559–82.

Farley, A. 2004. The relative effects of processing instruction and meaning-based output instruction. In *Processing instruction: Theory, research, and commentary,* ed. B. VanPatten, 143–68. Mahwah, NJ: Lawrence Erlbaum Associates.

———. 2005. *Structured input: Grammar instruction for the acquisition oriented classroom.* New York: McGraw-Hill.

Fernández, C. A. 2005. The role of explicit information in processing instruction: An on-line experiment. Ph.D. diss., University of Illinois at Chicago.

Gass, S. 1997. *Input, interaction and the second language learner.* Mahwah, NJ: Lawrence Erlbaum Associates.

Harrington, M. 2004. Commentary: Input processing as a theory of processing input. In *Processing instruction: Theory, research, and commentary,* ed. B. VanPatten, 79–92. Mahwah, NJ: Lawrence Erlbaum Associates.

Hulstijn, J. 1995. Not all grammar rules are equal: Giving grammar instruction its proper place in foreign language teaching. In *Attention and awareness in foreign language learning,* ed. R. Schmidt, 359–86. Honolulu: University of Hawai'i Press.

Izumi, S. 2002. Output, input enhancement, and the noticing hypothesis: An experimental study on ESL relativization. *Studies in Second Language Acquisition* 24 (4): 541–77.

Izumi, S., M. Bigelow, M. Fujiwara, and S. Fearnow. 1999. Testing the output hypothesis: Effects of output on noticing and second language acquisition. *Studies in Second Language Acquisition* 21 (3): 421–52.

Krashen, S. 1982. *Principles and practice in second language acquisition.* London: Pergamon.

Lafford, B., and R. Salaberry, eds. 2003. *Spanish second language acquisition: State of the science.* Washington, DC: Georgetown University Press.

Lantolf, J. 2000. *Sociocultural theory and second language learning.* Oxford: Oxford University Press.

Larsen-Freeman, D., and M. Long. 1991. *An introduction to second language acquisition research.* New York: Longman.

Lee, J. F., and B. VanPatten. 1995. *Making communicative language teaching happen.* New York: McGraw-Hill.

———. 2003. *Making communicative language teaching happen.* New York: McGraw-Hill.

Leeman, J. 2003. Recasts and L2 development: Beyond negative evidence. *Studies in Second Language Acquisition* 25 (1): 37–63.

Leeser, M. J. 2004. Learner proficiency and focus on form during collaborative dialogue. *Language Teaching Research* 8 (1): 55–81.

Long, M. H., S. Inagaki, and L. Ortega. 1998. The role of implicit negative feedback in SLA: Models and recasts in Japanese and Spanish. *Modern Language Journal* 82 (3): 357–71.

Long, M. H., and P. Robinson. 1998. Focus on form: Theory, research, and practice. In *Focus on form in classroom second language acquisition*, ed. C. Doughty and J. Williams, 15–41. Cambridge: Cambridge University Press.

Lyster, R. 2004. Differential effects of prompts and recasts in form-focused instruction. *Studies in Second Language Acquisition* 26 (3): 399–432.

Mackey, A., S. Gass, and K. McDonough. 2000. How do learners perceive implicit negative feedback? *Studies in Second Language Acquisition* 22 (3): 471–97.

Mackey, A., and J. Philp. 1998. Conversational interaction and second language development: Recasts, responses, and red herrings? *Modern Language Journal* 82 (3): 338–56.

Morris, F. A., and E. Tarone. 2003. The impact of classroom dynamics on the effectiveness of recasts in second language acquisition. *Language Learning* 53 (2): 325–68.

O'Grady, W. 2003. The radical middle: Nativism without universal grammar. In *Handbook of second language acquisition*, ed. C. Doughty and M. Long, 43–62. Malden, MA: Blackwell.

Pfaff, C. W. 1987. Functional approaches to interlanguage. In *First and second language acquisition processes*, ed. C. W. Pfaff, 81–102. Rowley, MA: Newberry House.

Pienemann, M. 1998. *Language processing and second language development: Processability theory.* Amsterdam: John Benjamins.

Pinker, S. 1994. *The language instinct.* New York: William Morrow.

Robinson, P. 1995. Aptitude, awareness, and the fundamental similarity of implicit and explicit second language learning. In *Attention and awareness in foreign language learning*, ed. R. Schmidt, 303–58. Honolulu: University of Hawai'i Press.

Salaberry, M. R. 1997. The role of input and output practice in second language acquisition. *Canadian Modern Language Review/Revue canadienne des langues vivantes* 53 (2): 422–51.

———. 1998. On input processing, true language competence, and pedagogical bandwagons: A reply to Sanz and VanPatten. *Canadian Modern Language Review* 54 (2): 274–85.

Sanz, C., and K. Morgan-Short. 2004. Positive evidence versus explicit rule presentation and explicit negative feedback: A computer assisted study. *Language Learning* 54 (1): 35–78.

Sanz, C., and B. VanPatten. 1998. On input processing, processing instruction, and the nature of replication tasks: A response to Salaberry. *Canadian Modern Language Review* 54 (2): 263–73.

Schmidt, R. 1995. Consciousness and foreign language learning: A tutorial on the role of attention and awareness in learning. In *Attention and awareness in foreign language learning*, ed. R. Schmidt, 1–63. Honolulu: University of Hawai'i Press.

Schwartz, B. 1993. On explicit and negative data effecting and affecting competence and "linguistic behavior." *Studies in Second Language Acquisition* 15 (1): 147–63.

———. 1998. The second language instinct. *Lingua* 106 (1–4): 133–60.

Sharwood-Smith, M. 1993. Input enhancement in instructed SLA: Theoretical bases. *Studies in Second Language Acquisition* 15 (2): 165–79.

Spada, N., and P. Lightbown. 1999. Instruction, first language influence, and developmental readiness in second language acquisition. *Modern Language Journal* 83 (1): 1–22.

Swain, M. 1985. Communicative competence: Some roles of comprehensible input and comprehensible output in its development. In *Input in second language acquisition*, ed. S. Gass and C. Madden, 235–53. Rowley, MA: Newbury House.

———. 1995. Three functions of output in second language learning. In *Principles and practice in applied linguistics: Studies in honour of H. G. Widdowson*, ed. G. Cook and B. Seidlhofer, 125–44. Oxford: Oxford University Press.

————. 1998. Focus on form through conscious reflection. In *Focus on form in classroom second language acquisition*, ed. C. Doughty and J. Williams, 64–81. Cambridge: Cambridge University Press

Towell, R., and R. Hawkins. 1994. *Approaches to second language acquisition*. Philadelphia: Multilingual Matters.

Trahey, M., and L. White. 1993. Positive evidence and preemption in the second language classroom. *Studies in Second Language Acquisition* 15 (2): 181–204.

Truscott, J., and M. Sharwood-Smith. 2004. Acquisition by processing: A modular perspective on language development. *Bilingualism: Language and Cognitive* 1:1–20.

VanPatten, B. 1993. Grammar teaching for the acquisition-rich classroom. *Foreign Language Annals* 26 (4): 435–50.

————. 1996. *Input processing and grammar instruction*. New York: Ablex.

————. 2002a. Processing instruction: An update. *Language Learning* 52 (4): 755–803.

————. 2002b. Processing the content of input-processing and processing instruction research: A response to DeKeyser, Salaberry, Robinson, and Harrington. *Language Learning* 52 (4): 825–31.

————. 2003. *From input to output: A teacher's guide to second language acquisition*. New York: McGraw-Hill.

————. 2004a. Input processing in second language acquisition. In *Processing instruction: Theory, research, and commentary*, ed. B. VanPatten, 5–31. Mahwah, NJ: Lawrence Erlbaum Associates.

————. 2004b. Input and output in establishing form-meaning connections. In *Form-meaning connections in second language acquisition*, ed. B. VanPatten, J. Williams, S. Rott, and M. Overstreet, 29–47. Mahwah, NJ: Lawrence Erlbaum Associates.

————. 2004c. Several reflections on why there is good reason to continue researching the effects of processing instruction. In *Processing instruction: Theory, research, and commentary*, ed. B. VanPatten, 325–35. Mahwah, NJ: Lawrence Erlbaum Associates.

————. 2006. Input processing in adult SLA. In *Theories in second language acquisition*, ed. VanPatten and J. Williams. Mahwah, NJ: Lawrence Erlbaum Associates.

VanPatten, B., and T. Cadierno. 1993. Explicit instruction and input processing. *Studies in Second Language Acquisition* 15 (2): 225–43.

VanPatten, B., and C. Fernández. 2004. The long-term effects of processing instruction. In *Processing instruction: Theory, research, and commentary*, ed. B. VanPatten, 273–89. Mahwah, NJ: Lawrence Erlbaum Associates.

VanPatten, B., and S. Oikkenon. 1996. Explanation versus structured input in processing instruction. *Studies in Second Language Acquisition* 18 (4): 495–510.

VanPatten, B., and J. Williams, eds. 2006. *Theories in second language acquisition*. Mahwah, NJ: Lawrence Erlbaum Associates.

VanPatten, B., J. Williams, and S. Rott. 2004. Form-meaning connections in second language acquisition. In *Form-meaning connections in second language acquisition*, ed. B. VanPatten, J. Williams, S. Rott, and M. Overstreet, 1–26. Mahwah, NJ: Lawrence Erlbaum Associates.

VanPatten, B., and W. Wong. 2004. Processing instruction and the French causative: Another replication. In *Processing instruction: Theory, research, and commentary*, ed. B. VanPatten, 97–118. Mahwah, NJ: Lawrence Erlbaum Associates.

White, J. 1998. Getting the learners' attention: A typographical input enhancement study. In *Focus on form in classroom second language acquisition*, ed. C. Doughty and J. Williams, 85–113. Cambridge: Cambridge University Press.

White, L. 1987. Against comprehensible input: The input hypothesis and the development of L2 competence. *Applied Linguistics* 8 (1): 95–110.

————. 1989. *Universal grammar and second language acquisition.* Amsterdam: John Benjamins.

————. 2003. *Second language acquisition and universal grammar.* Cambridge: Cambridge University Press.

Williams, J., and J. Evans. 1998. What kind of focus and on which forms? In *Focus on form in classroom second language acquisition,* ed. C. Doughty and J. Williams, 139–55. Cambridge: Cambridge University Press.

Wong, W. 2004a. The nature of processing instruction. In *Processing instruction: Theory, research, and commentary,* ed. B. VanPatten, 33–63. Mahwah, NJ: Lawrence Erlbaum Associates.

————. 2004b. Processing instruction in French: The roles of explicit information and structured input. In *Processing Instruction: Theory, research, and commentary,* ed. B. VanPatten, 187–205.

————. 2005. *Input enhancement: From theory and research to the classroom.* New York: McGraw-Hill.

————. In press. *Enhancing the learner's attention: A study with textual enhancement, orientation, and sentence- and discourse-level input.* Columbus: Ohio State University Press.

Concept-Based Instruction and the Acquisition of L2 Spanish

Eduardo Negueruela *University of Miami*
James P. Lantolf *Pennsylvania State University*

The rekindling of interest in teaching grammar in foreign language classrooms is arguably the result of concern about the lack of control over the grammatical features of the L2 (secondary language) observed among learners who have passed through pedagogical programs in which opportunities to communicate are given greater emphasis than are the formal features of learners' performance. A problem confronting those who wish to bring grammar back into focus is the need to develop a clear understanding of what grammar consists of in the first place (Odlin 1994). For instance, Ellis (2004) notes that L2 researchers do not seem to agree on either the relevance or even the relationship between such concepts as implicit versus explicit grammatical knowledge, automatic and controlled processing of grammar, metalinguistic knowledge versus grammatical rules, deductive versus inductive learning of grammatical features, and so on (see also Ellis 1997, 2002; Hinkel and Fotos 2002).

In their meta-analysis of the effects of instruction of learning, Norris and Ortega (2000) conclude that explicit form-focused and form*s*-focused instruction, where learners are made aware of grammatical forms, have substantial positive effects on learning and are more effective than implicit instruction. On the other hand, they note that in studies in which rules are explicitly taught, the impact on learning was not significant. One problem with these studies, however, is that grammar presentation was not carried out in a consistent manner across the studies. In some studies rules were presented paradigmatically "with various forms and functions of a linguistic subsystem presented together" (484). In others, the rules were presented in stages "with aspects of a structure explained in small steps accompanied by intervening practice or exposure activities" (ibid.). In most studies rule-based explanations were presented prior to engaging learners in other instructional activities. In some studies, however, explanations were available for consultation as learners participated in instructional activities; in others, the rules were reintroduced at intervals throughout the instructional intervention (ibid.).

As far as we can determine, the previous research has not concerned itself with the quality of the grammatical rules presented to learners, and this, along with the functionality of this knowledge—that is, how instruction promotes the appropriation of grammatical knowledge to make it accessible to learners when they use the language—form the primary focus of this chapter. Specifically, our concern is with instruction of Spanish verbal aspect. However, we are not interested in accuracy of morphological endings but in learner understanding of, and control over, the concept of aspect as it is manifested in the distinction in Spanish between preterit and imperfect. Consequently, we propose that the key to the development of conceptual understanding of grammar is the construction of appropriate didactic models that learners can use to guide their performance and ultimately internalize as a means of regulating their meaning-making ability in the L2.

We first explicate the pedagogical implications of Vygotsky's sociocultural theory of mind. It is important to point out that research within the Vygotskyan tradition generally has been grounded in the dialectical concept of praxis, which draws instruction and development into an organic unity that arises in concrete practical activity. Accordingly, the true test of a theory resides in its ability to promote development in the very sites where ordinary activity transpires, and this includes pedagogical activity in the school setting (see Cole 1996; Scribner 1997).[1] In Vygotsky's praxis-based framework, instruction is understood as "any directive which elicits new activity," and development is conceived of as "the reorganization of consciousness through this activity" (Axel 1997, 131). What all of this means is that from a sociocultural perspective, pedagogical research is part and parcel of SLA research.[2]

In what follows we propose an approach to grammar instruction that is predicated on the Vygotskyan principle that schooled instruction is about developing control over theoretical concepts that are explicitly and coherently presented to learners as they are guided through a sequence of activities designed to prompt the necessary internalization of the relevant concepts.[3] The primary value of theoretical concepts is that unlike spontaneous, everyday concepts, they are not connected to an individual's personal experience; rather, they represent the generalized experience of a community (Karpov 2003, 66). Control of theoretical concepts enables learners to operate independently of a specific context as it allows them to transfer the concept to all relevant contexts as needed. According to Karpov (2003, 70), "Rote skills are meaningless and nontransferable, and pure verbal knowledge is inert"; true control over theoretical concepts entails conceptual as well as procedural knowledge.

While Vygotsky proposed the principle that instruction must focus on the coherent presentation of theoretical concepts, scholars such as Gal'perin and Davydov have worked out systematic pedagogies for promoting concept-based instruction (CBI). In the remainder of the chapter we are concerned primarily with systemic-theoretical instruction (STI), an approach to grammar instruction based on Gal'perin's pedagogical model (for an approach to L2 writing based on the model of Davydov [1988], see Ferreira 2005). A few researchers (Carpay 1974; Carpay and Van Oers 1999; Kabanova 1985; Van Parreren 1975) have carried out studies of L2 instruction using Gal'perin's approach; however, virtually all of these have been brief, lasting no more than a few hours or a few days. The only extended study of CBI applied to foreign language instruction was conducted by the first author of this chapter as reported on in Negueruela (2003). We limit ourselves here to an overview of Negueruela's project.

1.0 Vygotsky and the Importance of Concepts in Development

According to Vygotsky (1978, 90), "Properly organized learning results in mental development and sets in motion a variety of developmental processes." As mentioned above, for Vygotsky there is an organic and dialectical connection between instruction and development that coheres in conceptual knowledge. Concepts not only form the minimal unit of higher forms of verbal thinking (intentional memory, voluntary attention, planning, imagination, and abstract thinking) but also are the foundational units of instruction. Human consciousness develops and is transformed through the internalization of culturally organized concepts during communication with others. Eventually, we begin to use these concepts to communicate with ourselves in private speech as the primary means of mediating our own cognitive activity. As Vygotsky puts it, the "relationship between thought and word is a living process; thought is born through words. A word devoid of thought is a dead thing" (Vygotsky 1986, 255). Keeping in mind that in the Vygotskyan view, cognition and language activity are interconnected, learning a second language is a matter of not only learning new forms but also internalizing new or reorganizing already existing concepts.

2.0 Gal'perin's Systemic-Theoretical Instruction and CBI

The focus of Gal'perin's work (Gal'perin 1969, 1989, 1992a, 1992b) is on the concretization of Vygotsky's proposal that education as CBI is about promoting the cognitive development of students through concepts formation. Gal'perin and his collaborators, especially Karpova (1977) and Talyzina (1981), developed a complete and specific heuristic for teaching that takes account of such constructs as orientation, minimal unit of analysis, action, materialization, speech, and internalization.

Gal'perin's program reconceptualizes the subject matter of instruction, beginning with the development of an appropriate conceptual unit of instruction implemented as a didactic model that materializes in a coherent way the properties of what is to be learned. To promote internalization of the concept, speaking is necessary to liberate students from the immediate concrete experience and to transform learning actions and concepts from the material to the ideal plane. The challenge, as Gal'perin himself recognized, is integrating these principles into a real class (see Podolskij 1990). As Haenen (1996) observes, an ideal implementation of STI to the classroom requires the reorganization of the entire curriculum, since mental actions and concepts are not formed in isolation but are systematically connected to one another. Each concept should be coherently connected to the next.

In Gal'perin's approach, "both understanding and ability are basically inseparable; they are conceived as a unity" (Haenen 1996, 149). For Gal'perin, only a proper orienting basis, provided to the learner through systematic instruction, can lead to full-fledged mental actions. According to Talyzina (1981), the orienting basis of an action is crucial because it not only guides the action to its completion but also allows for generalization of an ability across actions. In the orienting stage, learners need to become aware of and gain control over all of the elements that must be deployed in the execution of an action.

Different approaches to language teaching seem to emphasize one or the other component. It could be argued that certain grammar-based approaches emphasize orientation with a focus on understanding grammatical structures and rule-based regularities. However, the orientation provided by structural explanations based on rules of thumb is certainly not systematic and general in Gal'perin's sense (see below). Furthermore, the quality of the conceptual explanation is only a first step to internalization. Equally important to the quality of a concept is its functionality. Performance-based approaches to language teaching, whether communicative or not, seem to privilege the executive component of an action and in so doing separate fluency from accuracy, treating each as a unique problem. More important, accuracy is understood as matching a learner's behavior with an external benchmark (e.g., native or expert speaker) that supposedly reflects correct use of a rule, rather than the learner's ability to use the concept in question to construct her own meanings.

3.0 The Minimal Unit of Instruction

Concept-based instruction supports explicit instruction in grammar to promote the learner's awareness and control over specific conceptual categories as they are linked to formal properties of the language. Aspect in Spanish, the focus of this discussion, allows the user to adopt a range of temporal perspectives, which are formally signaled through a set of morphological suffixes. The key task for the learner is not so much to master the suffixes as to understand the meaning potential made available by the concept of aspect and to learn to manipulate this in accordance with particular communicative intentions. The concept that is the object of instruction and learning (e.g., aspect) must be organized into a coherent pedagogical unit of instruction. This unit must have two fundamental properties: It must retain the full meaning of the relevant concept and be organized to promote learning, understanding, control, and internalization (Negueruela 2003). The rules of thumb presented in most textbooks are inadequate on both counts. That is, they fail to reflect the full meaning of the concept and are not organized in a way that promotes understanding, control, and internalization.

Both Vygotsky and Gal'perin recognized that effective pedagogical practice was not simply a matter of direct teaching of constructs, as, say, might occur in an introductory linguistics class. Thus, CBI must link grammatical concepts to communication, understood as the locus where symbolically mediated intentions are made manifest through the concepts themselves. It is through communicative activities—spoken as well as written—that learners come to realize that they can express construct meaning through the conceptual properties of the new language rather than behaving as if there were right or wrong ways of saying things in this language. In this respect, learner reflection on the various meanings that can be created during communicative activities is a central component of CBI. How this is achieved in STI is illustrated in our consideration of Negueruela's study.

4.0 Rules of Thumb

As several scholars have already pointed out (see, among others, Garrett 1986; Danserau 1987; Langacker 1987; Hubbard 1994; Westney 1994; Blyth 1997), grammatical explanations found in the majority of current Spanish textbooks consist by

Table 5.1 Uses of preterit and imperfect according to Dasilva and Lovett (1965)

Imperfect	Preterit
Tells what was happening	Records, reports, and narrates
Recalls what used to happen	With certain verbs causes a change of meaning
Describes a physical, mental emotion	
Tells time in the past	
Describes the background and sets the stage upon which another action occurred	

Source: Whitley (1986)

and large of incomplete and unsystematic rules of thumb that learners are somehow expected to master in order to perform appropriately in the L2. For instance, verbal aspect, usually discussed as the difference between preterit and imperfect, is often presented as a menu of unrelated rules that learners are expected to master in order to make "the right choice" when using the language. Interestingly, two of the leading applied linguists of their day, Dwight Bolinger and William Bull, attempted to remedy the situation, but without much lasting impact on Spanish pedagogical practice (see Bolinger 1991; Bull 1965). While most of their ideas only sporadically found their way into mainstream Spanish pedagogy, Bull and his colleagues (Bull et al. 1972) published an introductory textbook with the title *Communicating in Spanish,* which contained coherent conceptual explanations of the grammar of the language. However, focus on grammatical explanations soon became incompatible with how communicative language teaching was defined, largely, in our view, as a result of the profound impact of Krashen's (1981, 1985) input hypothesis and the claim that grammatical explanations did not promote acquisition unless they were simple.

Whitley (1986) discusses the inadequacies of grammatical explanations found in most Spanish textbooks. Although the example he uses to illustrate his point with regard to aspect (see table 5.1) is taken from a popular textbook published nearly forty years ago (Dasilva and Lovett 1965), even a cursory examination of texts published today reveals that not much has changed in four decades.

The rules in table 5.1 are capricious to the extent that some are semantic in referring to a complete event, others are functional as when the preterit is used for foregrounding, while others are perceptual and concrete, as when the imperfect is used to tell time. Simplified and reductive rules of thumb have the potential to do more harm than good because, for one thing, they depict language as a sedimented entity that appears to have a life of its own independent of people. Rules of thumb easily lead students down a garden path of confusion and frustration. Whitley makes this point forcefully:

> The defects are manifold here [table 5.1]. First, this treatment represents the two
> categories as arbitrary groupings of independent uses: five different imperfects,

two different preterits; and the fact that recordings end up as preterit rather than imperfect seems as capricious as the classification of tomatoes as vegetables rather than fruits. Second, it suggests that the imperfect is used more frequently.. . . Third, it is extremely difficult to apply because its vagueness in specific contexts robs it of any criterial value. If students wish to convey their *I slept all day,* should they opt for 'what was happening,' 'describes physical state,' 'describes background,' or 'records, reports'? All these seem applicable and conflicting; thus, students are baffled when their teacher recommends *Dormí todo el día* over *Dormía todo el día.* (Whitley 1986, 109)

As has been pointed out in the research literature on aspect (see, for instance, Givon 1982; Bardovi-Harlig 2000; and Montrul and Salaberry 2003), there is more to aspect than the semantic distinction between an ongoing and a punctual action. Discourse factors such as the organization of narrative grounding as a global discourse function (see, for instance, Reinhart 1984 for textual criteria to mark narrative foreground) and the distributional bias hypothesis (Andersen 1984 and Andersen and Shirai 1994) must also be taken into account. However, from a teaching perspective and, more important, for the arguments developed in this chapter, it seems that the explanations that Spanish students receive are based on incomplete simplifications of grammatical rules derived from textbooks. The effects of textbook explanations emerge in our analysis of learner data.

5.0 Materialization of Concepts through Didactic Models

Once a minimal unit of instruction is determined (e.g., the concept of aspect for teaching of Spanish preterit and imperfect), the development and use of didactic models to capture the complexities of the concept forms the critical next step. Didactic models are the material tools that learners have at their disposal to help understand and internalize the concept. Engestrom (1996) stresses the importance of adequate didactic models for all school subjects and argues that approaches that simplify the object of study lead to what Wagenschein (1977, 42–43) provocatively calls "synthetic stupidity," a type of ignorance that emerges from the encapsulated study of the world that often occurs in the educational setting. For instance, many adults—regardless of their educational background—tend to offer a quick but absurd explanation for the phases of the moon (full moon, half moon, quarter moon, and new moon) based on the common misconception that "it is the shadow of the earth that makes the moon time and time again into a crescent" (Wagenschein 1977, 42–43).[4]

For Gal'perin, learning that fosters development is first based on material aids that can be manipulated by learners to represent structural, procedural, functional, and content properties of the object of study (see Karpova 1977). Didactic models such as charts are often times the better option to represent the properties of sophisticated and complex objects of instruction such as grammatical concepts (see figure 5.1). Two aspects of these diagrams are salient: their quality (empirical or theoretical) and manner of presentation to students (prefabricated or exploratory). With regard to quality, the models must raise learners' awareness of what linguistic resources are available to them to carry out concrete linguistic actions with specific purposes across all contexts. In essence, they must be maximally informative and at the same time generalizable. In addition, the models must allow students to explain their communicative intentions in actual performances.

Although the use of flow charts is not unique to CBI approaches to teaching grammar (see, for example, Massey 2001), in a CBI approach they are not primarily aimed at ensuring that students get the right answer to teacher questions, as often happens in encapsulated education (Engestrom 1996). Rather, they are but one component in

Figure 5.1 Didactic model constructed by Negueruela (2003) based on Bull (1965)

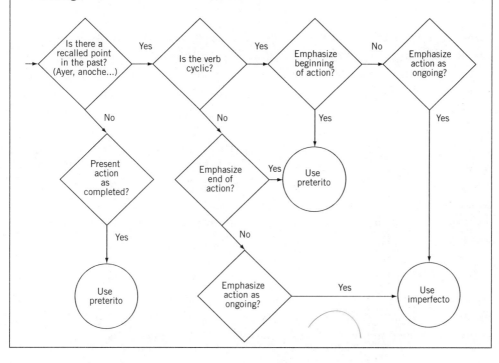

VERBALIZATION for ASPECT

- The concept of "aspect" is, simply put, the perspective on an action. That is, what is the part/aspect of the action that you, as the speaker/writer, want to emphasize?

- The meaning aspect of a verb is determined by two components:

  - Lexical aspect: based on the meaning of the verb (cyclic or noncyclic)

  - Grammatical aspect: based on the verbal tense used (preterito/imperfecto)

- When these two elements are combined, you can emphasize the beginning, end, middle (ongoing), or completion of an action.

- Follow the flow chart below to explain to yourself why you can select preterit or imperfect to present an action as completed, ongoing, beginning, or ending.

an integrated approach to instruction whose purpose is to help learners develop new meaning-making resources, a different thinking for speaking framework, as Slobin (1996) might put it.

6.0 Verbalization Activities

For Vygotsky, it is the functional use of speech in selecting and focusing attention on the important elements in concept formation that facilitates the process of internalization and the formation of the ideal or internal plane of understanding (Vygotsky 1986, 109). Following Vygotsky's lead, Gal'perin argues that using language as the tool for internalization frees learners from the material properties of specific contextualized actions and allows them to recontextualize concepts as needed. In CBI, therefore, verbalization is an instructional tool for attention focusing, selection analysis, and synthesis and thus is directly connected with internalization and concept formation. Although verbalization has been broadly interpreted by different sociocultural theory (SCT) scholars interested in classroom learning to include dialogic interaction between learners (e.g., Haenen 2001; Haenen, Schrijnemakers, and Stufkens 2003; Carpay and Van Oers 1999; Swain 2000), Negueruela (2003) defined it in fairly narrow terms as the intentional use of overt self-directed (i.e., private speech) to explain concepts to the self (see also Kabanova 1985).

In Negueruela's study, students were free to choose between the L1 (English) or the L2 (Spanish) for their verbalization activities. The meanings of our L1 serve as the basis of our reasoning and self-regulation; thus, to proscribe use of the L1 is to inhibit the very learning process we are attempting to promote. For this reason, "Gal'perin advocates that the orienting basis be built from the native language" (Carpay 1974, 171). Which language to use to promote conceptual development is a more complicated matter than it may at first appear. Internalization of certain grammatical concepts in all its functionality requires deep understanding. Given that (by definition) learners are in the process of attempting to develop the capacity to understand how meaning is constructed in the new language, it is unlikely that they will have the ability to simultaneously learn the new language and use this same language as a psychological tool to mediate their learning of the language. From our perspective, therefore, it makes perfect sense that learners should rely on their L1 as the metacognitive tool to understand and guide internalization of the new language. This is not an argument that the L1 should be allowed in interpersonal communication (as a social tool). It most certainly should not. It is, however, an argument that the L1 should be allowed in intrapersonal communication (as a psychological tool).

7.0 The Study

Negueruela's study was conducted in an intermediate-level university course in Spanish grammar and composition (sixth semester of study). A total of twelve students participated in the course, which ran for sixteen weeks.

7.1 Course Description

The course concentrated on the development of writing skills and grammatical knowledge. Although the majority of students at this level generally begin their study of Spanish in secondary school, they usually continue to have problems with aspect (as well as with other notoriously problematic grammatical domains such as mood). The students were provided with the conceptual model depicted in figure 5.1. Communicative activities designed to proceduralize the conceptual knowledge presented in the didactic model were based on Di Pietro's (1987) strategic interaction approach to language teaching. Strategic interaction is predicated on what Howatt (1984) calls a "strong understanding of communicative language teaching" (CLT), in which communication leads to learning, versus a "weak" understanding of CLT, in which learning leads to communication.

7.2 Data Collection

Two primary types of data were collected: conceptual development and personal. The former consists of three subsets of data: learners' definitions of grammatical concepts designed to tap into their conscious and explicit knowledge of the relevant concept, spontaneous performance data comprising several oral and written tasks, and verbalization data consisting of students' home recordings in which they were asked to explain to themselves specific grammatical concepts relying on explanatory charts provided by the instructor. Definition data were collected before a particular grammatical concept was introduced and then again at the conclusion of the course.

Six verbalization activities, designed so that students could explain to themselves specific grammatical points using the concepts represented diagrammatically, were included in the course. These activities were carried out as homework assignments and were audio recorded by the students for later analysis and discussion. They began at the level of the sentence but quickly moved to discourse-level features of the language. This shift in focus was important because it encouraged students to reflect on how they created meaning in specific communicative scenarios.

The performance data were collected at the beginning, at various points in the course, and again at the conclusion of the course. Personal data consisted of responses to an online questionnaire as well as students' reflections on the course collected in the eighth week (midsemester) and sixteenth week of the semester (final week of classes).

7.3 Data Analysis

In this section we present samples of the various types of data that were collected during the course, as described in the preceding section.

7.3.1 Definition Data

Conceptual definitions are important data because they reveal the quality of the resources that learners can bring to bear during communicative activity, and according to Valsiner (2001, 87) they are "functional for the future of the person." As Valsiner further points out (87), this type of knowledge does not equate with actual behavior (i.e., linguistic performance); however, it plays a critical role in guiding development of performance ability because it serves to orient learners to the meaning-making possibilities offered by the language. It is therefore important to uncover relationships between the development of coherent and complete theoretical concepts on the part of learners and the development of their actual performance. Thus the data on conceptual definitions must be viewed in light of linguistic performance data (see the earlier commentary by Karpov on conceptual and procedural knowledge). As will become evident in the data analysis, prior to STI, students' understanding of grammatical concepts is frequently fragmented and lacking in coherence, no doubt a reflection of their past experience with rules-of-thumb instruction.[5]

In an interesting small-scale study, Seliger (1979) investigated the relationship between grammatical rules of thumb and performance and found no connection between the two. Learners knew the correct rules but could not apply them, while others, including natives, did not know the correct rules but still could produce the correct forms. From the CBI perspective this is not a surprising outcome, because rules of thumb are not concepts and are very difficult to transfer beyond the bounds of the specific contexts (e.g., grammatical exercise) in which they were encountered. It is precisely this situation that theoretical concepts seek to ameliorate.

Due to space limitations, we cannot consider anything near the full set of rich and complex data from the sixteen learners reported on in Negueruela (2003). We instead examine the data from one of the learners for one of the grammatical concepts addressed in the STI course: verbal aspect. The following definition of aspect was provided by participant 1 at the point in the course where aspect was about to become the object of study (time 1, the second week of classes and before CBI): "The idea behind imperfect and preterit is for expressing things in the past. I use preterit when it wants to express something that is finished, or that it has a definitive time. The imperfect is used to describe things that happened with frequency in the past, or general things. The imperfect is used in the past to describe characteristics of people, to tell age of a person, and also to tell time." At time 2, the last week of classes, the student produced the following definition of verbal aspect: "The imperfecto is used to describe a point in the past that isn't specific. It is also used when describing the background of a story. The pretérito is used when you are talking about a recalled point in the past, something specific that happened at a specific time."

In the first definition, provided at time 1, the student's understanding emphasizes a nonspecific explanation of the use of preterit based on completeness of an action, but there is no parallelism for use of imperfect since its use is defined in terms of perceptual concrete criteria. The student no doubt externalized knowledge of aspect that she had appropriated in previous instruction, and it seems clear that this knowledge was based on a rules-of-thumb approach. Moreover, one can easily present counterexamples to the rules she presented. At time 2, on the other hand, the definition incorporates the importance of establishing a point of reference in determining the aspectual meaning of preterit in a specific utterance. The definition is more coherent and it shows sensitivity to the relevance of speaker perspective in marking aspect and thus takes on a more semantic and functional tone. To be sure, the definition still fails to manifest full conceptual understanding of aspect, but it is greatly improved over the original definition provided.

7.3.2 Discourse Data

Discourse data come from L2 learners' spontaneous performance collected before and after STI instruction through written and oral language diagnostic tasks administered during the first three weeks and again during the final two weeks of the semester. The written diagnostic used for assessing development of aspect was a nine-picture sequence taken from Mayer's (1979) well-known book, *Frog Goes to Dinner*.

In example 1 we include examples of written performance collected at time 1, and in example 2 we document samples of the student's writing at the end of the course. Words in bold indicate coherent use of relevant aspect morphology and underlined words indicate incoherent use of the morphology. The translations provided are literal in order to capture to the extent possible the full meaning and, where relevant, the awkwardness of the Spanish sentences:

1. Written performance: Frog story before CBI

(1a) ... *para celebrar el cumpleaños de él, la familia de Roberto vayan a un restaurante.*

' ... in order to celebrate his birthday, the family of Roberto be gone to a restaurant.'

(1b) ... *y la familia fueron muy excited a ir.*

' ... and the family were very excited to go.'

(1c) *Cuando Roberto y su familia estaron en el restaurante, Jorge [rana] **dejó** el jaquete [sic] de Roberto y **fue** en el saxofono de un miembro [sic] del grupo musical.*

'When Roberto and his family were in the restaurant, Jorge [rana] left the jacket of Roberto and went in the saxophone of a member of the musical group.'

(1d) *Todos los clientes del restaurante no **querían** que hay un frog en el restaurante.*

'All the clients in the restaurant did not want that there is a frog in the restaurant.'

(1e) *Toda la familia era furioso con Roberto porque él **trajó** Jorge al restaurante.*

'All the family was furious with Roberto because he brought Jorge to the restaurant.'

(1f) *Cuando regresaban a su casa, el padre de Jorge **mandó** a él a ir a su cuarto.*

'While Roberto came back, the father of Jorge sent him to go to his room.'

(1g) *Roberto aparece sentir malo por sus acciones.*

'Roberto seems to feel bad for his actions.'

2. Written performance: Frog story after CBI

(2a) *Este es un cuento de un chico, Juan, que **iba** a la cena con su familia.*

'This is a story about a boy, Juan, that went to have dinner with her family.'

(2b) *Toda la familia **estaban** felices con la excepción de Juan.*

'All the family was happy with the exception of Juan.'

(2c) *Mientras ellos **estaban** leyendo el menu, la drana [sic] de Juan, jumped . . . **saltó** (no sé la palabra pero está en la forma de pretérito) de la chaqueta al instrumento de uno de los miembros del grupo.*

'While they were reading the menus, Juan jumped (I don't know the word but it is in the preterit form) of the jacket to the instrument of one of the members of the group.'

(2d) *Todos los clientes del restaurante no **podían** creer lo que **pasó**.*

'All the clients in the restaurant could not believe what happened.'

(2e) *Juan **se dió** cuenta de que la drana [sic] **era** de él, y su familia **estaba** 'horrified.'*

'Juan realized that the frog was his, and his family was "horrified."'

(2f) *Cuando **llegó** a la casa el padre **mandó** que Juan <u>fue</u> a su cuarto.*

'When he got home, his father sent John to go to his room.'

(2g) ***Estaba** muy feliz porque no **necesitó** pasar toda la noche celebrando los cumpleaños [sic] de su hermana.*

'He was very happy because he did not need to spend the whole night celebrating the birthdays of her sister.'

The improvement from time 1 to time 2 is marked. Before CBI, participant 1 had problems with verbal aspect. In 1a, she used present subjunctive, most likely a random selection on her part, deploying a meaning that is incoherent in the context of use. In 1b, the learner should have used imperfect morphology and the verb *estar* to convey the emotions of the family, instead of using the Spanish verb *ser* in the preterit, which conveys an incoherent meaning in this context. Following CBI, 2a and 2b show a marked improvement in how the learner uses aspect, with imperfect used consistently in both cases (*iban* and *estaban*) and with appropriate lexical choices. The copula *estar* is also used appropriately, whereas in time 1 (example 1b) it was not. Furthermore, the participant is able to coherently ground her narrative by using preterit and imperfect morphology. In 2a she uses imperfect with a telic event, *ir a la cena,* which shows the ability to ground an event whose telicity would seem to call for a preterit construction, such as *fue a la cena.* Instead, she chooses to construct the event with the imperfect, infusing her utterance with an ongoing aspect, while at the same time grounding her narrative effectively.

We have underlined *fue* in 1c (coherent use of aspect) because the meaning conveyed by the verb in the particular context is what one might expect. Example 2c is especially interesting. The learner used *saltó*, which conveys the meaning depicted in the sequence, despite the fact that she first wrote the verb in English ("jumped"), then in Spanish, and then said that she did not know the word (when indeed she did), stating that she desired to render it in the preterit form. Also, the learner is able to construct the background *estaba leyendo* in order to foreground the salient event that takes place at this point in the narrative: *la rana saltó*. Importantly, with regard to the learner's development, both constructions occurred in the same utterance.

Finally, 1d is one of the few instances in which participant 1 used imperfect appropriately before instruction. However, she constructs a complex sentence that would require her to use imperfect subjunctive in the subordinate verb. Instead, she used the present tense. After CBI, in 2d, she used a different construction where she coherently deployed imperfect and preterit.

All of the examples confirm marked improvement in the use of verbal aspect. Item 2e shows how the learner was able to first use the preterit and then the imperfect form of both *ser* and *estar* in the same sentence. Example 1f produced prior to instruction nicely reflects the application of a rule of thumb that resulted in an inappropriate formation. The student attempted to use imperfect after *cuando*, since this is one of the adverbs that is often taught as a trigger for the imperfect. Learners are instructed that they should use the imperfect to set the scene in a narrative and then use the preterit in the next verb. Following this rule of thumb, the meaning participant 1 conveyed in 1f was not coherent in the context of the narrative. The pictures in the story are not about the father sending the little boy to his room while they were coming back home in the car; the father sent the boy to his room once they came home. Following instruction, in example 2f, participant 1 used two verbs in the preterit with the word *cuando*, thus violating her previous rule of thumb but conveying a coherent meaning—the two actions were sequential and not simultaneous with regard to the story she was trying to construct (when the family arrived home, the father sent the boy to his room).

The emergence and frequent use of the Spanish imperfect to construct narratives in the past, which parallels the semantic and functional conceptualizations of Spanish verbal aspect, is especially interesting. It is important to remember that before CBI the learners had no doubt studied verbal aspect numerous times in their previous courses. In fact, participant 1, as most of the participants in Negueruela's study (nine out of twelve learners), had been given the traditional rule-of-thumb explanation in the Spanish course they participated in the semester prior to enrolling in the STI course.

7.3.3 Verbalization Data

A total of 558 verbalizations were collected and compiled into a corpus. In addition to documenting developmental trends showing enhanced conceptual understanding of the relevant grammatical feature, the corpus also reflects the learners' struggle to overcome their previous, rule-of-thumb-based understanding of the concept. In what follows we consider a few examples relating to aspect.

The first example comes from participant 1:

> I was trying to say, one day, my friend and I were going shopping. Entonces I used the imperfect. "Ir" no es un verbo cíclico y no hay un tiempo específico. If I wanted to say: "my friend and I went shopping," I could've use the preterit, but because I was telling the background of the story es mejor decir "íbamos."

Participant 1, through reflecting on the notion of lexical aspect and her own intent of portraying the event as durative, is able to realize that in most contexts both preterit and imperfect are indeed possible. She is still intermingling semantic reasons, the meaning of aspect, with functional ones, providing the background of a story, but she is beginning to realize the personal significance of the grammatical choices she makes, as is documented in the continuation of her verbalization:

> "Entonces cuando estábamos en esta tienda los mismos dos que nos vimos en otra tienda caminaba por la puerta." First verb: "estábamos," imperfect because it was the ongoing action of us being in the store. Second verb: "The same two men that we saw," here I used the "pretérito" (vimos) because it was a completed action. Third verb: "They walked," here I should've said, "caminaron por la puerta," but "caminaba" could work if I had intended to say "those men were walking through the door."

Here participant 1 once again reflects on how she has the option of choosing between the two morphological forms that manifest aspect—action completed or ongoing—and, crucially, that it is possible to utilize either aspect depending on the meaning she as speaker wishes to express.

Although participant 1 came a long way in her understanding of aspect, the road to conceptual development is not, as Vygotsky (1986) cogently argues, a smooth, linear process. In a later verbalization, the same participant resorts to a rule-of-thumb approach to explain her choice of aspect:

> "Como siempre mi familia y yo fuimos a la casa de mi tío." En esta frase usé el pretérito y debí usar el imperfecto porque es el "background" y es una acción habitual.

Here participant 1 not only uses a rule of thumb for imperfect (imperfect is used for habitual actions), but the rule she invokes leads her to argue that the imperfect is a better option for the utterance she has created, when indeed it is not. Both options are possible; it is simply a question of perspective. Notice also that in this case she relies on the L2 in formulating her explanation. An interesting topic for future research would be to investigate the impact of L1 versus L2 verbalizations on conceptual development.

As it turns out, participant 12 was able to explain his use of aspect quite effectively, even at the time of the initial verbalization:

> *El seis de junio fui a la escuela a mi dormitorio para comenzar mis clases.* [June 6th, I went to school to my dorm to begin my classes.] I used preterit here because it's referring to a recalled point: "el seis de junio" and since "fui" is a non-cyclic verb, it's referring to the beginning of the action.

This explanation seems to show that participant 12 understands the importance of temporal perspective in the selection of the appropriate morphological marker of aspect. However, despite continued STI instruction, which we might anticipate resulting in even greater understanding of the concept, a time 2 verbalization reveals an inconsistency in which influence of a rule-of-thumb account slips into his explanation:

> *Siempre había mucho para comer.* [There was always a lot to eat.] Imperfect because it's emphasizing an ongoing action because I am saying "*siempre,*" so I use Imperfect cause it's a habitual action.

The learner begins his explanation by stating that his use of imperfect reflects an ongoing action but then confuses things by keying in on the temporal adverb *siempre,* frequently pointed to by textbooks and teachers as a trigger for imperfect because it indicates "habitual action."

Participant 2 is able to incorporate semantic reasoning when explaining grammatical features at time 2, but she continues to explain her use of imperfect as relating to habitual actions, again, reflecting a rules-of-thumb approach:

> *Como cada día de las fiestas mi abuelo se dormía* [Like each day of the holidays my grandfather slept.] "*Dormía*" because the action is ongoing. It's something that occurs all the time, so it's cyclic in a sense and it emphasizes that he slept until the dessert was ready, so therefore I used imperfect.

Participant 2 begins by explaining her choice of imperfect appropriately, an ongoing action. However, when she attempts to explain its meaning, her account becomes incoherent and fails to present a coherent and complete understanding of verbal aspect. In fact, she says that the verb *dormía* is cyclic (which it is not), and she adds that the verb is cyclic because the action happened all the time. It appears that the learner accesses the everyday meaning of cyclic—occurring repeatedly at regular intervals, as with the seasonal cycles—to construct her understanding of aspect. The problem is that this meaning does not jive with Bull's special understanding of cyclic aspect as entailing a simultaneous beginning and end of an event. In this sense, the learner appropriates the term "cyclic" for her explanation but personalizes its meaning based on the everyday meaning of the concept. This sense of the term will not help the learner understand the relationship between verbal aspect and lexical aspect and the meaning expressed by imperfect morphology in the context of use. The fact that the grandfather's sleeping occurred "all the time" is not conveyed by imperfect morphology but by the adverbial phrase *como cada día* (like every day). Thus the preterit option is also possible in this example. Rules of thumb still permeate this explanation.

7.3.4 *Personal Reflections*

Students were also asked to reflect on their experiences learning Spanish grammar through CBI. They submitted their reflections via email during the eighth week and again during the sixteenth (final) week of the semester. These reflections provide a unique opportunity to understand the feasibility of implementing CBI in a L2 classroom. The reflections were organized according to how they related to the main principles of CBI: understanding grammar through meaning and not mechanical rules, the "cognitive need" that arises from instructional activities based on understanding instead of memorization, and the relevance of charts and verbalizations in learning grammatical concepts.

7.3.4.1 UNDERSTANDING GRAMMAR

One of the critical issues in the application of CBI instruction was the importance of understanding grammatical categories through understanding the complexities of the conceptual meanings carried by specific forms while avoiding the misleading shortcuts provided by grammatical rules of thumb. In this regard participant 3, in her reflections collected the last week of classes, stressed the importance of explaining grammar to herself to really know if she understood it:

> When I explain concepts to myself, I always understand the concepts better. If I can explain it to myself, then I know that I really do understand the information. I feel as though I have learned so much about the language. I have really improved my writing, and now in my writing I am able to use preterit, imperfect, subjunctive, indicative and future tenses. Before this class I only used present tense.

As Vygotsky (1986) stated, if one cannot put something into language, one does not really understand it. More important, this participant connects her newfound understanding of grammar to her ability to use a wider array of forms in performance.

Participant 5, in his midsemester reflections, comments on how he struggled between the old grammatical explanations and the new conceptual understanding of grammar:

> It's more difficult to speak and rationalize using a certain tense for me, mainly because the reasoning is different from what I've been taught in the past. I'm still stuck on trying to rationalize it using old methods and it gets confusing sometimes.

CBI has generated a conflict for this student—a conflict that can lead to positive developmental outcomes. Indeed, as we see in the student's final reflection, the conflict is resolved and there emerges a much clearer understanding of the importance of personal agency in creating contextualized meaning through grammatical resources:

> [Verbalizations and recordings] have helped a lot because it's a more abstract way of thinking about it, so instead of saying "ok, this situation uses this particular rule, so I need to use this tense" I say "what is the point I'm trying to express here, and which tense best accomplishes that." I think I've learned how to effectively communicate my ideas better.

The learner's discovery of the importance of meaning makes this learner feel that she had not only learned about grammatical forms or even concepts but had also learned something about communication in the new language. This is clearly an important goal of any communicative language pedagogy.

The following two comments, from participants 7 and 8, respectively, reveal an appreciation of the difference between a rules-of-thumb approach to grammar instruction and a CBI approach, in which user agency is central to meaning making:

> In past classes, we have studied every part of grammar that we studied in this course. The difference is this: throughout Spanish 200, we were taught a different way of looking at the material. Yes, we reviewed it and realized our previous mistakes, but we also learned how to look at the grammar abstractly. It's no longer, "use subjunctive when you say 'es importante,'" etc., now we can look at the meaning of the sentence and realize indirect reasons for using the subjunctive, for example.
>
> In earlier Spanish classes they would tell us to choose a tense or mood based on very specific guidelines, but in this class I learned that the guidelines are not always exact and that it also depends on how you are trying to express the action or situation.

7.3.4.2 VERBALIZATIONS

With regard to verbalizations aimed at self-explanations of their performances, participant 12 made the following remarks:

> These assignments help me justify my reasoning for my decision. Even though I'm not sure if they are correct, it helps to explain vocally. Also the reasoning comes from actual concrete aspects that you gave us. For example, just because it says "para que" should not indicate that the sentence will take the subjunctive form.

These reflections show again the conflict between prepackaged menus of rules and the conceptual way of understanding of grammar, which the learner feels makes it "easier" to remember than rules.

An especially interesting comment comes from participant 7, who reports that it was beneficial for her to explain her performance not only to herself but also to someone else, even if the other person did not understand what she was talking about:

> Now that I think about it though, I made my roommate (who isn't a Spanish major, mind you, so she had no idea what I was talking about) listen to me explain when you use which pronoun, etc. Again, I always have found it helpful to explain to someone else (or a machine for that matter) the information. . . . I really liked the idea of the tape—at first it was weird to talk to yourself into a recorder, but it helped me so much. . . . By recording myself speaking, it was basically the same thing—and I think it helped me learn the information.

This is reminiscent of the nineteenth-century German writer Heinrich von Kleist, who in a short piece titled *On the Gradual Working Out of One's Thoughts in the*

Process of Speaking, quoted in Appel and Lantolf (1994, 438), nicely illustrates the importance of speaking for understanding:

> If you want to understand something and can't figure it out by pondering, I would advise you, my dear ingenious friend, to speak of it to the next acquaintance who happens by. It certainly doesn't have to be a bright fellow; that's hardly what I have in mind. You're not supposed to ask him about the matter. No, quite the contrary; you are first of all to tell him about it yourself.

Living in a more technologically advanced age than von Kleist, participant 7 found not only a friend who did not understand anything about Spanish but also a machine, which functioned equally well. The point is, however, that the primary addressee for participant 9's utterances was neither the friend nor the machine but the self. In essence, the verbalization activities were a form of private speech, which, as we know from the work of Vygotsky (1986) and others (Lantolf 2003; Ohta 2001; among others), is the primary mechanism through which concepts are internalized.

Participant 7 remarked that it was also useful for her to talk to others during group work in class:

> I found that the best way for me to learn is to try to teach others what I know. That's why I like working in groups and trying to explain to others the information. (It shows me what I know, and what I don't know.)

Wells (1999) notes that even when someone is engaged in social speech, as in the example above, the speech may be at the same time self-reflexive and thus have a private as well as a social function. Learner 7 seems to attest to just this type of circumstance.

The final two commentaries on the verbalization activities come from participants 2 and 1, respectively:

> I enjoy doing the verbalizations because it helps me internalize the rules of grammar more effectively. After the recordings I did silently explain the assignments to myself. I have a tendency to talk to myself when I have to remember things. I think it helps no matter what you are studying.

Interestingly enough, the learner appropriated the terminology "internalization," which had been used by the instructor in explaining grammatical concepts through the diagrams. Moreover, it appears that the assigned verbalization activity triggered the learner's use of subvocal private speech, a common strategy he is aware of deploying in the past.

Participant 1, as we see below, reports a similar awareness of using private speech as a way of understanding concepts, regardless of domain. However, it seems that although the effectiveness of this strategy was confirmed for the learner as a result of the required verbalization assignments, he now realized that overt vocalization was even more powerful than subvocal speech:

In all honesty, I never really consciously silently explained anything to myself. I think when I am studying that is basically what I am doing, and when I am trying to learn a concept, I do the same thing. But I never really sat down and thought to myself, "hey, now I'm going to explain this concept to myself." I think that these techniques have taught me a different way of studying and learning.

7.3.4.3 CONCEPT DIAGRAMS

The students consistently reported that they found the concept diagrams to be effective mediators of their learning. Participant 12, for instance, notes that not only did CBI provide him with a different perspective on grammar, but the diagrams were actually easier to recall than lists of rules:

Explaining things to myself helps me a lot, but using the subjunctive flow chart was a little more challenging than using the conditional one. I think that it is because I learned subjunctive a different way in Spanish 4 and 5 in high school. While I did learn NEW uses for it when we covered it in this class that I hadn't been taught in high school, the way in which it was taught to me first was that there are certain situations in which to use it (change of subjects, expressing doubt, expressing an opinion) but not that they follow a set of steps, like our flow chart. The flow charts worked well for me—they're easier to remember than lists of individual rules—and the conditional one was much easier. I think that my only difficulty with using the first handout was the result of the fact that it was a different way of explaining the subjunctive than I had originally been given.

In his final sentence, this student also further documents the initial struggles the learners had with CBI, because it conflicted with their past experience and with what they had already internalized.

Participant 4 also compares the effectiveness of the diagrams with her past experiences with rule-based pedagogy:

The charts are a grammar-figuring-out-guide that work better than the rules (like the rules for preterit and imperfect) that we had learned in Spanish 100. It was very helpful to see the concepts in a visual structure because the concept of grammar is a very structural concept, and being able to visualize it made it make much more sense.

Participant 1 remarks that the diagrams generated better understanding of the grammatical feature but that they also compelled him to think about why a particular feature (in this case tense) is used (as we have said earlier, this is an essential aspect of CBI):

I think they helped me learn the grammar better. Rather than using a certain tense just because you know a certain phrase requires it, you actually think about why that tense is used.

8.0   Concluding Comments

In this chapter, we have briefly explored the main principles of CBI as it relates to the L2 classroom and, specifically, instruction in Spanish grammar. Learners in Negueruela's class still need to develop a complete and systematic conceptual understanding of the grammatical notion of aspect along with the capacity to automatically utilize this concept to regulate their written and oral performance in the new language. This is the critical point: establishing the connection between visible explicit knowledge and its functionality in performance. From an SCT perspective, the connection between the two is not causal but genetic.[6] The source of conceptualizations is conscious reflection, but for any conceptualization to achieve functionality requires that the user attain automatic control over the feature in question—in this case, aspect. To be sure, robust opportunities for communicative interaction (written as well as oral) are necessary for automaticity to emerge; however, the ability to deploy appropriate meanings, often in innovative ways, emerges from a conscious understanding of the relevant theoretical concept. The data considered here evidence both conceptual development and improvement in performance. Indeed, all of the learners in Negueruela's (2003) full study exhibit development in both domains; however, and this is an important point, development was not uniform across learners.

It is important to reiterate that CBI in itself does not constitute a pedagogy but a theoretical claim about the appropriate object of instruction in any educational domain that originated in the writings of L. S. Vygotsky. To bring the theoretical stance into the classroom in a concrete way requires an appropriate pedagogy. The pedagogical framework adopted and adapted by Negueruela (2003), on whose larger study the present chapter is based, was Gal'perin's systemic-theoretical instruction. As we discussed, STI, as developed by Gal'perin, follows a preferred procedure to promoting the internalization of the relevant concepts.

However, we also must keep in mind that the goal of CBI is not simply the internalization of concepts, in the banal sense of memorization, but also development of the learner's capacity to use the concepts to mediate (i.e., self-regulate) their language performances. Thus communicative activities are an important component for CBI. These activities, in Negueruela's study, were based on strategic interaction, and although we did not have space to discuss this aspect of the course, we do not wish to leave the impression that such activities are less important. They are not, but we leave it to the interested reader to consult the full study as well as the work of Di Pietro on this intriguing way of stimulating classroom communication of both the spoken and written variety.

We also want to point out that STI is only one way of implementing CBI. In fact, Negueruela's study, while relying on many of the features of STI, implemented this approach to teaching in a more flexible way, which is described in the writings of Gal'perin and his colleagues and students (see also Fariñas León 2001). Instead of rigidly adhering to the linear six-stage discrete sequence proposed by Gal'perin— motivation, orientation, materialization, overt-verbalization, subvocal verbalization, and silent verbalization—the approach advocated here is more flexible. At the same

time, it maintains focus on the three foundational principles of STI: appropriate pedagogical unit for instruction, materialization through didactic models, and verbalization
of concept-based explanations of user performance. Moreover, it argues that language
instruction is about communication and not about internalizing grammatical concepts
per se. Any concept-based approach to instruction, regardless of its object of study, must
concern itself with the proceduralization of concepts in concrete material activity. In the
case under consideration, this means the ability to engage in effective communicative
(spoken and written) activity where conceptual understanding of grammar in the service of the user's efforts to construct appropriate meaning is the goal of instruction.

Notes

1. More than thirty years ago Jakobovits and Gordon (1974) made a similar proposal with
   regard to the relationship between basic and pedagogical research on language learning.
   Unfortunately, in our view, their proposal seems to have made little impact on the field.
2. The intent in the following pages is to illuminate a pedagogy based on concepts as tools of
   the mind and not to recapitulate everything that has been said before about the acquisition of preterit/imperfect. Interested readers should consult the companion volume of
   Spanish Second Language Acquisition (see Lafford and Salaberry 2003). Relevant to the
   present chapter, one should consult Montrul and Salaberry (2003) on tense and aspect
   morphology in Spanish acquisition, Grove (2003) on the role of instruction in Spanish
   SLA, and Anton, Dicamilla, and Lantolf (2003) for an overview on sociocultural principles and recent research combining Spanish SLA and SCT.
3. Vygotsky uses the term *scientific* rather than *theoretical;* however, we opt for the latter term
   because *scientific* is often misinterpreted to mean concepts that have been exclusively
   developed by what is traditionally understood as the field of science. Clearly, as Karpov
   (2003, 66) notes, Vygotsky understood science in the broadest sense to include not only
   the field of natural science but also the social sciences and the humanities.
4. See his account of the confusion that often arises when adults are asked to explain the
   phases of the moon versus a lunar eclipse—a topic that most high school science classes
   treat in detail but with inappropriate if not confusing information.
5. One anonymous reviewer suggests that there are more sophisticated explanations for
   Spanish aspect than those presented in textbooks. While this is indeed the case, textbooks
   and in our experience language teachers do not bring these into their lessons, particularly
   not in the fourth semester of study. In this chapter we are concerned with classroom practices as based on textbook explanations and on how these are instrumental in the development of problematic learner knowledge of grammatical concepts.
6. This distinction, that explanations are based not on causality but on transformative development, leads Vygotsky to propose the genetic method to study the human mind, learning, and development. Consequently, the use of control groups to isolate variables, calcu-
   late correlations, and infer causality is incommensurate with an understanding of mind
   in which people with their agencies are not explained through "causes" but through
   reasons/meaning mediating activity.

References

Andersen, R. 1984. The insider's advantage. In *Italiano Lingua Seconda/Lingua Straniers,* ed.
   A Gaiacalone-Ramat and M. Vedovelli, 1–26. Roma: Bulzoni.
Andersen, R., and Y. Shirai 1994. Discourse motivations for some cognitive acquisition prin-
   ciples. *Studies in Second Language Acquisition* 16:133–56.

Anton, M., F. Dicamilla, and J. P. Lantolf. 2003. Sociocultural theory and the acquisition of Spanish as a second language. In *Spanish second language acquistion: State of the science.* eds. B. Lafford and R. Salaberry, 262–86. Washington, DC: Georgetown University Press.

Appel, G., and J. P. Lantolf. 1994. Speaking as mediation: A study of L1 and L2 text recall tasks. *Modern Language Journal* 78:437–52.

Axel, E. 1997. One developmental line in European activity theories. In *Mind, culture, and activity: Seminal papers from the Laboratory of Comparative Human Cognition,* ed. M. Cole, Y. Engestrom, and O. Vasquez, 128–46. Cambridge: Cambridge University Press.

Bardovi-Harlig, K. 2000. *Tense and aspect in second language acquisition: Form, meaning, and use.* Malden, MA: Blackwell.

Blyth, C. 1997. A constructivist approach to grammar: Teaching teachers to teach aspect. *Modern Language Journal* 81 (1): 50–66.

Bolinger, D. 1991. *Essays on Spanish: Words and grammar.* Newark, NJ: Juan de la Cuesta.

Bull, W. E. 1965. *Spanish for teachers.* Malabar, FL: Robert E. Krieger.

Bull, W. E., L. A. Briscoe, E. Lamadrid, C. Dellaccio, and M. J. Brown.1972. *Spanish for communication: Level one.* Boston: Houghton Mifflin.

Carpay, J. A. M. 1974. Foreign language teaching and meaningful learning: A Soviet Russian point of view. *I.T.L. Review of Applied Linguistics* 25–26:161–87. Belgium: Leuven.

Carpay, J., and B. Van Oers. 1999. Didactic models and the problem of intertextuality and polyphony. In *Perspectives on activity theory,* ed. Y. Engestrom, R. Miettinen, and R. Punamaki, 288–309. Cambridge: Cambridge University Press.

Cole, M. 1996. *Cultural psychology: A once and future discipline.* Cambridge, MA: Belknap Press.

Danserau, D. 1987. A discussion of techniques used in the teaching of the passé compose/imparfait distinction in French. *French Review* 61:33–38.

Dasilva, Z., and G. Lovett. 1965. *A concept approach to Spanish.* New York: Harper and Row.

Davydov, V. V. 1988. The concept of theoretical generalization and problems of educational psychology. *Studies in Soviet Thought* 36:169–202.

Di Pietro, R. 1987. *Strategic interaction.* Cambridge: Cambridge University Press.

Ellis, R. 1997. *SLA research and language teaching.* Oxford: Oxford University Press.

———. 2002. The place of grammar instruction in the second/foreign language curriculum. In *New perspectives on grammar teaching in second language classrooms,* ed. E. Hinkel and S. Fotos, 17–34. Mahwah, NJ: Lawrence Erlbaum Associates.

———. 2004. The definition and measurement of L2 explicit knowledge. *Language Learning* 54:227–75.

Engestrom, Y. 1996. *Non scolae sed vitae discimus:* Toward overcoming the encapsulation of school learning. In *An introduction to Vygotsky,* ed. H. Daniels, 151–70. Routledge: New York.

Fariñas León, G. 2001. Toward a hermeneutical reconstruction of Gal'perin's theory of learning. In *The theory and practice of cultural-historical psychology,* ed. S. Chaikli, 260–82. Aarhus N, Denmark: Aarhus University Press.

Ferreira, M. 2005. An application of the concept-based approach to academic writing instruction. Ph.D. diss., Pennsylvania State University.

Gal'perin, P. I. 1969. Stages in the development of mental acts. In *A handbook of contemporary Soviet psychology,* ed. M. Cole and I. Maltzman, 248–73. New York: Basic Books.

———. 1989. Organization of mental activity and the effectiveness of learning. *Soviet Psychology* 27 (3): 65–82.

———. 1992a. Stage-by-stage formation as a method of psychological investigation. *Journal of Russian and East European Psychology* 30 (July/August): 60–80.

————. 1992b. Linguistic consciousness and some questions of the relationships between language and thought. *Journal of Russian and East European Psychology* 30 (July/August): 80–92.

Garrett, N. 1986. The problem with grammar: What kind can the language learner use? *Modern Language Journal* 70:133–48.

Givon, T. 1982. tense–aspect modality: The Creole prototype and beyond. In *tense–aspect: Between semantics and pragmatics,* ed. J. P. Hopper, 115–63. Amsterdam: John Benjamins.

Grove, Ch. 2003. The role of instruction in Spanish second language acquisition. In *Spanish second language acquisition: State of the science,* ed. B. Lafford and R. Salaberry, 287–319. Washington, DC.: Georgetown University Press.

Haenen, J. 1996. *Piotr Gal'perin: Psychologist in Vygotsky's footsteps.* New York: Nova Science Publishers.

————. 2001. Outlining the teaching-learning process: Piotr Gal'perin contribution. *Learning and Instruction* 11:151–70.

Haenen, J., H. Schrijnemakers, and J. Stufkens. 2003. Sociocultural theory and the practice of teaching historical concepts. In *Vygotsky's theory of education in cultural context,* ed. A. Kozulin, B. Gindis, S. Miller, and V. Ageyev, 246–66. New York: Cambridge University Press.

Hinkel, E., and S. Fotos. 2002. *New perspectives on grammar teaching in second language classrooms.* Mahwah, NJ: Lawrence Erlbaum Associates.

Howatt, A. P. R. 1984. *A history of English language teaching.* Oxford: Oxford University Press.

Hubbard, P. L. 1994. Non-transformational theories of grammar: Implications for language teaching. In *Perspectives on pedagogical grammar,* ed. T. Odlin, 49–71. Cambridge: Cambridge University Press.

Jakobovits, L. A., and B. Gordon. 1974. Freedom to teach and freedom to learn. In *The context of foreign language teaching,* ed. L. A. Jakobovits and B. Gordon, 76–106. Rowley, MA: Newbury House.

Kabanova, O. Y. 1985. The teaching of foreign languages. *Instructional Science* 14:1–47.

Karpov, Y. V. 2003. Vygotsky's doctrine of scientific concepts. In *Vygotsky's educational theory in cultural context,* ed. A. Kozulin, B. Gindis, V. S. Ageyev, and S. M. Miller, 138–55. Cambridge: Cambridge University Press.

Karpova, S. N. 1977. *The realization of the verbal composition of speech by preschool children.* Paris: Mouton.

Krashen, S. D. 1981. *Second language acquisition and second language learning.* Oxford: Pergamon.

————. 1985. *The input hypothesis: Issues and implications.* New York: Longman.

Lafford, B., and R. Salaberry, eds. 2003. *Spanish second language acquisition: The state of the science.* Washington, DC: Georgetown University Press.

Langacker, R. W. 1987. *Foundations of cognitive grammar: Theoretical perspectives.* Stanford, CA: Stanford University Press.

Lantolf, J. P. 2003. Intrapersonal communication and internalization in the second language classroom. In *Vygotsky's theory of education in cultural context,* ed. A. Kozulin, V. S. Ageev, S. Miller, and B. Gindis, 349–70. Cambridge: Cambridge University Press.

Massey, A. 2001. In pursuit of preterit: A flow-chart of conjugations. *Hispania* 84 (September): 550–52.

Mayer, M. 1979. *Frog goes to dinner.* New York: Dial Books for Young Readers.

Montrul, S., and R. Salaberry. 2003. The development of tense/aspect morphology in Spanish as a second Language. In *Spanish second language acquisition: State of the science,* eds. B. Lafford and R. Salaberry, 47–73. Washington, DC: Georgetown University Press.

Negueruela, E. 2003. Systemic-theoretical instruction and L2 development: A sociocultural approach to teaching-learning and researching L2 learning. Ph.D. diss., Pennsylvania State University.

Norris, J. M., and R. Ortega. 2000. Effectiveness of L2 instruction: A research synthesis and quantitative meta-analysis. *Language Learning* 50:417–528.

Odlin, T., ed. 1994. *Perspectives on pedagogical grammars.* New York: Cambridge University Press.

Ohta, A. 2001. *Second language acquisition processes in the classroom.* Mahwah, NJ: Lawrence Erlbaum Associates.

Podolskij, A. 1990. Formation of mental actions. Using cases, simulations, and games: Gal'perin's perspective. In *International conference on case method research and case method application,* ed. H. E. Klein, 36–58. Enschede, Netherlands: Twente University.

Reinhart, T. 1984. Principles of Gestalt perception in the temporal organization of narrative texts. *Linguistics* 22:779–809.

Scribner, S. 1997. Mind in action: A functional approach to thinking. In *Mind, culture and activity: Seminal papers from the Laboratory of Comparative Human Cognition,* ed. M. Cole, Y. Engestrom, and O. Vasquez, 354–68. Cambridge: Cambridge University Press.

Seliger, H. W. 1979. On the nature and function of language rules in language teaching. *TESOL Quarterly* 12 (3): 359–69.

Slobin, D. I. 1996. Two ways to travel: Verbs of motion in English and Spanish. In *Grammatical constructions: Their form and meaning,* ed. M. Shibatani and S. A. Thompson, 195–219. Oxford: Clarendon Press.

Swain, M. 2000. The output hypothesis and beyond: Mediating acquisition through collaborative dialogue. In *Sociocultural theory and second language learning,* ed. J. P. Lantolf, 97–115. Oxford: Oxford University Press.

Talyzina, N. F. 1981. *Psychology and the learning process.* Moscow: Progress Press.

Valsiner, J. 2001. Process structure of semiotic mediation in human development. *Human Development* 44:84–97.

Van Parreren, C. F. 1975. Grammatical knowledge and grammatical skill. In *The context of foreign language learning,* ed. A. J. van Essen and J. P. Menting, 117–31. Assen, Netherlands: van Gorcum & Comp. B.V.

Vygotsky, L. S. 1978. *Mind in society: The development of higher mental processes,* ed. M. Cole, V. John-Steiner, S. Scribner, and E. Souberman. Cambridge: Harvard University Press.

———. 1986. *Thought and language.* 1934. Reprint, Cambridge, MA: MIT Press.

Wagenschein, M. 1977. *Verstehen lehren: Genetisch—sokratisch—exemplarisch.* Weinheim: Beltz.

Wells, G. 1999. *Dialogic inquiry: Toward a sociocultural practice and theory of education.* Cambridge: Cambridge University Press.

Westney, P. 1994. Rules and pedagogical grammar. In Odlin, *Perspectives in pedagogical grammar.* 72–96. Cambridge: Cambridge University Press.

Whitley, M. S. 1986. *Spanish/English contrasts: A course in Spanish linguistics.* Washington, DC: Georgetown University Press.

The Effects of Study Abroad and Classroom Contexts on the Acquisition of Spanish as a Second Language

From Research to Application

Barbara Lafford   *Arizona State University*
Joseph Collentine   *Northern Arizona University*

Study-abroad (SA) contexts have traditionally been assumed by language professionals, school administrators, and students (and their parents) to be the best environments in which to acquire a foreign language and understand its culture. In the United Kingdom the "year abroad" had its origin in the "grand tour" of Europe by aristocratic children of means, who spent time abroad to attain the level of cultural knowledge (of Western civilization) that their status required. For many years American university administrators and foreign language instructors believed that a "junior year abroad" experience living with host families from the target culture would help students broaden their cultural horizons and become "fluent" speakers of the target language (L2), with more improved L2 pronunciation, grammar (morphosyntactic) usage, vocabulary knowledge, and discursive abilities than those possessed by learners who acquired the target language in the classroom at home.[1]

These assumptions were substantiated by Carroll's (1967) widely cited study, which looked at the language skills of 2,782 college seniors who went abroad. Carroll found that even a short duration abroad (touring or summer) had a positive effect on foreign language (FL) proficiency. Today, study-abroad experiences are still encouraged in the United States, as evidenced by the fact that 160,920 students went abroad in 2003 (NAFSA 2003). Moreover, in the United Kingdom a study-abroad experience has been obligatory for language majors for the last thirty years.

Recently, assumptions about the benefits of an SA experience have been challenged by Meara (1994) and Coleman (1996), who noted weaknesses in SA research in the 1960s to 1980s. Freed (1995a) also noted methodological shortcomings of empirical studies on study abroad during the same period: small size (N) of informant pool or short duration of treatment period, the lack of a control group, and extensive use of only test scores to measure gains. More controlled empirical studies on the effects of the SA experience on the development of learners' interlanguage systems appeared in earnest in the 1990s. Freed (1995a, 1998) noted that most research carried out on SA data from several languages (French, Spanish, Russian, Japanese) still confirmed old assumptions about the benefit of study-abroad experiences on the SLA process; however, some "surprising results" also came out of this research, especially regarding the lack of gain on measures of grammatical competence in learners who had studied abroad (see Collentine and Freed 2004).

This chapter critically examines the research on the development of interlanguage systems of learners of Spanish as a second language (SSL) in study-abroad and classroom ("at-home," or AH), contexts. Even though, as Freed has noted in various forums (1995a, 1998), it is generally assumed in educational circles that some sort of immersion setting—be it intensive domestic immersion (IDI) or study abroad—offers superior learning conditions over the domestic, at-home learning environment, the research on Spanish SLA to date has shown advantages for SA contexts on some measures (e.g., oral proficiency, fluency, pronunciation, lexical acquisition, narrative and discursive abilities) while finding that learners in AH contexts are either equal or superior to their SA counterparts in other areas (e.g., grammatical and pragmatic abilities).

In order to explore how the results of this research could be applied to the teaching of Spanish as a second/foreign language in SA and AH contexts and to the improvement of various aspects of study-abroad programs, we first review research that has been carried out on the acquisition of Spanish in study-abroad and classroom contexts and then comment on methodological factors that could affect and/or limit the generalizability of the findings of these studies. We conclude with thoughts about possible programmatic and classroom applications of this research and suggestions for future avenues of inquiry on this topic.

1.0 Review of SA Research

The study-abroad literature on the acquisition of Spanish is, in large part, reflective of the general findings on the efficacy of study abroad to date in the SLA literature (see Freed 1995a, 1998; Collentine and Freed 2004).[2] It is also reflective of this literature in terms of its methodological shortcomings. Collentine and Freed (2004), who examine the literature on SLA in study-abroad, intensive-domestic-immersion and at-home settings, surmise that, while the data presented to date are scant in comparison to the corpus available on SLA as a whole, learners studying abroad develop enhanced fluency, lexical abilities, and sociolinguistic awareness, but their grammatical development is slow to develop. Nonetheless, the findings in general show that the aspects of language learning that are traditionally the focus of research (e.g., lexical and grammatical development) are difficult to develop quickly in the study-abroad context (Collentine and Freed 2004).

This is interesting upon examination of the fact that, although the study-abroad data are scant, the "treatment periods" of such studies almost always qualify them as longitudinal studies (most are a semester long). This begs the question of whether study abroad is less beneficial than other learning contexts (in these traditionally studied realms) and/or whether the short-term learning conditions that are the focus of SLA research may not have the long-term effects that their results would suggest (see Norris and Ortega 2001). In other words, is SLA under any conditions a long, protracted process that progresses more in geological-like terms than during the course of a few "semesters"?

1.1 Research on the Effects of Spanish Study Abroad

The results discussed in this paper on empirical Spanish study abroad research were initially reported in sections 4.1–4.6 of Lafford (2006).

1.1.1 Global Oral Proficiency

Improvements in global oral proficiency (as measured by the Oral Proficiency Interview, or OPI) in AH and SA learners were investigated by Segalowitz and Freed (2004).[3] First a Mann-Whitney U test comparing OPI ratings of the two groups revealed no significant difference in the pretest scores (median rating for both groups was Intermediate-Low). However, the SA group showed significant improvement from the pretest to the posttest (n = 22; 12 students improved, 10 did not, $p < .001$), whereas the AH group showed no significant improvement (n = 18; 5 students improved, 13 did not; $p > .2$, *n.s.*). Students who did make gains only increased one level of proficiency (e.g., Intermediate-Low to Intermediate-Mid).

Studies without a control group have also noted global oral profiency gains abroad. For instance, Guntermann's (1992a, 1992b) studies of Peace Corps workers during their initial training and time abroad in Latin America showed that after four months of immersion, these learners had achieved an Intermediate-High ranking (on the American Council on the Teaching of Foreign Languages, or ACTFL, scale) on the OPI. After a year abroad, these workers had attained an Advanced/Advanced High rating.

It is important to note, nevertheless, that similar to Díaz-Campos (2004), Segalowitz and Freed (2004) emphasize that predicting success abroad is complex since not only does oral proficiency interact with development but also with cognitive abilities and with the amount of contact learners have with the target language.

1.1.2 Pronunciation

The development of phonetic and phonological abilities have been studied by Simões (1996), Stevens (2001), Díaz-Campos (2004), and Díaz-Campos (2006). In an acoustic analysis without a classroom control group, Simões (1996) found that learners improved their vowel quality during their five weeks abroad. Both Stevens (2001) and Díaz-Campos, Collentine, and Lazar (2004) report better phonological abilities in SA than in AH learners, yet Díaz-Campos (2004) was not able to completely confirm this finding. These results may be due, in part, to the fact that both Stevens (2001) and Díaz-Campos, Collentine, and Lazar (2004) used conversational data as part of their studies, whereas Díaz-Campos (2004) used only a reading task. However, Stevens (2001) and Díaz-Campos (2004) did find some advantage for the study-abroad group on the loss of aspiration with unvoiced stops.

Interestingly, in the Díaz-Campos, Collentine, and Lazar (2004) study, whether a student was abroad or at home, the number of years one had studied Spanish was the best predictor of phonological gains; this is even more robust of a predictor than the use of Spanish outside of the classroom (at least in the pronunciation of consonants).

1.1.3 Grammatical Abilities

Several studies examined the development of global grammatical abilities by looking at learners' progress via a variety of grammatical data points (SA vs. AH: DeKeyser 1986, 1990, 1991; Collentine 2004; SA alone: Guntermann 1992a, 1992b; Ryan and Lafford 1992; Lafford and Ryan 1995; Schell 2001; Isabelli 2001).

Some of the studies without a control group focused on examining the developmental stages of the acquisition of grammatical and lexical phenomena in learners' interlanguages during their time abroad. For instance, Schell (2001) examines the acquisition of the preterit/imperfect distinction by attempting to determine whether the (inherent) lexical aspect of a predicate affects an SA learner's choice of grammatical aspect (preterite or imperfect forms) (e.g., *romper* is a punctual verb and "tends" to occur in the preterit in the input that learners receive whereas statives such as *necesitar* are imperfective and appear often in the imperfect). Schell found that the lexical aspect hypothesis does not predict patterns of acquisition at the earliest developmental stages.[4]

Using SA data, Ryan and Lafford (1992) replicated VanPatten's (1987) classroom research on the order of acquisition of *ser* and *estar* vis-à-vis various syntactic collocations (e.g., conditional adjectives, present participles) and found basically the same order of acquisition as did VanPatten (1987) for the copulas *ser* and *estar*. However, unlike the classroom learners in VanPatten (1987), the SA learners in Ryan and Lafford's (1992) study experienced an extended period of zero copula and in conditional adjective contexts they tended to use the more unmarked form *ser* (e.g., *Mi hermana *es enferma hoy*).

Studies also investigated grammatical progress in the interlanguage of SA learners during their time abroad. For example, Guntermann (1992a, 1992b) concentrated on the benefits of the Peace Corps experience, showing that these learners improved significantly on their copula (*ser/estar*) and prepositional abilities (i.e., *por/para*). Lafford and Ryan (1995) also found evidence for the improvement of the use of the prepositions *por/para* in various linguistic contexts by learners in an SA context.

In addition, Isabelli (2001) studied the progress of five L2 intermediate learners of Spanish over a twenty-week period in an SA setting. Data on the learners was gathered through the use of OPI and SOPI (Simulated Oral Proficiency Interview) exams administered as pretests and posttests. The results showed improvement in the grammatical abilities of these learners over the five-month period abroad. However, since none of the aforementioned studies of global grammatical studies contained an AH control group, one can draw few generalizations from their findings.

In fact, in studies in which an AH control group was used, the positive effects of an SA context on grammatical development found in the studies without a control group are called into question. For instance, DeKeyser (1986, 1990, 1991) found that residence abroad had little impact on the development of overall grammatical abilities and that SA learners were equal to or inferior to their AH counterparts in their use of grammar. Collentine (2004) gauged study-abroad learners' acquisition of a variety of morphosyntactic features, showing that they do not make as much progress as AH learners on precisely those grammatical aspects that Spanish formal instruction emphasizes, namely, verbs and subordinate conjunctions (which are treated with some degree of detail when attention turns to the subjunctive; cf. Collentine 2003).

Four research studies on Spanish acquired in an SA context have examined the acquisition of syntax and morphosyntax (López-Ortega 2003; Torres 2003; Isabelli 2004; Isabelli and Nishida 2005).

López-Ortega (2003) studied SA learners' acquisition of the Spanish subject pronouns (for instance, null subjects vs. overt pronominal subjects). She found that while intermediate level learners acquire nativelike behaviors in general (e.g., proper use of null subjects), discourse factors such as speaker's identity and topic involvement, semantic features of the referents, interlinguistic narrative structures, type of verb, and conjunctions/adverbials also influence the presence or absence of a null subject.

Isabelli (2004) also studied the acquisition of Spanish null subjects by SA learners by examining the structural effects/ramifications of the null subject parameter. With this in mind she found that learners do exhibit nativelike null-subject behaviors as well as subject-verb inversions in embedded clauses (e.g., *Creen que vienen los muchachos mañana* 'They believe that the boys are coming tomorrow'). Even advanced learners do not, however, evidence more sophisticated behaviors, such as recognizing that "that-trace" effects are treated differently in Spanish (e.g., *¿Quién dice el FBI asesinó al presidente?* 'Who says the FBI assassinated the president?').

Torres (2003) examined the development of clitic accuracy, finding that study abroad does not appear to be more beneficial than classroom learning. In the initial stages, study-abroad learners use much ellipsis and formulaic dative experiencers. Afterward, learners tend to assign the preverbal position only to first person because third-person clitics are multifunctional, that is, the same clitic can refer to several different people in different roles (e.g., *le* can refer to second-person [*Ud.*] or third-person [*él, ella*] indirect or direct [in Spain] objects) and lack the one-to-one correspondence between referent and linguistic sign present in the first-person clitic "me" (only refers to the speaker).

Finally, Isabelli and Nishida (2005) studied the acquisition of the Spanish subjunctive in complement clauses by both study-abroad and classroom advanced learners. In comparing the two groups, they found that the at-home students did not progress noticeably either in their subjunctive abilities or in their abilities to produce complex syntax over the course of nine months, whereas the study-abroad group did.

In sum, these studies indicate that the appreciable development of general grammatical abilities and morphosyntax is not robust, at least within the timeframe of a semester to a year abroad. Indeed, two of these studies (DeKeyser 1986; Collentine 2004) suggest that the at-home experience affords certain advantages as regard overall grammatical development for intermediate learners. The notable exception is Isabelli and Nishida's (2005) study, which revealed a significant advantage for study abroad with respect to subjunctive development. However, the fact that Isabelli and Nishida (2005) used subjunctive data from Advanced learners with more developed syntactic abilities (rather than from Intermediate learners, who may still be at the presyntactic stage; see Collentine 1995) may account in part for these findings.

1.1.4 *Pragmatic and Communicative Abilities*

Four studies concentrated on the development of pragmatic and communicative abilities abroad (DeKeyser 1991; Lafford 1995; Rodríguez 2001; Lafford 2004). The use of communication strategies by learners in both SA and AH contexts was investigated by DeKeyser (1991), who found no statistically significant difference in the number and type of CSs in the two groups for the picture description and interview tasks. DeKeyser admits that the small sample size (SA = 7; AH = 5) could have contributed to these results.

Lafford (1995, 2004) examined the effects of SA contexts on learners' use of communication strategies, or conscious learner strategies that bridge a perceived communication gap from a lack of L2 knowledge, performance problems, or interactional problems. In both studies she presents data indicating that communication strategies may become less important to learners as they gain greater access to opportunities to use the L2 for communicative purposes. Interestingly, her research suggests that the AH experience promotes significantly more extensive use of these strategies due to the fact that pragmatic constraints presented by the SA environment may discourage their use (see Lafford 2004, 2006). In the 1995 study, Lafford found that SA learners possessed a wider range of conversational management strategies than the AH group. Rodríguez (2001) tracked the development of learners' pragmatic abilities to recognize and use request formulas, such as negative interrogatives (e.g., ¿No puedes traerme un vaso de agua? 'Could you bring me a glass of water?'), finding no advantage for the study-abroad group over classroom learners.

1.1.5 Narrative Abilities

What is notable about the study of narrative abilities is that we find evidence that phenomena on which the typical classroom (be it at home or abroad) places little or no organized emphasis (i.e., an ad hoc process at best) do indeed develop nicely abroad. To be sure, Isabelli (2001) (no control group) and Collentine (2004) (SA vs. AH groups) both present evidence that students' narrative abilities develop significantly in an abroad context. Collentine (2004) demonstrated that the narrative abilities of SA learners surpassed those of AH learners. The suggestion here is, as Collentine and Freed (2004) note, that what is important to the typical second language syllabus may not be so important to the learner abroad (or at least in the same proportion). For instance, while vocabulary is an important aspect of any curriculum, there is really no systematic treatment or guidance for teaching it in materials for classroom teachers; the same can be said about the (perhaps) nebulous realms of fluency and sociolinguistics.

1.1.6 Lexical Development

DeKeyser (1986) showed increases in vocabulary development by learners in a study-abroad context. Nevertheless, Collentine (2004) presents scaled data (normed over 1,000 words) that suggests that the SA experience does not promote significantly higher levels of acquisition of semantically dense words (such as nouns and adjectives) than those found in the classroom group. Indeed, the two groups only differed significantly in their use of adjectives (the AH group produced proportionally more unique adjectives than the SA group after the treatment). When he used nonscaled data, Collentine (2004) showed that the SA group generated many more semantical-ly dense utterances. This may be partially due to the fact that the SA students were more fluent (produced more words per syntactic unit at a greater speed with fewer pauses) than the classroom group.

Ife, Vives Boix, and Meara (2000) found that learners who stayed abroad for an entire academic year improved their vocabulary abilities more than those who only stayed for one semester. In addition, this study found that intermediate learners improved their acquisition of discrete vocabulary items while advanced learners enhanced their ability to make meaningful associations among Spanish words.

1.1.7 Fluency

De Keyser (1986), C. L. Isabelli (2001), and Segalowitz and Freed (2004) demonstrate that the most powerful advantage that the study abroad experience provides students is improvement in their L2 fluency (e.g., words per syntactic unit, speed, segments without pauses/hesitations).

1.1.8 Sociolinguistic Variables

What are wholly understudied in SA-versus-AH Spanish contexts are sociolinguistic variables. The only study in this regard is Talburt and Stewart (1999), and their data begs one to wonder whether the observed lack of overall advantage for the study-abroad experience is due to the day-to-day interpersonal experiences that various individual students have. They present a compelling case that affective variables abroad, such as race and gender issues that students may experience, can have deleterious effects on acquisition. As Kramsch (2000) and Collentine and Freed (2004) note, when the context of learning is expanded beyond the typical classroom, there may be unexpected results. Most likely this is due to the fact that immersed settings often show the student that what was on the radar screen of the teacher/student in the typical classroom (e.g., grammatical accuracy) is not the same as what comes on the learner's radar screen when the learner is confronted with the interpersonal dynamics of the target culture (e.g., pragmatic constraints on the use of language) (cf. Lafford 2004, 2006).

1.1.9 Cognitive Abilities

Another area that needs future research attention is the role that working memory plays in the development of interlanguages in SA and AH contexts. According to Harrington and Sawyer (1990), working memory is the space where learners process and store input in real time. As learners advance and automatize some processes, more space is freed up for controlled processing and conversion of new input forms (even redundant grammatical forms with low communicative value) into intake and for storage of these new forms, which are then available for integration into the learner's interlanguage system. One study that has begun to look at this issue in SA contexts is Lord (2006). The results of her research show increased working memory capacity (as measured by their ability to imitate L2 strings) in SA Spanish learners who participated in a summer study-abroad program.

1.2 Methodological and Experimental Design Issues

It may be interesting to note that the majority of the studies reviewed above have been authored quite recently (1999–2004). This is not unusual, since the importance of study abroad only came into its own right upon the publication of Freed's 1995 initial, comprehensive volume on the "state of the art" in this field of research. Most new fields of study emerge from small, loosely controlled, and exploratory studies.

In the following section, we critique the methodologies and the experimental design of the studies reviewed above with the goal of providing future researchers with important "lessons learned" so that the internal and external validity of study-abroad research might improve. All in all, sweeping generalizations stemming from this research must be tempered by the fact that certain design features of these studies could be greatly improved (e.g., experimental controls on the specific types of learning conditions and their contextualization and the ecological validity of the testing instruments).[5]

Future researchers will do well to consider the following factors concerning experimental controls on learning contextualization and conditions: duration and seat hours, type of instruction, living conditions, treatment design, sample (types and size), testing instruments, and preexperimental proficiency levels.

1.2.1 Duration and Seat Hours

More than half of the studies examined study-abroad gains during the course of one semester, approximately sixteen weeks (DeKeyser 1986, 1990, 1991; Rodríguez 2001; Schell 2001; Stevens 2001; Ryan and Lafford 1992; Lafford and Ryan 1995; Torres 2003; López-Ortega 2003; Segalowitz and Freed 2004; Lafford 2004; Díaz-Campos 2004; Díaz-Campos, Collentine, and Lazar 2004; Collentine 2004). All things considered, a semester is a sizable amount of time for a treatment period within the field of SLA. Five studies went beyond the typical semester time period (Guntermann 1995; Ife, Vives Boix, and Meara 2000; Isabelli 2001; Isabelli 2004; Isabelli and Nishida 2005), and four studies (Simões 1996; Talburt and Stewart 1999; Hokanson 2000; Lord 2004) used subjects on short-duration (five- to seven-week) programs.

Ife, Vives Boix, and Meara (2000) on vocabulary acquisition by SA learners was the only study that systematically investigated the effect of more time spent abroad (two vs. one semester).[6] In addition, the only comparative study that showed better grammatical (subjunctive) abilities in SA over AH learners was Isabelli and Nishida (2005), whose advanced subjects stayed in-country for nine months instead of just a semester (the usual treatment period for SA vs. AH grammatical studies). Clearly, more comparative studies of programs of differing lengths are called for in order to understand the effect of the duration of the SA program on SLA development.

The varying length of the SA programs in these studies makes more difficult the comparison and generalizability of their results. Considering the fact that there is a documented trend toward shorter programs abroad, as evidenced in the open doors report from NAFSA (2003), research on what learners can (or cannot) accomplish in short-term programs is valuable to SLA researchers, pedagogues, and program administrators alike.

In general, students in all of the studies are enrolled in university courses, taking a combination of "language" courses and direct enrollment (e.g., business, anthropology, sociology) courses. The seat hours, which are not always reported nor in a consistent format, appear to emulate American university "full loads" (twelve to fifteen contact hours per week).

1.2.2 Type of Instruction

The lack of information on the type of instruction that takes place in the SA contexts constitutes the weakest aspect of the study of study-abroad research. For the most part, researchers have not examined the effects of different types of teaching methodologies on acquisition abroad; this is an area ripe for future research. As Huebner (1998) noted, very little is known about the type of language instruction taking place in SA language and content-based (literature, history, art) classrooms (e.g., course design features such as syllabus and resources, focus on form vs. focus on meaning, type of oral and written feedback provided by instructor, pragmatics, and type of evaluation). Consequently, the effects of different types of instruction on student outcomes and the various types of input and feedback provided to students in both AH and SA contexts need to be investigated.

In addition, Brecht and Robinson (1995) showed that some SA learners try to apply what they learn in class; others do not see a connection between what they are taught in class and the reality of the target culture. This condition makes it difficult to judge the effect that such instruction has on the development of learners' interlanguage systems in SA contexts.

1.2.3 Living Conditions

With the exception of C. L. Isabelli (2001), C. A. Isabelli (2004), and Isabelli and Nishida (2005), study-abroad learners in these studies have lived with host families. Researchers such as Díaz-Campos (2004), Lazar (2004), and Segalowitz and Freed (2004) observe that the actual amount of time that learners spend with their host families varies in quantity and quality, and these interactions have an appreciable effect on acquisition in general.[7]

Lafford (2004) found a significant negative correlation between the amount of time spent talking with host families and the use of communication strategies to bridge communication gaps. Similar to the above observations on type of instruction, the host family as a standard "methodological" modus operandi of the study-abroad condition deserves closer attention in the future.

1.2.4 Treatment Design

Most of the studies employed a pretest-posttest design (DeKeyser 1986, 1990, 1991; Ryan and Lafford 1992; Guntermann 1995; Lafford and Ryan 1995; Simões 1996; Hokanson 2000; Ife, Vives Boix, and Meara 2000; Rodríguez 2001; Isabelli 2001; Stevens 2001; López-Ortega 2003; Torres 2003; Isabelli 2004; Collentine 2004; Díaz-Campos 2004; Lafford 2004; Segalowitz and Freed 2004; Lord 2004). However, no studies were carried out that contained several posttests over the course of several months or years. Freed (1998) contends that future research would need to gather this type of data in order to study the long-term effects of an SA experience.

Only about half of these studies (DeKeyser 1986, 1990, 1991; Lafford 1995; Rodríguez 2001; Stevens 2001; Torres 2003; Díaz-Campos 2004; Díaz-Campos, Collentine, and Lazar 2004; Collentine 2004; Lafford 2004; Segalowitz and Freed 2004; Isabelli and Nishida 2005) contrasted study-abroad findings to a comparable AH group using a quasi-experimental design. Therefore, for those studies lacking an AH control group it is difficult to contribute any observable gains (or lack thereof) to the learning condition(s) of the SA experience itself. At best, the SA investigations lacking an AH group (see table 6.1) comment on the learning that takes place while students "happen to be abroad"; these studies cannot comment on the uniqueness of the SA experience from an experimental design perspective. Indeed, to qualify study abroad as a unique experience implies that it is not the same as (and it is usually assumed to be more beneficial than) the typical classroom experience. Thus studies examining SA's effects in isolation lack an important contextualization for SLA research as a whole.

1.2.5 Sample

All of the Spanish L2 study-abroad and comparative SA-versus-AH studies carried out to date used subjects whose native language was English. It is quite possible that the use of subjects with other L1s (primary languages) would have resulted in different learner outcomes.

Regarding group size, the studies that had no AH group tended to use small samples (fewer than 10 informants) and qualify more as case studies than the quasi-experimental designs typical of many of the SA-versus-AH studies. The notable exceptions here are Hokanson (2000) (N = 27); Ife, Vives Boix, and Meara (2000) (N = 36); Isabelli (2004) (N = 31), Lord (2004) (N = 22) and Ryan and Lafford (1992) (N = 16).[8] Most (eight out of thirteen) of the studies employing both SA and AH groups were rather robust in size as SLA research goes, with 11 to 32 participants in the AH condition and 11 to 29 in the SA group.

A consideration for future researchers is that, as Mellow, Reeder, and Forster (1996) note, SLA research using small samples would achieve much greater validity (and statistical power) with repeated sampling "bootstrapping" techniques, such as time series experimental designs, as opposed to the typical pretest-posttest comparison.[9] This seems an especially critical consideration given that there appear to be a variety of unforeseen factors that influence study-abroad results.

1.2.6 Testing Instruments

For the most part, the testing procedures for about one-third of the studies reflect those employed in SLA research today (DeKeyser 1986, 1990, 1991; Hokanson 2000; Ife, Vives Boix, and Meara 2000; Schell 2001; Stevens 2001; Isabelli 2004; Díaz-Campos 2004; Segalowitz and Freed 2004; Lord 2004; Isabelli and Nishida 2005),

Table 6.1 Spanish study abroad research

SA vs. AH	Number of Subjects	Duration	Instrument	Preexperimental Level	Results
Collentine (2004)	AH = 20; SA = 26	16 weeks	OPI	3rd semester	SA > AH narrative abilities and lexical density; SA = AH or AH > SA in grammar abilities
DeKeyser (1986)	AH = 5; SA = 7	16 weeks	Grammar test; interview; picture description; recall	Intermediate	SA = AH in grammar and CS; SA > AH in fluency
DeKeyser (1990)	AH = 5; SA = 7	16 weeks	Grammar test; interview; picture description; recall	Intermediate	SA = AH monitoring grammar
DeKeyser (1991)	AH = 5; SA = 7	16 weeks	Grammar test; interview; picture description; recall	Intermediate	SA = AH in grammar and CS
Díaz-Campos (2004)	AH = 20; SA = 26	16 weeks	OPI	3rd. semester	SA = AH in pronunciation (reading task)
Díaz-Campos (2006)	AH = 20; SA = 26	16 weeks	OPI	3rd semester	SA > AH in pronunciation (conversational task)
Isabelli and Nishida (2005)	AH = 32; SA = 29	9 months	SOPI; questions involving hypothesizing, beliefs, etc.	3rd year	SA > AH in grammar (subjunctive)
Lafford (1995)	AH = 13; SA = 28	N/A	OPI (at end of 4th semester)	N/A	SA > AH in repertoire of CS and conversational management strategies
Lafford (2004, 2006)	AH = 20; SA = 26	16 weeks	OPI	3rd semester	SA < AH in frequency of CS use
Rodríguez (2001)	AH = 11; SA = 11	16 weeks	Judgment task; recall	1st or 2nd year	SA = AH in pragmatics (perception of requests); both groups improved over time
Segalowitz and and Freed (2004)	AH = 18; SA = 22	16 weeks	OPI; various cognitive	3rd semester	SA > AH in fluency and proficiency level
Stevens (2001)	AH = 13; SA = 9	16 weeks, 7 weeks	Reading task and storytelling task	1st or 2nd year	SA > AH in pronunciation
Torres (2003)	AH = 5; SA = 10	16 weeks	OPI	Intermediate	SA = AH in use of clitics
SA (no control group)					
Isabelli (2004)	SA = 31	1 year	GJ & oral interview	Intermediate	Learners improved null-subject behaviors and subject-verb inversions in embedded clauses
Isabelli (2001)	SA = 5	20 weeks	OPI; SOPI	Intermediate	Learners improved in fluency and ingrammatical abilities
Guntermann (1992a, 1992b)	SA = 9	1 year, 12 weeks	OPI	Novice	Learners improved in overall proficiency and in use of copulas and *por/para*
Ife, Vives Boix, and Meara (2000)	SA = 36	1 and 2 semesters	Vocabulary and translation tests	Intermediate = 21 Advanced = 15	Learners with more time abroad improved more in vocabulary abilities; both groups improved = Intermediate: discrete items; Advanced: vocabulary associations
Lafford and Ryan (1995)	SA = 9	16 weeks	OPI	Novice	Examined stages of *por/para*

(continued on next page)

Table 6.1 *(continued)*

	Number of Subjects	Duration	Instrument	Preexperimental Level	Results
López Ortega (2003)	SA = 4	16 weeks	OPI	4th semester	Learners acquire proper use of null subjects; discourse factors at play
Lord (2006)	SA = 22	7 weeks	Mimicry test	3rd year	Learners improved ability to imitate longer strings of L2
Ryan and Lafford (1992)	SA = 16	16 weeks	OPI	Novice	Examined stages of *ser/estar*
Schell (2001)	SA = 5	16 weeks	Cloze-like tests (with infinitive prompts)	2nd year at university and 3rd year at university	Found evidence against lexical aspect hypothesis in early developmental stages
Simões (1996)	SA = 5	5 weeks	OPI	Intermediate Low to Advanced	Learners improved pronunciation abroad
Talburt and Stewart (1999)	SA = 6	5 weeks	Ethnographic interviews	4th semester	Affective variables (race and gender issues) that students experience can have deleterious effects on acquisition

entailing grammaticality judgments, translations, cloze tests, picture description, recall tasks, reading tasks, storytelling, vocabulary tests, domain specific production/ recognition tests (e.g., mimicry tasks [for working memory], a read-aloud task), tests of various cognitive measures, measures of cognitive syle preferences; standardized tests of listening and reading (American Association of Teachers of Spanish and Portuguese National Exam–Level II), discrete point grammar exams, short essays, ethnographic interviews, and observations of students' oral performance and behavior. The great variety of instruments used by various investigators in this body of research makes it difficult to compare results across studies.

Half of the research to date has depended on the OPI interview as either a database for a corpus study of sorts or a measure of proficiency level (to gauge improvement). Most of the OPI studies were corpus-based to one extent or another, in which the researchers used the transcribed interview data as a source for linguistic analysis of more specific phenomena (e.g., grammar, fluency). Thus even though a large number of these studies depend on the OPI interview as their most important data-collection instrument, the OPI scale (Novice to Advanced) is a measure of global proficiency and is not fine-grained enough to measure progress on specific items within a semester's time or to measure gains by advanced learners In addition, the OPI interview format does not allow for natural interaction between interlocutors (e.g., the interviewer is not permitted to provide direct help to learner), so that generalizations about learner interactions and linguistic behavior must be restricted to interview settings.

In order to understand factors that affect the dynamics of interlanguage production, there need to be more studies that utilize qualitative methods of data analysis, such as ethnographic interviews and recall protocols; examples of studies that have implemented these assessment measures include DeKeyser (1986, 1990, 1991), Talburt and Stewart (1999), and Rodríguez (2001).

1.2.7 Preexperimental Proficiency Levels

The results of various Spanish SA studies are hard to compare since preexperimental proficiency levels vary among studies (Novice to Advanced on the ACTFL scale). All in all, subjects range from first year to fourth before their sojourn abroad; yet when there was a comparable AH treatment group, the experiments tended to examine learners at the Novice or Intermediate level in their first or second year of university study of Spanish (DeKeyser 1986, 1990, 1991; Lafford 1995; Rodríguez 2001; Stevens 2001; Torres 2003; Díaz-Campos 2004; Díaz-Campos, Collentine, and Lazar 2004; Collentine 2004; Lafford 2004; Segalowitz and Freed 2004). This fact limits the generalizability of the results of these comparative SA–AH studies and does not permit scholars to extend these conclusions to studies of advanced learners.

Ife, Vives Boix, and Meara (2000) found that preexperimental proficiency levels may affect vocabulary acquisition. The authors show that both intermediate and advanced groups improve equally in SA contexts; however, more gains are made in associative vocabulary knowledge by advanced learners and more gains in discrete items are seen in intermediate learners. Lantolf (1999) suggests that L2 conceptual restructuring toward native speaker (NS) norms only takes place after extended periods abroad.

The research of Isabelli and Nishida (2005) also suggests that preexperimental proficiency levels may affect grammatical acquisition. These authors showed that Advanced learners who studied abroad possessed better grammatical (subjunctive) abilities than AH learners at the same level. This contradicts all other SA-versus-AH grammatical studies using Novice-Intermediate subjects, which found classroom learners to be equal or superior to SA learners in grammatical abilities.

2.0 Discussion

The preceding critical analysis of the research done to date on the acquisition of Spanish in SA and AH environments opens several avenues of fruitful discussion and thoughts about the need for future research in certain areas. Factors that seem to have significant effects on the development of learners' interlanguage in SA contexts include the length of the SA program, the living conditions abroad, and the preproficiency level of the students. The only study discussed above that compared student outcomes from programs of different lengths (Ife, Vives Boix, and Meara 2000) found that both Intermediate and Advanced learners who spent two semesters abroad improved in vocabulary abilities more than those that only stayed for one semester. What is needed is more research on progress in several areas (pronunciation, morphosyntax, lexical development, and pragmatics, for instance) among similar groups of students who go abroad to the same destination under the same living conditions, but for various lengths of time.

It is important to note that the average time spent on study-abroad programs has been steadily reduced during the last century; what was the original "junior year abroad" is now normally the "semester abroad," with summer programs gaining in popularity. This trend toward shorter SA programs, especially in the last two decades, may be due to several factors: learners' financial considerations, increasing general studies requirements, the rise in popularity of professional programs that do not encourage study abroad, equivalencies issues, and the financial benefit of short-term programs.

Despite the surface attractiveness of shorter programs abroad for students and their educational institutions, Lantolf (1999) has suggested that in order for foreign/second language students to structure their L2 interlanguage system along NS lines (see Furstenberg et al. 2001), they need to spend extended periods abroad in the target culture. As mentioned earlier, Ife, Vives Boix, and Meara (2001) found more examples of nativelike lexical restructuring by advanced students abroad than by their intermediate SA counterparts, suggesting that daily exposure to the perspectives, practices, and products of the target culture allow more advanced students to restructure their cognitive associations (lexical schemata) as native speakers do; consequently, these students begin to "think like a native" and even dream in the target language, especially after spending at least a semester or year abroad.

Since most of the SA studies reviewed above used data collected from semester-long programs, little is known about the developmental effects of year-long or short-term SA programs. Until data are gathered from learners from SA programs of differing lengths, the effects of various types of SA experiences on Spanish L2 learners cannot truly be understood or appreciated.

Learners' living conditions abroad may also prove to be a crucial factor in the development of their interlanguage systems. Most of the students in the aforementioned studies lived with host families during their time abroad. Díaz-Campos (2004), Lazar (2004), and Segalowitz and Freed (2004) found that although the actual amount of time learners spend in conversation with their host families varies in quantity and quality, these interactions were found to have a positive effect on acquisition in general. Lafford (2004) also found a significant negative correlation between the amount of time spent talking with host families and the use of communication strategies to bridge communication gaps.

In light of the Wilkinson (2002) study of SA learners of French, in which she notes a great deal of variation in the qualitative interaction taking place among learners and their host families, similar research needs to be carried out on learners of Spanish in SA contexts in order to understand the dynamics behind this factor on interlanguage development. Research such as that carried out by Brecht, Davidson, and Ginsberg (1995) on the effects of homestays versus other environments in Russia should be undertaken on Spanish SA learners. These findings would provide more insight into the types of interactions that promote the attainment of a higher level of target-language proficiency abroad.

Another important factor affecting student outcomes on Spanish SA programs is the predeparture proficiency level of the subjects. As mentioned earlier, although proficiency levels in Spanish SA studies varied widely (from Novice to Advanced) over the entire array of investigations (table 6.1), most of the comparative SA–AH Spanish studies used data from intermediate learners. These studies showed that Intermediate classroom (AH) learners evidence grammatical abilities equal to or superior to their SA counterparts. Although grammatical L2 data from Advanced Spanish SA and AH learners was not extensively gathered or studied, the one study that did find a grammatical advantage for SA learners (Isabelli and Nashida 2005) was based on data from Advanced speakers. The question then arises: Is there a threshold level of grammatical or cognitive abilities that facilitates second language acquisition in a study-abroad context?

The need of a threshold level of grammatical competence before going abroad was first addressed by the pioneering work of Brecht, Davidson, and Ginsberg (1995), who studied the effects of SA contexts on the acquisition of Russian and found that grammatical and reading scores were the best predictors of proficiency gains in the SA context. In addition, the idea of a cognitive threshold for effective SLA was proposed by Segalowitz and Freed (2004) and Segalowitz et al. (2004). These studies of Spanish L2 learners found that an initial threshold level of basic word recognition and lexical access processing abilities may be necessary for oral proficiency and fluency to develop. Moreover, Hulstijn and Bossers (1992) found that more advanced learners have developed a larger working memory capacity, due in part to their having automatized a great deal of lexical retrieval. This capacity to retain material can prove to be a valuable resource in the acquisition process that allows learners to process longer segments of input and hold longer strings in their heads for incipient output (Payne and Whitney 2002).

Thus, intermediate learners who lack a well-developed lexical and grammatical base may also have less working memory capacity with which to process both content and grammatical form. These learners, having more of a burden placed on their phonological loop (Levelt 1989), are unable to hold long strings of new input or output in working memory, and so less information (input) can be converted to intake. Out of frustration caused by their limited working memory capacity, and perhaps other pragmatic factors (see Lafford 2004, 2006), these intermediate learners in an SA environment may choose to focus on meaning over form and, therefore, may neglect to work on acquiring redundant target language grammatical markers (which do not contain as much communicative value in the input). According to VanPatten's (1996) principles for input processing, learners process input for meaning before form and forms with low communicative value are processed only after the learner's processing of the input for comprehension has been automatized and has left space in working memory to process redundant grammatical markers. Therefore, more advanced SA learners, who possess a better cognitive, lexical, and grammatical base (threshold), may not experience this type of frustration when having to attend to new forms and meanings at the same time, since they have more cognitive resources to focus on and acquire redundant grammatical markers.

Thus we could tentatively propose a kind of "threshold hypothesis" for students studying abroad: those students with a well-developed cognitive, lexical, and grammatical base will be more able to process and produce grammatical forms more accurately after their experience in an SA context.[10] This hypothesis would help explain why Isabelli and Nishida's (2005) study found positive results for grammatical (subjunctive) improvement among Advanced learners while SA–AH studies using data from Intermediate learners did not find such an advantage for the SA group.

As a result of the relative lack of data on more advanced learners and comparative intermediate-advanced level studies, the results of the SA–AH Spanish studies cannot be generalized to all learners in these two contexts. Thus, Freed's (1995a) questions regarding the efficacy of study abroad experiences for beginning and intermediate (not advanced) learners cannot be answered without testing the "threshold hypothesis" test with further comparative SA–AH studies on learners at different pre-experimental levels of proficiency.

In addition to the aforementioned suggestions for directions for future research, scholars should also investigate the potential effects of other factors on student outcomes abroad: learners' type of home institution (large public vs. small private school), demographic profile, native language, prior experience abroad, individual factors (e.g., personality, learning styles), field of study, and the type of instruction s/he received in the SA setting.

Furthermore, despite the attention given to case studies of individual differences in SA studies involving learners of other languages (e.g., Russian [Brecht and Robinson 1995; Pellegrino 1997), Japanese [Siegal 1995; Marriot 1995; Dewey 2002], and French [Regan 1995; Freed 1995b; Wilkinson 1998, 2002]), only DeKeyser (1986, 1990, 1991) investigated the contribution of those differences to Spanish L2 learner outcomes in SA or SA versus AH environments. In addition, Hokanson (2000) showed that learners gravitated toward activities associated with their cognitive style (extroverts, for example, sought out communicative interaction with NSs). Interestingly, similar oral and written gains were found among students with different cognitive styles (extroverts vs. introverts, intuitives, and sensers). Hokanson proposes that the flexibility of the study abroad program that encouraged students to participate in activities of their own choice outside the SA classroom may explain the lack of difference in gains by students with different cognitive styles.

Thus, in order to investigate the effects of a SA or AH context on different types of Spanish learners, future qualitative and quantitative research should take individual factors (e.g., personality, cognitive styles, learning styles) and differences among learners into account. In addition to standardized tests to evaluate personality, learning styles, language learning strategies, and motivation, the use of attitude and demographic questionnaires, retrospective protocols, and participant observation notes would prove to be valuable instruments for gathering data on individual differences among learners.[11]

Finally, in order to get an in-depth understanding of the linguistic progress learners make in SA and AH environments, the types of instruments used to gauge linguistic abilities in SA and AH contexts also need to be reassessed. The reevaluation of the instruments used in Spanish SA–AH studies also needs to take into account what constitutes communicative "success" in classroom and study-abroad contexts. In other words, should we be measuring the same type of linguistic development in both contexts, or should we recognize that the types of improvement that SA learners make at different levels of proficiency abroad may differ from the types of gains normally seen in classroom contexts during the same period of time? As Collentine and Freed (2004) point out, what is on the "radar screen" of most classroom students and instructors (e.g., focus on grammatical forms) is often not given as much importance by learners in their daily communication in SA contexts.

In fact, the abilities that constitute true "communicative competence" abroad (understanding of the appropriate pragmatic uses of language, routine formulas, courteous ways of performing everyday linguistic functions with different interlocutors, fluency, vocabulary, etc.) have often not been the type of data (e.g., mophosyntactic and grammatical abilities, pronunciation) measured by the instruments used to date in SA–AH studies. Future research should include studies that gather both oral and written data to measure pragmatic abilities, use both multiple tasks and fine-grained assessment measures, use videotaped sessions of learners interacting with nonnative speaker (NNS) and NS interlocutors in various contexts, and multiple posttests to measure long-term effects of SA and AH environments on interlanguage development. Finally, qualitative analyses (e.g., introspective diary studies, interviews, retrospective protocols) should be used to complement quantitative studies on the effect of context on Spanish SLA.

3.0 Conclusion

We hope that the preceding critical review of research on the acquisition of Spanish in study-abroad and classroom contexts has served to raise awareness of the need to carry out more empirical studies on this topic in order to more fully inform administrative decision makers and instructors who wish to understand the programmatic and pedagogical implications of this research. In this final section, we propose some tentative suggestions for programmatic and pedagogical reform in these two environments based on the research reviewed above.

A simplistic reading of much of the aforementioned research might lead instructors to suggest the following to prospective study-abroad students: Go later! Stay longer! Live with a family! However, without also asking a student about his or her goals for the study-abroad experience (e.g., really improving grammar, vocabulary, and fluency in the target language and acquiring a deep understanding of the target culture or just absorbing some cultural knowledge and picking up a few phrases for communicative purposes) and for what purpose he or she intends (or not) to use the target language or knowledge of the target culture in the future, one cannot truly provide useful advice to students at different levels of proficiency about the length and type of SA program best suited to their needs and what linguistic outcomes he or she might expect from participating in SA programs of varying duration and living conditions. Nevertheless, we can use the results of some of the general study-abroad research already carried out to more intelligently inform prospective SA students about the best way to make the most of their experience in the target culture.

A new volume by Paige et al. (2003), *Maximizing Study Abroad*, bases its information and suggestions on research in the field of SLA and cultural studies. This book contains predeparture, in-country, and post-SA units on culture- and language-learning strategies. This volume could be used by the student in predeparture orientation sessions, in-country awareness meetings held by the resident director abroad, and post-SA reflective sessions. This book could also be supplemented by country- or region-specific units on appropriate pragmatic courtesy formulas to be used with various types of people in the target culture (e.g., host families, friends, instructors, strangers) and information regarding what kind of linguistic assistance they should or should not expect from their instructors in language and content courses abroad and from their host families.

In addition to providing predeparture orientations for students, prospective resident directors (or NS on-site instructors), who are often not SLA researchers, could be trained to give good target language feedback to the SA students in conversations or tutoring sessions in which they require students to negotiate meaning, rather than just providing them with target language forms. It might also be possible to have a short training session for host families to heighten their awareness of the need to focus on form as well as content when giving feedback to the students living with them. The families could also be made aware of communication strategies they can use with the SA students to help them develop their language skills (e.g., circumlocution, clarification requests, comprehension checks).

Another issue in need of mention is the possible pedagogical application of some of the insights gained from the Spanish SA and SA–AH research reviewed above to the assessment of linguistic progress in the two environments. For years we have been assessing SA students using instruments that measure what is important in an AH context (e.g., grammar and pronunciation). It is time to use more assessment instruments that measure the kinds of gains made by learners in an SA context (e.g., pragmatic ability, vocabulary associations, fluency). However, until more is known about the nature of the SA classroom—type of interaction, focus on form(s), and so on— no suggestions for pedagogical reform in the SA context would be appropriate.

After reviewing the aforementioned research, one might also ask, What insights from the Spanish SA and SA–AH research could also be applied to the classroom context? One of the distinguishing positive features of the SA context is the copious amount of target language input and the opportunities for interaction with L2 native speakers of various ages, socioeconomic conditions, professions, and so on. It is through these interactions that SA learners become aware of appropriate ways to communicate with various members of the target culture.

In order to provide more of these types of communicative opportunities for classroom learners, instructors could make efforts to find ways to bring students into contact with various L2 native speakers. For instance, language houses, language clubs, and honorary societies (such as Sigma Delta Pi) can provide other venues for authentic language practice. Frequently inviting native speakers to the classroom to interact with students and helping to set up conversation partners between Spanish and English L2 students on campus provide additional opportunities for interaction. Internships and service-learning opportunities in the community at large, in which students need to interact with monolingual Spanish speakers, can also be advantageous. Establishing controlled chatrooms in which English-speaking Spanish L2 speakers communicate with Spanish-speaking English L2 speakers living in target culture settings (Spain and Latin America) may also help to improve students' oral ability and cultural awareness.

The more AH students interact with native speakers of the target language, the more they become sensitive to pragmatic exigencies of the context that discourage learners from imposing on their interlocutor for corrective feedback or from stopping the flow of conversation to self-correct (see Lafford 2004, 2006); these pragmatic pressures (based on Grice's [1975] cooperative principle and maxim of manner and Brown and Levinson's [1987] concept of negative "face") to focus on meaning over form, that is, to "keep the conversation going" at the expense of grammatical accuracy, is something that SA learners frequently experience. However, both SA and AH learners should be made aware of the need to overcome these pragmatic pressures and notice the errors in their output, use communication strategies to negotiate meaning and to focus on form in order to polish their grammatical abilities and restructure their interlanguage system along NS lines.

More interaction with different types of native speakers of Spanish would also allow classroom learners the chance to acquire pragmatic awareness and become more proficient at using language appropriately in different communicative contexts. The use of target language authentic video materials, films or television, or live or taped role plays between native speakers of the target language in the classroom can serve to illustrate how natives use pragmalinguistic elements to perform various linguistic functions (e.g., inviting and apologizing).[12] While SA learners are exposed to this type of interaction on a daily basis, classroom instructors need to deliberately provide NS models of this kind of NS-NS interaction for AH learners in order for them to acquire these abilities. Production activities that follow these NS models of interaction should be task-based, in that they should mirror real-world activities in which NSs are often engaged (Doughty and Long 2003). In this way, learners engage in situated cognition (Brown, Collins, and Duguid 1989) and acquire certain linguistic forms in situations that simulate the social contexts in which those forms are normally utilized in the target culture. This type of task-based classroom activity will better prepare AH learners to converse with NSs at home or, if they have the chance to go abroad, at a later time.

One last pedagogical application of the SA research to be discussed is the need for AH learners to engage in activities that will help them restructure their interlanguage L2 word associations to more closely resemble the target language system. Ife, Vives Boix, and Meara (2000) found that advanced SA learners were able to readjust their schemata to conform to NS lexical association patterns after a semester or year abroad. This type of attention to L2 word associations rarely forms a part of foreign language classroom instruction, and yet it is precisely the development of these L2 associations and pragmatic abilities that allows L2 learners to attain advanced levels of proficiency and to begin to think like native speakers of the target language (Lantolf 1999). Authentic oral and written materials can be used in AH contexts to make learners aware of L2 word associations within semantic fields and of target language collocations (words that "go together," e.g., *carne y hueso*).[13]

In conclusion, after critically reviewing the extant research on Spanish SLA in study-abroad and classroom contexts, we propose that the research on the acquisition of Spanish in study-abroad and classroom contexts needs to be expanded along the lines suggested above in order for scholars to understand more fully the interaction of contextual and cognitive factors in the process of acquiring the target language and how those insights can be applied to improve study-abroad programs and pedagogical practices in the foreign language classroom.

Notes

1. This assertion is based on the reports on study-abroad programs from the 1920s to the 1970s by Hullihen (1928), Smith (1930), Diez (1946), Dougherty (1950), Graham (1962), and Berg, Cholakian, and Conroy (1975). These traditional views of the purpose and expectations of study-abroad programs were corroborated by Prof. William Davey, director of the Office of International Programs at Arizona State University.
2. All known Spanish SA or SA-versus-AH studies have been included in this reveiw.
3. See Lafford (2006) for an exploration of the social and cognitive factors that may account for the results of the studies on the effects of SA and AH contexts on student outcomes.
4. Andersen's (1986, 1991) lexical aspect hypothesis states that there is a relationship between the grammatical aspectual category (preterite/imperfect) of a verb chosen by the L2 speaker and the lexical aspect (e.g., states, activities, accomplishments, achievements) of the verb itself. In Andersen's (1986, 1991) data, the imperfect appears first in states, then in activities, accomplishments, and achievements, whereas the preterite is first acquired in achievements, then accomplishments and activities, and lastly in states.
5. See Lazar (2004) for an expanded discussion on this topic with respect to monitoring learning in different contexts of learning.
6. The positive effects of length of stay on linguistic gains have recently been attested by Davidson (2005).
7. Wilkinson (2002) found that although French SA learners have more exposure to the target language, host families vary in type of feedback given to learners.
8. Isabelli (2004) also made use of a sizable NS baseline group for the grammaticality judgment tasks she employed.
9. See Lazar (2004) for an extensive discussion of this bootstrapping in the study-abroad context.
10. This threshold hypothesis corresponds to what has been found for AH postsecondary immersion (Klee and Tedick 1997; Lynch, Klee, and Tedick 2001).
11. See Lafford (2006) for a more in-depth discussion of the importance of studying individual differences in SA and AH contexts.
12. See Olshtain and Cohen (1991) for ideas on how to teach pragmatic competence to L2 learners. See also the website "Dancing with Words: Strategies for Learning Pragmatics in Spanish" created by Julie Sykes and Andrew Cohen at the University of Minnesota. http://www.carla.umn.edu/speechacts/sp_pragmatics/home.html
13. See Batstone (2002) for ideas on how to incorporate more communicative activities into classroom (learning) environments.

References

Andersen, R. 1986. El desarrollo de la morfología verbal en el español como segundo idioma. In *Adquisición del lenguaje—Aquisição da linguagem,* ed. J. Meisel, 115–38. Frankfurt: Klaus-Dieter Vervuert Verlag.

———. 1991. Developmental sequences: The emergence of aspect marking in second language acquisition. In *Crosscurrents in second language acquisition and linguistic theories,* ed. T. Huebner and C. A. Ferguson, 305–24. Amsterdam: John Benjamins.

Batstone, R. 2002. Contexts of engagement: A discourse perspective on "intake" and "pushed output." *System* 30:1–14.

Berg, W. J., R. Cholakian, and P. V. Conroy. 1975. The year abroad in France: An inside look. *French Review* 48 (5): 819–35.

Brecht, R. D., D. E. Davidson, and R. B. Ginsberg. 1995. Predictors of foreign language gain during study abroad. In *Second language acquisition in a study abroad context,* ed. B. Freed, 37–66. Philadelphia: John Benjamins.

Brecht, R. D., and J. L. Robinson. 1995. On the value of formal instruction in study abroad: Student reactions in context. In *Second language acquisition in a study abroad context,* ed. B. Freed, 317–34. Philadelphia: John Benjamins.

Brown, J. S., A. Collins, and P. Duguid. 1989. Situated cognition and the culture of learning. *Educational Researcher* 18 (1): 32–42.

Brown, P., and S. C. Levinson. 1987. *Politeness: Some universals in language usage.* Cambridge: Cambridge University Press.

Carroll, J. B. 1967. Foreign language proficiency levels attained by language majors near graduation from college. *Foreign Language Annals* 1:131–51.

Coleman, J. 1996. *Studying languages: A survey of British and European students.* London: CILT.

Collentine, J. 1995. The development of complex syntax and mood-selection abilities by intermediate-level learners of Spanish. *Hispania* 78:122–35.

———. 2003. The development of subjunctive and complex-syntactic abilities among FL Spanish learners. In *Studies in Spanish second language acquisition: The state of the science,* ed. B. Lafford and R. Salaberry, 74–97. Washington, DC: Georgetown University Press.

———. 2004. The effects of learning contexts on morphosyntactic and lexical development. *Studies in Second Language Acquisition* 26 (2): 227–48.

Collentine, J., and B. Freed. 2004. Learning context and its effects on second language acquisition: Introduction. *Studies in Second Language Acquisition* 26 (2): 153–72.

Davidson, D. 2005. L-2 gain in the study abroad context: Examining the roles of pre-program proficiency, duration of immersion, and individual learner differences. Paper presented at the Georgetown University Roundtable on Languages and Linguistics. March.

DeKeyser, R. 1986. From learning to acquisition? Foreign language development in a U.S. classroom and during a semester abroad. Ph.D. diss., Stanford University.

———. 1990. From learning to acquisition? Monitoring in the classroom and abroad. *Hispania* 73:238–47.

———. 1991. Foreign language development during a semester abroad. In *Foreign language acquisition research and the classroom,* ed. B. Freed, 104–19. Lexington, MA: D. C. Heath.

Dewey, D. 2002. The effects of study context and environment on the acquisition of reading by students of Japanese as a second language during study-abroad and intensive domestic immersion. Ph.D. diss., Carnegie Mellon University.

Díaz-Campos, M. 2004. Context of learning in the acquisition of Spanish second language phonology. *Studies in Second Language Acquisition* 26 (2): 249–73.

———. 2006. The effect of style in second language phonology: An analysis of segmental acquisition in study abroad and regular-classroom students. *In Selected proceedings of the 7th conference on the acquisition of Spanish and Portuguese as first and second languages,* eds. C. A. Klee and T. L. Face, 26–39. Somerville, MA: Cascadilla Proceedings Project.

Diez, M. 1946. A junior year in Zurich for 1946–47. *German Quarterly* 19 (2): 152–56.

Dougherty, D. M. 1950. The value of a year of study in France for undergraduates. *French Review* 23 (4): 304–7.

Doughty, C., and M. Long. 2003. Optimal psycholinguistic environments for distance foreign language learning. *Language Learning and Technology* 7 (3): 50–80.

Freed, B. 1995a. Introduction. In *Second language acquisition in a study abroad context,* ed. B. Freed, 3–34. Philadelphia: John Benjamins.

———. 1995b. What makes us think that students who study abroad become fluent? In *Second language acquisition in a study abroad context,* ed. B. Freed, 123–48. Philadelphia: John Benjamins.

———. 1998. An overview of issues and research in language learning in a study abroad setting. *Frontiers. Special Issue: Language Learning in a Study Abroad Context* 4:31–60.

Furstenberg, G., S. Levet, K. English, and K. Maillet. 2001. Giving a virtual voice to the silent language of culture. *Language Learning and Technology* 5 (1): 55–102.

Graham, P. G. 1962. Why an undergraduate year abroad is so worthwhile—a reply. *German Quarterly* 35 (1): 1–4.

Grice, H. P. 1975. Logic and communication. In *Syntax and semantics.* Vol. 3, *Speech acts,* ed. P. Cole and J. L. Morgan, 41–58. New York: Academic Press.

Guntermann, G. 1992a. An analysis of interlanguage development over time: Part I, *por* and *para. Hispania* 75:177–87.

———. 1992b. An analysis of interlanguage development over time: Part II, *ser and estar. Hispania* 75:1294–1303.

Guntermann, Gail. 1995. The Peace Corps experience: Second language acquisition in a study-abroad context. In *Second Language Acquisition in a Study Abroad Context,* ed. B. Freed, 149–69. Amsterdam: John Benjamins.

Harrington, M., and M. Sawyer. 1990. Working memory in L2 reading: Does capacity predict performance? In *Variability in second language acquisition: Proceedings of the tenth meeting of the second language research forum,* ed. H. Burmeister and P. L. Rounds, 365–79. Eugene: University of Oregon.

Hokanson, Sonja. 2000. Foreign language immersion homestays: Maximizing the accommodation of cognitive styles. *Applied Language Learning* 11:239–64.

Huebner, T. 1998. Methodological considerations in data collection for language learning in a study abroad context. *Frontiers. Special Issue: Language Learning in a Study Abroad Context* 4:1–30.

Hullihen, W. 1928. Present status of the "junior year" abroad. *French Review* 1 (2): 25–37.

Hulstijn, J. H., and B. Bossers. 1992. Individual differences in L2 proficiency as a function of L1 proficiency. *European Journal of Cognitive Psychology* 4 (4): 341–53.

Ife, A., G. Vives Boix, and P. Meara. 2000. The impact of study abroad on the vocabulary development of different proficiency groups. *Spanish Applied Linguistics* 4 (1): 55–84.

Isabelli, C. A. 2004. The acquisition of null subject parameter properties in SLA: Some effects of positive evidence in a natural learning context. *Hispania* 87 (1): 150–62.

Isabelli, C. A., and C. Nishida. 2005. Development of Spanish subjunctive in a nine-month study-abroad setting. In *Selected proceedings of the 6th conference on the acquisition of Spanish and Portuguese as first and second languages,* ed. D. Eddington, 78–91. Sommerville, MA: Cascadilla.

Isabelli, C. L. 2001. Motivation and extended interaction in the study abroad context: Factors in the development of Spanish language accuracy and communication skills. Ph.D. diss., University of Texas at Austin.

Klee, C. A., and D. J. Tedick. 1997. The undergraduate foreign language immersion program in Spanish at the University of Minnesota. In *Content-based instruction in the foreign language classroom,* ed. S. Stryker and B. L Leaver, 140–73. Washington, D.C.: Georgetown University Press.

Kramsch, C. 2000. Social discursive constructions of self in L2 learning. In *Sociocultural theory and second language learning,* ed. J. Lantolf, 133–53. New York: Oxford University Press.

Lafford, B. A. 1995. Getting into, through and out of a survival situation: A comparison of communicative strategies used by students studying Spanish abroad and "at home." In *Second language acquisition in a study abroad context,* ed. B. Freed, 97–121. Philadelphia: John Benjamins.

———. 2004. The effect of context of learning on the use of communication strategies by learners of Spanish as a second language. *Studies in Second Language Acquisition* 26 (2): 201–26.

———. 2006. The effects of study abroad vs. classroom contexts on Spanish SLA: Old assumptions, new insights and future research directions. In *Selected proceedings of the 7th conference on the acquisition of Spanish and Portuguese as first and second languages,* ed. C. A. Klee and T. L. Face, 1–25. Somerville, MA: Cascadilla Proceedings Project.

Lafford, B., and J. Ryan. 1995. The acquisition of lexical meaning in a study abroad context: The Spanish prepositions POR and PARA. *Hispania* 75 (3): 528–47.

Lantolf, J. P. 1999. Second culture acquisition: Cognitive considerations. In *Culture in second language teaching and learning,* ed. E. Hinkel, 28–46. Cambridge: Cambridge University Press.

Lazar, N. 2004. A short survey on causal inference, with implications for context of learning studies of second language acquisition. *Studies in Second Language Acquisition* 26 (2): 329–48.

Levelt, W. J. M. 1989. *Speaking: From intention to articulation.* Cambridge, MA: MIT Press.

López-Ortega, N. 2003. The development of discourse competence in study abroad learners: A study of subject expression in Spanish as a second language. Ph.D. diss., Cornell University.

Lord, G. 2006. Defining the Indefinable: Study Abroad and Phonological Memory Abilities. In *Selected proceedings of the 7th conference on the acquisition of Spanish and Portuguese as first and second languages,* eds. C. A. Klee and T. L. Face, 40–46. Somerville, MA: Cascadilla Proceedings Project.

Lynch, A., C. A. Klee, and D. Tedick. 2001. Social factors and language proficiency in postsecondary Spanish immersion: Issues and implications. *Hispania* 84:510–25.

Marriot, H. 1995. The acquisition of politeness patterns by exchange students in Japan. In *Second language acquisition in a study abroad context,* ed. B. Freed, 197–224. Philadelphia: John Benjamins.

Meara, P. 1994. The year abroad and its effects. *Language Learning Journal* 10:32–38.

Mellow, J. D., K. Reeder, and E. Forster. 1996. Using the time-series design to investigate the effects of pedagogic intervention on SLA. *Studies in Second Language Acquisition* 18 (3): 325–50.

National Association of Foreign Student Advisors (NAFSA). 2003. Open doors online: Report on international educational exchange. http://opendoors.iienetwork.org (May 15, 2006).

Norris, J. M., and L. Ortega. 2001. Does type of instruction make a difference? Substantive findings from a meta-analytic review. *Language Learning* 51:157–213.

Olshtain, E., and A. D. Cohen. 1991. Teaching speech act behavior to nonnative speakers. In *Teaching English as a second or foreign language,* ed. M. Celce-Murcia, 154–65. New York: Newbury House.

Paige, R. M., A. D. Cohen, B. Kappler, J. D. Chi, and J. P. Lassegard. 2003. *Maximizing study abroad: A students' guide to strategies for language and culture learning and use.* Minneapolis: University of Minnesota, Center for Advanced Research on Language Acquisition (CARLA).

Payne, S., and P. J. Whitney. 2002. Developing L2 oral proficiency through synchronous CMC: Output, working memory and interlanguage development. *CALICO Journal* 20 (1): 7–32.

Pellegrino, V. 1997. Social and psychological factors affecting spontaneous second language use during study abroad: A qualitative study. Ph.D diss., Bryn Mawr College.

Regan, V. 1995. The acquisition of sociolinguistic native speech norms: Effects of a year abroad on second language learners of French. In *Second language acquisition in a study abroad context,* ed. B. Freed, 245–67. Philadelphia: John Benjamins.

Rodríguez, S. 2001. The perception of requests in Spanish by instructed learners of Spanish in the second- and foreign-language contexts: A longitudinal study of acquisition patterns. Ph.D. diss., Indiana University.

Ryan, J., and B. Lafford. 1992. Acquisition of lexical meaning in a study abroad environment: *Ser* and *estar* and the Granada experience. *Hispania* 75:714–22.

Segalowitz, N., and B. Freed. 2004. Context, contact, and cognition in oral fluency acquisition: Learning Spanish in at home and study abroad contexts. *Studies in Second Language Acquisition* 26 (2): 173–99.

Segalowitz, N., B. Freed, J. Collentine, B. Lafford, N. Lazar, and M. Díaz-Campos. 2004. A comparison of Spanish second language acquisition in two different learning contexts: Study abroad and the domestic classroom. *Frontiers* 10 (4): 21–38.

Schell, K. 2001. *Functional categories and the acquisition of aspect in L2 Spanish: A longitudinal study.* Ph.D.diss., University of Washington, Seattle.

Siegal, M. 1995. Individual differences and study abroad: Women learning Japanese in Japan. In *Second language acquisition in a study abroad context,* ed. B. Freed, 225–44. Philadelphia: John Benjamins.

Simões, A. 1996. Phonetics in second language acquisition: An acoustic study of fluency in adult learners of Spanish. *Hispania* 79 (1): 87–95.

Smith, H. 1930. The junior year in France. *French Review* 4 (1): 41–48.

Stevens, J. J. 2001. The acquisition of L2 Spanish pronunciation in a study abroad context. Ph.D. diss., University of Southern California.

Talburt, S., and M. Stewart. 1999. What's the subject of study abroad? Race, gender, and "living culture." *Modern Language Journal* 83 (2): 163–75.

Torres, Jenna. 2003. A cognitive approach to the acquisition of clitics in L2 Spanish: Insights from study abroad and classroom learners. Ph.D. diss., Cornell University.

VanPatten, B. 1987. The acquisition of *ser* and *estar*: Accounting for developmental patterns. In *Foreign language learning: A research perspective,* ed. B. VanPatten, T. Dvorak, and J. Lee, 61–75. New York: Newbury House.

———. 1996. *Input processing and grammar instruction.* Norwood, NJ: Ablex.

Wilkinson, S. 1998. Study abroad from the participant's perspective: A challenge to common beliefs. *Foreign Language Annals* 31 (1): 23–39.

———. 2002. The omnipresent classroom during summer study abroad: American students in conversation with their French hosts. *Modern Language Journal* 86 (2): 157–73.

Online Language Learning
The Case of Spanish Without Walls

Robert Blake   *University of California at Davis*
Ann Marie Delforge *University of California at Davis*

Two factors dominate the recent interest in distance learning courses for foreign languages: (1) their potential to make language education available to those who cannot attend traditional classes because of time constraints or geographical location, and (2) their capacity to provide increased access for the study of less commonly taught languages (LCTLs). In reality, both motivations respond to the broader issue of increasing opportunities for language study that is so desperately needed in the United States (Simon 1980). In recognition of how important knowledge of languages other than English is to the security and economy of the United States, Congress declared 2005 to be the Year of Languages.

Naturally, there are also financial motivations for distance language learning. Some educators are beginning to propose that university students be allowed to satisfy graduation requirements by participating in distance education courses or replacing a portion of class time with some form of independent learning as a viable means of alleviating the enrollment pressures experienced by consistently affected language programs (Rogers and Wolff 2000; Soo and Ngeow 1998). Likewise, perennially resourse-poor language departments—most of the LCTL departments—are looking for ways to keep their programs vibrant and even increase student access to their courses.

Online courses are a particularly effective option for meeting the needs of foreign language education. Various other types of distance-learning formats, including live satellite and cable transmission, as well as pretaped video and audio materials, have been employed to deliver language instruction to distance learners over the years, but none of these methods is capable of providing the type of interactivity or scaffolding that current theories cite as necessary to promote second language learning (Long and Robinson 1998; Gass 1997).

Recent innovations in computer technology, however, which include multimedia computer-assisted language learning (CALL) materials as well as the availability of systems capable of supporting computer-mediated communication (CMC), make it possible for participants in online courses to engage in the active construction of L2 knowledge and to interact with one another in ways considered conducive to language learning. Unfortunately, only a limited number of outcome studies exists for online language courses (see the review of the literature in section 3.0).

In this chapter, we evaluate the effectiveness of one such online course, Spanish Without Walls (SWW), taught through the University of California, Davis Extension, using both quantitative output data (i.e., grammar tests and compositions) and qualitative measures (i.e., student surveys).[1] SWW is a totally virtual first-year Spanish course that combines CD-ROM materials (Blake, Blasco, and Hernández 2001), web readings with online content-based activities, and bimodal CMC (i.e., sound and text) in both a synchronous and asynchronous format.[2] Our data (section 5) showed that students enrolled in the SWW course fared at least as well as the undergraduates enrolled in conventional introductory Spanish classes at UC Davis in terms of grammatical accuracy. The results suggest that well-designed distance language instruction can offer a viable option for learners without access to the traditional classroom setting or for those who prefer the online learning environment to the sit-down class format.

This study is unique in that few completely virtual language courses such as SWW exist and even fewer have been evaluated for their effectiveness (see the review of the literature in section 3.0). Furthermore, researchers have primarily examined the use of chat tools that support only textual exchanges, mostly within the context of experimental CMC projects carried out with second- or third-year (Intermediate or Intermediate-Advanced) students carrying out their conversations in the same room (e.g., Kern 1995). In contrast, this study looks closely at a fully implemented virtual language curriculum for beginners with daily access to bimodal oral and written chatting.

1.0 Multimedia CALL

While early CALL programs were exclusively text-based and typically limited to providing rote practice activities, the multimedia forms of CALL presently available are capable of providing not only interesting and authentic materials but also content-based activities that appear to promote acquisition rather than just mechanical, rote learning (Soo and Ngeow 1998; Jones 1999). From the learner's standpoint, it has also been argued that CALL materials may have a positive effect on the language learning process because they stimulate metalinguistic awareness, allow for self-directed learning (Lee 2005; Murray 1999), and can accommodate different learning styles (Bull 1997). Likewise, high interactivity, once thought the exclusive domain of the classroom, now takes place in the virtual classroom, as well, thanks to an array of CMC tools. For the SWW course, the communications component crucially helps to maintain student interest in learning Spanish, as described in section 2.0.

2.0 Synchronous Computer-Mediated Communication

Although online distance learners do not enjoy access to face-to-face in situ interactions, synchronous CMC makes it possible for online classmates to communicate with one another in real time as well as deferred time.[3] While distance language education may never provide the same quantity of interaction as in situ courses, recent research indicates that the quality of textual CMC interaction is similar to the exchanges that take place in face-to-face conversations in conventional classes (Blake 2000). Payne and Whitney (2002) have also found that even pure textual chatting has a positive impact on oral proficiency. It also could be argued that each CMC tool and educational setting provides inherent advantages that promote SLA (Salaberry 2000).

As a result, online students may reap special benefits, or many of the same SLA benefits, from CMC with their classmates and, consequently, not be at any disadvantage in the language learning process.

For example, Blake (2000), Pellettieri (2000), Smith (2003), and Sotillo (2000) all analyzed language students' synchronous computer-mediated communication and found that virtual exchanges contain the same type of negotiation of meaning typically found in face-to-face classroom discourse and hypothesized to play a fundamental role in second language acquisition by adherents of the *Interaction Hypothesis* (Gass 1997; Gass, Mackey, and Pica 1998; Long and Robinson 1998). Other benefits often associated with CMC are reduced anxiety (Chun 1998), fewer asymmetrical power relationships (Warschauer 1996), and more collaborative efforts and sociocultural affordances (Belz 2002).

The technology that supports spoken computer-mediated communication in online classes is now widely available. Audio-graphic collaboration tools such as Lyceum, currently being piloted by the Open University (Hampel 2003; Hampel and Hauck 2004), and Flash-based chat tool utilized in Spanish Without Walls (see section 4.1 below) allow students in online classes to engage in audio exchanges and practice. These tools give students the opportunity to speak to one another in real time via their computers while at the same time augmenting their spoken communication with the additional support of written text as desired. By permitting learners to develop and practice their oral communication skills, this technology offers a way of addressing, at least to some degree, the lack of in situ speaking practice, one of the apparent shortcomings of learning language at a distance.

3.0 The Evaluation of Online Language Learning

Although it appears probable that online courses combining multimedia CALL and opportunities for interaction have the potential to provide efficacious language instruction, very little empirical research has addressed the overall effectiveness of online language learning, compared the progress of students participating in such courses with the performance of those enrolled in traditional classes, or examined students' perception of the online learning experience (see sections 3.1 and 3.2). Providing more data to address these issues is one of the goals of this chapter.

3.1 Hybrid Courses

Most studies of online language learning for beginners to date have evaluated hybrid courses that combine regular class meetings with computer-mediated instruction. Their results indicate that online activities can be substituted for some of the class time normally required in language courses without adversely affecting students' progress. As a whole, they also suggest that students who learn language online may develop literacy skills that are superior to those of students enrolled in traditional courses (Warschauer 1996).

Adair-Hauck, Willingham-McLain, and Earnest-Youngs (1999) and Green and Earnest-Youngs (2001) compared the achievement test scores of students enrolled in standard elementary French and German classes that met four days per week with the scores of learners who attended class three days a week and participated in technologically enhanced learning activities in lieu of a fourth hour of in-class contact. Adair-Hauck and colleagues found that students participating in the treatment group did as well as those in the control group on tests of listening, speaking, and cultural knowledge and performed significantly better than the control group on measures of reading and writing ability. The authors speculate that online students were more motivated to write, which might explain the differences, but they offer no explanation with respect to the reading results. In contrast, Green and Earnest-Youngs found no significant difference between the treatment and control classes' scores on the same type of tests used in the Adair-Hauck, Willingham-McLain, and Earnest-Youngs study but adapted for the web. It is not immediately clear why the results diverge so much in these two studies and whether or not the authors sufficiently controlled for individual class differences.

Chenoweth and Murday (2003) examined the outcomes of an elementary French course, *French Online,* conducted mostly online and including an hour-long, face-to-face class meeting once per week as well as weekly twenty-minute individual or small-group meetings with a native speaker tutor. The progress of students in the online group was compared to that of those who attended a traditional class four hours per week on tests of oral production, listening comprehension, reading comprehension, grammar knowledge, and written production. Scores for the treatment and control groups differed significantly only in the case of the writing samples, with essays by students in the online learning group being judged superior to those of the control group on a variety of measures, including grammatical accuracy, syntactic complexity, use of transitions, and cohesive devices and organization. It was also found that the online students spent approximately one hour per week less studying than did those in the traditional class. Thus these findings suggest that the online course was more efficient as students achieved results similar to those attained by learners in the conventional class with less time expenditure.

Nieves (1996) reported on the performance of students enrolled in Exito, an introductory Spanish course offered at George Mason University in a format very similar to the online French program studied by Chenoweth and Murday. As originally developed (for employees of the CIA), the Exito program was a ten-day survival course; each day was devoted to learning to survive in Spanish with regard to some aspect of daily life, such as obtaining food and driving. Nieves expanded this program into a semester-long course in which students primarily worked on their own with the materials and attended a one-hour face-to-face class meeting per week. The multimedia component for each lesson includes newscast video and various types of activities to do with the software. There were no activities using the web, since the study was done in 1994, when the web was still not widely employed as a teaching tool. In complete contrast to Chenoweth and Murday's (2003) data, Nieves's results from her own set of outcome listening measures showed that students who participated in the multimedia-based course outperformed those enrolled in traditional courses on measures of aural and oral communication skills but scored slightly lower on a test of writing abilities.

These studies make the case that online learning can contribute to the student's L2 learning, but much depends on the learning environment, pedagogical materials, and tasks. However, since these studies combine online instruction with face-to-face class meetings, it is difficult to generalize their results to language courses conducted entirely online. Specifically, it should be noted that, although the regular small group or individual meetings with instructors included in the online French course studied by Chenoweth and Murday and in the Exito program were probably extremely beneficial for students, they complicate the interpretation of outcome data. Such opportunities for more intimate interaction with fluent speakers of the target language are rarely available in any introductory language class, either conventional (with twenty-five students or more) or online, with the SWW course being no exception.

3.2 Courses Taught Entirely Online

Thus far, only two studies (Cahill and Catanzaro 1997; Soo and Ngeow 1998) have evaluated completely online language courses based on empirical data. In both cases, online learners were found to outperform students from conventional courses on the grammar output measures administered.

Cahill and Catanzaro (1997) reported on an introductory online Spanish class that might be considered somewhat low tech, as it did not have a multimedia component. Instead, the *Dos Mundos* text along with the accompanying audiocassettes and lab manual were used as the core course materials. Online activities included synchronous chat sessions, open-ended web assignments, practice tests, and a substantial number of pen-pal letter writing assignments. Responses to two essay questions were used to compare the progress of students participating in the experimental group to that of students enrolled in conventional Spanish classes.

Based on ratings of global quality and percentage error scores, the writing samples of students in the online course were judged to be significantly better than those from the traditional classes. Although not discussed by the authors, it seems clear that in this study more writing was demanded of the online students, which makes the effect due simply to the online teaching format hard to ascertain.

Soo and Ngeow (1998) compared the performance of 77 students enrolled in conventional English classes with 111 students who studied English exclusively through use of a multimedia CALL program. Pretest and posttest TOEFL scores were compared for both groups, and it was found that the students in the online group showed significantly more improvement than did those who took part in conventional classes. In addition, given that the experimental group started studying five weeks later than students in the control group due to technical difficulties, it can be said that the online students not only made more progress than learners in the control group but also improved their language skills more rapidly.

As is the case for the hybrid courses reviewed above, the outcome data from these two studies suggest that online language learning can be effective, at least as a means of improving writing, reading, and listening comprehension abilities. However, these authors did not make it clear why the online course brought about these results. Perhaps the online students had a higher engagement level with the texts themselves. More research is necessary to substantiate these initial observations. Again, Cahill and Catanzaro's results must be viewed with caution, since it could be argued that students in their distance course wrote better final essays simply because of the exceptional amount of writing practice they had to endure in the online format. The extent to which their results can be said to support the overall effectiveness of online language learning remains unclear.

3.3 Students' Perceptions of the Online Learning Experience

A handful of studies have asked students to describe and rate the quality of their experience in online language classes. The studies by Adair-Hauck, Willingham-McLain, and Earnest-Youngs (1999), Green and Earnest-Youngs (2001), and Chenoweth and Murday (2003) all included such an evaluative component.

Adair-Hauck and colleagues used a self-report questionnaire to compare the attitudes and opinions of students in their hybrid French course with those of students taking a conventional class. They found that a greater percentage of students in the hybrid class reported meeting their personal language-learning goals over the course of the semester. A number of students in the technology-enhanced class also indicated that the flexibility of the multimedia materials contributed to their progress in the class, noting the advantage of being able to spend more time on activities they found particularly difficult—in short, more student-centered learning. This is not to say that student-driven materials cannot be incorporated into the regular classroom, but rather that students often perceive that the classroom is teacher driven in most cases as opposed to the necessarily student-driven nature of the online format.

Responses to a self-report questionnaire administered to online and offline students by Green and Earnest-Youngs and the results of course evaluations collected by Chenoweth and Murday shed a less positive light on the online language learning experience. Students in the hybrid and conventional courses studied by Green and Earnest-Youngs reported equal levels of satisfaction with the progress they had achieved. However, the students who completed web-based activities in place of a fourth hour of class time found some website pages too difficult and some of the activities not sufficiently well organized. The mostly online French course evaluated by Chenoweth and Murday received a lower overall rating on student evaluations than did a conventional class taken by learners in the control group. The authors note that, since students' principal complaints were related to the organization of the online course and to grading standards, this rating may be due to the fact that the course was being offered for the first time rather than to its technological component.

Murray (1999) also reports on students' assessment of their experiences learning language with CALL materials. He interviewed Canadian university students who used an interactive videodisc program to study French for one semester and obtained responses very similar to those mentioned above by Adair-Hauck, Willingham-

McLain, and Earnest-Youngs. For example, students in Murray's study commented that they liked the ability to work at their own pace and focus their efforts on activities that were particularly difficult for them—once again, the benefit of student-directed learning. Also, a number of students stated that they found working independently with the video disc materials much less anxiety-provoking than participating in a conventional language class.

A recent study by Lee (2005) examined college students' experiences in a Spanish course that included essay writing assignments and chat sessions conducted in Blackboard. In this case also, students found the self-directed nature of the web-based tasks particularly helpful. In oral interviews at the end of the semester, a number of participants indicated that they learned to improve their organizational skills and take more responsibility for their own language learning as a result of the Blackboard activities.

Thus, according to the limited amount of research available at this time, students' reactions to the experience of learning language online cannot be considered universally positive. However, it does appear that students respond favorably to the flexibility afforded by CALL materials and to their potential for self-directed learning. Murray's results also indicate that working with CALL may make language learning less stressful for some students.

3.4 This Study

Although existing studies found that students who learn language online tend to equal or surpass the progress of students in traditional sit-down courses, further research is necessary in order to more thoroughly evaluate the quality of online language courses, especially those conducted entirely online. More information regarding students' perceptions of the online learning experience also needs to be gathered in order to improve the design of such courses in the future.

This study seeks to address the need for more outcome research bearing on the relative efficacy of online language learning. The progress of students enrolled in Spanish Without Walls at UC Davis Extension was compared to that of undergraduate students enrolled in a regular, year-long introductory Spanish language courses (i.e., SPA 1, SPA 2, and SPA 3) at UC Davis.

4.0 Research Methods

Several measures were used to rate performance, including results from multiple-choice tests of grammatical knowledge, instructors' judgments of short compositions, and attitude surveys regarding the quality of the online learning experience. The online students' spoken interaction with their instructors via sound/text chat were also transcribed and analyzed.

4.1 Course Design

Spanish Without Walls (a year-long course divided into three quarters) combines multimedia language materials from (1) *Tesoros,* a five-disk CD-ROM detective story

(Blake, Blasco, and Hernández 2001), (2) content-based website readings (e.g., *One Hundred Years of Solitude* and writings on the Americas, the Mexican Revolution, the Aztecs, Hispanics in the United States, etc.) and Flash activities designed by María Victoria González Pagani (UC Santa Cruz), and (3) a collaborative CMC tool based on a Flash communication server (by Macromedia) that allows for both asynchronous and synchronous communication with half-duplex (i.e., walkie-talkie) sound.[4]

Tesoros' five CD-ROMs served as the textbook for this three-part, first-year course. The remaining online materials were originally packaged into a course management system (programmed using a ColdFusion database) and now resides in a Moodle server. The materials are designed to teach first-year Spanish grammar and vocabulary, provide exercises, conduct testing, present authentic Spanish-language readings, and enable oral conversations with teachers and peers alike. Students alternated between use of the CD-ROMs and the SWW website in order to cover the scope and sequence of a normal university Spanish language course. Students were held accountable for the CD-ROM material by means of online exams that cover the vocabulary, storyline, and grammar presented by *Tesoros*.

Students were also required to chat live with their instructor in groups of no more than three students at least once a week for one hour and several more times with their assigned partners as time and schedules permitted in order to complete the collaborative content-based tasks. For example, one student might have researched the capital cities for four Latin American countries while the partner investigated the same type of information for four different countries. During the chat, the students shared their results with one another in jigsaw fashion.

This chat tool allows three different CMC modalities (see fig. 7.1): (1) the exchange of half-duplex sound (the TALK button), (2) individual keyboard chat delimited by a carriage return (the CHAT window), and (3) a shared writing space that updates output character by character (the TEXTPAD window). Students must take turns using either the TALK or TEXTPAD functions because only one individual can hold the floor or cursor at a time, but CHAT text can be sent by anyone at any time without waiting.

4.2 First-Year Spanish Program at UC Davis

First-year Spanish courses at UC Davis use *Dos Mundos* (Terrell et al. 2002) as a textbook and follow a communicative approach to language instruction. Classes meet five hours per week and include a variety of activities, including information-gap tasks, skits, role plays, and songs. Students are also required to listen to audiotapes and complete the workbook exercises (hard copy) that accompany the text. The exams for this level primarily consist of fill-in-the-blank and multiple-choice items that test grammatical structures, vocabulary, listening comprehension, and reading ability with short essay.

4.3 Participants

SWW students enroll in this online class through the UC Davis Extension and are for the most part adults who work full time. Out of 147 enrollments over the last year, 96 students completed the course (and the others dropped), which translates into a 65

Figure 7.1 CHAT Interface

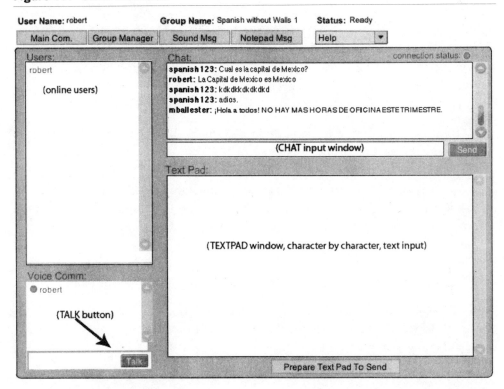

percent retention rate, well above the standard rate of 50 percent often quoted in the literature as the norm for a distance-learning format (Carr 2000, A39).

A sample cohort, 21 of these 96 students, participated in our survey. More students were invited to participate, but data collection from virtual students is difficult because students can not be forced to comply with the surveys or with other activities that are not part of the course. After the course is finished, virtual students feel no compulsion to participate in course evaluations, and it is illegal to contact them and follow up by email. Information on previous language experience in high school and reasons for studying Spanish for this cohort of 21 online students can be found in tables 7.1 and 7.2.[5]

Table 7.1 SWW students' experience with Spanish in high school (percent)

Student experience	None	One year	Two or more years
SWW I and II	71	11	18

Table 7.2 Students' reasons for taking Spanish in the online format (percent)

Student level	Professional development	Personal interests	Satisfy language requirement
SWW I and II	57	38	5

Tables 7.1 and 7.2 make it clear that most of the SWW students (71 percent) are taking Spanish for the first time and are motivated by career-related factors (57 percent)—this should not be surprising for the adult continuing-education setting. One experienced student was clearly using the online format for reasons of retention and/or further perfection of her existing L2 knowledge because she was required to teach Spanish by her school employer. The following quotes are a representative of the responses of those taking Spanish for professional reasons:

- "I run a small vineyard in Napa, and would like to be able to communicate better with the people I work with."
- "I am an elementary school teacher and am trying to get my CLAD certificate. ... It requires two semesters of a second language."
- "I am a part-time teacher at the San Francisco Conservation Corps. The corps members who are working toward their GED or high school diploma are 80% native Spanish speakers."
- "I am a specialist in diabetes/nutrition. Learning Spanish is good for my job."
- "I work with many Spanish-speaking people in my work with the labor unions."

Nine students preferred the online format to the notion of taking Spanish in a conventional setting, mostly for reasons dealing with managing a busy schedule of work and family commitments:

- "With three children and an at-home business my schedule allows for evening/night study and this seems to be the best way."
- "I took the online class because I am a single mother and didn't want to rely on somebody else in order for me to attend class."
- "I chose this course because I did not want to sit in a traditional classroom. I wanted the flexibility to 'attend class' on my own schedule."

For purposes of comparison, we also gathered biodata from forty-six UC Davis students enrolled in traditional language classes during the winter quarter of 2004: twenty-three undergraduates in a UCD first-quarter Spanish course (SPA 1) and twenty-three from a section of second-quarter Spanish (SPA 2). The corresponding data for these students are found in tables 7.3 and 7.4.

The data in Tables 7.3 and 7.4 reveal that language students in UC Davis's introductory courses are principally fulfilling a language requirement, despite the fact that most of them (61 percent) have taken one or more years of Spanish in high school. This pattern stands in sharp contrast to the SWW students and their more professional orientation, given that they have already entered the work force. Logically enough, the main objective of the university students is finishing up the language requirement for graduation (76 percent).

5.0 Outcome Measures and Data Collection

In this section we describe the methods of data collection in more detail. This description is important, given that not all tasks were exactly the same in each group.

Table 7.3 UC Davis students' experience with Spanish in high school (percent)

Student level	None	One year	Two or more years	Four or more years
SPA 1	39 (9/23)	13 (3/23)	44 (10/23)	4 (1/23)
SPA 2	22 (5/23)	39 (9/23)	35 (8/23)	4 (1/23)

Table 7.4 Students' reasons for taking Spanish at UC Davis (percent)

Student level	Satisfy language requirement	Personal interests
SPA 1 and 2	76	24

5.1 Tests of Grammatical Knowledge

Several grammar tests from the Spanish Without Walls course were administered to the undergraduate subjects during weeks five to eight of the course in order to compare their grammatical knowledge with that of online students. These SWW tests included multiple-choice and fill-in-the-blank items that were slightly adapted for use in this study in order to maintain parity. First, certain vocabulary items and grammar structures were modified to ensure that the material was also covered in the *Dos Mundos* curriculum used by the undergraduate students. In all such cases, an attempt was made to preserve the difficulty level of the original question (e.g., stem-changing verbs were replaced with other stem-changing verbs, etc.). Second, most of the tests were divided into two sections and administered to the undergraduates at different times to accommodate slight differences in the respective syllabi's scope and sequence. Accordingly, the SWW Grammar Tests 3, 4, 5, 6, and 7 were transformed into Tests 3.1, 3.2, 4, 5, 6, 7.1, and 7.2 for the purposes of this investigation, which explains why the total points differed from test to test.

The scores obtained by undergraduates on these modified exams were compared with those achieved on the original tests by SWW students enrolled in all sections of the course that have been offered by the UC Davis Extension thus far. Data for all SWW were aggregated in order to increase sample size because the number of students in each online class at any one time tended to be relatively small. Since the SWW course content and instructional methods remained consistent from term to term, the data from all SWW students were amalgamated and treated as belonging to a single class (see section 6.0).

5.2 Student Compositions

The final SWW content-based task asks the online students to complete a writing assignment. For the purposes of comparison, two classes of Spanish 1 and Spanish 2 at UC Davis were asked to carry out similar short writing assignments based on the same web reading materials. Students enrolled in SPA 1 were asked to write a brief description (at least five sentences) of a Velázquez painting, while the SPA 2 class wrote a minimum of ten sentences reporting on the Mexican indigenous cultures. As in the case of the grammar tests, writing samples from all SWW sections were combined to maximize sample size.

The writing samples from both groups (SWW and UC Davis) were typed and randomized to allow for blind rating by two independent judges. Criteria used in the evaluation process included the calculation of a percentage error score (total number of errors divided by total number of words) and the assignment of scores on a series of Likert-type scales adapted from Chenoweth and Murday (2003). Specifically, each essay was given a score ranging from one to five on the following dimensions: variety and appropriateness of vocabulary, syntactic complexity and variety, grammatical accuracy, organization and use of transitions, mechanics, and overall quality.

5.3 Self-Report Questionnaire

This instrument was completed on a voluntary basis by SWW students from the winter and fall terms of 2003 and from the winter, spring, and summer quarters of 2004 (see the questionnaire at http://philo.ucdavis.edu/zope/home/rblake/survey_SWW.html). As explained above, some items on the questionnaire asked students to describe previous coursework they had taken in Spanish and to give their reasons for choosing to take an online rather than traditional language course. Other items requested that students discuss the advantages and disadvantages of taking an online Spanish course and compare that experience with any conventional classes they might have taken in the past. In addition, students were asked to indicate whether or not they were satisfied with the progress they had made in Spanish Without Walls and if they would be interested in taking another online language course in the future. Students enrolled in the fall, spring, and summer sections of the course used the Flash-based chat collaboration tool, and the version of the questionnaire administered to these groups requested that they rate its effectiveness.

6.0 Results

In this section, the students' performance in the distance learning course will be assessed from a variety of perspectives: discrete grammar tests, writing samples, self-reports, and an analysis of selected chat transcripts.

6.1 Tests of Grammatical Knowledge

For comparative purposes, UC Davis students enrolled in a traditional classroom course were given the same grammatical tests that the SWW students took online. These grammar quizzes had to be divided into smaller units (i.e., the rubric "Total points" found in tables 7.5 and 7.6) for the classroom students in order to accommodate both curriculum and time constraints. For the classroom students, these exams were administered in weeks five through eight of the quarter (which correspond to chapters 3 and 4 in the SWW curriculum), again, with an eye to avoiding the typical stress encountered at the beginning and end of a classroom curriculum.

On all of the discrete-point grammar tests, the SWW students scored significantly higher as judged by their *t*-test values than did the undergraduates enrolled in the classroom Spanish 1 and Spanish 2, respectively. Individual means, number of points possible, and sample size for both groups are presented for all tests in tables 7.5 and 7.6. It should be noted that the total points varied slightly from test to test both for reasons already discussed above. In the case of the online students, the same number of scores was not available for each test due to student attrition. Fluctuation in the number of classroom undergraduate scores is due to absences on days when the data were collected.

Why the SWW should so soundly outperform the classroom students invites speculation. Both curricular programs teach approximately the same grammar scope and sequence. The SWW students must rely on grammar self-study and practice through a predominately textual medium, whereas the classroom students are more accustomed to oral practice in small groups and choral rehearsal led by the teacher. Perhaps the more textual emphasis required by an online course affords the SWW students greater textual concentration and, therefore, greater awareness of grammatical details. Likewise, the SWW online readings and activities provide students with very engaging self-study materials designed to maintain their interest. It

Table 7.5 *T*-test comparison between SWW I and SPA 1 grammar scores

Grammar tests	Total points	SWW I		SPA 1 classroom		Significance level
		Mean	SD	Mean	SD	
3.1	8	7.14 (N = 42)	1.03	5.83 (N = 18)	1.10	$p < .001$
3.2	17	15.5 (N = 42)	1.92	14.2 (N = 20)	2.12	$p < .02$
4	21	17.3 (N = 35)	4.31	14.5 (N = 19)	4.55	$p < .03$

Table 7.6 *T*-test comparison between SWW II and SPA 2 grammar scores

Grammar tests	Total points	SWW I		SPA 1 classroom		Significance level
		Mean	SD	Mean	SD	
5	6	7.69 (N = 35)	1.69	6.26 (N = 23)	1.54	$p < .002$
6	14	11.8 (N = 13)	2.30	8.76 (N = 21)	2.17	$p < .001$
7.1	10	7.70 (N = 10)	2.91	5.61 (N = 23)	2.13	$p < .03$
7.2	17	13.7 (N = 10)	3.40	10.2 (N = 20)	2.62	$p < .004$

is impossible to measure what impact these curricular materials, specifically designed for home study, had on grammatical accuracy. In any event, the SWW students do not appear to be disadvantaged in the least with respect to their progress learning grammar. We will return to this issue in the conclusion.

6.2 Comparative Writing Samples

As can be seen from table 7.7, a two-way t-test revealed no significant differences ($p < 0.05$) between the SWW and regular classroom groups for either the first-quarter or second-quarter levels, although the mean scores for the SWW group were consistently slightly higher.

If the SWW I and SWW II students were more accustomed to the textual modality of the online environment, this factor did not manifest itself in the writing results. Why did the SWW students fail to achieve significantly better writing scores than their counterparts in the traditional classroom? Writing at the first-year level follows a series of basic patterns often characterized by many transfers from L1. It is also restricted in terms of the quantity that can be demanded from students. The prose of students at this level is also hard to graduate into distinct levels, and this tends to create the impression that the students are all writing about the same, even in the eyes of experienced teachers. Perhaps, when we have data from SWW III, the writing samples will present enough linguistic development and complexity to reveal more obvious differences between these groups. At the very least, the SWW students, once again, are holding their own against the UC Davis classroom students, but these results are tempered by the inability to obtain larger writing samples from beginning students.

6.3 Responses to the Self-Report Questionnaire

Four of the ten students enrolled in the SWW during the winter quarter of 2003, and four of the five students who took the class in the fall term of that year returned the online questionnaire. Given this low rate of response, it is difficult to draw definitive conclusions about the online language learning experience. Not surprisingly, given our review of previous research, the SWW respondents singled out flexibility—working within the online learning format—in discussing the course's advantages:

> I like the flexibility of working at my own pace. There were days when I could not work at all but others that I was able to devote several hours and complete several assignments at one time.

Table 7.7 *T*-test comparison of written samples from SWW and UC Davis students*

T-test comparison	Vocabulary	Syntax complexity	Grammar accuracy	Organization	Mechanics	Percentage of errors	Global score
SWW I/SPA 1	0.957	0.322	0.541	0.566	0.787	0.730	0.399
SWW II/SPA 2	0.668	0.950	0.200	0.918	0.232	0.205	0.577

*$p < 0.05$

Another student was able to carry on with the SWW course despite being unexpectedly assigned to a job on the East Coast for two months. Another student continued on with the course even though he was assigned to check plant production quality for a lemon juice factory in Mexico. Students appreciated the ability to work at their own pace and around busy schedules.

Others commented on what might be called the course's potential for self-directed learning, indicating that they liked being able to dedicate more time and effort to concepts that they found to be difficult and only skim over those they found less difficult. In addition, two SWW students indicated that they found the online language learning environment much less stressful than the conventional classroom setting. Both felt that the lower anxiety level of the online format helped improve their performance.

The few students who returned the questionnaire assessed the online language learning experience as generally positive. All eight of these respondents stated that they would be interested in taking more online language courses in the future, and seven indicated that they were satisfied with the progress they had made in the course. One student said she was satisfied with the grammar and vocabulary aspects of the course, but not with the reading materials or with the opportunities for interaction.

Several respondents expressed the desire for more interaction and speaking practice. Technical difficulties, when they occurred, tended to aggravate these feelings. Both criticisms are to be expected: every participant to an online course brings a slightly different hardware and system configuration. The Flash communication server has the advantage of only requiring students to install an up-to-date Flash plug-in and browser for their respective system. Nevertheless, user inexperience and low-end modem connections can still confound even the simplest technical solutions. The other criticism—the lack of face-to-face interactions—is an obvious, if not inherent, shortcoming of the online format. Unfortunately, the desire for flexibility directly conflicts with the possibility of having face-to-face interactions.

Again, these reactions should be viewed with caution because of the sample size, but we suspect that these observations, which are remarkably similar to findings previously reported in the literature (see Adair-Hauck, Willingham-McLain, and Earnest-Youngs 1999, as cited in section 3.2), will be confirmed by further data collection from the SWW project.

Many language professionals continue to be skeptical about online language learning, especially since the review of the literature turns up a relatively thin track record. This skepticism was shared by the student quoted below, which makes her final appraisal all the more convincing:

> The lack of a classroom setting made it less stressful to take the class. I didn't have to worry so much about not being able to properly pronounce the words in front of the whole class. It reduced the embarrassment factor considerably. . . . It allowed me to be successful in starting to learn the language. When I took Spanish the traditional way, I hated it and did poorly. . . . I was skeptical about how it would work to take a language course online and would probably have preferred to take the

course in a traditional manner when I signed up for it. Now, however, I think that the online course is a more effective way for me to learn the language.

6.4 Interaction via the Chat Tool

The Flash-based chat collaboration tool was first integrated into the Spanish Without Walls course in the fall of 2003. (Before that, we used asynchronous Wimba voice boards.) This technology primarily has been used as a means for holding virtual office hours between students and their instructors but also has facilitated pair work among students. An informal examination of student-instructor sound exchanges via the chat tool that occurred every week for an hour gives the impression that these conversations are similar to exchanges that typically occur among instructors and students during face-to-face classroom contact or office hours. A more detailed analysis of these interactions (Blake 2005) confirms that they include negotiations of meaning, noticing of gaps, and the types of collaboration that, ideally, would occur in face-to-face language instruction. Much of the focus for these exchanges revolves around issues of formal accuracy and correct pronunciation; they are, for the most part, teacher centered, with both English and Spanish used freely. The following exchange with a SWW student parallels what Jepson (2005) found: many of the repairs in voice chats between nonnative speakers address pronunciation problems:

Exchange 1:

Student: So I would say *mi familia es piqiña,* I think. *Mi hermana se llama,* I think; I'm not sure if I'm saying that right.

Instructor: Yes, you're on target: *Mi familia es pequeña.* And then you're talking about your sister and what her name is: *mi hermana se llama.* You're saying it correctly, the *ll* is pronounced as a *y.* Remember, don't pronounce any of the *h*'s. Give it another try.

Student: *Mi familia es pequeña. Mi hermana se llama Alexanne.*

Instructor: *Mi hermana* [the *h* is not pronounced]. And careful with the vowels. [Models the Spanish vowels: a, e, i, o, u.]

Student: OK, here goes. *Mi familia es pequeña, mi hermana se llama Alexanne.*

Exchange 2:

Instructor: For the tap, the tongue goes up to the roof of the mouth once. For the trill, it goes up more than once. Let me demonstrate; *caro, carro.*

Student: So the double *r* is longer than the single *r? Pero, perro. Caro, carro.*

Instructor: That's getting there. Be sure you don't loose your very tense pronunciation of the vowels. So, *pero, perro. Caro, carro.*

Student: *Pero, perro. Caro, carro.* [With noticeably improved pronunciation.]

Exchange 3:

Student: *Yo soy Valencia, California.*

Instructor: Perfect. Don't forget the *de* because you have to be from somewhere. So it's *Soy de Valencia, California.*

Student: *Soy de Valencia, California.*

Exchange 4:

Student: *No estoy quejando . . . quejar . . .* to complain?

Instructor: *El verbo que tienes que usar es "quejarse."* [Writes *no estoy quejándome* and *no me estoy quejando.*]

Student: *No estoy quejándome o no me quejo. Sí, lo veo y lo entiendo.*

Students also had to work with other students to finish a series of content-based tasks as described in section 4.1. These exchanges were entirely student directed and can be characterized within an interacionist framework (Blake 2000) in which pairs of students mutually supported each other in order to reach closure on the task. Exchange 5 (below) is representative of this type of student-student interaction. A misunderstanding arises here when one student is unable to break down and comprehend a calendar date. The more advanced student (Student T) provides the necessary scaffolding in order to move forward on their assignment as a team:

Exchange 5:

Student K: Could you repeat that slowly? I'd like to hear how you say the year.

Student T: *Claro que sí. Mil* is 1,000. A hundred is *cien.* But when it's plural, it's *cientos.* So you want 800, so you say *ochocientos.* And you want *cuarenta,* which is 40. *Cuarenta y ocho* is 48; you add the one's place like that.

Student K: *Mil ochocientos cuarenta y nueve.*

In the same questionnaire discussed in section 4.3, the SWW students evaluated the chat tool as positive, except when they experienced technical problems.

7.0 Conclusion

The quantitative results of this study indicate that students in the completely online SWW course performed at least comparable to and often better than undergraduates enrolled in the conventional introductory Spanish courses with respect to grammatical accuracy.[6] These findings are consistent with the results of previous research evaluating the effectiveness of online learning. Soo and Ngeow (1998) found that students enrolled in a completely online English class made greater gains in proficiency as measured by the Test of English as a Foreign Language (TOEFL) than did a similar group enrolled in traditional English courses. Adair-Hauck, Willingham-McLain, and Earnest-Youngs (1999), Cahill and Catanzaro (1997), and Chenoweth and Murday (2003) found that students who participated in online learning received higher scores on measures of written ability than did learners enrolled in conventional classes, demonstrating superior grammatical accuracy as well as a more cohesive writing style.

Several researchers (Warschauer 1997; Blake and Zyzik 2004) have speculated about why online students might perform in this way. Written language is the primary mode of instruction for online learning, and this fact might correlate closely with an increased sense of metalinguistic awareness of the type interactionist researchers have alluded to as being a crucial priming mechanism for language acquisition (Gass 1997, 104–32).

The qualitative results of this study are also in agreement with other findings concerning the experiences of online language learners. Many SWW students, in like fashion to those surveyed by Adair-Hauck, Willingham-McLain, and Earnest-Youngs (1999) and Murray (1999), praised the flexibility of the course materials and indicated that they liked being able to work at their own pace as well as spend more time on the material that was most difficult for them. As was the case in the studies by Adair-Hauck and colleagues and by Murray, a small number of SWW students mentioned that they found it much less stressful to learn language online than in a conventional language class. These SWW students also stated that they felt they made much more progress in the online format than they had in traditional language courses previously taken. Their comments lend support to Liontas's (2002) contention that CALL materials may have the effect of lowering students' affective filters by allowing them to work with the target language without having to be embarrassed by making a mistake in front of other learners. SWW students' positive evaluations of the chat tool, despite the technical difficulties involved in its use, are also similar to those reported in the literature by Hampel (2003) and Hampel and Hauck (2004).

Taken as a whole, the results of our study suggest that online courses can be an effective means of providing foreign language instruction and may be especially conducive to the development of grammatical competence and written expression. Whether or not keyboard chatting and voice-IP sound exchanges will have a significant effect on oral proficiency is a topic that has only just begun to attract researchers' attention (Payne and Whitney 2002). Confirming a link between keyboard chatting and oral proficiency development will be crucial to the long-term student success and acceptance of this language learning format by the foreign language profession. Language teachers will not easily swap oral proficiency for gains in written skills, nor should they.

Despite this mostly rosy outlook for the online format, several extraneous factors may have influenced some of the findings reported here. First, the superior performance of SWW students on some of the measures of language abilities included in this study may be, in part, the result of motivational factors. The majority of the undergraduate participants in the study, as well as of the SWW students, stated that they were studying Spanish because they felt that knowledge of the language would be helpful to them in their careers. However, in the case of the adult professionals enrolled in the Spanish Without Walls course, the potential benefits of being able to communicate in Spanish may have been a much more tangible, compelling, and, consequently, immediate overall motivation. Motivational factors are especially likely to have played a role in the performance of the two groups on the grammar examinations; SWW students undoubtedly did their best on these tests because the results affected their course grade, whereas the undergraduates may not necessarily have made their best effort because their scores did not count toward their grade in any significant way.

More data are needed to clarify these issues. Fortunately, the SWW project and similar efforts will continue to generate more information on these aspects of online learning in the near future. Practitioners should be acutely aware that more is always better with regard to language learning. Hybrid forms are particularly attractive in this light, but a completely online delivery will do nicely when no other access is available.

Notes

1. The Spanish Without Walls project was funded by a three-year FIPSE grant, P116–000315. For a brief description of the project, see Jeff van de Pol, Spanish Without Walls: Using technology to teach language anywhere, an article at http://ittimes.ucdavis.edu/mar2001/blake.html (accessed June 20, 2006).
2. By content-based activities, we mean those for which the purpose of the task is to have the students focus first on meaning and, second, on the linguistic forms—grammar is learned by studying content and meaning.
3. Although the focus of this paper deals with online language courses and synchronous chat, we readily acknowledge other benefits from a synchronous CMC that have an impact on writing and other scaffolding activities from both a linguistic and sociocultural perspective. These aspects, however, fall outside the scope of this particular study.
4. For a review of the *Tesoros* CD-ROMs, see Lafford 1995.
5. Not all twenty-one SWW students answered every question, which accounts for the slightly fewer responses (seventeen).
6. We also asked the same cohort of twenty-one SWW students at the end of the respective courses (SWW I or SWW II) to take the Spanish Computer Adaptive Placement Exam (S-CAPE) developed at BYU and used as a placement test at UC Davis and many other institutions. Again, the online students tended to not complete any task not directly related to their grade; only eight students took the online S-CAPE exam. All eight placed above the level of the SWW course they were enrolled in. However, the sample is too small to draw any reliable conclusions.

References

Adair-Hauck, B., L. Willingham-McLain, and B. Earnest-Youngs. 1999. Evaluating the integration of technology and second language learning. *CALICO Journal* 17 (2): 269–306.

Belz, J. A. 2002. Social dimensions of telecollaborative foreign language study. *Language Learning & Technology* 6 (1): 60–81.

Blake, R. 2000. Computer-mediated communication: A window on L2 Spanish interlanguage. *Language Learning & Technology* 4 (1): 120–36.

———. 2005. Bimodal CMC: The glue of language learning at a distance. *CALICO Journal* 22 (3): 497–511.

Blake, R., J. Blasco, and C. Hernández. 2001. Tesoros CD-ROM: A multi-media-based course.

Blake, R., and E. Zyzik. 2003. Who's helping whom? Learner/heritage speakers' networked discussions in Spanish. *Applied Linguistics* 24 (4): 519–44. Boecillo, Valladolid: Boecillo Editorial Multimedia (BeM); New York: McGraw-Hill.

Bull, S. 1997. Promoting effective learning strategy use in CALL. *Computer Assisted Language Learning* 10 (1): 3–39.

Cahill, D., and D. Catanzaro. 1997. Teaching first-year Spanish on-line. *CALICO Journal* 14 (2–4): 97–114.

Carr, S. 2000. As distance education comes of age, the challenge is keeping the students. *Chronicle of Higher Eduction,* February 11, 2000, A39.

Chenoweth, N. A., and K. Murday. 2003. Measuring student learning in an online French course. *CALICO Journal* 20 (2): 284–314.

Chun, D. 1998. Using computer-assisted class discussion to facilitate the acquisition of interactive competence. In. *Language learning online: Theory and practice in the ESL and L2 computer classroom,* ed. J. Swaffar, S. Romano, P. Markley, and K. Arens, 57–80. Austin, TX: Labyrinth Publications.

Gass, S. 1997. *Input, interaction, and the second language learner.* Mahwah, NJ: Lawrence Erlbaum Associates.

Gass, S., A. Mackey, and T. Pica. 1998. The role of input and interaction in second language acquisition. *Modern Language Journal* 82 (3): 299–305.

Green, A., and B. Earnest-Youngs. 2001. Using the web in elementary French and German courses: Quantitative and qualitative study results. *CALICO Journal* 19 (1): 89–123.

Hampel, R. 2003. Theoretical perspectives and new practices in audio-graphic conferencing for language learning. *ReCALL* 15 (1): 21–36.

Hampel, R., and M. Hauck. 2004. Towards an effective use of audio conferencing in distance language courses. *Language Learning & Technology* 8 (1): 66–82.

Jepson, K. 2005. Conversations—and negotiated interaction—in text and voice chat rooms. *Language Learning & Technology* 9 (3): 75–95.

Kern, R. 1995. Restructuring classroom interaction with networked computers: Effects on quantity and characteristics of language production. *Modern Language Journal* 79 (4): 457–76.

Jones, C. M. 1999. Language courseware design. *CALICO Journal* 17 (1): 5–7.

Lafford, P. 1995. Tesoros: Curso Multimedia intensivo de español. *CALICO Software Review.* http://calico.org/CALICO—Review/review/tesoros00.htm (accessed September 30, 2005).

Lee, L. 2005. Using web-based instruction to promote active learning: Learners' perspectives. *CALICO Journal* 23 (1): 139–56.

Liontas, J. I. 2002. CALLMedia digital technology: Whither in the new millennium? *CALICO Journal* 19 (2): 315–30.

Long, M., and P. Robinson. 1998. Focus on form: Theory, research and practice. In *Focus on form in classroom second language acquisition,* ed. C. Doughty and J. Williams, 15–41. Cambridge: Cambridge University Press.

Murray, G. L. 1999. Autonomy and language learning in a simulated environment. *System* 27:295–308.

Nieves, K. A. 1996. The development of a technology-based class in beginning Spanish: Experiences with using EXITO. Ph.D. diss, George Mason University.

Payne, S., and P. J. Whitney. 2002. Developing L2 oral proficiency through synchronous CMC: Output, working memory and interlanguage development. *CALICO Journal* 20 (1): 7–32.

Pellettieri, J. 2000. Negotiation in cyberspace: The role of chatting in the development of grammatical competence. In *Network-based language teaching: Concepts and practice,* ed. M. Warschauer and R. Kern, 59–86. Cambridge: Cambridge University Press.

Rogers, D. M., and A. Wolff. 2000. El Español . . . ¡A distancia!: Developing a technology-based distance education course for intermediate Spanish. *Journal of General Education* 49 (1): 44–52.

Salaberry, R. 2000. Pedagogical design of computer mediated communication tasks: Learning objectives and technological capabilities. *Modern Language Journal* 84 (1): 28–37.

Simon, P. 1980. *The tongue-tied American: Confronting the foreign language crisis.* New York: Continuum.

Smith, Bryan. 2003. Computer-mediated negotiated interaction: An expanded model. *Modern Language Journal* 87 (1): 38–57.

Soo, K., and Y. Ngeow. 1998. Effective English as a second language (ESL) instruction with interactive multimedia: The MCALL project. *Journal of Educational Multimedia and Hypermedia* 7 (1): 71–89.

Sotillo, S. M. 2000. Discourse functions and syntactic complexity in synchronous and asynchronous communication. *Language Learning & Technology* 4 (1): 82–119.

Terrell, T. D., M. Andrade, J. Egasse, and M. Muñoz. 2002. *Dos mundos.* New York: McGraw-Hill.

Warschauer, M. 1996. Comparing face-to-face and electronic discussion in the second language classroom. *CALICO Journal* 13 (2): 7–26.

———. 1997. Computer-mediated collaborative learning: Theory and practice. *Modern Language Journal* 81 (4): 470–81.

Testing Spanish

Rafael Salaberry *University of Texas–Austin*
Andrew D. Cohen *University of Minnesota*

One of our major goals is to consider the design and administration of Spanish tests for students at U.S. universities in light of the social implications attached to any specific testing (and teaching) framework. A second goal is to substantiate the need for test administrators to engage in the type of reflective practice (Schön 1983) that will lead them to adapt and modify as needed currently available tests to make them more appropriate to accomplish their specific teaching/learning objectives.

Currently, numerous methods are being used for assessing language in Spanish courses, including

- traditional fill-in-the-blank grammar tests;
- *n*th word or rational-deletion cloze tasks;
- multiple-choice and open-ended reading comprehension questions on a seen or unseen text;
- listening comprehension checklists of various kinds;
- structured and open writing tasks, usually in response to a prompt;
- structured or improvised oral interviews.

All of the above testing activities, as well as others, are regularly used in Spanish courses taught in most universities in the United States. The fact that these methods of assessment are used rather routinely, however, does not necessarily mean that they are reliable (i.e., that their use would produce the same results each time) or valid (i.e., measuring what they purport to measure). In fact, it may be a challenge to obtain an accurate measure of language ability in the classroom. Yet the construction of reliable and valid assessment measures can have crucial relevance in supporting learners in their efforts to develop Spanish language skills. Hence, it behooves language teachers to enhance their knowledge of what assessing Spanish language ability can entail and to update their knowledge of ways to assess this ability.

1.0 Methods to Assess Classroom Learning

In this section we will briefly describe some selected theoretical aspects of language testing in classrooms, concentrating on the qualities of a test and the models of language competence that inform the field of language testing.

1.1 Assessing the Usefulness and Relevance of a Test

Just as assessment may benefit from the use of multiple measures of language proficiency like the ones described in the previous section, so the worth of any assessment instrument depends on a combination of methodological factors. Bachman and Palmer (1996) have identified six qualities that they would argue will determine the value of a language testing instrument:

1. Reliability: the consistency of measurement

2. Construct validity: an indicator of the ability we want to measure

3. Authenticity: the correspondence between the characteristics of the test task and the features of the real task

4. Interactiveness: the interaction between the test taker—including language ability, topic knowledge, and the affective situation—and the task

5. Impact: on society and the individuals

6. Practicality: the demands of test specifications can be met with existing resources

Bachman and Palmer (1996) warn us that the evaluation of the usefulness of a test is essentially subjective, predicated on value judgments as well as specific goals and conditions for the test. For instance, they point out that for large-scale testing, reliability and validity are likely to be crucial, whereas for most types of classroom testing, authenticity, interactiveness, and impact are the likely factors to be most relevant (19). Therefore, national standardized tests should not necessarily be viewed as better or more appropriate than locally produced tests. Furthermore, we specifically highlight the importance of the impact of a test, a factor that is sometimes regarded as irrelevant to determine a test's ultimate overall usefulness.

Consistent with Bachman and Palmer's list of test qualities, Byram (1997) would remind us that "foreign language teaching is a social phenomenon which is in part determined by the nature of the particular context in which it takes place. . . . The context includes the educational institution and the societal and geo-political factors to which educational institutions and the education system as a whole must respond" (87). Needless to say, Spanish instruction in the United States cannot remain oblivious to the realities of Spanish use in the United States (see Gutiérrez and Fairclough, this volume).

1.2 Models of Communicative Ability

In what has become the seminal work on communicative ability, Canale and Swain (1980) and Canale (1983) offered a four-component model of communicative competence in a second language: (1) grammatical competence (morphology, syntax, lexicon, phonology), (2) sociolinguistic competence (appropriate use of language), (3) discourse competence (cohesion and coherence), and (4) strategic competence (verbal and nonverbal coping mechanism used when communication breaks down). The model served to make certain distinctions that until that point had remained somewhat blurred. For example, they grouped those matters of discourse relating to cohesion (i.e., textual elements that link elements of the text) and coherence (i.e., the comprehensibility of the text) within their own separate category, whereas prior to this they may have been subsumed within, say, grammar or perhaps even sociolinguistics. In addition, they added a category for strategic ability—perhaps the first official recognition in applied linguistics that strategic ability is not a given but appears to a greater or lesser degree, depending on the learner.

Some years later, Bachman (1990) provided his revised model of communicative ability in which he combined under organizational competence the grammatical and the discourse or textual aspects that Canale and Swain had separated. He also grouped under the category *pragmatic competence* both sociolinguistic ability and a new component he referred to as *illocutionary competence.* The latter was defined as the ability to understand and express a wide range of language functions, including but not limited to speech acts (e.g., promising, apologizing), ideational, and heuristic functions. He also included in his model strategic competence, though he left it outside of the scope of language ability per se (although it is still assumed to have an effect on language performance). In addition, he gave it a more rigorous subgrouping into strategies for assessing, planning, and executing language tasks (see Johnson 2001 for an in-depth analysis of these models).

A coauthor of this chapter further distinguished sociolinguistic ability into both sociocultural ability and sociolinguistic ability (Cohen 1994). *Sociocultural ability* refers to knowledge about (1) whether the speech act can be performed at all, (2) whether the speech act is relevant in the situation, and (3) whether the correct amount of information has been conveyed. *Sociolinguistic ability,* in contrast, refers to whether the linguistic forms (words, phrases, and sentences) used to express the intent of the speech act are acceptable in that situation (e.g., intensifying an apology for hurting someone physically with "really" to indicate regret, rather than with "very," which may be more an indication of etiquette). Thomas (1995) also saw the need for a distinction of sociolinguistic ability into two categories, though she referred to them as *sociopragmatic* and *pragmalinguistic ability,* respectively. As is true with many dichotomies, this one has been criticized by Beebe and Waring (2001) for being too simplistic a distinction and one that is difficult to validate empirically. Still there is some conceptual salience in the sociopragmatic versus pragmalinguistic distinction, and so it continues to enjoy relative popularity in the field of L2 pragmatics and assessment of interlanguage pragmatic ability (see Roever 2004).

More recently, the early models have been revisited. He and Young (1998, 3), for example, contend that Bachman's model "is largely a psychological model that neglects the social, dialogic dimension of cognition and emotion—that is to say, cognition and emotion are not located in the mind of a single individual, but are instead embedded in distributed systems and are shaped and accomplished interactionally." They also assert that "we must now add competence in (at least) the five interactional features: Knowledge of rhetorical scripts, contextually-relevant lexicon and syntax, strategies for managing turns, management of conversation topics and the means to signal boundaries in a conversation" (He and Young 1998, 6–7). Furthering the argument about the role of interactional competence, Chalhoub-Deville (2003, 372) proposes that "ability, language users, and context are inextricably meshed." She goes on to add, "It is likely that the interplay between the more and less stable ability features is what researchers need to account for to explain situated language use" (Chalhoub-Deville 2003, 377). A brief introduction to models of communicative competence is found in McNamara (2000, chap. 2), and a more substantive coverage is provided in Johnson (2001, chap. 8).

2.0 Types of Tests

In this section we will critically analyze some concrete methodological issues that have relevance to classroom testing, namely, the distinction between discrete-item and integrative testing, the use of tasks as tests, the validity of real-life tests and semi-direct tests, and the use of complementary measures to assess L2 ability.

2.1 Discrete-item and Integrative Tests

Discrete-item tests focus on the testing of specific (discrete) aspects of language. For instance, a passage with blank spaces to be filled in with past tense forms of verbs provided in their infinitive form in parenthesis is an example of a discrete-item test of grammar. The main advantage of this type of test is that it can be easily designed, scored, and graded. In contrast, an integrative test of past tense use may be represented in the form of a personal narrative about some adventurous situation the test taker may have experienced in the past. It is clear that the latter type of test may have some advantages over the discrete-item test. For one thing, it may appear to the test takers to have a higher level of face validity—that is, to seem like a more realistic measure of language than the discrete-point focus-on-form approach. Second, an integrative test, by definition, brings several aspects of language competence together. Here are a few examples of more integrative testing formats:

Cloze
- A text with every *n*th (e.g., 7th word) deleted or with words deleted on some rational basis (e.g., key function words or major content words).
- Reverse-cloze, where students decide which words have been added to a text.
- A C-test, where the second half of every second word is deleted.

Dictation
- A traditional written dictation, delivered at a slow pace.
- A *dictogloss* where the passage is read at the pace of natural speech. Students take note as they listen and then they are given the chance to fill in missing information.
- Oral repetition, where students repeat or reproduce orally what they have heard.

Summary
- Students need to identify the main ideas while reading a text and then organize these into a coherent summary of the text.

In an effort to avoid being simplistic in making this distinction between discrete-point and integrative measures, we need to point out that some rational-deletion cloze tests are discrete-point in actuality. When we have interviewed learners about how they have answered cloze tests (Cohen 1984), we have found that they may well have treated sections of such tests as local, focus-on-form exercises rather than as exercises in more integrated language processing. Likewise, it is possible to give a dictation where the focus is just on, say, students' ability to use the appropriate tenses of the verb. Then it would be an integrative task in principle but used in a more discrete-point manner.

2.2 Using Tasks as Tests

The notion of using a series of tasks to serve as a test has been around for many years, though it has looked more like a classroom project than a test per se (e.g., Swain 1984; Brill 1986). More recently, Hughes (2003) describes another example of a series of writing tasks on the same topic that can be assigned to elicit many representative samples of the test taker's writing ability. In his test, Hughes proposes the use of four writing tasks centered around the theme of work at a summer camp for children:

1. Having learners write a letter to inquire about a position at a summer camp (the period of employment, accommodations, the pay, and the like)

2. Having them fill out an application form

3. Having them send a postcard to a friend telling him or her where they are, why they are there, and two things they like about the summer camp

4. Writing a note to their friends to apologize for not being able to meet them and to suggest a different day to go out

As the reader can see, all of the examples described above are written tests. It is obvious that a written test represents a more efficient way of collecting performance data from students. The same tests, however, can be easily transformed into oral tasks should teachers desire to do so.

In recent years, task-based instruction has gained considerable prominence. Consistent with this trend, Norris (2002, 343) would argue that task-based assessment has a key role in the classroom as a type of performance test in that it

- serves to determine whether a test taker "can use the target language to engage in and accomplish a given task" (e.g., an exchange student convinces his or her host family to let him or her travel to a nearby city and stay overnight on his or her own);
- focuses on "complex tasks and the criteria by which they are judged beyond the instructional setting" (expressing embarrassment after spilling coffee over another customer at a local coffee shop—this task requires much more than simply linguistic information to be accomplished successfully);
- can be "based on criteria specific to a given genre, setting or audience" (e.g., asking a friend's mom for more food while having dinner at his or her house as opposed to making the same request from our friend while having dinner alone with him or her.

A performance assessment instrument is defined by the following three characteristics: (1) examinees must perform a task, (2) the task should be as authentic as possible, and (3) success or failure is based on the outcome of the task (Norris et al. 2002). We note that these features of task-based tests are also features of task-based instruction in general. Willis (1996), for instance, outlines the various stages of task-based instruction. Lest we embrace task-based assessment too quickly, Bachman (2002) would offer several caveats. He warns that there are two serious challenges in the design of tasks: (1) precisely how "real-life" task types are identified, selected, and categorized, and (2) how we actually go about linking pedagogic or assessment tasks to these task types. His concern is that vagueness in task specification inevitably leads to vagueness in measurement.

2.3 Real-life Tests

The Oral Proficiency Interview (OPI), a performance test originally developed by the Foreign Service Institute (FSI) and later adapted by the American Council for the Teaching of Foreign Languages (ACTFL), uses the criteria in the ACTFL guidelines (1986, 1999) to assess mostly speaking proficiency. Most important, second language performance tests, such as the ACTFL-OPI test, have been portrayed as authentic real-life direct tests of second language ability. Barnwell (1996, 151), however, warns us about the "test makers' traditional hubris: the fallacy that a test always measures what its designers say it measures" (see also Lantolf and Frawley 1988, for the same critique). With regard to its authenticity in particular, there are important objections to the claim that the ACTFL-OPI measures real-life oral conversation (e.g., Johnson 2001; van Lier 1989). For instance, Johnson argues that "the OPI lacks both the empirical evidence and theoretical rationales to justify the claim about the conversational nature of its interaction" (143). Furthermore, there are concerns about the validity of the ACTFL-OPI test. In fact, even proponents of the OPI, such as Dandonoli and Henning (1990, 11), acknowledge that "the most significant" criticism against the use of the ACTFL-OPI is that there is no study that supports the validity of such a testing procedure.[1] Finally, it appears that the ACTFL-OPI makes use of an outdated concept of validity to justify its claims. For instance, Messick's (1994) reconceptualization of validity, specifically incorporated into Bachman's (1990) model of second language assessment, has not become part of the theoretical framework of the revised version of the ACTFL tester training manual, published in 1999 (cf. Johnson 2001; Salaberry 2000a).

2.4 Semidirect Tests

Semidirect tests simulate an oral interview through prerecorded questions that the respondent is to answer in a recorded session. The Simulated Oral Proficiency Interview (SOPI) is the best known of such measures (see Malone 2000). The SOPI follows the general structure of the OPI, but it relies on audiotaped instructions and a test booklet to elicit language from the examinee. The SOPI makes an effort to contextualize tasks so that they appear as authentic as possible. The prototypical SOPI follows the same four phases as the OPI: warm-up, level checks, probes, and wind-down. The warm-up phase, designed to ease examinees into the test format, begins with background questions, then level checks and probe phases follow, assessing the examinee's ability to perform different functions at the ACTFL's Intermediate, Advanced, and Superior levels. The prototypical SOPI includes picture-based tasks that allow examinees to perform activities such as asking questions, giving directions based on a simple map, describing a place, or narrating a sequence of events based on the illustrations provided.

The Center for Advanced Research on Language Acquisition (CARLA) at the University of Minnesota has developed a tape-mediated instrument for assessing speaking, the Contextualized Speaking Assessment (CoSA), requiring students to listen to a master cassette. The test can also be administered to large groups in a language lab or large room. After listening to the instructions, a sample response, and a description of the overall theme for the test, the test takers are presented with situations and topics for their responses. All instructions are provided in English. (See www.carla.umn.edu/assessment/MLPA/CoSA.html for more on the CoSA.)

2.4.1 Do Direct and Indirect Tests Measure the Same Construct?

Stansfield and Kenyon (1992) report correlations of .89 and .95 between the OPI and the SOPI in various languages. Considering the substantive criticism against the conversational nature of the face-to-face OPI (e.g., van Lier 1989), such high correlations may exist because neither test allows candidates to demonstrate interactive skills. Despite the findings from Stansfield and Kenyon, however, Shohamy (1994) argues that the functions and discourse features elicited in the face-to-face OPI and the tape-mediated SOPI are not necessarily the same. Along the same lines, Chalhoub-Deville's (2001) analysis of data from the OPI, the University of Minnesota's CoSA, and the San Diego State's Video/Oral Communication Instrument (VOCI) revealed that each test seemed to be tapping different language abilities. With respect to the testing of Spanish in particular, Koike's (1998) empirical study revealed differences between the OPI and the SOPI, especially with regards to the effect of the live interlocutor (e.g., more turns, more use of English).

2.4.2 Advantages of Semidirect Tests

There are various factors that can make a semidirect format attractive and help explain why it has been used widely in China and elsewhere in the world. For one thing, it allows for a uniformity of elicitation procedures, which helps to promote reliability. In addition, it is economical to administer, since there is no need to hire test administrators to interact with each respondent. Furthermore, it eliminates the interview effect which can play a role in oral interviews. Brown (2003, 3), for instance, argues that interviewers may influence the outcome of an interview by means of factors such as their level of rapport with the test takers, their choice of topics and functions, their phrasing of questions and prompts, and the extent to which they accommodate to the test taker's abilities. The dilemma is that differences in interviewer reactions to various test takers are actually supportive of the nonscripted natural variation we normally find in most conversations, where a change in interlocutor will often naturally lead to changes in the type of interaction. Brown (2003, 20), nevertheless, claims that such changes in interviewer behavior may turn out to be relevant for the construct of language proficiency.

To help underscore the inconsistency across interviewers, Brown (2004) conducted a study that demonstrated how two different interviewers could rate the same nonnative English speaker differently. Through close conversational analysis of the two interviews, she demonstrated how oral assessment instruments can be dramatically different from ordinary conversation and how the individual interviewer conducts the session can sway the subsequent ratings made by outside raters. In our view, for the sake of economy, the semidirect approach is the only feasible alternative for classroom Spanish teachers with limited resources who wish to obtain a measure of speaking from all students. An alternative mixed format would be to have students interacting with each other with prompts from a computer or a tape. As Hughes (2003, 121) points out, "An advantage of having candidates interacting with each other is that it should elicit language that is appropriate to exchanges between equals." This mixed format, although in principle potentially as valid as any one of the other test formats, has not been sufficiently researched, nor have teachers used it often enough yet in order to have substantive information on its usefulness.

2.5 Complementary Measures to Assess Second Language Ability

Regardless of efforts made to ensure that a given measure is a true estimate of a learner's ability in that area, there are bound to be method effects. These effects result from differences in discourse tasks (e.g., reporting vs. interviewing), elicitation methods (e.g., personal vs. machine, direct vs. indirect), genres (e.g., narrative vs. expository texts), item types (e.g., multiple-choice vs. open-ended tests), and even test consequences (e.g., declared vs. undeclared purposes of tests) (Shohamy 1997). To address the limitations of a single testing instrument, several researchers have promoted the use of a battery of alternative assessment instruments in complementary ways (e.g., Liskin-Gasparro 1996; Lynch 1997). Spolsky (1997, 246) expresses it best when he states, "What we are starting to do, I am pleased to see, is accept . . . the inevitable uncertainty, and turn our attention to the way tests are used, insisting on multiple testing and alternative methods, and realizing that the results need cautious and careful interpretation."

An early effort at demonstrating how a multiple-measure instrument can improve on measurement was that described by Shohamy, Reves, and Bejarano (1986). They report on the construction of an oral proficiency test to replace the existing English as a Foreign Language (EFL) Oral Matriculation Test administered by the Ministry of Education in Israel. The results showed that the experimental test had better linguistic, educational, and testing qualities than the existing Oral Matriculation Test; namely, it produced a better distribution of scores, showed reasonable rater reliability, tested a broader range of speech styles, and produced favorable attitudes on the part of the test takers. A somewhat scaled-down variety of this multimeasure test is still being used in Israel a decade later.

Thus language assessment can involve various types of measures, from the more traditional formats to the more innovative ones, such as the following (adapted and expanded from Liskin-Gasparro 1996):

- Portfolios (sample materials plus reflective assessment/longitudinal)
- OPIs and SOPIs (face-to-face or tape-mediated interviews as described above)
- Mixed OPI and SOPI (students interact with each other and the tape)
- Computer adaptive testing (competency level modified as responses are entered)
- Tasks (news broadcast program, writing letters, preparing websites)
- Self-assessment (usually guided with specified criteria)
- Collaborative assessment (both teachers' and students' opinions)
- Learning logs (students quantitatively evaluate their own progress)
- Journals (students qualitatively evaluate their own progress)

3.0 Testing Effects on the Spanish Curriculum

In this section we analyze the relationship between testing objectives and program/course objectives. For that purpose we will identify and describe the pedagogical role of tests and, in particular, the washback effect of tests on teaching.

3.1 Testing Objectives

Tests are usually defined according to specific objectives such as achievement versus proficiency tests, formative versus summative tests, or process- versus product-oriented tests. Achievement tests focus on measuring whatever topics and components of language abilities were taught in a given course, whereas proficiency tests measure language abilities independently of the process of acquiring such language competence (Shohamy 1992). Achievement tests would be expected to restrict themselves to that material which is specified by course objectives, whether it be focused more broadly on communicative language abilities or more narrowly on grammatical functions. The challenge, however, is to clearly identify such program objectives.

For instance, assessing the achievement of the objective of "successfully paying a compliment in Spanish" may be easier said than done. For one thing, there are several dimensions to be taken into account to measure the successful accomplishment of complimenting. Notice that not only is verbal information relevant for meeting this objective but also paralinguistic (e.g., intonation) and physical cues (e.g., face gestures, hand movements). Second, as with any other speech act, there are various complex social cues that need to be taken into account to successfully compliment someone in Spanish (e.g., the relative status and relationship of the interlocutors, the setting, and the expected responses to compliments in that society.). Finally, we note that it is not easy to developmentally grade levels of complimenting. For instance, if a learner is not successful at complimenting someone else, should we conclude that this learner conveyed a less intense sense of the compliment? The problem with this approach is that it is not easy to measure what these different degrees of complimenting mean or how they should be measured. In other words, can complimenting be graded? Or should we consider it a dichotomous category? In sum, the dichotomy between achievement and proficiency assessment is not a clear-cut distinction since the same test items and tasks could be assessing both. The only factor that might make a task involving complimenting an achievement item rather than a general proficiency one would be a very narrow definition and specification of what the teacher had specifically taught in class to compliment others.

There are other distinctions of note as well, such as that between formative assessment, aimed at getting an ongoing picture of performance, and summative assessment, which is intended to assess learner achievement and program effectiveness after a determined period of time, such as a unit of instruction, a semester, an academic year, and so on. Associated with formative versus summative assessment is the distinction between assessing the process whereby learners perform a task and the product obtained. So assessment could, for example, look only at a finished written composition or measure incremental gain through a series of drafts (as would be the case with a writing portfolio). Additionally, tests may be created for placement purposes, including the awarding of advanced credit. For instance, several commercial tests in Spanish are geared toward this goal: College Board's CLEP (College Level Examination Program), SAT II, and the Educational Testing Service's Spanish AP (Advanced Placement) test.

It also is possible to gather information about the strategies that the learners use and evaluate their selection of strategies in the processing stage of the task (independent of how successful they are with the product) (see Cohen 1998a; in press). A final distinction is between internal assessment, aimed at giving feedback to the classroom teacher, participating students, and perhaps the parents, versus external assessment, which is meant to inform the school district, the language program, an association such as ACTFL, and even the federal government (e.g., the National Assessment of Educational Progress has recently generated a test of Spanish for administration nationwide in the United States).

3.2 Washback Effect

Whereas Bachman and Palmer propose six qualities to account for the usefulness of a test, Hughes (2003) would limit the list of qualities to four: validity, reliability, practicality, and a new category not explicitly mentioned by Bachman and Palmer: "beneficial washback." *Washback* refers to the impact of the language assessment measures on the teaching syllabus, the course materials, and the classroom management (Taylor 2004). Washback can be beneficial, as in the case where changing or instituting language measures leads to beneficial changes in teaching and curriculum. Washback can also refer to negative effects, such as when the testing program fails to recognize course goals and learning objectives to which the test is supposed to relate (Cheng and Curtis 2004). Taylor (2004, 143) points out that the impact is now often used to describe the washback or consequences that a test may have not just at the micro, or local, educational level, but also its impact at a macro, or societal, level. Both the local and macro influence contribute to the consequential validity of the test.

The link between curriculum and assessment of the objectives pursued in a curriculum needs to be bidirectional. That is, changes in the curriculum should have a beneficial impact on testing content and on criteria as well. Consider, for instance, how notions and goals of cross-cultural awareness are routinely mentioned in Spanish L2 program objectives. Barnwell (1996, 185), for instance, points out, "It is not uncommon to hear language teaching justified in terms of rather tenuous notions of opening students' minds to other cultures, imparting a more sophisticated awareness of the nature of human language itself." The concern is for whether such lofty goals are actually implemented in course objectives and syllabi and, more important, whether they are carried out in actual classroom practices.

4.0 Testing Pragmatics and Cultural Knowledge

In this section we analyze in detail two aspects of Spanish L2 competence (pragmatics and culture) that tend to be neglected in the explicit testing of the target language.

4.1 Can We Test for Knowledge of Spanish Pragmatics?

An important component of communicative language competence that is frequently glossed over in the testing of Spanish is that of pragmatics and, more specifically, speech acts (e.g., apologizing, requesting, complimenting, and complaining). Pragmatics focuses on the functional use of language within a social, cognitive, and cultural context (see Koike, Pearson, and Witten 2003). The relevance of teaching and testing pragmatic knowledge cannot be overemphasized, given the importance of pragmatic abilities for communicating successfully in the second language and the daunting challenges facing learners in attempting to be pragmatically appropriate.

Numerous research studies have documented the role of pragmatics. Let us take, for example, a study that compared the linguistic expression of Spanish and English speakers in their own native language in six specific situations that prompted various speech acts such as requests and apologies (Fulcher and Márquez Reiter 2003, 335). In the first situation the participants had to borrow a book from a professor. The following were typical ways in which English and Spanish native speakers phrased their requests in their native language:

1a. I was just wondering if you have the book and if I could borrow it?
1b. *¿Me puedes prestar el libro?* 'Can you lend me the book?'

Fulcher and Márquez Reiter concluded that "English speakers used more conditional or embedded conditional sentences than the Spanish speakers. They also used softening devices and provided reasons for making a request." Needless to say, full proficiency in Spanish would imply knowledge about how to express specific speech acts in ways that are nativelike. Yet nonnative speakers of a language may take years to master these speech functions, if at all. And in fairness to students, instructional programs usually do not provide adequate instruction in this area (see Cohen and Ishihara 2005).

Notice that important differences in pragmatic information may exist even in cases where the surface utterances are almost direct equivalents of each other across the languages. For instance, Koike, Pearson, and Witten (2003) describe how the direct translation of a suggestion in Spanish to English can be misleading at best or confrontational at worst. Spanish suggestions expressed in the negative form acquire a much stronger connotation in English:

2a. *¿No has pensado en leer este libro?*
2b. Haven't you thought about reading this book?

It is open to question whether Spanish learners can actually offer suggestions with this particular phrasing of the question in the negative form.[2]

Ironically, the type of test that the teaching profession was hoping would help assess language abilities beyond grammar or vocabulary, the real-life performance test exemplified in the ACTFL-OPI, failed to deliver on its promise. For instance, Raffaldini (1988) pointed out that the ACTFL-OPI evaluated numerous aspects of grammatical competence and certain aspects of discourse competence, such as grammatical and lexical features in cohesive discourse. But the OPI, she argued, did not properly or thoroughly evaluate sociocultural and sociolinguistic abilities. Raffaldini proposed that one particular component of the traditional OPI, the role play, be used more extensively and across all levels of proficiency to address this serious shortcoming of a test of overall communicative language ability.

Raffaldini's Oral Situation Test was intended to assess more areas of language proficiency in a wider range of language-use situations than the ACTFL/ETS Oral Proficiency Interview. It was aimed at college-level study-abroad students to France and added something that other measures were not assessing, namely, tone (e.g., courteous, regretful, persuasive). The following are two examples from the test:

Tone: persuasive; *Stimulus:* You will be leaving France in a few weeks and all the students in the program would like to get together for a final party. The only place big enough is the house where you are living. You ask the parents if you can have the party there. You say:

Tone: annoyed; *Stimulus:* The parents of the family with whom you are living have gone away for the day and left you in charge of their little boy. He went out to play and disappeared for quite a while. You went out looking for him but couldn't find him. When he finally returns you are upset at what he has done and tell him not to do it again. You say:

The rating scales for the oral test were comprehensive, including ratings for discourse competence, sociolinguistic competence, and linguistic competence. It would appear that the call to assess pragmatic tone fell largely on deaf ears because now, many years later, Beebe and Waring (2002, 2004a, 2004b) are once again raising the issue since tone has continued to be neglected in measurement.

Along the same lines, Cohen (2004) has offered a basic framework for the teaching and testing of speech acts:

1. Keep the speech act situations realistic for the students and engaging.

2. Check for the sociocultural (= sociopragmatic) appropriateness of the strategies in the given situation and the appropriateness of the sociolinguistic (= pragmalinguistic) forms used with regard to level of formality, degree of politeness, and amount of language used.

3. Have a discussion afterward with the students as to whether the setting was clear and as to the factors that most contributed to the students' responses.

4. Use verbal reports to help in reconstructing why the students responded as they did.

Cohen (2004, 320–21) described how learners could be asked to reconstruct retrospectively (while viewing their own videotaped speech act performance) the processes that they went through while responding to prompts that required the use of specific speech acts, and to describe the strategies that they selected in performing the given speech acts. García (1996, 2001) has specifically adapted some of Cohen and Olshtain's (1993) recommendations for the teaching of Spanish speech acts. In her earlier publication she described how results from sociolinguistic research studying a group of Spanish speakers declining an invitation, along with models from several researchers, led to the design of listening and speaking activities for developing students' ability to communicate and their avoidance of cross-cultural miscommunication (García 1996).

4.2 Can We Test Cultural Knowledge in Spanish?

An even more elusive target than the testing of pragmatically appropriate uses of Spanish language is the testing of cultural knowledge. As argued by Byram (1997), second language speakers are attempting to attain several goals at once when they engage in a sociocultural analysis of the uses of the second language:

- To be pragmatic, by attempting to communicate appropriately with native speakers of the target language community
- To be critical, by trying to understand others
- To be hermeneutic, by getting to understand oneself in the process

But is it possible to teach and test culture and in so doing to assess the degree of critical thinking brought about by second language learning?

Moore (1994, 164) argues that "testing culture has traditionally measured the knowledge of bits and pieces of information, rather than insights and awareness of the essence of a culture or society." In fact, in a review of various proficiency rating scales, North (2000, 95) concludes that "inter-cultural skills are an aspect of Socio-cultural Competence not found in any of the scales analyzed." Echoing the opinions held by Moore and North, Storme and Derakhshani (2002, 663) stated that "the profession has only begun to give serious thought to developing the requisite measures to cultural proficiency." Arguably, at least part of the blame for the lack of adequate focus of classroom and curricular practices on the development of cultural competence—beyond the trivial and superficial facts—can be associated with testing practices and logistical concerns. Byram (1997, 111), for one, recognizes the difficulties in assessing the overall range of complex competences that make up intercultural communicative competence: "It is the simplification of competences to what can be 'objectively' tested which has a detrimental effect: the learning of trivial facts, the reduction of subtle understanding to generalizations and stereotypes, the lack of attention to interaction and engagement because these are not tested."

Identifying the intercultural skills that should be taught and implementing appropriate assessment measures that would hopefully have a beneficial washback effect on the curriculum may be a challenging task. In order to understand the true nature of this challenge, let us define in more detail the actual objective of teaching and testing culture. For one thing, we need to remember that learning a second language cannot be simplistically reduced to becoming a monolingual speaker of that language because, in fact, learners add a second language to the first (not to mention the fact that a second language could also have effects on the first one). With regard to culture in particular, North (2000, 95) argues, "The curriculum aim of 'intercultural skills' is to create '150% persons' who understand (empathy), find value, and have positive sentiments towards (favorableness) both cultures."

Second, the assessment of intercultural skills is multifaceted. For instance, the National Standards in Foreign Language Education Project (1996, 439) established that learners "must be able to participate appropriately in a range of social relationships and in a variety of contexts." It posits further that the "capacity to communicate requires not only an awareness of the linguistic code to be used, but also an understanding of the cultural context within which meaning is encoded and decoded." Third, there are no right or wrong answers when it comes to the testing of culture, and although this same point can in principle be made about other aspects of a second language (such as morphology or syntax), it is clear that such variability is most noticeable when it is predicated on the assessment of cultural knowledge. With regard to the testing of intercultural pragmatic ability (which clearly involves the intricate interweaving of language and culture), coauthor Cohen (2004, 322) explains that "sociocultural and sociolinguistic behavior are by their very nature variable. Thus, there will be few 'right' and 'wrong' answers in comparing L2 to L1 responses, but rather tendencies in one direction or another." Therefore, he concludes that "the variable nature of speech act behavior has made tested outcomes less reliable and valid than those for more circumscribed language performance and helps explain why such measures do not abound in the field."

There are, nevertheless, proposed solutions to the problem of testing cultural knowledge. Byram (1997, 103), for instance, argues that for the assessment of intercultural competence, language testers need to take into account metacognitive capacities for self-analysis, proposing that "neither the testing of knowledge nor the evaluation of observable performance are sufficient. It is in the self-analytical and often retrospective accounts by a learner of their interaction, their *savoir faire* and *savoir s'engager,* that the main evidence will be found." Storme and Derakhshani (2002, 663), however, conclude that some of Byram's recommendations for the testing of intercultural knowledge may not be appropriate or practical for a second language classroom. They, in turn, suggest that the program of action outlined in the National Standards project may be more suitable for the teaching and testing of cultural knowledge.

5.0 Spanish Developmental Sequences and Testing

We turn now to the discussion of the benefits of taking into account potential developmental sequences in the acquisition of Spanish in an effort to make language testing procedures more congruent with learning processes.

5.1 What Do We Know about Developmental Sequences in Spanish?

North (2000, 13) suggests that scales of proficiency "have the potential to exert a positive influence on the orientation, organization and reporting of language learning." North sees the potential for scales in that they provide learners with

1. explicit goals and descriptions of them,

2. coherent internal links for curriculum development and testing,

3. behavioral evidence of progress,

4. a means for increasing the reliability of subjective ratings, and

5. a common metric for comparisons among different populations of learners.

North acknowledges, however, that scales of proficiency have serious limitations if they do not conform to actual developmental stages of acquisition (see Brindley 1988, for an extensive discussion). The problem is that we still know very little about developmental sequences in language acquisition in Spanish as the chapters in Lafford and Salaberry (2003) show.

Such paucity of clear research findings about stages of acquisition should make us wary of blindly following traditional and almost categorical sequences of acquisition typically espoused by publisher's textbooks. For instance, there are well-attested developmental patterns and developmental processes in the acquisition of Spanish past tense morphology in both classroom and naturalistic environments (Andersen 1986; Salaberry and Ayoun 2005; Salaberry 2000b; Schell 2000; Shirai 2004). Learners in classroom environments are clearly focused on the acquisition of morphological markers of Spanish tense aspect. Furthermore, there appears to be a tendency to use some default markers of past tense during beginning stages of development, gradually incorporating a past tense marking system that is shaped by frequency-based distributional tendencies, and eventually using more sophisticated notions of viewpoint aspect marked by discursive grounding (e.g., García and vanPutte 1988). This is one of the areas of L2 development more akin to Pienemann's (1988) agenda of profiling L2 development, and an area where testing procedures could match developmental stages of acquisition that are now becoming better known to researchers. Other components that make up any one of the models of L2 competence reviewed above are also subject to similar analyses of developmental stages of acquisition. For a more in-depth analysis, the chapters in Lafford and Salaberry focus on developmental trends in the acquisition of pragmatics, pronunciation, the subjunctive, object pronouns, tense and aspect, and vocabulary.

5.2 Developmental Nature of Institutionalized Rating Criteria

We now turn to the analysis of developmental criteria used in one specific test of Spanish as a second language. The ACTFL guidelines constitute a widely recognized standardized criteria used to measure second language proficiency in U.S. universities. The guidelines, although successful in bringing the attention of teachers to the use of standards in language assessment, are nevertheless problematic with respect to developmental criteria. Arguably, the more troublesome aspect of the guidelines is the notion of an implicit degree of complexity (linguistic or cognitive) assigned to particular registers, discourse genres, or topics of discussion. Our discussion will lead us to the conclusion that Spanish teachers should view such a set of scales with caution.

The ACTFL guidelines assign particular language abilities to specific stages of development (or levels of proficiency): "Each major level subsumes the criteria for the levels below it" (ACTFL 1986, 2–5). For instance, the guidelines propose that only Superior level speakers are able to "explain and defend opinions and develop effective hypotheses," that not until the Advanced level can speakers "narrate and describe in major time frames with good control of aspect," and that not until Intermediate level can speakers "obtain and give information by asking and answering questions." Along the same lines, the ACTFL hierarchy proposes that the formal registers of the language are not managed successfully until learners are at the Superior level, and that speakers cannot control most informal and some formal registers until they are at the advanced level. More specifically, some informal registers are assumed to be controlled at the Intermediate level and only the most common informal settings are successfully controlled by novices. Similarly, only Superior level speakers are able to manage abstract and unfamiliar topics whereas concrete and factual topics are controlled at the Advanced level.

To the best of our knowledge, however, there is no empirical evidence that shows that classroom learners, for instance, will develop proficiency in informal registers of the language before they achieve such proficiency in formal registers—or, for that matter, that they will be able to discuss concrete and factual topics before they manage more abstract topics or from familiar to unfamiliar. For instance, it would not be out of the question to propose that formal registers of the language may actually be easier to learn for classroom learners for several reasons. For one thing, native English speakers learning Spanish have access to a lexicon based on both Germanic and Latin roots, the latter mostly represented in formal registers of English (compare "liberty" and "velocity" [Latin roots] with "freedom" and "speed" [Germanic roots]). Furthermore, the standard register of the language, the academic subjects of discussion, and academic discourse in general (not surprising given the university setting in which this type of instruction is embedded) are typically favored in classroom instruction (see, for example, a learner's testimonial in a diary study with regard to university-level Japanese instruction in Cohen 1997). More important, the more standard forms of vocabulary and syntax are typically preferred in classroom instruction in order to avoid dealing with any type of dialectal variation.

More important, proponents of ACTFL acknowledge this significant limitation about the hierarchical (developmental) distribution of communicative functions. For instance, Lowe (1985, 47) states, "In everyday life we tend to speak at Level 3, with forays into higher levels as required for technical topics." Thus one could argue that the levels may not be hierarchical but complementary, as they represent, according to the distinction made by Lowe, different registers of the language. Following this line of argumentation, one could reasonably expand Lowe's claim and argue for the complementarity of discourse genres, registers of the language, and other components of language competence, as opposed to assuming a hierarchy as proposed by the ACTFL scale. In practice this means that teachers can introduce learners to the linguistic features of several registers and genres of Spanish without concerns about the students not being developmentally ready to put such sociolinguistic information into use. In fact, it may even be more pedagogically sound (in keeping with the proposal of the National Standards) to explicitly point out to learners the linguistic and interactional contrasts that different genres and registers exhibit in Spanish.

Furthermore, the developmental hierarchy of skills and functions proposed for listening and reading tasks by the ACTFL guidelines has been questioned on both theoretical and empirical grounds. For instance, Phillips (1988, 138) concedes that the hierarchical skills or competencies described in the guidelines for reading may not be developmental after all. Lee and Musumeci's (1988) findings lend empirical justification to making the same argument against the hierarchical nature of the reading scale. Similarly, the developmental progression for listening abilities is also questioned by Valdés et al. (1988). In principle, the hierarchy of developmental stages proposed by the guidelines (1986, 1999) may represent a possible theoretical hypothesis.

In sum, despite their conspicuousness in the profession, the ACTFL criteria for testing Spanish in the classroom are not particularly helpful because they are nondevelopmental (see above), vague, and disregard the relevance of the learning context. The main problem with using scales such as the ACTFL guidelines for testing Spanish learning in the classroom is that "the progressions described . . . could appear to present a picture of universal patterns of second language development" (Brindley 1988, 133). At the same time, we do recognize that the ACTFL guidelines have become the only widely available set of language proficiency criteria. Thus in our opinion, a practical solution to this dilemma is to adapt the current rating criteria of proficiency (from ACTFL or other models) as necessary, as it is feasible to incorporate changes apparent in our current understanding of SLA.

6.0 Recommendations for Classroom Testing

Even though it is true that throughout the 1980s and 1990s language teachers were particularly concerned with standardized measurement of proficiency (Liskin-Gasparro

1996, 173), the day-to-day operation of a language program relies heavily on language tests developed by textbook publishers. Barnwell (1996, 188) explains that "in the foreign language classroom many, if not most, of the tests used come with the textbook that has been adapted [*sic*]. Hence, in one sense the most influential testers are those who write the test manuals for publishers and provide teachers with entire banks of tests and items to measure the progress and achievements of their students." Given the importance of tests developed by publishers, Barrette (2004, 68) suggests "putting pressure on publishing companies to provide testing programs . . . that are written by the text's authors to increase the level of comparability between the teaching and testing approaches, thereby providing a quality model for other tests developed by the textbook adopters." In the meantime, however, language teachers need to be aware of some practical procedures at their disposal to improve and expand the tests made available to them by publishers.

We believe that the following considerations regarding the design and writing of tests for the Spanish classroom will address some of the issues we raised in previous sections of this chapter and will hopefully provide a clear framework for the assessment of interactional communicative competence.

6.1 Giving Primary Importance to the Context of Learning

Classroom interactions will likely have a significant effect on the acquisition of the L2, not only in terms of content areas but also in terms of preferred language learning and language use strategies. For instance, students from various regions of the country not only relate more or less to different topics that may or may not be relevant locally but also bring with them specific predispositions toward learning languages related to academic specializations, social networks, and so on. As Chalhoub-Deville (2003, 377) points out, the "language user has a set of preferred abilities that are typically activated in contexts with particular features. The more familiar the language user is with these ability structures–contextual features, the more efficient and fluid learners become at activating them: combining and recombining knowledge structures as needed to engage in a given situation." She further notes that "variation is inevitable if we view ability within context as the construct" (Chalhoub-Deville 2003, 379). Johnson (2001) would underscore the importance of drawing on local rather than general models of language ability and use these for measuring sociocultural competence. For instance, regions where Spanish-English bilingualism is common may bring about specific dialectal features of Spanish that cannot be ignored from our model of language competence and ideally should be incorporated to it.

6.2 Identifying, Describing, and Operationalizing the Goals of Learning as Objectives

The use of any one of the communicative ability models briefly described in section 2 (or a modification of them) represents a good first step to determine the specifics of what a particular Spanish course is intended to achieve in terms of learning goals. For instance, programs which are intent on developing learners' awareness of the pragmatic, social and cultural aspects of the target language group cannot remain oblivious to the most recent changes in the definition of communicative ability, especially with regards to the notions of interactional competence, situated language use and overall pragmatic abilities. On the other hand, programs that for specific reasons prefer to maintain a focus on more traditional aspects of language learning such as the structure of the language should specifically and explicitly identify such goals as part of their objectives. In our view, the recent trend to operationalize almost any conceivable learning goal as a part of a program's objective is not only unrealistic but also detrimental to the achievement of the specific objectives that are indeed targeted by any program.

6.3 Testing the Course Objectives

We would concur with Hughes (2003, 13–14) in his recommendation that test content be based on course objectives (as opposed to course content) in that this "will provide more accurate information about individual and group achievement, and it is likely to promote a more beneficial backwash effect on teaching." In addition, we would recommend incorporating the testing of abilities/strategies/processes that will further develop the L2 outside of the classroom environment/after the course. For instance, conversational management techniques and awareness of register and dialectal differences could also be assessed.

6.4 Obtaining a Robust Sampling of the Course Objectives

Not only should course objectives be sampled, but those language interactions that take place regularly in classroom interactions should be included in testing tasks as well. This would assure better congruency between actual classroom language and what is measured on tests.

6.5 Writing Good Tests

Despite all good intentions, tests are not necessarily well written. Barrette (2004) has recently identified five areas in which a series of draft language achievement tests written by college-level instructors were lacking:

1. Criteria for correctness: Criteria for scoring writing sections were vague.

2. Weighting of the test components: There was a lack of correspondence in the weight assigned to the different components of the test with regard to the goals of the program (e.g., assigned points tended to favor the grammar component of the test).

3. Length of the input: Inconsistency in the length of both listening and reading passages, which, as Bachman (1990) noted, could heighten the potential effects of the other characteristics on performance.

4. Representation of the construct: The intended language component was under-represented—tests elicited only "the most common vocabulary items and the most regularized grammatical forms."

5. Extraneous factors: Ambiguous questions and overly demanding tasks created what would amount to error variance in the measures.

Among various recommendations for improving the writing of tests proposed by Barrette, we highlight the following:

- Reviewing test drafts both from the perspective of students and from that of scorers (see also Hughes 2003, 62–65)
- Making explicit and unambiguous the scoring criteria and the standards for correct target language use
- Making judicious judgments about what is taught in class and what is tested, especially with regard to the relative importance of different components of the test and the relative length of aural and written texts
- Engaging in networking (Barrette suggests sharing the burden of materials development by sharing test materials among institutions using the same textbooks or similar programs of study)
- Making ample use of verbal report as a means of validating the measures (verbal reports [see Cohen 1998b, chap. 3] may be useful to assess the effectiveness of testing materials and to determine whether the objectives of the testing program are actually met and which changes may be needed)

7.0 Conclusion

In closing, we summarize the major points that we have made in this chapter. We have argued for the importance of using a clear definition of teaching and testing objectives as exemplified by the many models of communicative competence. We have briefly described some of the most relevant formats of tests for classroom learning, and we have advocated reaching a balance between efficient and valid measures of language proficiency. Further, we have highlighted the symbiotic relationship that exists between teaching and testing and the implications of changing testing procedures without considering concomitant changes in teaching processes. We have advocated the expansion of the traditional objectives of language tests to explicitly incorporate central aspects of later communicative ability models such as culture and pragmatics, components that to date, in our opinion, have been vaguely incorporated into the assessment of language proficiency. In addition, we have assessed the consequences of the use of developmental criteria for the creation of proficiency scales and have warned readers about the potential liabilities in blindly following the criteria from models that may disregard the most recent findings from SLA research. Finally, we have outlined some practical recommendations for the actual design and implementation of classroom-based language tests.

Notes

1. We should note that although the study carried out by Dandonoli and Henning (1990) was claimed to be the first to quantitatively validate the OPI as a testing instrument, it appears to contain various significant methodological weaknesses pointed out by Fulcher (1996).

2. Even though Koike, Pearson, and Witten (2003) report that only a few learners thought the above Spanish question expressed a rebuke, their analysis was based on results from a listening comprehension task.

References

American Council on the Teaching of Foreign Languages (ACTFL). 1986. *ACTFL proficiency guidelines.* Hasting-on-Hudson, NY: ACTFL.

———. 1999. *ACTFL proficiency guidelines.* Hasting-on-Hudson, NY: ACTFL.

Andersen, R. 1986. El desarrollo de la morfología verbal en el español como segundo idioma. In *Adquisición del lenguaje—Acquisicição da linguagem,* ed. J. Meisel, 115–38. Frankfurt: Klaus-Dieter Vervuert Verlag.

Bachman, L. 1990. *Fundamental considerations in language testing.* Oxford: Oxford University Press.

———. 2002. Some reflections on task-based language performance assessment. *Language Testing* 19 (4): 453–76.

Bachman, L. F., and A. S. Palmer. 1996. *Language testing in practice: Designing and developing useful language tests.* Oxford: Oxford University Press.

Barnwell, D. 1996. *A history of foreign language testing in the United States: From its beginnings to the present.* Tempe, AZ: Bilingual Press.

Barrette, C. 2004. An analysis of foreign language achievement test drafts. *Foreign Language Annals* 37.1: 58–69.

Beebe, L. M., and H. Z. Waring. 2001. Sociopragmatic vs. pragmalinguistic failure: How useful is the distinction? Paper presented at the NYSTESOL Applied Linguistics Winter Conference. CUNY Graduate Center, February 3.

———. 2002. *The pragmatics in the interlanguage pragmatics research agenda: The case of tone.* Paper presented at the AAAL Colloquium titled "Revisioning Interlanguage Pragmatics Research." Salt Lake City, April 7.

———. 2004a. The linguistic encoding of pragmatic tone: Adverbials as words that work. In *Study speaking to inform second language learning,* ed. D. Boxer and A. D. Cohen, 228–52. Clevedon, U.K.: Multilingual Matters.

———. 2004b. Understanding the perception of tone: A cross-cultural study. Paper presented at the Annual Conference of the American Association for Applied Linguistics. Portland, OR, May 1–4.

Brill, H. 1986. *Developing a communicative test of reading comprehension and determining its effectiveness.* Seminar paper, School of Education, Hebrew University, Jerusalem (in Hebrew).

Brindley, G. 1988. Describing language development? Rating scales and SLA. In *Interfaces between second language acquisition and language testing research,* ed. L. Bachman and A. D. Cohen, 112–40. New York: Cambridge University Press.

Brown, A. 2003. Interviewer variation and the co-construction of speaking proficiency. *Language Testing* 20 (1): 1–25.

———. 2004. Discourse analysis and the oral interview: Competence or performance? In *Studying speaking to inform second language learning,* ed. D. Boxer and A. D. Cohen, 253–82. Clevedon, U.K: Multilingual Matters.

Byram, M. 1997. *Teaching and assessing intercultural communicative competence.* Clevedon, U.K.: Multilingual Matters.

Canale, M. 1983. On some dimensions of language proficiency. In *Issues in language testing research,* ed. J. W. Oller Jr., 333–42. Rowley, MA: Newbury House.

Canale, M., and M. Swain. 1980. Theoretical bases of communicative approaches to second language teaching and testing. *Applied Linguistics* 1 (1): 1–47.

Chalhoub-Deville, M. 2001. Task-based assessments: characteristics and validity evidence. In *Researching pedagogic tasks,* ed. M. Bygate, P. Skehan, and M. Swain, 210–28. Edinburgh: Longman.

———. 2003. Second language interaction: Current perspectives and future trends. *Language Testing* 20 (4): 369–83.

Cheng, L., and A. Curtis. 2004. Washback or backwash: A review of the impact of testing on teaching and learning. In *Washback in language testing: Research contexts and methods,* ed. L. Cheng and Y. Watanabe, 3–17. Mahwah, NJ: Lawrence Erlbaum Associates.

Cohen, A. D. 1984. On taking language tests: What the students report. *Language Testing* 1 (1): 70–81.

———. 1994. *Assessing language ability in the classroom.* 2nd ed. Boston: Newbury House/Heinle & Heinle.

———. 1997. Developing pragmatic ability: Insights from the accelerated study of Japanese. In *New trends and issues in teaching Japanese language and culture,* ed. H. M. Cook, K. Hijirida, and M. Tahara, 137–63. Technical Report 15. Honolulu: University of Hawai'i, Second Language Teaching and Curriculum Center.

———. 1998a. Strategies and processes in test taking and SLA. In *Interfaces between second language acquisition and language testing research,* ed. L. F. Bachman and A. D. Cohen, 90–111. Cambridge University Press.

———. 1998b. *Strategies in learning and using a second language.* Harlow, UK: Longman.

———. 2004. Assessing speech acts in a second language. In *Study speaking to inform second language learning,* ed. D. Boxer and A. D. Cohen, 302–27. Clevedon, U.K.: Multilingual Matters.

———. In press. The coming of age of research on test-taking strategies. In *Language testing reconsidered,* ed. J. Fox, M. Weshe, D. Bayliss, L. Cheng, C. Turner, and C. Doe. Ottawa: Ottawa University Press.

Cohen, A. D., and N. Ishihara. 2005. *A web-based approach to strategic learning of speech acts.* Report to the Center for Advanced Research on Language Acquisition (CARLA). www.carla.umn.edu/speechacts/Japanese%20Speech%20ACT%20Report%20Rev.%20June05.pdf (accessed September 12, 2006).

Cohen, A. D., and E. Olshtain. 1993. The production of speech acts by EFL learners. *TESOL Quarterly* 27 (1): 33–56.

Dandonoli, P., and G. Henning. 1990. An investigation of the construct validity of the ACTFL proficiency guidelines and oral interview procedure. *Foreign Language Annals* 23 (1): 11–22.

Fulcher, G. 1996. Invalidating validity claims for the ACTFL oral rating scale. *System* 24 (2): 163–72.

Fulcher, G., and R. Márquez Reiter. 2003. Task difficulty in speaking tests. *Language Testing* 20 (3): 321–44.

García, C. 1996. Teaching speech act performance: Declining an invitation. *Hispania* 79:267–79.

———. 2001. Perspectives in practices: Teaching culture through speech acts. In *Teaching cultures of the Hispanic world: Products and practices in perspective,* ed. V. Galloway, 95–112. Mason, OH: Thomson Learning.

García, E., and F. vanPutte. 1988. The value of contrast: Contrasting the value of strategies. *IRAL* 26:263–81.

He, A. W., and R. Young. 1998. Language proficiency interviews: A discourse approach. In *Talking and testing: Discourse approaches to the assessment of oral proficiency,* ed. R. Young and A. W. He, 1–24. Amsterdam: John Benjamins.

Hughes, A. 2003. *Testing for language teachers.* 2nd ed. Cambridge: Cambridge University Press.

Johnson, M. 2001. *The art of non-conversation*. New Haven: Yale University Press.

Koike, D. 1998. What happens when there's no one to talk to? Spanish foreign language discourse in oral proficiency interviews. In *Language proficiency interviews: A discourse approach,* ed. R. Young and A. He, 69–98. Amsterdam: John Benjamins.

Koike, D., Pearson, L., and C. Witten. 2003. Pragmatics and discourse analysis in Spanish second language acquisition research. In *Spanish second language acquisition: The state of the science,* ed. B. Lafford and R. Salaberry, 160–85. Washington, DC: Georgetown University Press.

Lafford, B., and R. Salaberry. 2003. *Studies in Spanish second language acquisition: State of the science.* Washington, DC: Georgetown University Press.

Lantolf, J., and W. Frawley. 1988. Proficiency: Understanding the construct. *Studies in Second Language Acquisition* 10 (2): 181–95.

Lee, J., and D. Musumeci. 1988. On hierarchies of reading skills and text types. *Modern Language Journal* 72 (2): 173–87.

Liskin-Gasparro, J. 1996. Assessment: From content standards to student performance. In *National standards: A catalyst for reform,* ed. R. Lafayette, 169–96. Lincolnwood, IL: National Textbook.

Lowe, P. 1985. The ILR scale as a synthesizing research principle: The view from the mountain. In *Foreign language proficiency,* ed. C. James, 9–53. Lincolnwood, IL: National Textbook.

Lynch, B. K. 1997. In search of the ethical test. *Language Testing* 14 (3): 315–27.

Malone, M. 2000. Simulated oral proficiency interviews: Recent developments. *Digest,* December, EDO-FL-00-14. Washington, DC: Center for Applied Linguistics. www.cal.org/resources/digest/0014simulated.html (accessed June 20, 2006).

McNamara, T. 2000. *Language testing.* Oxford: Oxford University Press.

Messick, S. 1994. The interplay of evidence and consequences in the validation of performance assessments. *Educational Researcher* 23 (2): 13–23.

Moore, Z. 1994. The portfolio and testing culture. In *Teaching, testing and assessment: Making the connection,* ed. C. Hancock and S. Brooks-Brown, 163–82. Lincolnwood, IL: National Textbook.

National Standards in Foreign Language Education Project. 1996. *Standards for foreign language learning: Preparing for the 21st century.* Yonkers, NY: ACTFL.

Norris, J. 2002. Interpretations, intended uses and designs in task-based language assessment. *Language Testing* 19 (4): 337–46.

Norris, J., J. Brown, T. Hudson, and W. Bonk. 2002. Examinee abilities and task difficulty in task-based second language performance assessment. *Language Testing* 19 (4): 395–418.

North, B. 2000. *The development of a common framework scale of language proficiency.* New York: Peter Lang.

Phillips, J. 1988. Interpretations and misinterpretations. In *Second language proficiency assessment,* ed. P. Lowe and C. Stansfield, 136–48. Englewood Cliffs, NJ: Prentice Hall.

Pienemann, M. 1988. Constructing an acquisition-based procedure for second language assessment. *Studies in Second Language Acquisition* 10 (2): 217–43.

Raffaldini, T. 1988. The use of situation tests as measures of communicative ability. *Studies in Second Language Acquisition* 10 (2): 197–216.

Roever, C. 2004. Difficulty and practicality in tests of interlanguage pragmatics. In *Studying speaking to inform second language learning,* ed. D. Boxer and A. D. Cohen, 283–301. Clevedon, U.K.: Multilingual Matters.

Salaberry, R. 2000a. Revising the revised format of the ACTFL Oral Proficiency Interview. *Language Testing* 17 (3): 289–310.

———. 2000b. *The Development of Past Tense Morphology in L2 Spanish.* Amsterdam: John Benjamins.

Salaberry, R., and D. Ayoun. 2005. The development of L2 tense–aspect in the Romance languages. In *Tense and aspect in Romance languages: Theoretical and applied perspectives*, ed. D. Ayoun and R. Salaberry, 1–33. Amsterdam: John Benjamins.

Schell, K. 2000. Functional categories and the acquisition of aspect in L2 Spanish: A longitudinal study. Ph.D. diss., University of Washington.

Schön, D. 1983. *The reflective practitioner: How professionals think in action.* New York: Basic Books.

Shirai, Y. 2004. A multiple-factor account for the form-meaning connections in the acquisition of tense–aspect morphology. In *Form-meaning connections in second language acquisition*, ed. J. Williams and B. VanPatten, S. Rott, and M. Overstreet, 91–112. Mahwah, NJ: Lawrence Erlbaum Associates.

Shohamy, E. 1992. Beyond proficiency testing: A diagnostic feedback testing model for assessing foreign language learning. *Modern Language Journal* 76 (4): 513–21.

———. 1994. The validity of direct versus semi-direct oral tests. *Language Testing* 11 (2): 99–123.

———. 1997. Testing methods, testing consequences: Are they ethical? Are they fair? *Language Testing* 14 (3): 340–49.

Shohamy, E., T. Reves, and Y. Bejarano. 1986. Introducing a new comprehensive test of oral proficiency. *ELT Journal* 40 (3): 212–20.

Spolsky, B. 1997. The ethics of gatekeeping tests: What have we learned in a hundred years? *Language Testing* 14 (3): 242–47.

Stansfield, C. W., and D. M. Kenyon. 1992. The development and validation of a simulated oral proficiency interview. *Modern Language Journal* 76 (2): 129–41.

Storme, J., and M. Derakhshani. 2002. Defining, teaching and evaluating cultural proficiency in the foreign language classroom. *Foreign Language Annals* 35 (6): 657–68.

Swain, M. 1984. Large-scale communicative language testing: A case study. In *Initiatives in communicative language teaching*, ed. S. J. Savignon and M. S. Berns, 185–201. Reading, MA: Addison-Wesley.

Taylor, L. B. 2004. Testing times: Research directions and issues for Cambridge ESOL Examinations. *TESOL Quarterly* 38 (1): 141–46.

Thomas, J. 1995. *Meaning in interaction.* London: Longman.

Valdés, G., M. P. Echeverriarza, E. Lessa, and C. Pino. 1988. The development of a listening skills comprehension-based program: What levels of proficiency can learners reach? *Modern Language Journal* 72 (4): 414–31.

van Lier, L. 1989. Reeling, writhing, drawling, stretching, and fainting in coils: Oral proficiency interviews as conversation. *TESOL Quarterly* 23 (3): 489–508.

Willis, J. 1996. *A framework for task-based learning.* Edinburgh: Longman.

Incorporating Linguistic Variation into the Classroom

Manuel J. Gutiérrez *University of Houston*
Marta Fairclough *University of Houston*

The following example of an online chat appears in an English as a Second Language (ESL) textbook recently published in a Latin American country:[1]

[sacha] *todos los marinos de Chile son pinochetistas y cagones*

[eduardo] *CUENTAME ESA VERSION QUE NO LA CONOZCO*

[GLORIA] *LLA ESTAN HABLANDO WUEVADAS LOS FOME*

[eduardo] *TODOS ES MUCHA GENTE*

[eduardo] *LO DICES POR LO DEL ESMERALDA?*

[Marco] *p*

[MORENAZO] *Y QUE ESTA HACIENDO=?*

[Shawn] *ich will*

[Marco] *pppp*

[sacha] *arturo prats era un viejo culiao cochino que ni se afeitava*[2]

(*La Tercera* online, March 19, 2004)

After receiving information about the content of the passage, the government of the country retrieved all 250,000 copies of the book from the schools (they had been delivered to the students free of charge). It was not the language style used by the chat participants but the content of the interaction that accounted for the response. However, the language style is the reason we decided to include this passage at the beginning of our chapter. The linguistic norms evident in this chat are at the non-formal extreme of the style continuum used by adolescents in Chile, yet they found a place in a language textbook. Although textbook authors hardly ever include nonstandard dialects such as the quoted sample, it is refreshing to know that some of them try to present at least a few examples of the variety used every day by the users of the textbook. Would it not be reasonable to offer adolescents a foreign language textbook written in the style they could relate to and likely use, in the same way that business professionals would expect a textbook written in the more formal style of interest to them? While this comparison may be an exaggeration, it seems obvious that the specific needs of students should be taken into account when constructing a language textbook.

A study of immersion classrooms conducted by Tarone and Swain (1995) corroborates this assertion. Their findings demonstrate that in an academic context students learn only a formal register, as opposed to a speech style that would allow them to communicate with their peers. Consequently, their competence is limited to certain domains that require use of the formal variant, such as exchanges with their teachers. Although Tarone and Swain admit that there are some difficulties in teaching an L2 (secondary language) vernacular in the classroom (e.g., teachers who are not comfortable teaching a non-academic variety, choice of vernacular to present, etc.), one of the options they propose is that sociolinguistic variation should be explicitly taught in immersion classrooms through TV programs, films, magazines, and other media to provide models of current vernacular usage (1995, 175).

Let us move now from the style variable to the geographical dimension. Consider the case of a textbook designed to teach Spanish in Madrid's primary schools that includes a section on the Argentine *voseo,* or a textbook printed in Spain for Latin American audiences that includes several sections on the use of the *vosotros* pronoun.[3] Any textbook that intends to impose nonlocal linguistic forms over local ones would probably not be taken out of the schools, but it would be foolish to expect students to produce these forms in their environment. The reason is obvious: As suggested by Kachru (1988) regarding World Englishes, no single model of a language meets local, regional, and international needs simultaneously. Varieties often develop innovations for practical reasons, such as regional dialect contact and social variation. When creating a pedagogical norm, therefore, not only student needs but also the local or regional sociolinguistic contexts need to be taken into account.

The situation is even more complex in the teaching of Spanish to students in the United States. As a nation with more Spanish speakers than most Spanish-speaking countries, the United States presents a reality characterized by extreme variation. This variation is based on a number of linguistic and social variables, including "generation," which is defined by place of birth, age upon arrival to the United States, and number of years speakers have been in contact with English. Common to most Spanish language textbooks used in this country are linguistic forms used in other Spanish-speaking countries, such as the pronoun *vosotros,* the morphological future, and many lexical items that are not necessarily found in the different varieties of Spanish spoken in the United States. Such inclusions are intended to supersede local norms, which are absent. The goal should be for students to communicate both with Spanish speakers in the United States and around the world. Bilingual speakers should not only be proficient in English and Spanish but also be able to communicate using the predominant local or regional vernacular norms. The dialect of Spanish learned also has professional implications. Students learning Spanish often work in a variety of professional sectors, including government, health, the arts, law enforcement, the judiciary, and business. In an article published in the *Los Angeles Times* in 2000, Kraul writes that many American companies need bilingual personnel not only in Latin America but also for the domestic market (Carreira 2002, 45).

The linguistic complexity of language learning and Spanish-English bilingualism in the United States necessitates a discussion of specific guidelines for teaching Spanish as a second language in such a context. Specifically, do we have to make available to students the full range of variation that occurs in the real world? Further, if this is the right thing to do, how can we do it? In this chapter, we intend to (1) examine linguistic variation in the Spanish-speaking world, focusing on some specific studies of U.S. Spanish, (2) offer a glimpse of the U.S. Spanish classroom and its students, and (3) consider the feasibility of incorporating local Spanish varieties into the classroom.

1.0 Language Variation

During the last several decades, many empirical and descriptive studies on Spanish dialects around the world have succeeded in showing synchronic and diachronic language variation, in both monolingual and contact situations. Using a sociolinguistic framework, research has been conducted based on the notion of space, on sociocultural factors, and on differences of style and register (Fontanella de Weinberg 1992; Silva-Corvalán 1994, 1995; Gutiérrez 1994a, 2001; Fairclough 1999; Klee and Ramos-García 1991; Bentivoglio 1987; DeMello 1995, 1996; Lipski 1994, 1998; Lope Blanch 1977, 1979; López Morales 1992; Martínez Sequeira 2000; Quilis et al. 1985; Samper Padilla 1990; Serrano 1994, 1995; and Valdivieso 1991, among many others). In addition to extensive variation present at all linguistic levels,[4] contradictions were often found between prescriptive and descriptive accounts of Spanish (De Sterck 2000; Fairclough 2000; Gutiérrez 1995, 1996, 1997; Lavandera 1984).

In the United States there is a very complex linguistic situation. Multiple varieties of Spanish with diverse origins (Mexican, Puerto Rican, Dominican, etc.) are spoken in major cities all over the country, and a language continuum has emerged that includes varying levels of proficiency. Most of these varieties of Spanish are used orally; written Spanish is used more sporadically. However, this situation may be changing due to the growing number of newspapers, magazines, and books published in Spanish in the last few decades (Carreira 2002). In studying variation within these dialects, investigators often use the variable *generation* to explain the differences in language forms and structures. Intergenerational studies have been useful in providing evidence on the diverse degrees of Spanish language simplification and loss. These investigations have revealed not only the existing variation at the lexical and phonological levels but also the variation and processes of linguistic change present in the grammatical system of Spanish (Silva-Corvalán 1994; Ocampo 1990; Lynch 1999).

Perhaps the most important contribution that has emerged from the sociolinguistic research on the Spanish spoken in the United States has been the "revelation" of U.S. Spanish as a variety of a language spoken by more than 350 million in the world, but with distinctive characteristics due to its contact with English. At the same time, this variety has been shown to be as diverse as many of the Spanish varieties spoken around the world (Amastae and Elías-Olivares 1982; Bergen 1990; Roca and Lipski 1993; Klee and Ramos-García 1991; Silva-Corvalán 1995, etc.).

Fairclough (2003), among others (Álvarez 1991; De Jongh 1990; Keller and Keller 1993; Montes-Alcalá 2000; Otheguy 1993; Otheguy et al. 1989; Callahan 2001), examines some of the phenomena of transfer that result from the Spanish-English contact in spoken Spanish and in literature, teaching, media, the legal system, and the business world. Mixing or alternating between the two languages are options bilinguals have, provided that certain functional, structural, semantic, and communicational constraints are observed. Numerous studies have analyzed those constraints as well as the social and pragmatic functions of this type of interaction (Valdés-Fallis 1976; McClure 1981; Gumperz 1982; Zentella 1990; Torres 1997; Poplack 1982; Sánchez 1983; Pfaff 1982; Otheguy 1993) and found it to be widespread and systematic. The results of the mixture of English and Spanish often appear as single and multiple-word transfers as illustrated in figure 9.1.

Figure 9.1 Model of Linguistic Interaction: English/Spanish in the United States

Single-word Transfers

Switches: preserve English phonology
   *Ellas son más **educated***

(2) Borrowings: adapted to Spanish phonology
   (a) Loans (transfer of form + meaning)
      Troca (= '*truck*'→ *camioneta*)

   (b) Calques (transfer of meaning only)
      Aplicación (= '*application*' → *solicitud*)

Multiple-word Transfers

(1) Switches: preserve English phonology
   (a) Intersentential switches
      El no sabe hacerlo. **I'll do it.**
   (b) Intrasentential switches
      *Y luego **during the war,** él se fue al Valle.*

(2) Calques: adapted to Spanish phonology
   (a) Conceptual/cultural calques
      Estampillas de comida (= '*food stamps*')
   Calques of bound collocations, idioms and proverbs
      *So él sabrá si **se cambia su mente*** (= . . . *if (he) changes   his mind* → . . .
      si cambia de opinión/de idea)
   Lexico-syntactic calques
      Tuvimos un buen tiempo (= '*We had a good time*'/ *Lo pasamos bien*)

Source: Based on Silva-Corvalán 1994, Otheguy et al. 1989, and Otheguy 1993.

These phenomena are part of a natural process that takes place in language contact situations and cannot be interrupted, despite the opinion of those in favor of language purity. The number of speakers who were born in the United States and the permanent immigration from Spanish-speaking countries have helped (and probably will continue to help) maintain Spanish as not only the home language of many Americans but also one of the languages used in the media and the business world. Although loss of Spanish has been documented at the individual level, at the community level Spanish is maintained (Hudson, Hernández-Chávez, and Bills 1995; Silva-Corvalán 1994, 10); we might, therefore, expect the presence of the Spanish language to continue to be an integral part of the growing Hispanic community of the United States in the years to come.

The characteristics that distinguish the variety of Spanish spoken in the United States from other Spanish dialects are not reduced to the lexical component or to code switching, however. The grammatical system of U.S. Spanish has also been affected by contact with English. Variation phenomena present in monolingual varieties are also evidenced in U.S. Spanish. But in the bilingual context, research has attested to (1) an increment in the linguistic variation, and (2) an acceleration of the processes of change. Let us observe a couple of examples.

The extension of the Spanish copula *estar* has been studied by Silva-Corvalán (1986) in Los Angeles and by Gutiérrez (2001) in Houston. Uses such as those shown in example 1 are considered innovative because *estar* is being used where other Spanish varieties would use *ser:*

(1) *No, yo nací, pues no es Monterrey, es a ... como media hora de Monterrey ... viene siendo Nuevo León ... [en] un pueblito chiquito, no **está** muy grande ... y yo nací en la casa.*

In the case of the innovative *estar*, the speaker establishes a class frame of reference with its use; other varieties establish the class frame with *ser*. In Houston and Los Angeles similar rates of use for *estar* were found, at 36 and 34 percent, respectively. Table 9.1 shows the increment in *estar* use by generation in Houston.

In comparing these results with data from Michoacán, Mexico (Gutiérrez 1994a), a predominantly monolingual community, we notice that a 16 percent occurrence of innovative *estar* was found. Accordingly, it can be said that the change is present in

Table 9.1 Percentages of innovative *estar* in Houston by generation

	Percentage	Frequency innovative *estar* / innovative *estar* + prescriptive *ser*
Generation 1	24	(45/187)
Generation 2	39	(84/217)
Generation 3	46	(75/163)
Total	36	(204/567)

monolingual Spanish also but has been accelerated in bilingual situations. Thus, the phenomenon of innovative *estar* can be characterized as a variation or a linguistic change in progress in its first stages in the monolingual community; in the United States, however, it seemingly has advanced more rapidly and has taken over an important part of the semantic domain of *ser* there.

Research on the use of the subjunctive also show greater variation in the Spanish spoken in Los Angeles (Ocampo 1990; Silva Corvalán 1994), Houston (Gutiérrez 1994b; Fairclough 2005), New York (Torres 1997), and Miami (Lynch 1999). Similar variability has been noted with hypothetical discourse (Gutiérrez 1996, 1997; Fairclough 2005). There appears to be a tendency to replace the subjunctive and the conditional forms with the indicative (example 2) and the compound tenses with the simple tenses (example 3):

(2) *Me están arreglando un carro, el carro chiquito que estaba atrás; lo están arreglando ya por fin y ojalá* **puedo** [PRESENT INDICATIVE] *registrarlo este fin de semana.*[5]

(3) *— ¿Y qué crees tú que habría sido de tu vida si se hubiera quedado tu familia en México en vez de venir aquí a los Estados Unidos?*

—. . . Sí. o sea, es que no sé qué, qué **pasaría** [CONDITIONAL] *de nosotros, quizás yo, ya* **estaría** [CONDITIONAL] *trabajando, lo más probable o casada. Todas mis amigas y primas en México de mi edad ya están casadas.*

This same type of variation takes place in a number of regions (Central and South America, Spain, the United States) and in both monolingual and contact situations (Spanish/Basque, Spanish/English). Some representative studies in monolingual contexts include Navarro's study (1990) of Venezuelan Spanish. Navarro finds a high percentage of imperfect subjunctive usage (38 percent) in the apodoses of [−past] conditional sentences (example 4), while the standard form, the conditional, appears in the remaining contexts (62 percent):

(4) *Si yo tuviese esas fotos, te las* **enseñara.** [IMPERFECT SUBJUNCTIVE]

Another example of a noncontact variety is found in Lope Blanch's studies (1991) of Mexican Spanish. He observes that indicative forms often replace the subjunctive (example 5). Also, the conditional (simple or perfect) is frequently replaced by the imperfect subjunctive in the apodoses (example 6), and in some cases even by the imperfect or the present indicative (examples 5 and 7):

(5) *Si hubieras ido conmigo, no te* **pasa** [PRESENT INDICATIVE] *nada.*

(6) *No le* **guardara** [IMPERFECT SUBJUNCTIVE] *rencor si viniera a pedirme perdón.*

(7) *Si lo supiera, te lo* **decía.** [IMPERFECT INDICATIVE]

In Covarrubias (Northern Spain) Silva-Corvalán's (1985) research of spoken Spanish shows a high frequency of the conditional in the protasis of [±past] conditional sentences (Example 8). This is most likely due to the geographical proximity with Basque. Similar phenomena are found in Buenos Aires, as attested by Lavandera (1975).

(8) *Esta bota es para el vino, si se **pegaría*** [CONDITIONAL] *puede echarle un poco de agua.*

DeMello (1993) gives quantitative evidence that indicates that speakers favor the use of pluperfect subjunctive over compound conditional in apodoses of (+ past) conditional sentences in nine Spanish dialects: Bogotá (82 percent/18 percent), Buenos Aires (83 percent/17 percent), Caracas (100 percent/0 percent), La Habana (100 percent/0 percent), Lima (95 percent/5 percent), Madrid (94 percent/ 6 percent), Ciudad de México (93 percent/7 percent), San Juan (100 percent /0 percent), and Sevilla (86 percent/14 percent). Data from Houston (Gutiérrez 1997) however, indicates that there is greater variety in the forms that appear in these apodoses. The results suggest that the process of change, almost complete in some monolingual varieties, has possibly had further developments in the bilingual community of Houston. Table 9.2 illustrates the different forms used by three generations.

Table 9.2 shows that several forms are in competition in the apodosis (shown in the "Other" category in table 9.3). In the monolingual community of Michoacán only 6 percent of forms used were not pluperfect subjunctive or conditional perfect. In Houston, however, the conditional perfect has disappeared and forms other than the pluperfect subjunctive represent half of the forms used in the apodoses. The differences could be explained by intergenerational transmission or by incomplete acquisition by second- and third-generation speakers due to the scarce frequency of this type of discourse.

Table 9.2 Percentages of forms in apodoses in Houston by generation

Form	First generation	Second generation	Third generation	Total
Imperfect subjunctive	15 (3)	14 (8)	37 (11)	21 (22)
Pluperfect subjunctive	60 (12)	63 (36)	27 (8)	52 (56)
Conditional	25 (5)	3 (2)	17 (5)	11 (12)
Imperfect indicative	–	2 (1)	3 (1)	2 (2)
Pluperfect indicative	–	2 (1)	–	1 (1)
Fuera + participle	–	16 (9)	17 (5)	13 (14)
Total	(20)	(57)	(30)	(107)

Note: Numbers in parentheses indicate frequency.

Table 9.3 Percentages of forms in apodoses in Michoacán and Houston

	Michoacán	Houston
Conditional perfect	17 (8)	–
Pluperfect subjunctive	77 (36)	52 (56)
Other	6 (3)	48 (51)
Total	(47)	(107)

Note: Numbers in parentheses indicate frequency.

Examples 9–11 illustrate the use of diverse verbal forms in the mentioned context:

(9) — *y si hubieran seguido viviendo en México, ¿cómo habría sido la situación?*

— *... pues yo creo que yo sí yo **estuviera** [IMPERFECT SUBJUNCTIVE] en una alguna una [escuela], universidad o algo ...*

(10) — *¿Y qué crees tú que habría sido de tu vida si se hubiera quedado tu familia en México en vez de venir aquí a los Estados Unidos?*

— *... Sí. O sea, es que no sé qué, qué **pasaría** [CONDITIONAL] de nosotros, quizás yo, ya estaría trabajando, lo más probable o casada. Todas mis amigas y primas en México de mi edad ya están casadas.*

(11) — *¿Cómo habría sido tu vida si te hubieras quedado a vivir en México?*

— *... quizás no me **fuera casado** ... [FUERA + PARTICIPLE]*

Fairclough (2005) corroborates these findings. Fairclough's research looks at the production of hypothetical discourse by bilingual Spanish/English speakers from the Houston area in different tasks (interviews, writing samples, and acceptability judgments). Patterns of variation similar to those found by Gutiérrez were also evident in this study.

2.0 Teaching New Varieties of Spanish

So what is the place of the variation and the tendencies (of the type presented in the previous discussion) in the pedagogical norm to be followed to teach Spanish in the United States? Will at some point the allophone [v] be considered an allophonic variant of the phoneme /b/ in Spanish? What about the allophone [š] as part of the phoneme /č/occurring in some monolingual Spanish dialects? And what about lexical loans: *troca, aplicación*; code switching; innovative *estar*; and variation in the subjunctive and conditional? Will we have to establish a pedagogical norm to be used with traditional foreign language learners and a different norm or norms to be used with heritage speakers of Spanish?

2.1 The traditional classroom

Traditional foreign language instruction in the United States has been based on the teaching of a standard variety of Spanish (almost exclusively the written form of the language) and therefore, on the rejection of local varieties. However, sociolinguistic studies of language heterogeneity have challenged key constructs in language education. Concepts such as "the standard language" (Joseph 1991; Hidalgo 1997; Villa 1996) and "the native speaker" (Train 2002; Spolski 2002; Davies 2003; Myhill 2003; Blyth 2002), on which most classroom instruction has been based, are being challenged (Kramsch 1997).[6] A good example of the gap between what is taught in the classroom and what happens in the real world is the teaching of the morphological future (synthetic future) in courses of Spanish as a second language. The future conjugations are introduced fairly early in Spanish textbooks, but in spoken Spanish they are practically nonexistent. In the written language, this form has diminished in frequency even in monolingual Spanish. The gap is even greater when we observe the reality in Spanish-speaking communities in the United States. Table 9.4 shows the use by bilinguals of synthetic and analytic future and the present indicative in contexts where the three alternate with future value. Table 9.5 illustrates the use of the same forms among monolingual speakers in Mexico City.

The tendency in both language varieties is similar. Both show a predominant use of the periphrastic form (synthetic future) over the other two forms. In the bilingual community, however, the difference between this form and the morphological future and the present indicative is greater than in the monolingual variety. The comparison between tables 9.4 and 9.5 supports the hypothesis that language contact situations accelerate changes that are in progress in monolingual varieties (Silva-Corvalán 1986; Gutiérrez 1994a). This process of linguistic change shows a progressive predominance of the periphrastic form in contexts that refer to future time in several Spanish

Table 9.4 Southwestern United States: Morphological future, periphrastic future, and present indicative use in alternation contexts

Form	Percentage	
Morphological future	4	(5)
Periphrastic future	89	(118)
Present indicative	7	(10)
Total	100 (133)	

Source: Gutiérrez (1995).
Note: Numbers in parentheses indicate frequency.

Table 9.5 Mexico City: Morphological future, periphrastic future, and present indicative use

Form	Percentage
Morphological future	23
Periphrastic future	51
Present indicative	26

Source: Moreno de Alba (1977, 146).

dialects, such as those spoken in Venezuela, the Dominican Republic, Chile, and Mexico (Silva-Corvalán and Terrell 1989). However, this process is more advanced in the dialect in contact with English in the southwestern United States. The periphrastic form has the potential to become the only one used to refer to future situations in spoken Spanish in the Southwest. In most other varieties of Spanish, even the present indicative has a higher frequency than the morphological future. Therefore, the question that arises is obvious: Why are we teaching the morphological form to express future?[7]

We must not forget that the typical student of Spanish is interested in the language, and also in the cultural aspects of the communities where Spanish is spoken. That student is, or should, therefore be interested in the varieties of Spanish spoken in the United States by more than 12 percent of the population. They should also likely be interested in the cultural diversity of U.S. Spanish communities. Learners of Spanish are aware of the Spanish-speaking communities around them, and they need to know about these different cultures. Language and culture go hand in hand.

This does not mean that we should not teach about the culture and civilization of Spain, about indigenous Hispanic American civilizations, or about colonial and modern Latin America. It is clear that to learn Spanish constitutes learning as much as possible about the diverse facets of the communities that speak the language around the world. In fact, content material on Spanish around the world is included in many of the language courses taught throughout the United States. However, today more than ever, it is imperative to teach about the Hispanic communities that exist in this country, and, at the same time, to teach about the linguistic norms that exist in those communities. We must remember that the interaction between a Spanish language student and a Spanish speaker in the United States (if we do not take into account the Spanish instructor), with a high degree of probability, will be between the student and one or more of the 35 million U.S. Spanish speakers.

Clearly, the Spanish spoken by these U.S. Spanish speakers is not homogenous. Some of them recently arrived and were educated in a Spanish-speaking country. Others were born in the United States and are third or fourth generation heritage speakers who learned Spanish as their first language at home, and may or may not have continued developing their language skills within the educational system or apart from it (Fairclough 2005). The complex linguistic situation described above is not uncommon. In fact, homogeneous linguistic communities are practically nonexistent around the world. Reality has taught us that a selection is made among all the local dialects found in a monolingual country (if we are able to find a monolingual country!) to be used as a means of instruction. The same process must be performed in the United States in teaching Spanish as a second language. Instructors should introduce students to sociolinguistic variation by familiarizing them with the full range of Spanish varieties.

2.2 The Students

To add to the complexity of language variation and the challenges to some key L2 constructs, different types of learners have been identified in the Spanish classrooms in the United States during the last few decades. Along with traditional foreign language students, we often find heritage learners and, occasionally, native speakers of Spanish who were born, raised, and educated in Latin America or Spain.[8]Although in some cases there are separate tracks for bilingual Spanish speakers (Valdés 1997; Feal 2002), often they share a classroom with traditional foreign language learners. All these factors make it extremely difficult to define a pedagogical norm to be used in the Spanish classroom.

It is clear that different needs should be addressed with different solutions, but this is only true regarding the methodological approach or the material to be used in class, and the language level of the group being taught. There is no reason to establish one pedagogical norm for traditional foreign language students and a different one for heritage learners of Spanish, unless we evaluate the norms in a different way. In fact, that is what happens with most of the textbooks that are available today. They privilege an invariant norm, which does not include the tools that will enable students to perform in the variety of contexts in which they will be required to perform outside of the classroom. Some scholars favor a bidialectal pedagogy for heritage speakers of Spanish (Porras 1997; Hidalgo 1993), which would allow them to maintain the local variety while mastering the standard dialect. However, this issue is seldom addressed when the students are traditional learners of Spanish as a second language, even though there are many professional opportunities in government, business, media and communications, the performing arts, the motion picture industry, healthcare, and education for example, for bidialectal or multidialectal Spanish speakers in the United States (Aparicio 1997; Carreira and Armengol 2001).[9]

2.3 The Teaching Context

The general attitude of those in charge of teaching Spanish at the different levels is also based on the superior value assigned to standard monolingual norms. Valdés et al. (2003) found such attitudes in a study about the teaching of Spanish in foreign language departments of the United States. Among the results, the variety spoken in this country is practically disregarded when appropriateness for academic use is considered. Almost all the respondents in the study saw varieties from Spain and Latin America as apt for the academic world (14–15). Spanish speakers of the United States are identified as a group that will have difficulties in acquiring academic Spanish. This is because they are thought to be limited by the variety of Spanish they speak, which is very different compared to what is taught in the classroom (18–19). Accordingly, attitudes toward Spanish spoken in the United States and toward speakers of this Spanish variety are negative, which represents a tremendous problem when attempts are made to incorporate variation into the Spanish language classroom. Bernal-Enríquez and Hernández-Chávez (2003), for example, find that New Mexican Hispanic students are aware of the negative attitude toward their Spanish on the part of the general public, yet they want to maintain it for affective reasons. The authors quote one of the participants in their study: "What I want to stop is being a 'Chicana falsa' and really speak my language like I once did with my great-grandma" (2003, 108). This is a good reason for incorporating language variation into the classroom, starting perhaps by teaching the culture of different Spanish-speaking groups in the United States.

Another step toward reinforcing the validity of U.S. Spanish in the classroom should come from the Spanish speakers who live in the United States. In addition to our language students, recent Spanish-speaking arrivals to the United States should familiarize themselves with the language variation found in the different Spanish-speaking communities in this country, and they should accept these as legitimate varieties of Spanish. The natural process of accommodation to the new reality will help with this because many of the immigrants will use the Spanish language in different situations in their life in the United States, and will slowly adapt to the new variety(ies). This phenomenon can be easily observed in Spanish immigrants in Latin America and in Latin American immigrants in Spain and in the different Latin American countries to which they have migrated. In most cases, they accommodate their linguistic behavior to the Spanish forms used by local speakers. A similar process can and should occur in the United States. In fact, this is a sociolinguistic phenomenon that is taking place at the lexical level and to some extent at the grammatical level, in spite of the opinion of a number of purists who insist on changing the course of this natural tendency. Even though this type of accommodation is unavoidable, negative views of the local varieties usually prevail among recent arrivals.

2.4 Interaction as a Learning Tool

Learning a language is a very complex task. Acquiring linguistic competence does not mean simply knowing the vocabulary and the grammar of a language. Bachman (1990, 87) shows the complexity of language competence and its many components: grammatical, textual, illocutionary, and sociolinguistic competence, which includes sensitivity to dialects and registers, ability to interpret cultural references, and so on. In most university undergraduate linguistic courses at the advanced level, students are taught about geographic language variation, both synchronic and diachronic. At the graduate level, more and more institutions are offering courses on sociolinguistics and language contact, which include U.S. Spanish and teaching Spanish to heritage learners, thus familiarizing future educators with this language variety. These practices will help to change attitudes toward local varieties of Spanish and facilitate the introduction of variation into the language class.

2.5 The Incorporation of Variation into the Spanish Language Class

Obviously the amount of variation that would be presented to the student will depend on the level of knowledge of Spanish. Besides teaching the hybrid and simplified form of the language that is the norm in most basic second language programs, instruction should gradually move from awareness of linguistic variation to productive use of alternative dialects, and from a focus on local varieties, registers, and styles to other varieties, registers, and styles of Spanish around the world.

In addition to teaching about the cultural realities of Hispanic groups in the United States, a basic first step in a language class would be to provide numerous and varied contexts to generate communication. In these situations, the student really uses the language with a purpose, and therefore, what the student learns through these activities are language phenomena related to the diverse contexts in which the communication takes place. Variation in contexts means sociolinguistic variation because students must accommodate linguistic uses to the communication tasks at hand. Without a doubt, these are the richest acts of learning, and through them, the learning processes get closer to becoming acquisition experiences.

Once students have mastered the basic aspects of a communication task, practice sessions using linguistic variation that may be simplified to make it more comprehensible (Long 1983) can be carried out in the classroom. In this way, language instructors will not only use the linguistic context, but also the extralinguistic content to make available to the students what is required in different communicative situations.

Another excellent way to introduce variation into the classroom is through the negotiation of meaning by using request clarification techniques. Rich lexical variation can be obtained through this metalinguistic practice, while using the diverse structures available to request clarification. In many situations, students will tend to simplify the communication by giving an English translation of the item being asked for clarification (for example, see Koike and Ramey 2001, in Koike and Klee 2003), but the reliance of the student's native language will diminish as the student's performance in Spanish advances.

It is obvious that the full spectra of situations in which the student might have to perform in the real world cannot be reproduced in the classroom, but some real situations can be created and class projects can be developed. The outside world and the culture of the communities that speak the language should be brought into the classroom so that the diverse Spanish communities of the United States become a central component of the Spanish class. A good introduction to particular varieties and their pragmatic and stylistic functions might include readings of literary texts written in different varieties of U.S. Spanish that include a wide range of topics and cultural issues, as well as different language modalities and styles. At the more advanced levels, students could partake in volunteer work and take advantage of internship opportunities in the Hispanic community, as well as work on class projects in which they can compare and contrast different varieties of Spanish by interviewing members of the Hispanic community (thus learning more about the cultural and linguistic diversity in their area). Although it is unrealistic to think that students will be exposed to a high number of communicative situations (the limitations of classroom learning are well known), they will acquire the necessary skills to transfer uses and create new ways to communicate in the new contexts they encounter.

The communicative context determines the forms that speakers select and creates opportunities for linguistic variation (Labov 1972). Since this affects all kinds of communication, situations that occur inside the classroom and in the real world, which are related to the language class, also will be affected by contextual differences. Stylistic variation has to be taught to students if our goal is to teach the real language. Tarone's (1983) suggestions for teaching the different points of the stylistic continuum work very well in incorporating variation into the classroom. Therefore, diverse tasks requested by the instructor should be taken into account—for instance, situations in which the students role play, such as requesting something from different interlocutors. This type of activity will place the student in more or less formal situations.

In any case, nothing compares to the experience of using language in the real world with native speakers of the language the student is studying. When one teaches Spanish in the United States, the real world is out there. Instructors should provide the students with the right language tools through formal instruction, and bring the communities and their language varieties into the classroom. Better yet, they should have the students interact with the local Spanish community. That is the linguistic norm that we all should be familiar with and use in the first place, without forgetting that there are other norms that might be acquired according to an individual's needs.

It is clear that at the beginner's level we cannot expect complex communicative abilities, but that is the best time to start incorporating awareness of other dialects and cultures. As the student advances, we should offer opportunities to develop their capacity to deal with different situations and increase their linguistic repertoire so that advanced students are prepared to interact with the real world and communicate with U.S. Spanish speakers as well as Spanish speakers from a variety of dialects.

3.0 Conclusion

What is taught in the classroom in high school and at beginning and intermediate university levels is generally restricted by time and instructional expertise constraints. Usually a glimpse of dialectal variation is introduced to students of Spanish in the United States through authentic materials introduced in the classroom. However, a pared-down version of Spanish is often taught in the classroom because of the limited number of classroom hours, the teachers' lack of sociolinguistic knowledge, and the quality of teaching materials available.

To avoid just teaching a "sanitized standard" Spanish, sociolinguistic variation should be incorporated into the classroom. But what variety(ies) should we teach? Clearly it would be impossible to develop productive abilities in the many different Spanish dialects, but increasing awareness of language variation and alternative dialects is worthwhile during the beginning stages of acquisition. As students advance in their L2 proficiency, the range of their linguistic abilities, including the command of different varieties, should increase considerably. Ideally, students should be exposed to all varieties of the language, but taking into account the fact that more than 35 million Hispanics live in the United States, the local variety(ies) of Spanish should have a priority.

So how do we achieve this goal? First, second language learning should begin in childhood and continue through higher education if we want our students to acquire a high level of proficiency in all aspects of linguistic competence. Second, teacher education programs should include extensive linguistic training as well as pedagogy and methodology courses on how to teach both heritage and traditional language learners. And third, key sociolinguistic concepts and samples of language variation should be included in all language textbooks and should be presented to students, even at the basic levels of instruction.

Notes

We would like to thank two anonymous reviewers and Jennifer Ayres and Tonya Wolford for their insightful comments on a previous version of this chapter.

1. This dialogue, curiously in Spanish, appeared under the title "This page is part of a chat room. What can you do if you want to chat?" Original orthography has been maintained. *La Tercera*, online edition, www.latercera.cl. (accessed March 19, 2004).
2. The topic of the conversation introduced by Sacha among the participants of the chat is related to the people in the Chilean navy who are followers of Gen. Augusto Pinochet, Chilean dictator between 1973 and 1989. Gloria qualifies the subject as a silly thing (*wuevadas*), and she thinks it is boring (*fome*). The conversation revolves around the navy and Pinochet because the *Esmerelda* is a school ship that was used a torture center during the first years of the Pinochet regime. At the end of the conversation, Sacha talks derogatively about Arturo Prat, the most important national hero of the Chilean navy. Prat was commander of the *Esmerelda*, a Chilean warship, during the Combate Naval de Iquique (May 21, 1879), in which he died, against Peruvian naval forces. Two high school students discovered the quoted chat and the Chilean navy complained, which triggered the retrieval of the book by the Chilean government.
3. These uses from other dialects are taught from time to time in some school systems with the purpose of helping students understand texts written in other dialects, but sometimes the goal is to make the students produce some of these forms.
4. For an overview of some of the key studies in Spanish variation, see Silva-Corvalán 2001.
5. Example from Ocampo (1990, 44).
6. Valdés (this volume) offers additional remarks on the notion of the native speaker.
7. It should be noted that the synthetic form of the future, while scarcely used with its temporal meaning, often appears in the expression of modality in the Spanish of the Southwest (Gutiérrez 1995, 223–24).
8. For a comprehensive summary of Hispanic heritage language education in the United States, see Fairclough 2005.
9. Some recently published textbooks are beginning to incorporate information about dialectal differences, specifically, variations from U.S. Spanish. For instance, the textbook *Impresiones* (Salaberry et al. 2004) explicitly incorporates activities with regional linguistic variations, including variations in the United States, in every chapter of the book, in the activities manual, and in the video program.

References

Álvarez, C. 1991. Code-switching in narrative performance: Social, structural, and pragmatic function in the Puerto Rican speech community of East Harlem. In *Sociolinguistics of the Spanish-speaking world: Iberia, Latin America, United States,* ed. C. A. Klee and L. A. Ramos-García, 271–98. Tempe, AZ: Bilingual Press/Editorial Bilingüe.

Amastae, J., and L. Elías-Olivares, eds. 1982. *Spanish in the United States: Sociolinguistic aspects.* Cambridge: Cambridge University Press.

Aparicio, F. 1997. La enseñanza del español para hispanohablantes y la pedagogía multicultural. In *La enseñanza del español a hispanohablantes: Praxis y teoría,* ed. M. C. Colombi and F. X. Alarcón, 222–32. Boston: Houghton Mifflin.

Bachman, L. F. 1990. *Fundamental considerations in language testing.* Oxford: Oxford University Press.

Bentivoglio, P. 1987. *Los sujetos pronominales de primera persona en el habla de Caracas.* Caracas: Universidad Central de Venezuela.

Bergen, J., ed. 1990. *Spanish in the United States: Sociolinguistic issues.* Washington, DC: Georgetown University Press.

Bernal-Enríquez, Y. and E. Hernández-Chávez. 2003. La enseñanza del español en Nuevo México: ¿Revitalización o erradicación de la variedad chicana? In *Mi lengua: Spanish as a heritage language in the United Status,* ed. A. Roca and M. C. Colombi, 96–119. Washington, DC: Georgetown University Press.

Blyth, C. 2002. Between orality and literacy: Developing a pedagogical norm for narrative discourse. In *Pedagogical norms for second language and foreign language learning and teaching: Studies in honour of Albert Valdman,* ed. S. Gass, K. Bardovi-Harlig, S. Magnan, and J. Walz, 241–79. Amsterdam: John Benjamins.

Callahan, L. 2001. Spanish/English codeswitching in fiction: A grammatical and discourse function analisis. Ph.D. diss., University of California, Berkeley.

Carreira, M. 2002. The media, marketing and critical mass: Portents of linguistic maintenance. *Southwest Journal of Linguistics* 21 (2): 37–54.

Carreira, M., and R. Armengol. 2001. Professional opportunities for heritage language speakers. In *Heritage languages in America: Preserving a national resource,* ed. J. K. Peyton, D. A. Ranard, and S. McGinnis, 109–42. Washington, DC: Center for Applied Linguistics.

Davies, A. 2003. *The native speaker: Myth and reality.* London: Multilingual Matters.

De Jongh, E. 1990. Interpreting in Miami's federal courts: Code-switching and Spanglish. *Hispania* 73 (1): 274–78.

DeMello, G. 1993. *-Ra* vs. *-Se* Subjunctive: A new look at an old topic. *Hispania* 76:235–44.

———. 1995. Alternancia modal indicativo/subjuntivo con expresiones de posibilidad y probabilidad. *Verba* 22:339–61.

———. 1996. Indicativo por subjuntivo en cláusula regida por expresión de reacción personal. *Nueva Revista de Filología Hispánica* 44:365–86.

De Sterck, G. 2000. *Registros y áreas geográficas en lingüística: Valores y usos de las formas verbales en -ra, -se, -ría, y -re.* Salamanca: Ediciones Universidad de Salamanca.

Fairclough, M. 1999. Discurso directo vs. discurso indirecto en el español hablado en Houston. *Bilingual Review* 24 (3): 217–29.

———. 2000. Expresiones de modalidad en una situación de contacto: "Deber (de)" vs. "Tener que" en el español hablado en Houston. *Southwest Journal of Linguistics* 19 (2): 19–30.

———. 2003. El (denominado) *Spanglish* en Estados Unidos: Polémicas y realidades. *Revista Internacional de Lingüística Iberoamericana* 2:185–204.

———. 2005. *Spanish and heritage language education in the U.S.: Struggling with hypotheticals.* Madrid/Frankfurt: Iberoamericana/Vervuert.

Feal, R. 2002. Foreign language study: World needs, now. *MLA Newsletter* 34 (4): 5–6.

Fontanella de Weinberg, M. B. 1992. *El español de América.* Madrid: Mapfre.

Gumperz, J. J. 1982. *Discourse strategies.* Cambridge: Cambridge University Press.

Gutiérrez, M. J. 1994a. **Ser** *y* **Estar** *en el habla de Michoacán, México.* México DF: Universidad Nacional Autónoma de México.

———. 1994b. Simplification, transfer, and convergence in Chicano Spanish. *Bilingual Review/La Revista Bilingüe* 19 (2): 111–21.

———. 1995. On the future of the future tense in the Spanish of the Southwest. In Silva-Corvalán, *Spanish in four continents.* 214–26.

———. 1996. Tendencias y alternancias en la expresión de condicionalidad en el español hablado en Houston. *Hispania* 79:316–26.

———. 1997. Discurso irreal de pasado en el español de Houston: La disputa continua. *Bulletin of Hispanic Studies* 74 (3): 257–69.

———. 2001. *Estar* innovador en el continuo generacional bilingüe de Houston. In *Proceedings of the VII Simposio Internacional de Comunicación Social*, 210–13. Santiago de Cuba.

Hidalgo, M. 1993. The teaching of Spanish to bilingual Spanish-speakers: A "problem" of inequality. In *Language and culture in learning: Teaching Spanish to native speakers of Spanish*, ed. B. J. Merino, T. Trueba, and F. A. Samaniego, 82–93. London: Falmer Press.

———. 1997. Criterios normativos e ideología lingüística: aceptación y rechazo del español de los Estados Unidos. In *La enseñanza del español a hispanohablantes: Praxis y teoría*, ed. M. C. Colombi and F. X. Alarcón, 109–19. Boston: Houghton Mifflin.

Hudson, A., E. Hernández-Chávez, and G. Bills. 1995. The many faces of language mainte- nance: Spanish language claiming in five southwestern states. In Silva-Corvalán, *Spanish in four continents*. 165–83.

Joseph, J. E. 1991. Levels of consciousness in the knowledge of language. In *Languages and standards: Issues, attitudes, case studies*, ed. M. L. Tickoo, 11–22. Singapore: SEAMEO Regional Language Center.

Kachru, B. B. 1988. Teaching World Englishes. *ERIC/CLL News Bulletin* 12 (1): 1, 3–4, 8.

Keller, G. D., and R. G. Keller. 1993. The literary language of United States Hispanics. In *Handbook of Hispanic cultures in the United States: Literature and art*, ed. F. Lomelí, 163–91. Houston: Arte Público Press.

Klee, C., and L. A. Ramos-García, eds. 1991. *Sociolinguistics of the Spanish-speaking world: Iberia, Latin America, United States*. Tempe, AZ: Bilingual Press/Editorial Bilingüe.

Kock, J., ed. 2001. *Lingüística con corpus: Catorce aplicaciones sobre el español*. Salamanca: Universidad de Salamanca.

Koike, D. A., and C. A. Klee. 2003. *Lingüística aplicada: Adquisición del español como segunda lengua*. New York: John Wiley and Sons.

Koike, D. A., and A. Ramey. 2001. Collaborative discourse in the Spanish second language acquisition context. Paper presented at TexFlec Conference, May 23–24.

Kramsch, C. 1997. Standard, norm, and variability in language learning: A view from foreign language research. In *Pedagogical norms for second language and foreign language learning and Teaching: Studies in honour of Albert Valdman*, ed. K. Bardovi-Harlig et al., 59–79. Amsterdam: John Benjamins.

Labov, W. 1972. *Sociolingüistic patterns*. Philadelpia: University of Pennsylvania Press.

Lavandera, B. 1975. Buenos Aires Spanish: Tense variation in Si-Clauses. *Pennsylvania Working Papers on Linguistic Change and Variation* 1:4.

———. 1984. *Variación y significado*. Buenos Aires: Hachette.

Lipski, J. 1994. El lenguaje afroperuano: Eslabón entre África y América. *Anuario de Lingüística Hispánica* 10:179–216.

———. 1998. Perspectivas sobre el español bozal. *América negra. Panorámica actual de los estudios lingüísticos sobre variedades hispanas, portuguesas y criollas*, ed. M. Perl and A. Schwegler, 293–327. Madrid: Iberoamericana.

Long, M. 1983. Native speaker/non-native speaker conversation and the negotiation of com- prehensible input. *Applied Linguistics* 4:126–41.

Lope Blanch, J. 1977. *Estudios sobre el español hablado en las principales ciudades de América*. México DF: Universidad Nacional Autónoma de México.

———. 1979. *Investigaciones sobre dialectología mexicana*. México DF: Universidad Nacional Autónoma de México.

———. 1991. *Estudios sobre el español de México*. México DF: Universidad Nacional Autónoma de México.

López Morales, H. 1992. *El español del Caribe*. Madrid: Mapfre.

Lynch, A. 1999. The subjunctive in Miami Cuban Spanish: Bilingualism, contact, and language variability. Ph.D. diss., University of Minnesota.

Martínez Sequeira, A. T. 2000. El dequeísmo en el español de Costa Rica: Un análisis semántico-pragmático. Ph.D. diss., University of Southern California.

McClure, E. 1981. Formal and functional aspects of the codeswitched discourse of bilingual children. In *Latino language and communicative behavior,* ed. R. Durán, 69–92. Norwood, NJ: Ablex.

Montes-Alcalá, C. 2000. Two languages, one pen: Socio-pragmatic functions in written Spanish-English code switching. Ph.D. diss., University of California, Santa Barbara.

Moreno de Alba, J. 1977. Vitalidad del futuro de indicativo en la norma culta del español hablado en México. In Lope Blanch, *Estudios sobre el español hablado en las principales ciudades de América.* 129–46.

Myhill, J. 2003. The native speaker, identity, and the authenticity of hierarchy. *Language Sciences* 25 (1): 77–97.

Navarro, M. 1990. La alternancia –ra/-se y –ra/-ría en el habla de Valencia (Venezuela). *Thesaurus* 45 (2): 481–88.

Ocampo, F. 1990. El subjuntivo en tres generaciones de hablantes bilingües. In Bergen, *Spanish in the United States.* 39–48.

Otheguy, R. 1993. A reconsideration of the notion of loan translation in the analysis of U.S. Spanish. In Roca and Lipski, *Spanish in the United States.* 21–45.

Otheguy, R., O. Garcia, and M. Fernandez. 1989. Transferring, switching, and modeling in west New York Spanish: An intergenerational study. *International Journal of the Sociology of Language* 79:41–52.

Pfaff, C. 1982. Constraints on language mixing: Intrasentential code-switching and borrowing in Spanish/English. In J. Amastae and L. Elías-Olivares, *Spanish in the United States.* 264–97.

Poplack, S. 1982. "Sometimes I'll start a sentence in Spanish y termino en español": A typology of code-switching. In *Sociolinguistic aspects,* ed. J. Amastae and L. Elías-Olivares, 230–63. New York: Cambridge.

Porras, J. E. 1997. Uso local y uso estándar: Un enfoque bidialectal a la enseñanza del español para nativos. In *La enseñanza del español a hispanohablantes: Praxis y teoría,* ed. M. C. Colombi and F. X. Alarcón, 190–97. Boston: Houghton Mifflin.

Quilis, A., M. Cantanero, M. J. Albalá, and R. Guerra. 1985. *Los pronombres le, la, lo y sus plurales en la lengua española hablada en Madrid.* Madrid: CSIC.

Roca, A., and J. Lipski, eds. 1993. *Spanish in the United States: Linguistic contact and diversity.* Berlin: Mouton de Gruyter.

Salaberry, R., C. Barrette, M. Fernández-García, and P. Elliot. 2004. *Impresiones.* Upper Saddle River, NJ: Pearson–Prentice Hall.

Samper Padilla, J. A. 1990. *Estudio sociolingüístico del español de Las Palmas de Gran Canaria.* Las Palmas de Gran Canaria: La Caja de Canarias.

Sánchez, R. 1983. *Chicano discourse: Socio-historic perspectives.* Rowley, MA: Newbury House.

Serrano, M. J., ed. 1994. *La variación sintáctica: Formas verbales del período hipotético en español.* Madrid: Entinema.

———. 1995. Sobre los usos de pretérito perfecto y pretérito indefinido en el español de Canarias: Pragmática y variación. *Boletín de Filología de la Universidad de Chile* 35:533–66.

Silva-Corvalán, C. 2001. *Sociolingüística y pragmática del español.* Washington, DC: Georgetown University Press.

———. 1985. Modality and semantic change. In *Historical semantics: Historical word formation,* ed. J. Fisiak, 547–72. Berlin: Mouton.

———. 1986. Bilingualism and language change: The extension of *estar* in Los Angeles Spanish. *Language* 62:587–608.

———. 1994. Language contact and change: Spanish in Los Angeles. Oxford: Clarendon Press.

————. 1995. *Spanish in four continents.* Washington, DC: Georgetown University Press.

Silva-Corvalán, C., and T. Terrell. 1989. Notas sobre la expresión de futuridad en el español del Caribe. *Hispanic Linguistics* 2:191–208.

Spolsky, B. 2002. Norms, native speakers and reversing language shift. In *Pedagogical norms for second language and foreign language learning and teaching: Studies in honour of Albert Valdman,* ed. K.Bardovi-Harlig et al., 41–58. Amsterdam: John Benjamins.

Tarone, E. 1983. On the variability of interlanguage systems. *Applied Linguistics* 4 (2): 143–63.

Tarone, E., and M. Swain. 1995. A sociolinguistic perspective on second language use in immersion classrooms. *Modern Language Journal* 79 (2): 166–78.

La Tercera. 2004. Online edition. Santiago de Chile. www.latercera.cl (accessed March 19).

Torres, L. 1997. *Puerto Rican discourse: A sociolinguistic study of a New York suburb.* Mahwah, NJ: Lawrence Erlbaum Associates.

Train, R. 2002. The (non) native standard language in foreign language education: A critical perspective. In *The sociolinguistics of foreign language classrooms: Contributions of the native, the near-native, and the non-native speaker,* ed. C. Blyth, 3–40. Boston: Heinle.

Valdés, G. 1997. The teaching of Spanish to bilingual Spanish-speaking students: Outstanding issues and unanswered questions. In *La enseñanza del español a hispanohablantes: Praxis y teoría,* ed. M. C. Colombi and F. X. Alarcón, 9–44. Boston: Houghton Mifflin.

Valdés, G., S. V. González, D. López García, and P. Márquez. 2003. Language ideology: The case of Spanish in departments of foreign languages. *Anthropology and Education Quarterly* 34 (1): 3–26.

Valdés-Fallis, G. 1976. Social interaction and code-switching patterns: A case study of Spanish/English alternation. In *Bilingualism in the bicentennial and beyond,* ed. G. Keller, R. Teschner, and S. Viera, 53–85. New York: Bilingual Press.

Valdivieso, H. 1991. Variación fonética de /s/ en el habla espontánea. *Revista de Lingüística Teórica y Aplicada* 29:97–113.

Villa, D. 1996. Choosing a "standard" variety of Spanish for the instruction of native Spanish speakers in the U.S. *Foreign Language Annals* 29 (2): 191–200.

Zentella, A. C. 1990. Lexical leveling in four New York City Spanish dialects: Linguistic and social factors. *Hispania* 73 (4): 1094–1105.

Making Connections
Second Language Acquisition Research and Heritage Language Teaching

Guadalupe Valdés *Stanford University*

In the United States, *heritage language teaching* refers to the teaching of indigenous and immigrant languages as academic subjects to students who have been raised in homes where these languages are spoken. For language-teaching professionals, the term refers to a group of young people who are different in important ways from English-speaking monolingual students who have traditionally undertaken the study of foreign languages in American schools and colleges. This difference has to do with actually developed functional proficiencies in the language in which instruction is given.

In general, there have been few connections between researchers engaged in the study of second language acquisition (SLA) and researchers and practitioners involved in the study of heritage language learners. As Valdés (2005) points out, heritage learners have been the focus of researchers engaged in the study of bilingualism, a field that has examined both individual and societal bilingualism and language contact from the perspectives of the disciplines of sociolinguistics, linguistics and psycholinguistics. Researchers in the field of applied linguistics have also been involved in the development of appropriate language pedagogies for heritage students. Much of the work on heritage learners (e.g., textbooks, pedagogical articles), however, has been carried out by individuals actually engaged in the teaching of heritage language classes. Unfortunately, the work is largely anecdotal, pretheoretical, and often not informed by research on bilingualism and language contact, language change, language variation, or language acquisition.

SLA researchers, on the other hand, have tended to distance themselves from the traditional concerns of applied linguistics (i.e., second language pedagogy) and have focused instead on the "developing knowledge and use of systems by children and adults who already know at least one other language" (Spada and Lightbown 2002, 115). Although recently criticized for what some (e.g., Firth and Wagner 1997; Block 2003) have referred to as a narrow psycholinguistic perspective, most mainstream SLA researchers have continued to engage in the theoretical and experimental investigation of the development of linguistic rather than communicative competence.

This chapter is an attempt to bridge these two worlds of professional practice by exploring potential areas of common interest. In organizing the chapter, I am assuming a limited background by SLA researchers in both the teaching of Spanish as well as in the study of societal bilingualism.

1.0 Teaching Spanish to Heritage Learners

According to a survey of college and university foreign language departments conducted by the Modern Language Association (MLA) (Goldberg, Lusin, and Welles 2004), Spanish heritage language classes are offered at 24 percent of 772 colleges and universities offering majors and advanced courses in Spanish. According to a survey conducted by the National Foreign Language Center (NFLC) and the American Association of Teachers of Spanish and Portuguese (AATSP) (Ingold et al. 2002), however, only 18 percent of 146 campuses responding have implemented special courses for heritage speakers. At the secondary level, only 9 percent of secondary schools in the country currently offer Spanish heritage language programs (Rhodes and Branaman 1999).

Interest and concern about how to teach Spanish to students who were raised in homes where Spanish is spoken has been present in educational circles since 1930s, but it was only in the late 1970s and early 1980s that teaching Spanish to Spanish speakers as an academic subject became more widely known.[1] At that time, increasing enrollment at state colleges and universities by nontraditional students (particularly Mexican Americans and Puerto Ricans) led to a realization that existing practices were inappropriate. The consensus, reflected in the textbooks of that period (e.g., Baker 1966; Barker 1972), was that bilingual Hispanophone students were in need of remediation, of techniques and pedagogies that would help undo the damage that had been done at home.

In the late 1970s and early 1980s, a number of articles appeared that attempted to define the field by discussing the difference between foreign language (FL) and native language (NL) instruction, the implications of the study of linguistic differences for the teaching of Spanish to bilingual student, and the teaching of the standard variety. A number of articles also appeared that described classroom practices and shared suggestions about what to teach and how, including the teaching of traditional grammar, spelling, and reading and writing. Also during this period, much activity in the field centered around the production of textbooks to be used in teaching bilingual students.

By the late 1980s however, it became clear that the problems surrounding the teaching of Spanish to bilingual speakers as an academic subject that was part of a "foreign language" program had not been solved. Few materials were available for the secondary level, and younger college faculty found themselves facing the same problems that others had faced a decade before. The profession had changed as well. The emphasis in FL teaching had shifted away from grammar-based instruction to a proficiency orientation, and there was much confusion about the right kinds of instruction and assessment. By the late 1980s and early 1990s articles that examined old issues in new ways or that posed new questions (e.g., the use of the oral proficiency interview with bilingual students, the question of dialect and standard, the role of FL teachers in teaching bilingual students, the relationship between theory and practice, and the role of the FL teaching profession in maintaining minority languages) began to appear.

Beginning in the late 1990s and continuing today, professional activities focusing on the teaching of heritage languages have increased enormously. The AATSP initiated its *Professional Development Series Handbooks for Teachers K–16* with volume 1, *Spanish for Native Speakers* (AATSP, 2000). The NFLC, in cooperation with AATSP, developed a language-based resource, Recursos para la Enseñanza y el Aprendizaje de las Culturas Hispanas, or REACH (see www.nflc.org/REACH), for teachers of Spanish to heritage speakers. NFLC also developed LangNet, a searchable database that includes Spanish and contains numerous resources for the teaching of heritage languages. In collaboration with AATSP, NFLC also conducted a survey of Spanish language programs for native speakers (Ingold et al. 2002). The Center for Applied Linguistics and NFLC launched the Alliance for the Advancement of Heritage Languages (on line at www.cal.org/heritage/).

2.0 Goals and Objectives of Heritage Language Instruction

While many minority language communities have undertaken efforts to maintain their languages by offering instruction to both children and adults (Fishman 1966, 1985), it is only in the last several years that a number of language groups (e.g., Chinese, Korean, Japanese) as well as native communities have seen themselves as engaged in activities analogous to those of the foreign-language teaching profession (Strang et al. 2002; Maheux and Simard 2001; Reyhner and NAU 2003).

The events of September 11, 2001, moreover, made evident what Brecht and Rivers (2002) have referred to as a "language crisis" surrounding national security. As a result of this growing perception of the importance of language resources for national defense, there has been an increasing interest by the intelligence and military communities (Muller 2002) in expanding the nation's linguistic resources by both teaching non-English languages and maintaining the heritage or home languages of the forty-seven million individuals who reported speaking both English and a non-English language in the latest census (U.S. Census Bureau 2003). For many individuals concerned about language resources, the development of strategic languages can only be brought about by expanding the mission of departments of foreign languages to include the maintenance and expansion of the varieties of non-English languages currently spoken by immigrants, refugees and their children.

To date, although one can identify various pedagogical goals and objectives in the literature on heritage language instruction, there is no clear articulated consensus about either goals or successful pedagogical practices. As compared to the goals of L2 (secondary language) instruction, which primarily involve the acquisition of linguistic competence (and, more recently, communicative competence), the goals of heritage language instruction primarily include the four goals identified by Valdés (1995): (1) the acquisition of a standard dialect, (2) the transfer of reading and writing abilities across languages, (3) the expansion of bilingual range, and (4) the maintenance of the heritage language. They also include two other goals identified more recently by Valdés et al. (in press) at the secondary school level: the development of academic skills and the increase of students' pride and self-esteem.

2.1 The Acquisition of the Standard Dialect

Within the Spanish-teaching profession, concern about the teaching of an educated standard variety of Spanish has been very much at the center of the teaching of Spanish to bilingual hispanophone students in the United States. For many practitioners, the ideal model of ultimate attainment for heritage learners is the *norma escolar* of the monolingual speaker of educated Spanish, and the central goal of heritage language (HL) instruction is the development of the grammatical, pragmatic, sociolinguistic, and textual competence of upper-class Spaniards or Latin Americans. While the condemnation of students' home varieties of Spanish is much less blatant than that found in the early textbooks (e.g., Baker 1966 and Barker 1972), most existing textbooks aimed at heritage learners include sections in which attention is given to the contrast between "popular" and "academic" Spanish. Such sections usually include a presentation of grammatical forms as well as exercises designed to focus students' attention on "lo correcto."

2.2 The Transfer of Reading and Writing Skills

Instruction aimed at helping heritage students to transfer existing literacy skills from English to their heritage language has been a very strong focus of heritage language instruction. Because heritage students have been educated primarily or exclusively through English, most have not developed reading and writing skills in their heritage language. Almost all existing Spanish textbooks and other materials designed for heritage learners, therefore, give a great deal of attention to these skills. There are many pedagogical articles that have focused on the teaching of writing conventions (e.g., spelling, the written accent). More recently, a number of articles have centered on the recognition and production of registers appropriate for writing in the academy (e.g., Schwartz (2003), Colombi (2003). With few exceptions (e.g., Colombi 2003; Chevalier 2004), there has been very little discussion of theories of reading and writing development that can inform pedagogies aimed at helping students to transfer developed reading skills in the L2 to an L1 or to use a primarily oral language to develop the written registers needed for academic writing.

2.3 The Expansion of Bilingual Range

The goal of expanding heritage students' bilingual range is one that is appealing to many practitioners.[2] It suggests that it is possible for instruction aimed at heritage speakers to expand their overall proficiency in a nondominant L1 so that it can then be used professionally and personally in a variety of contexts. This general objective is directly supported by the definition of communication established by the American Council on the Teaching of Foreign Languages in *Standards for Foreign Language Learning* (ACTFL 1996). From the point of view of the standards, communication in a language involves much more than simply speaking and listening. The standards recognize three "communicative modes" (interpersonal, interpretive, and presentational) that place primary emphasis on the context and purpose of the communication.

Interpersonal communication, for example, may involve the written language in the writing of informal notes to members of the family. It may also involve conversing with strangers, making requests, apologizing, or simply establishing personal contact. This mode requires linguistic, sociolinguistic, and pragmatic knowledge. The interpretive communication mode, on the other hand, involves understanding what is communicated by others in both oral and written texts. When students read literary texts, for example, or listen to lectures in the language they are studying, they are engaged in interpretive communicative activities. The abilities required for engaging in this type of communication are primarily the receptive skills of reading and listening. In contrast to the interpersonal mode, the presentational oral communication mode involves "one-too-many" communication with a group of listeners or readers. It can take place in both written and oral language but involves a sense of audience as well as planning and preparation in presenting an argument, explaining, or summarizing information.

Heritage learners may enter formal language instructional programs with considerable ability in the interpersonal mode. However, they may not have completely developed the interpretative and presentational communication modes. While many heritage learners are quite fluent in oral interpersonal language, many need to develop a greater bilingual communicative range in order to interact with a broad range of individuals of different backgrounds and ages for a variety of purposes. In terms of the interpretive and presentational communication modes, heritage language speakers need to learn how to read skillfully in the heritage language, to interpret subtle meanings found in both oral and written texts, and to present information in both oral and written forms intended for audiences with which they do not have immediate contact. The *Standards* framework supports the expansion of bilingual range in that it views ultimate attainment for these students as the development of proficiencies that will allow them to carry out both personal and academic interactions in two languages for a variety of purposes.[3]

2.4 Language Maintenance

The goal of language maintenance has not been identified specifically by current language-teaching professionals as central to classroom instruction. It is perhaps an implicit goal of heritage language instruction in general, but it has not received much attention in the literature focusing on classroom pedagogies. For the moment, instruction aimed at bilingual speakers of Spanish that purports to support language maintenance is operating according to what are, at best, very tentative hypotheses about the relationship between language instruction and language maintenance. What is clear is that, in developing a theory of classroom approaches to such maintenance, applied linguists and practitioners must establish a set of coherent principles about the precise role of language instruction in language maintenance and include the systematic examination of questions:What levels of linguistic development correlate with students' desire to maintain Spanish? What kinds of interactions with other Spanish speakers in the school context promote an increased interest in continuing to participate in such interactions? What kinds of readings promote an understanding of students' linguistic circumstances and a concomitant awareness of the efforts involved in maintaining language? Which classroom activities contribute to students' positive attitudes about themselves and their Spanish?

It is important to note that few sociolinguists and students of societal bilingualism are optimistic about developing simple principles about why and how individuals maintain minority languages in bilingual contexts. The variables are many, and the classroom is limited in what it can accomplish against the assimilative pressures of the wider society. Fishman (1991) is most persuasive in arguing that language maintenance depends on transmission across generations. He maintains that schools, *by themselves*, will not be able to reverse language shift, and he suggests steps that can be followed in those communities that are at level 6 of his Graded Intergenerational Disruption Scale (GIDS) in order to create a community—not school—context in which the minority language can both grow and thrive.

3.0 Development of Theories of Heritage Language Development/(Re)acquisition

Ideally, pedagogical approaches used with heritage learners would be based on an understanding of the linguistic knowledge systems of heritage speakers and on a familiarity with the processes involved when speakers of such nondominant first languages attempt to develop or reacquire these languages in formal instructional settings. At present, although we have some knowledge of the role of instruction in restructuring the interlanguages of L2 learners, we have no information about the role of formal instruction in restructuring or reshaping the knowledge systems of learners who are in many ways quite different from traditional classroom learners.[4] In this section, I briefly review key characteristics of heritage language speakers and outline elements of a research agenda directed at understanding both the development/(re)acquisition of heritage languages as well as the role of instruction in these processes.

3.1 Heritage Learners as L1/L2 Users

Rejecting the view that the ultimate state of L2 learning is to pass undetected among native speakers, Cook (2002, 9) emphasizes that "the minds, languages and lives of L2 users are different from those of monolinguals" and that "L2 users are not failures because they are different." In suggesting the term *L2 user* and rejecting the designation *bilingual*, Cook (2002, 4) points out that the term has "contradictory definitions and associations in both popular and academic usage."

Recently, Valdés (2005) argued that the term *L2 user* is not entirely appropriate for the description of heritage language learners. Pointing out that the term *L2 user* still tends to emphasize and focus attention primarily on the L2, she proposes the term *L1/L2 user* to describe heritage learners many of whom acquire the L2 in a combination of naturalistic and instructed settings and continue to use the L1 to some degree in their everyday lives. Here I use the term *L1/L2 user* interchangeably with the terms *bilingual* and *heritage speaker* in the discussion that follows to emphasize the difference between heritage speakers and second language learners.

3.2 Acquisition in L1/L2 Users

Romaine (1995) maintains that much of the work on bilingual acquisition has been methodologically flawed and that many studies do not describe the context of acquisition or the age or patterns of exposure to two languages. Few studies of bilingual language acquisition, for example, have been carried out in minority language contexts, that is, in communities that are home to both monolingual and bilingual speakers of both an immigrant and a societal language and in which both newly arrived immigrants and adult native-born individuals may be part of the same family. In such families the original varieties of the heritage language of its members may be converging with other immigrant varieties of the same language present in the community. Moreover, recently arrived individuals may be at different stages of acquisition of the societal language while at the same time, members of the family who have been in the country for many years might be at various stages of loss or attrition of the heritage language. For children of these families, exposure to one or the other of two languages used together or separately may vary significantly depending on which members of the household are present at particular points in time. Even though there is no consensus about the influence on parental or care-taker speech on bilingual children's language acquisition involving, for example, language mixing, Bialystok (2001) maintains that studies of monolingual language acquisition show that "the effect is pervasive enough . . . to acknowledge that the language children hear has a role in shaping the language they will speak" (115).

3.3 The Knowledge Systems of Heritage Learners

As Grosjean (1985) and Cook (1997) have argued, L1/L2 users are not two monolinguals in one but specific speaker-hearers who have acquired their two languages in particular contexts and for particular reasons. Viewed from a bilingualist rather than a monolingualist perspective, L1/L2 users have acquired two knowledge systems that they use in order to carry out their particular communicative needs, needs that may be unlike those of monolingual native speakers, who use a single language in all communicative interactions. Oksaar (1997, 9), for example, argues that bilingual individuals may have "not only two or more sets of rule complexes from their languages, regulating their communicative performance, but at least three, the third complex arising from LX," which consists to a large extent of items from L1 and L2. Oksaar maintains that LX itself is governed by its own norms of usage.

Also arguing for a bilingualist perspective on L1/L2 users, Grosjean (1997) contends that at any given moment, bilinguals are in states of activation of their languages and language processing mechanisms that are either monolingual or bilingual. Depending on the base language used and the interlocutors involved, an L1/L2 user will be in (1) a monolingual mode in language A, (2) a monolingual mode in language B, or (3) a bilingual mode. While in one or the other of the monolingual modes, the other language is deactivated to some extent and transfer between the two languages is reduced. In the bilingual mode, however, because both languages are active, transfer between the two languages as well as the tendency to code switch will be evident to a greater degree. Grosjean argues that since language behavior in different modes most probably reflects how bilinguals process their two languages, research on bilingual competence and performance must take into account language mode.

Unfortunately, as a number of researchers (e.g., Cook 1997; Mohanty and Perregaux 1997; Romaine 1995; Woolard 1999) have pointed out, bilingualism has generally been seen as anomalous, marginal, and in need of explanation. In spite of the fact that the majority of the populations of the world are bilingual or multilingual, the position that has been taken by many researchers is that the norm for human beings is to know a single language. While absolutely equivalent abilities in two languages are theoretically possible, except for rare geographical and familial accidents, individuals seldom have access to two languages in exactly the same contexts in every domain of interaction. L1/L2 users do not have the opportunity of using two languages to carry out the exact same functions with all individuals with whom they interact or to use their languages intellectually to the same degree. They thus do not develop identical strengths in both languages. More important, perhaps, it is not the case that all monolingual native speakers would be successful if measured against the norm of the educated native. It thus makes little sense to use a monolingual native-speaker norm to evaluate the competence of L1/L2 users. As Cook (1997, 294) has argued, it is not clear why we should "ever compare two types of people in terms of a bookkeeping exercise of profit and loss."

4.0 A Research Agenda on Heritage Language Development and (Re)acquisition

In order to design instruction aimed at developing the unique language strengths of heritage language learners, a systematic research agenda that can guide the multiple aspects of this research needs to be put in place. This agenda must focus not only on the linguistic characteristics of heritage learners but also on the role of instruction in the development/(re)acquisition of nondominant L1s. At a minimum, such an agenda must

- develop language evaluation/assessment procedures that can identify key differences among heritage learners;
- investigate the implicit systems of different types of heritage learners in their nondominant L1s;
- determine the degree of system restructuring that would need to take place in order for heritage speakers at different levels of heritage language proficiency to carry out particular functions in particular settings using appropriate linguistic forms;
- investigate the role of different types of instruction in such restructuring for different types of heritage speakers;
- determine whether pedagogies used to restructure the interlanguages of L2 learners can also be effective for various categories of heritage speakers.

4.1 Identifying Key Differences among Heritage Learners

Given the complexity of the bilingual experience and the fact that there are few L1/L2 users who are ambilingual, we can hypothesize that there are important differences in the implicit linguistic knowledge systems of various types of L1/L2 users who are grouped under the label *heritage speakers* in an academic context. A research agenda designed to support theories of the development/reacquisition of heritage languages that are acquired as L1s by these users, therefore, needs to begin by developing procedures for examining similarities and differences among individual heritage speakers of the same language as well as between categories of heritage speakers of different languages. These procedures must ultimately lead to the development of typologies of heritage speakers that are potentially important for classroom instruction. What are needed are typologies that go beyond traditional generational categorizations (first, second, third generation) of immigrant speakers that are commonly used in sociolinguistic research as well beyond other categorizations that have focused on recency of arrival, schooling and access to the standard language (e.g., Valdés 1995). For pedagogical purposes, useful classifications should be able to provide information about the linguistic proficiencies of heritage speakers, about the characteristics of their underlying implicit knowledge systems, and about the differences among heritage speakers of the same generation and background.

4.2 The Development of Proficiency Assessment Procedures

A starting point for establishing general typologies of heritage speakers of different types will require the development of proficiency assessments of various types that will allow researchers to compare and contrast various types of speakers along a variety of dimensions. Such procedures must be capable of providing information about the range of functions that can be successfully carried out by different speakers in different contexts as well as information about the linguistic characteristics of the various registers present in the language repertoires of individual L1/L2 users. A resulting language proficiency scale might, for example, resemble that used by Hallamaa (1998, 72–74) in his study of endangered languages.[5] Hallamaa's scale includes the following categories:

1. Speaks eloquently and knowledgeably.

2. Speaks fluently, prefers language for most interactions.

3. Speaks fluently but prefers another language.

4. Speaks with "minor" flaws including careless or uncertain words, grammar simplifications, limited vocabulary, use of unassimilated loan words.

5. Speaks a little. Makes "serious" grammatical errors. Tends to revert to other language when encountering difficulties.

6. Understands the language well but is not able to or does not speak it.

7. Understands some. Can understand topic of conversations carried out around him.

8. Understands standard set of questions and commands. May have had instruction in this language as a foreign language.

9. Understands at least two dozen words in the language.

10. Understands half a dozen words in the language.

11. Does not understand the language.

As will be noted, this set of categories, while not entirely satisfactory, is structured so that differences between various types of L1/L2 users can be identified. For Hallamaa's purpose, which was the creation of community profiles for potentially endangered languages, it was important to identify numbers and ages of speakers who were eloquent and knowledgeable and other types of speakers ranging from those who still preferred L1 to those who no longer had receptive proficiencies in the language.

In order to provide adequate instruction for heritage speakers, it will be important to determine not only speaking fluency in general but also the number of registers and varieties produced and understood as well as levels of literacy developed in the heritage language. One might imagine, for example, categorizing knowledgeable and eloquent heritage speakers as

- biliterate, eloquent, and knowledgeable speakers of *domestic and academic registers*;[6]
- monoliterate (or biliterate), eloquent, and knowledgeable speakers of a *domestic register* in an *urban/prestige variety* of the language;
- monoliterate (or biliterate), eloquent, and knowledgeable speakers of a *domestic register* in a *rural/nonprestige variety* of the language;
- monoliterate (or biliterate), eloquent, and knowledgeable speakers of a *domestic register* in a *contact variety* of the language.

Other fluent speakers might be identified as

- monoliterate (or biliterate) fluent speakers of a *domestic register* in an urban (or rural or contact) variety of the language *who still prefer that language*;
- monoliterate (or biliterate) fluent speakers of a *domestic register* in urban (or rural or contact) variety of the language who prefer the other language.

In the case of speakers who produce "flawed" language, the categorization of these speakers might take into account the possible sources of the identified flaws, and they might be identified as

- hesitant speakers of flawed language (speech suggests *incomplete acquisition* of obligatory categories and/or limited vocabulary);
- hesitant speakers of flawed language (speech suggests *language attrition*).

Fine-grained categorizations such as these, while detailed, are a necessary preliminary to the detailed study of both inter- and intraheritage learner variation in the various subsystems of their nondominant language. Assessment procedures might adapt or draw directly from methodologies used in the study of fossilization in L2 learners (Han 2003) and include oral and written proficiency tests, dialect- and register-sensitive cloze procedures (Gibbons and Ramirez 2004), and grammaticality/acceptability judgments. A focus on the linguistic forms frequently examined by L2 researchers might be especially useful in comparing L1/L2 users with L2 learners and in examining the role of instruction in the development/reacquisition of heritage languages in classroom contexts.

In sum, carrying out research on L1/L2 users designed to inform instruction in their heritage language will require that researchers attend carefully to questions such as those raised by Grosjean (1998), more recently recalled by Wei (2000, 481–82), and adapted here to apply to heritage speakers:

- Which languages (and language skills) have been acquired by heritage speakers?
- When and how was the heritage language acquired?
- Was the cultural context of acquiring the heritage and the societal language the same or different?
- What has been the pattern of heritage language use?
- What is the relationship between the heritage speaker's two languages?
- Are one or several languages still being acquired?
- Is the heritage speaker in the process of restructuring (maybe losing) a language or language skill because of a change of linguistic environment?
- Has a certain language stability been reached?
- Which languages (and language skills) are used currently, in what context, and for what purpose and to what extent?
- What is the heritage speaker's proficiency in each of the four skills (listening, speaking, reading and writing) in each language?
- What is the heritage speaker's proficiency in various dialects, registers, or styles of each language?
- How often and for how long is the bilingual in a monolingual mode (i.e., when one language is active) and in a bilingual mode (i.e., when both languages are active)?
- When the heritage speaker speaks in a bilingual mode, how much code switching and borrowing takes place?
- What is the heritage speaker's age, sex, socioeconomic and educational status, and so on?

In understanding the role of instruction in developing or maintaining heritage languages, what needs to be determined is whether heritage students—by formally studying their L1s—are involved in one or more of the following processes:[7]

- The acquisition of incompletely acquired features of the L1 as a "second" language
- First language (re)acquisition involving features that have undergone attrition
- The acquisition of a second dialect (D2 acquisition)

- The development of discourse skills in the written and oral language, including the acquisition of academic registers and styles (R2 acquisition)
- The acquisition of literacy

4.3 Incomplete Acquisition

Silva-Corvalán (2003a, 2003 b), for example, reports on the Spanish of young children in Los Angeles who at school age have not yet acquired the complete tense, aspect, and mood system of Spanish. She argues that, without school support, such children will not completely acquire the linguistic system of the language as used by normative L1 speakers because of limited access to Spanish language input. For Silva-Corvalán, the extended intensive contact with English in the school context appears to interrupt the normal process of Spanish acquisition in later childhood. Children move through the same stages of acquisition but at a slower rate and, once the L2 becomes dominant, their use of the L1 decreases significantly. According to Silva-Corvalán, as a result of a lack of input and fewer opportunities for using the L1, children who grow up in contexts in which one of their two languages has limited use will not fully acquire the subsystems of the language that are acquired by youngsters in monolingual settings at an early age. In her work on the Spanish of Los Angeles, Silva-Corvalán (1994) maintains that the Spanish of third-generation speakers who have grown up in this country is characterized by a reduced range of styles as a result of either language attrition or incomplete acquisition. She notes that the use of Spanish in Los Angeles appears to be much less frequent among both second- and third-generation speakers in the home domain.

The use of a simplified verb system as well as the uneven control of the heritage language (often made evident by the constant use of pauses, hesitations, and fillers) may not indicate that the language has been incompletely acquired by a heritage speaker. What will not be immediately clear from superficial assessments, however, is whether flawed production is due to interrupted acquisition, individual language attrition, or "full" acquisition of a contact variety of the heritage language that is now different from the varieties of the heritage language originally brought to the community. A theory of instruction supporting the development or (re)acquisition of a nondominant L1 for such learners will require an understanding of how and whether the implicit systems of speakers who have incompletely acquired the heritage language, speakers whose heritage language has undergone attrition, and speakers of a heritage language that has undergone extensive change are alike or different. What needs to be explored is how these different systems—if they are different—might be reshaped by formal instruction. In the case of incomplete acquisition, the instructional problem to be solved might involve, for example, the full acquisition of tense, aspect, and mood in the L1. Instructional approaches might, therefore, include second language methodologies used in the teaching of both the oral and written language to L2 learners.

In the case of language attrition (the erosion, decay, contraction, or obsolescence of a language) the process of (re)acquisition might be quite different. Without evidence to the contrary, one could not conclude that direct forms- or form-focused instruction or other typical pedagogies used in L2 instruction would be particularly beneficial in the process of (re)acquisition or reversal of attrition. This is, however, an empirical question, and one that can only be answered by examining the effects of different types of instruction designed to reverse attrition in a category of students who have been carefully identified as having undergone attrition in their heritage language.

4.4 Complete Acquisition of a Contact Variety

For the heritage speaker who has fully acquired a communal language that has undergone extensive changes through its contact with other varieties of the same language and with the dominant language, the instructional problem to be solved is quite different. If the goal is for such speakers to acquire the normative monolingual variety through formal instruction, what needs to be understood is the process of second dialect (D2) acquisition. These heritage speakers are not involved in acquiring parts of a system that they have incompletely acquired, nor are they involved in reacquiring subsystems that have been lost. In this case, heritage speakers are involved in acquiring an additional variety of the same language. What they must learn is which features of the communal language do and do not correspond to the features of the normative monolingual varieties of the language. A possible theory of D2 acquisition, for example, might parallel theories of L2 acquisition and propose that, in acquiring second dialects, learners move through a set of interdialect grammars until they reach the desired end state. Additionally, if the goal of heritage language instruction is also for these D2 learners to develop reading and writing skills, literacy instruction would ideally be based on an understanding of the differences and similarities between literacy acquisition in a second dialect and literacy acquisition in both a first and a second language.

If the goal of heritage language instruction for heritage speakers who are acquiring a second dialect is also for them to extend their repertoires to include styles and registers of the heritage language appropriate for communicating in academic or professional settings, instruction must be based on an understanding of the acquisition of additional registers by *monolingual* speakers who have not had access to contexts in which these particular registers are used. The instructional problem to be solved in this case is the acquisition of additional registers (R2 acquisition), that is, a set of discourse practices that are directly tied to values and norms of a particular social group (Gee 1990). As Gee has also pointed out, however, particular discourse practices are difficult to acquire in classroom settings because learners may have little or no access to speakers who use these particular specialized registers. In attempting to add such higher registers to their heritage language to their repertoires, L1/L2 users may attempt to imitate these registers by transferring and adapting features of similar registers from their L2.

A possible theory of R2 acquisition might, therefore, parallel theories of L2 and D2 acquisition and propose, as Valdés and Gioffrion-Vinci (1998) did, that in acquiring second or additional registers dialects, learners move through a set of interregisters until they reach the desired end state. Clearly, in order to develop adequate and effective instruction of heritage learners whose goal it is to acquire additional varieties and registers of the heritage language, careful research must be carried out on the process of D2 and R2 acquisition in naturalistic settings as well as on the effects of different types of instruction on both of these processes.[8] A final category of heritage speakers—in addition to those who have incompletely acquired the language, those whose language has undergone attrition, and those who speak a contact variety of the language—includes L1/L2 users who cannot or will not speak the heritage language although they are able to participate in interpersonal, face-to-face communication with bilingual individuals who speak to them in this language. These passive L1/L2 users exhibit strong receptive proficiencies in their heritage language, which, while limited, still exceed the receptive proficiencies acquired by beginning and even intermediate learners of a foreign language. At minimum, receptive L1/L2 users offer evidence of having acquired what Clark (2003) refers to as *C-representations,* that is, a system of representations for comprehension of the language that allows them to parse the stream of speech into meaningful units. How this system is related to the productive system in the L1 and to the receptive and productive systems in the L2 is of central importance to the development of pedagogical approaches for developing the existing proficiencies of such speakers in a classroom setting.

A theory of heritage language growth/development for such individuals must be based on a better understanding of comprehension and production grammars (Swain, Dumas, and Naiman 1974). We need to understand (1) how and why these two types of knowledge systems develop independently, (2) how comprehension and production grammars are related, (3) whether the presence of comprehension grammars supports the acquisition of production grammars in specific ways, and (4) whether these individuals are more similar to L2 learners than to L1 speakers. Unfortunately for educators, a single group of heritage learners enrolling in a heritage language class will in most cases include students who are quite dissimilar from each other and who are involved in very different processes of L1 (re)acquisition/development. Some language educators and researchers, moreover, are not entirely persuaded that heritage learners are entirely different from intermediate and advanced second language (L2) learners (e.g., Angelelli and Leaver 2002; Lynch 2003). Some maintain that because the language of both groups appears to be characterized by comparable flaws, the implicit L1 systems of heritage learners must be similar to the transitional L2 systems of L2 learners. These scholars conclude, therefore, that the same approaches to language instruction will be successful. Angelelli and Leaver (2002) for example, maintain that similar pedagogical approaches can be used with both groups of "advanced" students. These approaches include those described by Byrnes and Maxim (2003) and Kern (2003) as utilized by the New London Group (1996) with native English speakers—often with members of stigmatized minority groups—who are seen to be in need of acquiring a set of discourse practices, both oral and written, that are connected with standard English (Gee 1990). This particular approach to literacy studies focuses specifically on the discursive nature of knowledge construction by engaging in genre studies.

For researchers interested in examining the process of R2 (second register) acquisition, the focus on the development of genres, styles, and registers by L2 learners and
by heritage learners offer exciting possibilities for investigating the differences in rate
of acquisition, stages of acquisition, and ultimate attainment of registers and genres
of these two groups of learners. It is evident, however, that much research needs to be
done on the similarities and differences between the implicit systems of advanced language learners and heritage speakers of various types, before it can be assumed that
the processes of R2 acquisition will be similar in L2 learners and L1/L2 users. In sum,
the study of heritage learners raises a number of important theoretical issues for
researchers seeking to understand the human language faculty that involve the development of receptive versus productive grammars in heritage learners, the characteristics and sources of "flawed" language production in such learners as compared to L2
learners, the order of acquisition of particular features in both second registers and
second dialects, the existence of interdialects or interregisters in addition to interlanguages among learners of various types, and most importantly the types of instruction that can reverse language attrition and/or result in the acquisition of a range of
registers and styles.

4.5 The Implementation of a Research Agenda

The research agenda that I have outlined above was designed to suggest that the development of heritage language resources—if it is to be undertaken successfully—will
require the careful and systematic investigation of different types of heritage learners
and of the effect of various types of instruction on the development/(re)acquisition
of their heritage language. National investments in the simple adaptation of pedagogies currently used with L2 learners are based on unfounded assumptions about the
restructuring of the implicit systems of such learners and may be largely unsuccessful on a long term basis. As Hidalgo (1993) noted, direct instruction on normative
structures appears to lead to very limited changes in the language used by heritage
students for everyday communication. Retreating from the position she expressed in
Hidalgo (1987), she describes her previous practice as attempting to correct the three
most noticeable morphosyntactic characteristics of the "nonstandard structures
heard from immigrants from the countryside" (1997, 88):

> Given that correction implies criticism of that which is perceived as erroneous or
> mistaken, the reaction of the Mexican-American students is confusion, shame, or
> contained anger, since this correction reminds the individual of the speech of their
> grandparents, their parents, their older siblings, and all those people who they
> most love. The sporadic and asystematic correction of an adult implies, then,
> humiliation by what is one's own, contempt for what is authentic, disdain for the
> legitimacy of the dialect or idiolect. (1993, 80)

Hidalgo concludes that results in the acquisition of standard forms is a slow
process that "is subjected to a number of social and cultural variables that do not
depend on the individual" (89). She argues that professors of Spanish working with

heritage speakers "should not expect their students to attain a quasi-literate mastery of their mother tongue because the educational system has not offered them opportunities galore to educate themselves in their own language" (89).

5.0 Conclusion

As I have pointed out, Spanish heritage speakers (*L1/L2 users*) face a number of challenges in the formal study of Spanish, in part because there is little agreement among researchers and practitioners about appropriate goals and objectives for heritage instruction and no theories of the role of instruction in the (re)acquisition and development of their first language. It may also be the case that heritage language speakers appear to make little progress in reacquiring/developing the heritage language in classroom settings because, as Fishman suggests (Valdés et al. in press), "schools either do or must fail to teach HLs successfully because schools cannot reproduce anything like the total sociocultural and interpersonal reality that languages themselves require for post-adolescent language maintenance, not to mention linguistically fluid, native-like maintenance." Unfortunately, we have almost no empirical research on the effects of different types of instruction in developing heritage languages or about what might be reasonable goals and objectives.

There is much to be gained by establishing connections between Spanish SLA and the heritage-language teaching field. The involvement of SLA researchers in heritage language research would bring with it, for example, important research traditions involving the gathering and quantifying of data and the replication of research that have been largely absent in the work on classroom instruction of heritage learners. Such involvement would also result in the use of established methodologies and in the development of research instruments—including language assessments—that can more accurately measure the various language proficiencies of *L1/L2* users in each of their languages and provide information, not only about the knowledge systems of various types of heritage learners but also about the effects of instruction on, what might well be, interdialects and interregisters.

Finally, for Spanish SLA researchers, an involvement in the investigation of the process of development and (re)acquisition of the language(s) of U.S. Latinos could contribute in important ways to the solution of language problems that affect the lives of Spanish-speaking children in this country on an everyday basis. As Pennycook (1994, 297) has argued, schools are "cultural and political arenas within which various political, cultural and social forms are engaged in constant struggle." The problem of (re)acquisition and development of minority languages is not simple. However, there is much to be gained from a joint endeavor that addresses difficult problems by examining the ways they can be approached from the perspective of different areas of inquiry. Such an endeavor can lead not only to a better practice but also to a better understanding of what it means to generate theoretical knowledge that can directly contribute to the improvement of educational practice.

Notes

1. This presentation of the history of heritage language teaching from the mid-1970s to the late 1980s makes extensive use of the discussion in Valdés (2001).
2. The section draws extensively on Valdés (2001).
3. While not perfect, the classification of three communicative modes adopted by the *Standards* attempts to help teachers value the colloquial language of heritage speakers. It also establishes the notion that different types of language are used for different communicative purposes. In describing these modes, the Standards Writing Task Force (of which I was a member) deliberately avoided the terms *formal, informal, standard,* and *nonstandard.* It also sought to go beyond the distinction between *contextualized* and *decontextualized* language as well as the Basic Interpersonal Communicative Skills (BICS) and Cognitive Academic Language Proficiency (CALP) dichotomy made by Cummins (1979). (Bartolomé [1998] has written extensively about the problematic nature of such distinctions.)

   A further refinement of these modes may well be in order, but such a refinement would need to draw directly from increasingly sophisticated work on the definition of "academic language" currently being examined by a variety of scholars from different perspectives. For a review of recent work in this area, the reader is referred to Valdés (2004).
4. For a very thorough discussion of this topic, the reader is directed to Han (2003).
5. Hallamaa (1998) carries out the evalutation process by posting questions to informants about their proficiencies as well as by directly observing their speaking ability. Because Hallamaa's purpose is to create a profile for particular communities, much attention is given to the age of informants.
6. The terms *domestic* and *academic register* are used by Gibbons and Ramirez (2004) to refer to registers used at home by minority speakers and to registers used for more complex and public uses.
7. The discussion on this topic draws extensively from Valdés (2005).
8. It is not clear whether R(2) acquisition is guided by the same process as D(2) acquisition. The acquisition of a normative or standard dialect as a second dialect might involve, for example, the acquisition of additional grammatical structures. The acquisition of additional registers (linguistic systems used in particular contexts) might also involve the acquisition of what Halliday and Hasan (1985) and Halliday and Martin (1993) have referred to as *field* (specialization and technicalization of language), *tenor* (the characteristics of the language appropriate for social relationships between the interlocutors), and *mode* (the differences between written and oral language). Gibbons and Lascar (1998, 44) offer examples of the characteristics of field, tenor, and mode in different registers in Spanish by examining primary and secondary textbooks.

References

American Association of Teachers of Spanish and Portuguese (AATSP). 2000. *Spanish for native speakers: AATSP professional development series handbook for teachers K–12. A handbook for teachers.* (Vol. 1). Fort Worth, TX: Harcourt College Publishers.

American Council on the Teaching of Foreign Languages (ACTFL). 1996. St*andards for foreign language learning: Preparing for the 21st century.* Yonkers, NY: National Standards in Education Project.

Angelelli, C., and B. L. Leaver. 2002. Heritage speakers as learners at the superior level: Differences and similarities between Spanish and Russian student populations. In *Developing professional-level language proficiency,* ed. B. L. Leaver and B. Shekhtman, 197–218. Cambridge: Cambridge University Press.

Baker, P. 1966. *Español para los hispanos.* Skokie, IL: National Textbook.

Barker, M. E. 1972. *Español para el bilingüe.* Skokie, IL: National Textbook.

Bartolomé, L. 1998. *The misteaching of academic discourse: The politics language in the classroom.* Boulder, CO: Westview Press.

Bialystok, E. 2001. *Bilingualism in development: Language, literacy, and cognition.* Cambridge: Cambridge University Press.

Block, D. 2003. *The social turn in second language acquisition.* Edinburgh: Edinburgh University Press.

Brecht, R., and W. P. Rivers. 2002. The language crisis in the United States: Language, national security and the federal role. In *Language policy: Lessons from global models,* ed. S. Baker, 76–90. Monterrey CA: Monterey Institute for International Studies.

Byrnes, H., and H. H. Maxim, eds. 2003. *Advanced foreign language learning: A challenge to college programs.* Boston: Thomson.

Chevalier, J. F. 2004. Heritage language literacy: Theory and practice. *Heritage Language Journal* 2:1. www.international.ucla.edu/lrc/hlj/index.as.

Clark, E. V. 2003. *First language acquisition.* London: Cambridge.

Colombi, M. C.. 2003. Un enfoque funcional para la enseñanza del ensayo expositivo. In *Mi lengua: Spanish as a heritage language in the United States; Research and practice,* ed. A. Roca and C. Colombi, 78–95. Washington, DC: Georgetown University Press.

Cook, V. 1997. The consequences of bilingualism and cognitive processing. In *Tutorials in bilingualism: Psycholinguistic perspectives,* ed. A. M. B. de Groot and J. F. Kroll, 279–99. Mahwah NJ: Earlbaum.

———. 2002. Background of the L2 user. In *Portraits of the L2 user,* ed. V. Cook, 1–28. Clevedon, U.K.: Multilingual Matters.

Cummins, J. 1979. Linguistic interdependence and the educational development of bilingual children. *Review of Educational Research* 49:222–51.

Firth, A., and J. Wagner. 1997. On discourse, communication, and (some) fundamental concepts in SLA research. *Modern Language Journal* 81:285–300.

Fishman, J. A. 1966. *Language loyalty in the United States.* The Hague: Mouton.

———. 1985. Mother-tongue claiming in the United States since 1960: Trends and correlates. In *The rise and fall of the ethnic revival: Perspectives on language and ethnicity,* ed. J. A. Fishman, M. H. Gertner, E. G. Lowy, and W. G. Milan, 107–94. Berlin: Mouton.

———. 1991. *Reversing language shift.* Clevedon, U.K.: Multilingual Matters.

Fishman, J., and B. R. Markman. 1979. *The ethnic mother tongue school in America: Assumptions, findings and directory.* Final Report to the National Institute of Education, Ferkauf Graduate School, Yeshiva University.

Gee, J. 1990. *Social linguistics and literacies: Ideology in discourses.* London: Falmer Press.

Gibbons, J., and E. Lascar. 1998. Operationalising academic language proficiency in bilingualism research. *Journal of Multilingual Multicultural Development* 19 (1): 40–50.

Gibbons, J., and E. Ramirez. 2004. *Maintaining a minority language: A case study of Hispanic teenagers.* Clevedon, U.K.: Multilingual Matters.

Goldberg, D., N. Lusin, and E. B. Welles. 2004. Successful college and university foreign language programs, 1995–99: Part 2. *ADFL Bulletin* 35 (2–3): 27–70.

Grosjean, F. 1985. The bilingual as a competent but specific speaker-hearer. *Journal of Multilingual Multicultural Development* 6:467–77.

———. 1997. Processing mixed language: Issues findings and models. In *Tutorials in bilingualism,* ed. A. M. De Groot and J. F. Kroll, 225–54. Mahway NJ: Earlbaum.

———. 1998. Studying bilinguals: Methodological and conceptual issues. *Bilingualism: Language and Cognition* 1:131–49.

Hallamaa, P. 1998. Endangered languages: Methodology, reality and social advocacy. In *Language contact, variation, and change,* ed. J. Niemi, T. Odlin and J. Heikkinen, 70–97. Joensuu, Finland: University of Joensuu.

Halliday, M.A. K., and R. Hasan. 1985. *Language, context, and texts: Aspects of language in a social-semiotic perspective.* Geelong VIC: Deaking University Press.

Halliday, M.A. K., and J. R. Martin. 1993. *Writing science: Literacy and discursive power.* London: Falmer.

Han, Z. H.. 2003. *Fossilization in adult second language acquisition.* Clevedon, U.K.: Multilingual Matters.

Hidalgo, M. 1987. On the question of "Standard" vs. "Dialect": Implications for teaching Hispanic college students. *Hispanic Journal of the Behavioral Sciences* 9 (4): 375–95.

———. 1993. The teaching of Spanish to bilingual Spanish-speakers: A "problem" of inequality. In *Language and culture in learning: Teaching Spanish to native speakers of Spanish,* ed. B. J. Merino, H. T. Trueba, and F. A. Samaniego, 82–93. London: Falmer Press.

Ingold, C., W. Rivers, C. Chavez Tesser, and E. Ashby. 2002. Report on the NFLC/AATSP survey of Spanish language programs for native speakers. *Hispania* 85 (2): 324–29.

Kern, R. G. 2003. Literacy and advanced foreign language learning: Rethinking the curriculum. In Byrnes and Maxim, *Advanced foreign language learning.* 2–18.

Lynch, A. 2003. Toward a theory of heritage language acquisition. In *Mi lengua: Spanish as a heritage language in the United States; Research and practice,* ed. A. Roca and C. Colombi, 25–50. Washington, DC: Georgetown University Press.

Maheux, G., and D. Simard. 2001. The problematic of the practice of teachers' training in Inuit communities within a perspective of knowledge construction in collaboration. Paper read at International Congress of Arctic Social Sciences 4th. Quebec City, Canada, May 18.

Mohanty, A. K., and C. Perregaux. 1997. Language acquisition and bilingualism. In *Handbook of cross-cultural psychology: Basic processes and human development,* ed. J. W. Berry, P. R. Dasen, and T. S. Saraswathi, 217–53. Boston: Allyn and Bacon.

Muller, K. E. 2002. Adressing counterterrorism: U.S. literacy in languages and international affairs. *Language Problems and Language Planning* 26 (1): 1–21.

New London Group. 1996. A pedagogy of multiliteracies: Designing social futures. *Harvard Educational Review* 66 (1): 60–92.

Oksaar, E. 1997. Social networks, communicative acts and the multilingual individual. In *Language change: Advances in historical sociolinguistics,* ed. E. H. Jahr, 3–19. Berlin: Mouton de Gruyter.

Pennycook, A. 1994. *The cultural politics of English as an international language.* London: Longman.

Reyhner, J., and Northern Arizona University–Flagstaff (NAU). 2003. Native Language Immersion. http://jan.ucc.nau.edu/›jar/NNL (accessed July 6, 2005).

Rhodes, H. C., and L. E. Branaman. 1999. *Foreign language instruction in the Untied States: A national survey of elementary and secondary schools.* Arlington, VA: Center for Applied Linguisitics and Delta Systems.

Romaine, S. 1995. *Bilingualism.* 2nd ed. Oxford: Blackwell.

Schwartz, A. M. 2003. No me suena: Heritage Spanish speakers' writing strategies. In *Mi lengua: Spanish as a heritage language in the United States; Research and practice,* ed. A. Roca and C. Colombi, 235–56. Washington, DC: Georgetown University Press.

Silva-Corvalán, C. 1994. *Language contact and change: Spanish in Los Angeles.* New York: Oxford University Press.

———. 2003a. Narrating in English and Spanish: Story telling in the words of a 5-year-old bilingual. *Revista Internacional de Lingüística Iberoamericana* 1 (2): 35–58.

———. 2003b. *El español en Los Angeles: Adquisición incompleta o desgaste lingüístico?* Centro Virtual Cervantes website. http://cvc.cervantes.es/obref/espanol—eeuu/bilingue/csilva.htm (accessed November 5, 2004).

Spada, N., and P. M. Lightbown. 2002. Second language acquisition. In *An introduction to applied linguistics,* ed. N. Schmitt, 115–32. London: Arnold.

Strang, W., A. von Glatz, P. Cahape Hammer, and ERIC Clearinghouse on Rural Education and Small Schools Charleston WV. 2002. Setting the agenda: American Indian and Alaska native education research priorities. *ERIC Digest.* Charleston, WV: ERIC/CRESS. ED471718. Text on line at www.ael.org/eric/digests/edorc02-14.pdf.

Swain, M., G. Dumas, and N. Naiman. 1974. Alternatives to spontaneous speech: Elicited translation and imitation as indicators of second language competence. *Working Papers on Bilingualism* 3:68–79.

U.S. Census Bureau. 2003. October. Census 2000 brief: Language use and English-language ability. Washington, DC: U.S. Census Bureau.

Valdés, G. 1995. The teaching of minority languages as "foreign" languages: Pedagogical and theoretical challenges. *Modern Language Journal* 79 (3): 299–328.

———. 2001. Heritage languages students: Profiles and possibilities. In *Heritage languages in America: Preserving a national resource,* ed. J. K. Peyton, D. A. Ranard and S. McGinnis, 37–77. Washington, DC: Center for Applied Linguistics/Delta Systems.

———. 2004. Between support and marginalization: The development of academic language in linguistic minority children. *International Journal of Bilingualism and Bilingual Education* 7 (2) and (3): 102–32.

———. 2005. Bilingualism, heritage language learners and SLA research: Opportunities lost or seized. *Special Issue of the Modern Language Journal: Re-conceptualizing Research on L2 Learning across Education Contexts* 89 (3): 410–26.

Valdés, G., J. A. Fishman, R. Chávez, and W. Pérez. In press. *The development of minority language resources: Lessons from the case of California.* Clevedon, U.K.: Multilingual Matters.

Valdés, G., and M. Geoffrion-Vinci. 1998. Chicano Spanish: The problem of the "underdeveloped" code in bilingual repertoires. *Modern Language Journal* 82 (4): 473–501.

Wei, L. 2000. *The bilingualism reader.* London: Routledge.

Woolard, K. A. 1999. Simultaneity and bivalency as strategies in bilingualism. *Journal of Linguistic Anthropology* 8 (1): 3–29.

Spanish Second Language Acquisition
Applications to the Teaching of Professional Translation (and Interpretation)

Sonia Colina   *University of Arizona*

1.0 Applications of Spanish Second Language Acquisition to the Teaching of Professional Translation (and Interpretation)

This chapter deals with the application of L2 (second language) research, in particular Spanish second language acquisition (SLA), to the teaching of translation and interpretation. By *translation* and *interpretation* I mean cross-linguistic and crosscultural communicative acts for meaningful purposes as opposed to, for instance, translation as a formalistic language exercise. Consequently, I do not deal with translation as a language teaching method or task as used, for instance, in grammar translation; rather, it is concerned with showing how the findings of second language acquisition can inform the teaching (and thus the practice) of professional translation.[1] The emphasis will be on translation with some mention of interpretation.[2]

The chapter is divided in three sections. After a brief introduction, I focus on SLA applications to the teaching of translation by reviewing applications of general concepts first, followed by applications in the areas of reading and writing, pragmatics, discourse and transfer, testing and advanced proficiency, and think-aloud protocols.

1.1 Models of Competence and General Concepts

A significant number of applications of SLA theory to translation studies and, in particular, to the teaching of translation and interpretation are concerned with general models of competence and theoretical concepts, such as communicative competence, the acquisition and learning distinction, and so on. These are, therefore, concepts drawn from general SLA theory and not restricted to Spanish SLA.

Cao (1996) applies Bachman's (1991) model of the components of communicative language competence to the development of a model of translation proficiency (fig. 11.1) for the purpose of testing translator skills. What she terms *translational competence* includes organizational competence in the source language (SL) and target language (TL), consisting of grammatical and textual competence, and pragmatic competence in SL and TL, made up of illocutionary and sociolinguistic competence. Cao also applies standard SLA assumptions about developmental stages to translation competence: She concludes that in her model of translation, proficiency follows a developmental path and can be acquired/developed/learned from zero to professional levels (339).

Figure 11.1 Cao's Model of Translation Proficiency (1996)

Kiraly (1990) applies the *acquisition-learning distinction* in conjunction with the notion of *communicative competence* to translator training. He points out that the dominant educational paradigm in translator training is still the equivalence or linguistic transfer paradigm, in which students are expected to replace words and structures from one language by words and structures in the other, with little regard for the purpose of the text. This means that a great deal of time is spent on learning and not enough on using language for self-expression or communication. Kiraly contends that in translator training students must be given opportunities for acquisition as well as learning and that "the translator needs to acquire communicative competence in addition to linguistic knowledge and linguistic manipulation skills" (214). He also proposes an acquisitionist model of the translation process (ibid.).

In addition to reiterating the importance for a pedagogy of translation of the notion of communicative competence (see, for definitions, Savignon [1972, 1983] and many others after her) and of SLA proposals concerning the partial competencies comprised by communicative competence (Canale and Swain 1980), Kiraly (1995) stresses the relevance of language acquisition and language teaching in general for translator education. He argues that the "integration of language competences in overall translation competence links translation skills instruction to foreign language teaching" (26). He contends that language teaching—and therefore SLA—can clarify the L1 and L2 competencies that a professional translator must possess and use when translating. More specifically, he reminds translation researchers that the elaboration of translation pedagogy need not retrace the evolution of language teaching, as translation scholars in the area of pedagogy can benefit from the knowledge acquired in second language acquisition.[3]

Kiraly (2000), drawing on the case of German translation schools in which translators must learn their foreign languages as well as translate, proposes a socioconstructivist approach (Vygotsky 1986, 1978) to translator education. He brings to the foreground the connection between language teaching and translation by arguing that for a constructivist approach to translation to work, it must be preceded by the same type of approach to language learning. In a similar vein, Colina (2002) shows that many of the deficiencies of translation students today can be traced back to the type of language education that they were exposed to, in particular, methodologies based on behaviorist and formalist theories of language acquisition.[4]

Kiraly (1995) and Colina (2002, 2003a, 2003b) delve further into the connection between second language acquisition and translation teaching by observing that translation is a special form of communicative language use and therefore a unique form of second language education. Given the current communicative purpose shared by language teaching, SLA, and translation, it makes sense to suggest, as Kiraly does, that some of the important language and language learning concepts that have evolved within communicative approaches to second language education can serve as a point of departure for developing a systematic translation pedagogy, for example, language function, the monitor model, interlanguage theory, creative and active student participation, and so on (Kiraly 1995, 34). Colina (2002, 6) takes the analogy further by arguing that if, as SLA literature suggests, communicative competence is acquired by communicating, communicative translational competence is probably also acquired through authentic, communicative translation tasks. Consequently, the goal of translation teaching should be "to facilitate the acquisition of communicative translational competence by providing opportunities for engaging in communicative translation tasks and by working along with the natural process of acquisition" (2003a, 29).

Note that more recent trends in SLA incorporate some type of focus on form into communicative approaches (see Dussias 2003 and Grove 2003 for an overview), resulting in "instruction that endeavors to contextualize attention to the formal properties of the language within communicative interactions" (Grove 2003, 289). I am not aware of any studies that have explicitly drawn a connection between focus on form in SLA and the teaching of translation, yet such connection may be unnecessary for translation pedagogy. Focus-on-form instruction in language teaching can be seen as an attempt to reinstate the attention to form that was lost with some communicative approaches; attention to form, however, has always been present in the translation classroom, and even communicative approaches, as in Colina (2003a), include a focus-on-form approach, such as her Focus on Language sections (Colina 2003a, 81–82, 88–89, 95, 103–4, 110). The ever-present role of form in translation pedagogy is most likely the direct consequence of the translation process itself, specifically, the need to avoid the cognitive bias towards transfer (systemic and translational). Thus it can be argued that the translation classroom is in need of a focus-on-communication approach and that such an approach should not come at the cost of diminished attention to form (cf. Colina 2002 for other factors involved in the excessive focus on form present in translation teaching until very recently).

Arguing for the need to develop a translation teaching methodology based on research findings (vs. the current anecdotal basis), Colina (2003a, 6) singles out the relationship between SLA theory and language teaching as a model to be imitated in developing a research-based pedagogy of translation. She also contends that SLA is an area of knowledge that translation pedagogy needs to draw from in order to establish a solid, systematic research foundation (2003a, 6, 29–30).

1.2 Empirical and Area-specific Applications
1.2.1 Scarcity of Empirical Applications

Several of the studies mentioned in section 2.1 explicitly refer to the connection between SLA and translation teaching. In fact, a significant body of work in SLA and translation has to do with either general concepts or the intersection between SLA and translator training to the detriment of empirical studies. The reasons for this have to do with various factors generally related to the evolution of translation, translation studies, and language teaching (see Colina 2002). Kiraly puts it as follows:

> The wealth of articles . . . on translation studies over the past two decades is marked by a virtual absence of contributions dealing with the role of second language learning and teaching in translator education. This lack of research and discussion could suggest that there is basic agreement that translator education institutions are doing an adequate job of teaching foreign languages. I contend, however, that the still pervasive pedagogical view of translation as an interlingual transcoding process has perpetuated the stranglehold of transmissionist teaching approaches in translator education and has inhibited fruitful debate on the applicability of communicative teaching methods to translator education. (2000, 181)

In other words, because of the long-held view that SLA is not pertinent to translation, many translation and SLA scholars are still engaged in demonstrating its relevance in general terms (consider, for instance, the publication date of Colina 2002). Consequently, this section will present evidence that establishes the relevance of SLA research for the teaching of translation and interpretation and review some of the scarce empirical studies, focusing on Spanish, that draw an explicit connection between SLA findings and translation/interpretation as well as those areas of SLA that hold potential for application to the teaching of translation and interpretation.[5]

Translation and interpretation teachers, practitioners and scholars alike, have often considered second language acquisition unrelated to their goals. In general this position is rooted in firmly entrenched prescriptivist notions dictating that language acquisition should be complete before the start of translation and interpretation training and that translators should always translate into their native language. I argue that such views are inadequate to the current reality of the training and education of language mediators, mainly due to (1) the descriptive nature of translation studies (Toury [1980, 1995] and many others after him) and (2) oversimplified views of language acquisition and bilingualism.

If translation studies is to be consistent with the descriptive approach it has set for itself, research in translation cannot ignore the fact that translators across the globe do indeed translate into their nonnative languages. One case where this is found is among immigrant communities of recent arrival, where unavoidably translators are found within the community itself (Campbell 1998, 24). However, as time progresses and the number of second-generation speakers increases, the reverse scenario prevails: community members start to become dominant in the majority language and to experience language loss affecting the ethnic language, usually relegated to the home environment. A well-studied case of this type of translation practice is Australia, as described in Campbell (1998). Another significant, although much less discussed, example is that of heritage speakers in the United States (Valdés, this volume). Given that the heritage language is no longer the dominant language, translation into the heritage language is translation into the second language as defined by Campbell and therefore involves a directionality not recommended by the professional community of translators.[6] Translation into the nonprimary language, however, is not limited to immigrant communities and heritage speakers, since there are numerous countries where translators work into their nonnative language, usually due to a shortage in the supply of professionals working into certain primary languages. Well-known cases are, for instance, those of the former Soviet Union, Japan and other Asian countries, and Finland (Ahlsvad 1978; Campbell 1998; Mackenzie 1998). Even of countries like Spain, Wetherby (1998, 21) says that "in practice more than half of many professional translators' work is done into their L2." In sum, given the descriptive facts concerning translation practice around the world, it is obvious that considerable amounts of language acquisition take place during and after translation and interpretation training and that therefore SLA research must fall within the purview of descriptive translation studies and more specifically the teaching of translation and interpretation.

A second argument against the view that holds that language acquisition is irrelevant to translation studies is that such a statement is an overgeneralization based on oversimplified views of language acquisition and bilingualism. The concept of *native speaker* was originally formulated in cognitive linguistics to refer to the competence/mental representation of the language possessed by such speaker. Within the context of translation, an activity concerned more with language use and performance (vs. competence and ideal mental representations), the term *native speaker* is either ill-defined or ill-applied. The concept itself cannot be easily transferred to many translation situations. Clyne et al. (1997) say that "in the context of language acquisition and development in multicultural Australia, the terms 'native' and 'nonnative speaker' have little significance" (5). The same can be said of heritage speakers in the United States: while they can be considered native speakers for purposes of linguistic research, they should probably not translate into the "native language," as the lack of exposure to formal registers and to a variety of text types makes their textual competence rather limited.

The notion of native speaker as applied to translation also assumes that language acquisition is static, leaving no room for attrition. Language attrition may render translation into the native language less desirable than into the second language, especially when this is the language of current professional activity and education. Furthermore, the cognitive notion of native speaker fosters a monolithic view of acquisition that does not reflect different contexts of use and register. Native speaker competence does not entail native level competence in all registers and all discourse and text types.

In summary, the terms *native speaker* and *native language* reveal themselves as highly inadequate to describe the complexities of translation practice throughout the world. Their infelicitous application to translation can be seen as the generalization of a common practice in Western Europe and a simplification of translation requirements. An implication of this is the need for much more detailed descriptions of translator skills with regard to language proficiency. Furthermore, skill descriptions need to be correlated with the requirements of specific translation tasks, as various kinds of language proficiency will be required for different jobs. Obviously writing and applying such descriptions is a much more challenging endeavor than merely requiring translators to be native speakers of the language they are translating into, but this is also an area where the findings of second language acquisition research can inform translation teaching. SLA can help to identify competency levels/areas and help student translators progress to the next level.

Moreover, independent of the concept validity of the term *native speaker,* one can argue that second language acquisition is involved even when one translates into the first language, as second language comprehension, in particular reading comprehension, becomes activated in translation with respect to the source text. Marmaramidou (1996) puts it as follows:

> The translator mediates so that an unknown domain of experience such as the source text is understood in terms of another, the translation or target text. This implies that there is a mapping between the two domains such that the conceptual structures of the target language are mapped onto the source text. . . . A further implication of this position is that, even though *temporally* the translation process starts out with a source text and ends with the translation product, cognitively this process has the reverse directionality. (1996, 53)

In sum, the second language is always involved in translation, regardless of native language and directionality, and therefore second language acquisition is always pertinent to translation teaching.

1.2.2 Reading and Writing Research and the Lexicon

With regard to reading and writing, Colina (2002) applies SLA writing research, more specifically, the cognitive approach to writing of Flower and Hayes (1981), to translation teaching and shows how some of the components of the writing process mentioned by Flower and Hayes have also been documented by translation scholars in the translation process. She illustrates this point by providing some sample activities for the translation classroom.

Colina (2002) also reviews research in reading in SLA and its implications for translation teaching. She stresses the relevance of reading comprehension research on schemata and background knowledge (Rumelhart 1977, 1980; Johnson 1981; Lee 1987) that indicates that reading is an interactive process in which the reader's schemata/experience interact with the information on the page. An important consequence of such research is that knowing all the linguistic data in the text does not, in many cases, equal comprehension (2002, 10). This is in direct contradiction with traditional teaching approaches to translation that focus on learning terminology lists without any reference to their use and limitations.

Colina (2002) contends that current language teaching materials designed to help students to use their background knowledge and schemata more efficiently in order to compensate for possible linguistic deficiencies should have a positive impact on the translation student. As a consequence, she proposes the creation of lessons/activities for the translation classroom that isolate comprehension issues. She also provides some Spanish/English sample lessons (2002, 12–13; 2003a) containing activities that guide the student through the creation and identification of the relevant schemata, familiarize him or her with reading comprehension processes, and help him or her stay away from word-by-word translation.

The organization of the L1 and L2 lexicon, its storage and retrieval, is an area of research with clear connections to reading comprehension and writing. The contributions in Anderman and Rogers (1996) review L1 and L2 lexicon research and its implications for translation and translation teaching, although none of these studies focus on Spanish lexicon acquisition. Anderman (1996) considers the application of prototype theory to second language acquisition and reviews several attempts to apply the concept of prototype to translation. She observes that translators moving between languages need to revise their notions about prototypes just as children do when acquiring their native lexicon. This has important consequences for the way vocabulary is taught in translation classes, usually in a one-to-one equivalence fashion, as well as for the reading comprehension processes of the translator translating into his or her native language.

Applying prototype theory to translation, Aitchison (1996) points out that for a translator it may be better to replace a prototypical instance with another prototypical instance rather than with the exact lexical equivalent. For instance, the Spanish translator of a U.S. English nutritional brochure about food groups may find it appropriate to replace "tomatoes" with what would be a more prototypical instance of a fruit, at least for some Spanish-speaking groups, (e.g., *manzanas*), rather than with its lexical equivalent (*tomates*). Meara (1996) reviews findings related to subjects' learning and forgetting of words as presented in vocabulary lists and the implications for translation teachers and curriculum designers. Colina (2003a) and Kussmaul (1995) also apply research findings on word meaning and the lexicon, specifically, the scenes-and-frames semantics model (Fillmore 1976, 1977) to the teaching of translation. Colina (2003a, 123–24) includes some curricular suggestions and lesson samples on how to incorporate this in the Spanish translation classroom.

The interactive nature of the reading process revealed by the research reviewed here brings to the foreground the issue of transfer in second language reading and consequently in translating into the first language (Marmaramidou 1996). Odlin (1989, 62–64) discusses transfer, specifically transfer of discourse patterns and coherence and how they affect comprehension since "a passage may be more readable or less readable depending on readers' expectations, which are partially shaped by language and culture" (64). This type of second language transfer is not normally considered in the translation classroom. Using Spanish and English texts, Colina (2003a) proposes a pretranslation component in the design of translation lessons that would raise awareness of possible gaps in cultural and textual knowledge regarding the source text.

In addition to the extralinguistic resources that the reader brings to a text, the reading process encompasses areas of linguistic competence beyond the ones traditionally taught/focused upon in the classroom (e.g., phonology, morphology, syntax, and semantics). These areas are pragmatics and textual competence (discourse competence), which are starting to acquire their due place in second language acquisition (see, among many, Kramsch 1982; Rose and Kasper 2001; see also Koike 1996 and the references therein).

1.2.3 *Pragmatics, Discourse, and Transfer*

Pragmatics and discourse SLA studies are essential to translation independent of the directionality of translation because capturing the pragmatic and discourse content of the source text is as crucial to the effectiveness of the target text as producing the pragmatic force and discourse structure required by the function of the translation.

While much research has focused on contrastive pragmatics and discourse in both Spanish and in other languages, including pragmatic and discourse shifts and/or transfer, there have been fewer investigations of the acquisition of pragmatic knowledge and rhetorical structure (developmental stages, interlanguage pragmatics, etc.) (cf. Koike 1996 for review), and even fewer of the application of research findings to the teaching of translation. From the perspective of translation studies, research has focused mostly on contrastive rhetoric and how translated texts deviate from or approximate the rhetorical and pragmatic norms of the target community (e.g. Blum-Kulka 1986; van den Broeck 1986; Tobin 1986; Tirkkonen-Condit 1986; Weizman 1986; Colina 1997), as well as on various sorts of applications of pragmatics and discourse to the translation process (e.g., Hervey 1998; House 1998; Fawcett 1998).

Within translation teaching, some authors call for the need to incorporate contrastive rhetoric (Colina 1997), text types, and pragmatic factors in the translation classroom (Hatim 1997; Nord 1997; Schäffner 2002; Colina 2003a, 2003b). Colina (1997) reports significant improvement in the quality of student translations when the task was preceded by a short lesson on the rhetorical structure of recipes in Spanish and English original texts. Colina (2003a) incorporates pragmatic factors into a methodology of translation teaching by resorting to global considerations, functionalism, and text types in course and lesson design. This approach is also empirically justified as it has been shown that novice translators usually ignore pragmatic factors (function, addresses of the translation), regardless of language proficiency (Colina 1997, 1999; Jääskeläinen 1989, 1990, 1993, 1996; Königs 1987; Krings 1987; Kussmal 1995; Lörscher 1991, 1992, 1997). Note, however, that pragmatic transfer in translation (often leading to pragmatic inappropriateness of the target text) can be ascribed to deficient pragmatic competence or to translational transfer (without ignorance) (Toury 1986; James 1988; Colina 1997, 1999; Colina and Sykes 2004). Given that full pragmatic competence is acquired late, even in very advanced learners (Koike 1996), it becomes extremely challenging to discriminate between the two types of pragmatic transfer in translation.[7] This is one reason most studies focus on the descriptive aspects of pragmatic transfer in translation (rather than on their sources—language acquisition or translation).

In fact, I suggest that establishing a distinction between acquisitional and translational transfer may not be crucial and that the overlap may be beneficial for SLA and for teachers of translation. Since SLA researchers, language teachers, and translation scholars all emphasize awareness of pragmatic and rhetorical differences for language acquisition and translation, professional translation tasks that focus on the function of the translation can be incorporated in advanced language classes to foster awareness; similarly, the use of translation tasks with a pragmatic (rather than structural, linguistic) orientation in language classes will help translation students to become aware of pragmatic and discourse factors in translation and to move away from sign-based translation even before they enter the translation class.

As mentioned above, translation scholars do not usually make explicit connections between research on pragmatics/discourse and translation. It is often assumed that awareness will lead to improved teaching and learning. Similarly, there is a dearth of studies that explicitly apply the findings of Spanish SLA pragmatics research to the teaching of translation. Moreover, the connection is obvious. For instance, Koike (1996) in a study on the transfer of suggestion strategies from L1 English speakers to L2 Spanish in listening comprehension found that the transfer strategy (which leads to assigning incorrect illocutionary force) is applied even by the more advanced learners. She studies speech acts such as

1. *¿No has pensado en leer este libro?*
'Haven't you thought about reading this book?'

2. *¿Has pensado en leer este libro?*
'Have you thought about reading this book?'

Whereas in Spanish, 1 is a suggestion (2 is merely a request for information), direct transfer/translation into English results in a reproach. The same problem of transfer, which leads English learners of Spanish to assign much stronger force to 1 than the native speaker of Spanish, surfaces in translation as translators often focus on the syntactic form to the detriment of illocutionary force and pragmatics. Colina and Sykes (2004) found that many translations produced for local use by Spanish-speaking parents of school-aged children in Arizona exhibit pragmatic transfer from the source text and therefore convey inappropriate illocutionary force. On the basis of this, Colina and Sykes (2004) make recommendations for the teaching of translation to include pragmatic awareness. Translation teachers and students can benefit from a pedagogy of translation that takes into consideration these findings by raising awareness of pragmatic and rhetorical contrasts across languages and that forces student to consider them in their translations (see, for instance, Colina 2003a).

In dealing with applications of Spanish SLA pragmatics and discourse to translation teaching, transfer surfaced as a related topic. Although in translation teaching transfer in pragmatics, discourse and reading comprehension has not received much attention (see however Toury 1986), transfer in translation has been studied in a general fashion by SLA scholars such as Carl James. James (1988, 46–47) examines the relevance of transfer theory for translation (and vice versa). He identifies four transfer types—original, institutionalized, systemic, and translational—and applies them to translator training, presenting a complex but comprehensive picture for those engaged in translator training.

Original transfer refers to negative transfer from the L1; institutionalized transfer is not a property of the individual learner but of the community in a language contact situation; systemic transfer is the result of the confluence, in the speaker's mind, of two knowledge systems, independent of the task (negative and positive transfer); finally, translational transfer is a consequence of the presence of the source text in the translation process. James states that if the student is a natural bilingual, he or she will probably show all types of transfer. If the translation student is a foreign language student, he or she will supply the original transfer, his teachers the institutionalized, and the act of translation itself the other two.

From the point of view of translation and second language acquisition, teachers need to consider all these types of transfer; their different sources call for different pedagogical approaches. Institutionalized transfer is perhaps better dealt with as a specific geographical and/or social variety of a language that will be more or less appropriate to the translation task on the basis of the translation requirements/brief (audience, purpose, etc.).

1.2.4 Testing and Advanced Proficiency

Proficiency, in particular advanced proficiency, is an area of SLA research that directly affects translation and translation teaching. Angelelli and Kagan (2002, 211) compare the language proficiency of Spanish and Russian heritage speakers at the Superior level on the ACTFL scale (1999) to their nonheritage counterparts. They argue that effective programs for heritage speakers will both overlap and differ from L2 programs for nonnative speakers. Angelelli and Kagan also present instructional approaches that can help heritage language learners reach the Superior/Distinguished level in the ACTFL scale.[8] Heritage learner proficiency is a crucial issue for translation teaching in countries with large immigrant populations, such as Australia and the United States, given the fact that many students or practitioners of translation are heritage speakers. In fact, it is commonplace in the educational literature in the United States to refer to the need to develop this national linguistic resource. Similar observations have been occasionally made in translation and interpretation (Campbell 1998; Colina and Sykes 2004; Colina 2004b). In some cases pilot educational programs in translation and interpretation (for instance, the Professional Language Development Program at the University of Arizona) have been developed to take advantage of heritage speakers' linguistic skills in an effort to increase academic and professional involvement from minority populations in areas such as law, medicine, and so on. Initial findings indicate a positive outcome (Dueñas-González 2004).

Angelelli and Degueldre (2002) draw an explicit connection between Superior/ Distinguished level speakers and the language skills required for professional purposes, such as language teaching, translation, and interpretation. An important implication and observation of this study and others that deal with developing language skills for professional purposes is that the level of proficiency required when using a foreign/second language for work is higher than Superior/Distinguished. The ACTFL scale is therefore considered insufficient. The ACTFL Superior/Distinguished level corresponds to five numerical levels (3, 3+, 4, 4+, and 5) in the Interagency Language Roundtable (ILR) scale, from which the ACTFL scale originated (Liskin-Gasparro 1982). The highest level of proficiency attainable is that of (or equivalent to) an educated native-speaker. Both the ILR and ACTFL scales are insufficient to measure the proficiency of translators and interpreters because professional translation and interpreting usually require levels of metalinguistic awareness and linguistic skill absent even in many educated native speakers (those whose jobs do not focus on language use, for example, journalists, writers, literary critics, and scholars). Translation and interpretation teaching will therefore benefit from the development of advanced proficiency scales that would reach the highest level of proficiency as well as establish different proficiency levels and their adequacy for particular programs of study and/or translation tasks. These scales can be used in connection with exit requirements for graduation from training programs.

Colina (2003a, 130–34) applies concepts such as summative and formative assessment, proficiency and achievement testing, and criterion and norm-referenced testing to translation testing. Concerning test writing, she proposes a checklist for a quality translation test based on Carroll's (1980) criteria for language tests (2003, 134–35). Also following the lead of proposals in language teaching and SLA testing, Colina (2003a) develops componential grading criteria for translation tests on the basis of two models of translation competence (Cao 1996; Hatim 1997); she illustrates their application to student translations.

1.2.5 Think Aloud Protocols

Think aloud protocols (TAPs) is an experimental method of research that clearly brings out the overlap between language learning/acquisition and translation. TAPs have been used to investigate language acquisition (Cohen and Hosenfeld 1981; Cohen 1984) and the cognitive processes involved in translating (see Jääskeläinen 2002 for references). The first studies dealing with translating (Gerloff 1986; Krings 1986a, 1986b; Lörscher 1986; Königs 1987) have often been criticized by translation scholars on the basis that their subjects were language students (of French and German), not professional translators. While this is a valid objection if the results are to be extrapolated to describe professional behavior, the findings themselves are nevertheless important for language acquisition and translation teaching.

A translation pedagogy needs by definition to focus on the process of acquisition of translational competence from novice to expert, including developmental stages and factors that promote change. Consequently, the translation and linguistic competence of novice translators and other types of bilinguals needs to be described to under-stand how full professional competence is acquired. The studies mentioned above all found that language students translate in very small units, focusing on words or short phrases, resorting to a linguistic replacement approach. TAPs of nonprofessional, untrained translators also indicate similar behavior, regardless of language proficien-cy (Colina 1999; Lörscher 1997; Jääskeläinen 1990). In sum, TAPs of language stu-dents and more advanced learners reveal similar findings—a linguistic approach to interlingual language tasks that is indicative of either deficiencies in pragmatic com-petence or the inability to use pragmatic knowledge. Research findings in pragmatics acquisition in SLA have therefore an important application in the area of translator training.

2.0 Challenges and Suggestions for Application

The second section of this chapter deals with the challenges faced by initiatives to transfer findings from Spanish SLA research to the teaching of translation and interpretation.

2.1 Challenges for the Application of SLA Research to the Teaching of Translation

It is evident that the first challenge to overcome is the demonstration of relevance of SLA to the teaching of translation and interpreting (see section 2.3.1). An additional, perhaps greater, challenge faced by attempts to develop a translation pedagogy informed by SLA findings lies in the translation community itself. Angelelli (2000, 40) explains that language teaching pedagogy has benefited from a long empirical tradi-tion, resulting from the interaction of related research fields. Collaboration between educators and researchers has informed practice, which in turn sets different direc-tions for research.

This collaboration avoids what Angelelli calls a "closed circle" in which a field draws only from the knowledge of its own experts and practitioners. Angelelli argues that not all fields have evolved this way. For historical reasons, this is precisely the case of interpreting pedagogy. Colina (2003a, 2003b, 2004b) contends that the "closed cir-cle" situation also applies to translation, despite the somewhat different historical evolution.[9] The translation and interpretation teaching community is often made up of practitioners (translators and interpreters) with no research or pedagogical back-ground or at times of academics with a literary translation background who lack research and pedagogical expertise in nonliterary translation as well as practical expe-rience and access to the profession.

At the same time, much of the research conducted in translation and interpreta-tion is disconnected from related areas of investigation, such as bilingualism, lan-guage acquisition, sociolinguistics, educational linguistics, and so on, which cannot therefore contribute to the enrichment of the field and of teaching practices. As Angelelli puts it, "The crucial relationship arising from the interaction of both theo-ry and research (which normally would inform practice by helping a field move ahead) and teaching practice (which in other fields informs theory and research, thereby setting new directions in which the field needs to move) is almost nonexistent" (2000, 46).

In sum, the challenge then becomes one of research dissemination and of teacher education. In order to attain its goal, research dissemination must consider the needs of a teacher audience that is practice oriented and has severe time constraints, much more severe in the case of the translator/interpreter teacher. Teachers must be educated to discriminate and justify varied approaches to teaching, to become informed users of research findings and to be able to develop teaching materials and curricula on the basis of current research. In other words, a call for a research-based pedagogy that is not accompanied by the means to make it accessible to its users is doomed to failure.

Colina (2003a) takes that position as her point of departure. She argues for a research-based translation teaching methodology by showing teachers of translation how to apply research findings to the development of a pedagogy of translation. More specifically, after presenting a detailed review of the relevant empirical and theoretical research in SLA and other areas, Colina devotes an entire chapter to the design of an introduction to translation course in which for each course component proposed—classroom discussion and participation, theory, translation tools, translation activities, portfolio, translation project and revision—she identifies issues to be taught, research justification, and method (see Colina 2003a, 55–76). For instance, for the translation activities component, she identifies the skills, research justification, and teaching method shown in table 11.1.

Similarly, when addressing lesson and activity design, Colina (2003a) demonstrates how each activity type relates to specific goals connected to particular research findings (explained in detail earlier in the book) in the acquisition of translational

Table 11.1 Basic components of a research-based pedagogy of translation

Skill(s)	Research justification	Method
Translation as a process; importance of pragmatic, textual, and global considerations.	Students do not consider textual and pragmatic factors in their translations (Jääskeläinen and Tirkkonen-Condit 1991; Kussmaul 1995; Jääskeläinen 1993; Colina 1997, 1999); students view translation merely as a product; although pertinent information (textual and pragmatic) may be available for successful completion of the task, students have difficulty focusing on it (Shreve 1997).	Various types of translation activities accompany the assignments. Activities are process-oriented, guide the student through the translation process, and focus on textual and global considerations.

Table 11.2 Activity types

Activity type	Description	Example
Pretranslation	Activities that focus on pragmatic factors for the source and target texts, the translation brief or translator instructions (complete or partial, to help in determining contextual factors for the target text), transfer issues (How do the pragmatic factors studied relate to the transfer process and what are the consequences for textual features and organization?), and parallel text analysis.	Step 1. Indicate the pragmatic (situational) factors (function, addressees, time of reception, place of reception, medium of transmission, motive for production) that pertain to the source text. Step 2. Do the same for the target text on the basis of the brief provided. Step 3. Compare the situational factors in ST and TT. Notice the differences in the target pragmatic factors imposed by the translation brief. Skim the source text quickly and think of how this might affect translation decisions.
Reading comprehension	Activities that make up for difficulties in comprehension, incomplete schemas, and unclear terminology; aid in the understanding of reading and background knowledge and their role in translation; teach students how to use these processes to facilitate translation.	[Translation of a TV catalogue/ad that lists technical features. Discussion in the target language.] Step 1. What are some of the most common features you will find on big screen TVs? [Teacher makes a chart on board to summarize students' ideas.] Step 2. See if you find any of these features in the specifications list provided in the ad.
Focus on language	Activities that focus on smaller units of translation, langue use, well-known linguistic problems (e.g., negative transfer, sign translation, translation difficulties, and word- or phrasal-level linguistic issues), as they relate to the brief and global translation decisions.	Locate the segments provided (multiple choice) in the source text and choose the most appropriate target correspondent for the brief. Explain your choice. Recall that professional translation is a type of a communicative use of language and, therefore, you need to focus on the pragmatic factors surrounding the production of the target text and not on the structure of the source.

competence. She proposes the activity types seen in table 11.2; the goals and justification follow table 11.2. The reader is referred to Colina (2003a) for a more detailed review of the relevant research and for complete lesson samples.

A final challenge is related to the educational profile of many teachers of translation and interpreting. Unlike language teachers, who often start teaching in graduate school as part of a program of study and professional development, translation teachers are usually practicing translators. Having experienced professionals in the classroom is a desirable state of affairs; however, it also poses a serious difficulty with regard to teacher training, as most professionals are not able to embark on a full-time program of study.

2.2 Overcoming the Challenges

One possible way of overcoming the challenges in section 2.1 consists of an educational course of action that works in several fronts simultaneously. Teachers of translation and interpretation and program administrators have traditionally looked at the European schools as the model to imitate in program design. As a result, professional programs in the United States are in many cases staffed by practitioners (e.g., Monterrey Institute of International Studies, numerous community colleges) and isolated from the general academic and research communities of higher education. This situation fosters the preservation of the "closed circle." While the closed circle would not have been a problem in the academic and research environment of forty years ago, it presents itself as a real obstacle in an era of increased specialization, interdisciplinarity, and fast technological and research advances. New problems cannot be easily addressed through old models, hence the inadequacy of the European model.[10] Therefore, in addition to a wide-based, multipronged approach, possible solutions to the challenges of section 2.1 need to be innovative and nontraditional in method.

2.3 The Need to Be Innovative and Nontraditional in Method
2.3.1 Embedded Programs

Translation and interpretation research and pedagogy could be embedded in related, established programs of study such as applied linguistics, education, and even medicine, public health, and other professional fields. An example would be a master of arts degree in Spanish linguistics that focuses on Spanish SLA, bilingualism, and sociolinguistics, where students can do translation and interpretation research projects.[11] Another example would be a special research track within a master of arts and/or doctorate program of study in the fields mentioned.[12] Whether taught as an independent course or as a module in a language methods course, translation pedagogy can be useful not only to linguistics students but also to literature majors who teach language courses.

One of the benefits of this type of approach is that it is faster and more likely to succeed than designing new, specialized programs in translation studies. Another one is that contrary to the translation studies doctorate or master's degree aternative, the inclusion approach would foster understanding, dissemination, and research in related disciplines, thus facilitating the opening of the closed circle and the enrichment of translation teaching by incorporating the research findings of relevant fields.

2.3.2 Practice-oriented Translation and Interpretation Modules/Programs

Graduate research programs could be articulated with practice-oriented translation and interpretation modules/programs. These could consist of certificate degrees for bilingual professionals in various fields and would be staffed by graduate students with professional experience in translation and interpretation or by practitioners

Table 11.3 Goals and justifications for activity types

Pretranslation activities

To force students to consider pragmatic factors at the right time in the translation process, so that they will guide global and local translation decisions.

To help students understand translation as a communicative activity that goes well beyond its linguistic basis.

To start undoing the effects of traditional approaches (sentence-based, formalistic) to translation teaching.

To encourage top-down processing and the use of global processes.

To discourage sign translating and encourage sense translating.

Comprehension activities

To encourage global comprehension.

To understand the process of reading comprehension and how it affects translation.

To teach use of context.

To teach the nature of meaning and meaning potential (including more adequate use of dictionaries).

To teach the importance and the role of world knowledge and of background knowledge, and of schemata in reading and in translation.

To demonstrate that terminology is only one aspect of technical translation.

To undo the influence of traditional approaches to reading in the language classroom (which saw reading as the decoding and replacement of language terms).

To help students to develop strategies to deal with the multifarious requirements imposed by specific translation tasks (by providing a better understanding of reading comprehension).

Focus on language

To avoid sign translating and unjustified transfer.

To remind students of the importance of accuracy (grammar and spelling in addition to form and content).

To make sure that matters of detail do not get lost among global considerations.

To focus on lower level structures and show how global decisions made earlier materialize at these levels.

trained in pedagogy/methods of teaching translation.[13] This type of articulation provides teaching experience for graduate students, pedagogical training, and experience for practitioners and gives students in the practice courses exposure to both professional, research and pedagogical practice. Programs are staffed cooperatively by academics and professional translators and interpreters.

2.3.3 Articulation with Continuing Education and Workshops for Professional Translators

Graduate research programs and faculty research could be articulated with ongoing continuing education programs and workshops for professional translators (distance learning, online format) (see, for an example, Colina 2003c). In the case of working professionals, time constraints can be offset by the incentive of continuing education credits, which are required by many employers and by professional associations such as the American Translators Association. Research-based workshops can also be offered in connection with applied and grant projects (see, for instance, Colina 2004a, a workshop on translator qualifications and translation needs for hospital translators and administrators funded by the Robert Wood Johnson Foundation). A dissemination component through publications is also included.

Not all academic and research settings may be positioned to work in the broad fashion suggested above. However, even small language programs can contribute to the application of SLA research findings in translation teaching by fostering/benefiting from the exchange and overlap between the two areas. One possible way to do this is to incorporate simple, but authentic and communication-oriented, translation tasks in advanced language courses, such as hospital intake forms, medical histories, and so on. Another one is to include a translation and interpretation introductory course (survey type) in the language curriculum (see Colina 2003a and Dueñas-González 2004 for examples).

3.0 Conclusion

This chapter reviewed SLA applications to the teaching of translation and interpretation with regard to both general concepts and specific areas such as reading, writing, pragmatics, discourse and transfer, and testing and proficiency. One obvious conclusion that can be drawn is that the application of SLA findings to the teaching of translation and interpretation is very much in its infancy, especially when compared to other areas (see other contributions to this volume). At the root of this situation usually lie prescriptivist, oversimplified notions regarding the role of language proficiency in the education of translators and interpreters. Consequently, an important first step taken in this chapter was to lay out the hidden assumptions and present some solid argumentation for the relevance of SLA findings to the teaching of translation and interpretation.

Nevertheless, despite the arguments presented, and independent of their validity, it is likely that the weight of tradition and norms in translation and interpreting will continue to exert its influence by minimizing the role of SLA findings in translator and interpreter training. Thus the final suggestion is aimed at researchers, to encourage them to take the lead and carefully consider the potential and need for research and research applications at the intersection of SLA and translation and interpreting. One of the goals in writing this chapter was to prepare the ground for this type of effort. Language teachers, translators and interpreters, and translation and interpretation teachers will be the direct beneficiaries of it.

Notes

1. Note, however, that this does not mean that communicative translation tasks cannot be a useful component of a language education curriculum (Colina 2002; 2003a, 40–42). The role of translation and of its various types (formalistic, communicative, professional) in language acquisition remains to be defined and investigated in the acquisition and the translation studies literature. A renewed interest in translation within second language acquisition has uncovered some degree of confusion regarding types of translational activity and their relationship to language acquisition (see the review of Lunn and Lunsford 2003 in Colina 2005).
2. This was not the original intent behind this article. However, during the actual researching and writing of the chapter, it became obvious that time and space constraints would not allow for adequate treatment of interpreting pedagogy. Consequently, and given the importance of the written mode of communication in the second language acquisition literature, it seemed appropriate to focus on translation first. Interpretation is referred to as well when the implications and/or findings are shared by both modes of communication, regardless of medium.
3. Kiraly often uses language teaching and/or foreign language teaching rather than SLA.
4. Recent sociocultural models of SLA (Lantolf 2000; Johnson 2004) have not, to my knowledge, been applied to translation. Kiraly (2000) applies Vygotsky's sociocultural theory directly to translation teaching.
5. A logical consequence of this state of affairs is that there is a dearth of studies that apply Spanish SLA research findings to the teaching of translation. However, given the size of the Spanish translation market in the United States, it is reasonable to assert that Spanish SLA findings are the most pertinent to translation teaching.
6. Note that this could also be considered translation into the native language.
7. There seems to be near-consensus in the SLA field that contextualized language use is necessary for pragmatic acquisition.
8. Distinguished is the highest level of proficiency for the areas of Reading and Listening.
9. Among the reasons for this are the exclusion of professional, nonliterary translation from higher education in countries like the United States, as well as the discredit of translation following its association with grammar translation in the language teaching context (see Colina 2002).
10. Bear in mind also the characteristics of the students interested in translation and interpretation in the United States compared to their European counterparts (immigrant community background, second language context heritage speakers, older, professional student body, etc.).
11. See, for instance, the master of arts degree in Spanish linguistics at Arizona State University (www.asu.edu/languages) or the SLATE doctoral program at the University of Arizona. Some of the graduates of the latter work in applied translation research.
12. For instance, the health interpreting and health applied linguistics (HIHAL) concentration in the master of public health (M.P.H.) degree offered by the University of North Texas.

13. For illustration puposes, see Translation Certificate Program at Arizona State University (www.asu.edu/clas/dll/spa/certrans.htm).

References

American Council on the Teaching of Foreign Languages (ACTFL). 1999. *ACTFL Proficiency Guidelines*. Hastings-on-Hudson, NY: American Council on the Teaching of Foreign Languages.

Ahlsvad, K. 1978. Translating into the translator's non-primary language. In *Translating, a profession: Proceedings of the Eighth World Congress of the International Federation of Translators*, ed. Paul A. Horguelin, 183–88. Ottawa: Conseil des traducteurs et interpretes du Canada.

Aitchison, J. 1996. Taming the wilderness: Words in the mental lexicon. In *Words, words, words: The translator and the language learner*, ed. G. M. Anderman and M. A. Rogers, 15–26. Clevedon, U.K.: Multilingual Matters.

Anderman, G. M. 1996. The word in my oyster: The language learner and the translator. In Anderman and Rogers, *Words, words, words*. 41–55.

Anderman, G. M., and M. A. Rogers. 1996. *Words, words, words: The translator and the language learner*. Clevedon, U.K.: Multilingual Matters.

Angelelli, C. 2000. Interpretation pedagogy: A bridge long overdue. *ATA Chronicle* 29 (11): 40–47.

Angelelli, C., and C. Degueldre. 2002. Bridging the gap between language for general purposes and language for work: An intensive Superior-level language/skill course for teachers, translators, and interpreters. In *Developing language proficiency at the professional level*, ed. B. Leaver and B. Shekhtman, 77–95. Cambridge: Cambridge University Press.

Angelelli, C., and O. Kagan. 2002. Heritage speakers as learners at the Superior level: Differences and similarities between Spanish and Russian student populations. In *Developing language proficiency at the professional level*, ed. B. Leaver and B. Shekhtman, 197–218. Cambridge: Cambridge University Press.

Bachman, L. F. 1991. *Fundamental considerations in language testing*. New York: Oxford University Press.

Blum-Kulka, S. 1986. Shifts of cohesion and coherence in translation. In *Interlingual and intercultural communication*, ed. J. House and S. Blum-Kulka, 7–35. Tübingen: Narr.

Campbell, S. 1998. *Translation into the second language*. London: Longman.

Canale, M., and M. Swain. 1980. Theoretical basis of communicative approaches to second language teaching and testing. *Applied Linguistics* 1 (1): 1–47.

Cao, D. 1996. A model of translation proficiency. *Target* 8 (2): 341–64.

Carroll, J. B. 1980. *Testing communicative performance*. London: Pergamon.

Clyne, M., S. Fernández, I. Chen, and R. Summo-O'Connell. 1997. Background speakers: Diversity and its management in LOTE programs. Belconnen: Language Australia.

Cohen, A. 1984. Studying second-language learning strategies: How do we get the information. *Applied Linguistics* 5:101–12.

Cohen, A., and C. Hosenfeld. 1981. Some uses of mentalistic data in second language research. *Language Learning* 31:285–313.

Colina, S. 1997. Contrastive rhetoric and text-typological conventions in translation teaching. *Target* 9 (2): 353–71.

———. 1999. Transfer and unwarranted yranscoding in the acquisition of translational competence: An empirical investigation. In *Translation and the (re)location of meaning: Selected Papers of the CERA Research Seminars in Translation Studies*, ed. J. Vandaele, 375–91. Leuven: CERA

———. 2002. Second language acquisition, language teaching and translation studies. *Translator* 8 (1): 1–24.

————. 2003a. *Translation teaching from research to the classroom: A handbook for teachers.* New York: McGraw-Hill.

————. 2003b. Towards an empirically-based translation pedagogy. In *Beyond the ivory tower: Rethinking translation pedagogy,* ed. B. Baer, G. Koby, F. Arango Keeth, and S. Bell, 29–59. American Translators Association Monograph Series, vol. 12. Amsterdam: Benjamins.

————. 2003c. Teaching translation: A pedagogy workshop for translators. Workshop presented at the 44th Annual Meeting of the American Translators Association. Phoenix, November.

————. 2004a. "*Make or Buy*" decision-making. Workshop presented at the *Hablamos Juntos* Grantee Meeting, Spanish Materials Development. Fort Worth, Texas, January.

————. 2004b. Issues in translation pedagogy. Paper presented at the conference of the American Translation Studies Association. Amherst, MA, April.

————. 2005. Review of *En otras palabras: Perfeccionamiento del español por medio de la traducción,* by P. Lunn and E. Lunsford. *Modern Language Journal* 89:307–8.

Colina, S., and J. Sykes. 2004. Parental education in the Spanish-speaking community: A look at LEP guidelines and translated educational materials. *Bilingual Research Journal* 28 (3): 299–317.

Dueñas-González, R. 2004. The Arizona initiative to improve Latino access and academic success. Tucson, AZ: NCITRP.

Dussias, P. E. 2003. Cognitive perspectives on the acquisition of Spanish as a second language. In *Spanish second language acquisition: State of the science,* ed. B. Lafford and R. Salaberry, 233–61. Washington, DC: Georgetown University Press.

Fawcett, P. 1998. Presupposition and translation. In *The pragmatics of translation,* ed. L. Hickey, 114–23. Clevedon, U.K.: Multilingual Matters.

Fillmore, C. 1976. Frame semantics and the nature of language. In *Origins and evolution of language and speech,* ed. J. Harnard, H. Steklis, and J. Lancaster, 20–32. New York: Annals of the New York Academy of Sciences.

————. 1977. Scenes and frames-semantics. In *Linguistic structure processing,* ed. A. Zampolli, 55–88. Amsterdam: North Holland.

Flower, L., and J. R. Hayes. 1981. A cognitive process theory of writing. *College Composition and Communication* 32:365–87.

Gerloff, P. 1986. Second language learner's reports on the interpretive process: Talk aloud protocols of translation. In *Interlingual and intercultural communication,* ed. J. House and S. Blum-Kulka, 243–62. Tübingen: Narr.

Grove, Ch. 2003. The role of instruction in Spanish second language acquisition. In *Spanish second language acquisition: State of the science,* ed. B. Lafford and R. Salaberry, 287–319. Washington, DC: Georgetown University Press.

Hatim, B. 1997. *The translator as communicator.* London: Routledge.

Hervey, S. 1998. Speech acts and illocutionary function in translation. In *The pragmatics of translation,* ed. L. Hickey, 10–24. Clevedon, U.K.: Multilingual Matters.

House, J. 1998. Politeness and translation. In *The pragmatics of translation,* ed. L. Hickey, 54–71. Clevedon, U.K.: Multilingual Matters.

Jääskeläinen, R. 1989. Translation assignment in professional vs. non-professional translation: A think-aloud protocol study. In *The translation process,* ed. C. Séguinot, 87–98. Toronto: H. G. Publications, School of Translation, York University.

————. 1990. Features of successful translation processes: A think-aloud protocol study. Licentiate thesis, University of Joensuu, Savolinna School of Translation Studies.

————. 1993. Investigating translation strategies. In *Recent trends in empirical translation research,* ed. S. Tirkkonnen-Condit and J. Laffling, 99–120. Joensuu: University of Joensuu, Faculty of Arts.

———. 1996. Hard work will bear beautiful fruit. *Meta* 41 (1): 45–59.

———. 2002. Think-aloud protocol studies into translation: An annotated bibliography. *Target* 14 (1): 107–36

Jääskeläinen, R. and S. Tirkkonen-Condit 1991. Automatised processes in professional vs. non-professional translation: A think-aloud protocol study. In *Empirical research in translation and intercultural studies,* Tirkkonen-Condit, S., ed.. Tübingen: Gunter Narr. 89–109.

James, C. 1988. Perspectives on transfer and translation. *Linguist* 27 (1): 45–49.

Johnson, M. 2004. *A philosophy of second language acquisition.* New Haven: Yale University Press.

Johnson, P. 1981. Effects of reading comprehension of Language complexity and cultural background. *TESOL Quarterly* 15:169–81.

Kiraly, D. 1990. A role for communicative competence and the acquisition-learning distinction in translator training. In *Second language acquisition/Foreign language learning,* ed. B. VanPatten and J. Lee, 207–15. Clevedon, U.K..: Multilingual Matters.

———. 1995. *Pathways to translation.* Kent, OH: Kent State University Press.

———. 2000. *A social constructivist approach to translator education.* Manchester: St. Jerome.

Koike, D. 1996. Transfer of pragmatic competence and suggestions in Spanish foreign language learning. In *Speech acts across cultures,* ed. S. Gass and J. Neu, 257–81. Berlin: Mouton de Gruyter.

Königs, F. 1987. Was beim Übersetzern passiert: Theoretische Aspekte, empirische Befunde und praktische Konsequenzen. *Die Neueren Sprachen* 86 (2): 182–85.

Kramsch, C. 1982. *Discourse analysis and second language teaching.* Washington, DC: Center for Applied Linguistics.

Krings, H. 1986a. Translation problems and translation strategies of advanced German learners of French. In *Interlingual and intercultural communication,* ed. J. House and S. Blum-Kulka, 263–76. Tübingen: Narr.

———. 1986b. *Was in den Köpfen von Übersetzern vorgeht: Eine empirische Untersuchung zur Struktur des Übersetzungsprozesses an fortgeschrittenen Französischelernern.* Tübingen: Narr.

———. 1987. Der Übersetzungprozeb bei Berufsübersetzern—Eine Fallstudie. In *Textlinguistik und Fachsprache: Akten des Internationalen übersetzungwissenschaftlichen AILA-Symposiums,* ed. R. Arnts, 396–412. Hildesheim: Olms.

Kussmaul, P. 1995. *Training the translator.* Amsterdam: John Benjamins.

Lantolf, J. P., ed. 2000. *Sociocultural theory and second language learning.* Oxford: Oxford University Press.

Lee, J. 1987. The Spanish subjunctive: An information-processing perspective. *Modern Language Journal* 71:50–57.

Liskin-Gasparro, J. 1982. *ETS oral proficiency testing manual.* Princeton, NJ: Educational Testing Service.

Lörscher, W. 1986. Linguistic aspects of translation processes: Towards an analysis of translation performance. In *Interlingual and intercultural communication,* ed. J. House and S. Blum-Kulka, 277–92. Tübingen: Narr.

———. 1991. *Translation performance, translation process, and translation strategies: A psycholinguistic investigation.* Tübingen: Narr.

———. 1992. Process-oriented research into translation and implications for translation teaching. *Traduction, terminologie, redaction (TTR)* 5:145–61.

———. 1997. A process-analytical approach to translation and implications for translation teaching. *Ilha do Desterro* 33:69–85.

Lunn, P., and E. Lunsford. 2003. *En otras palabras: Perfeccionamiento del español por medio de la traducción.* Washington, DC: Georgetown University Press.

Mackenzie, R. 1998. The place of language teaching in a quality-oriented translator's training programme. In *Translation and language teaching: Language teaching and translation,* ed. K. Malmkjaer, 15–19. Manchester: St. Jerome.

Marmaramidou, S. 1996. Directionality in translation processes and practices. *Target* 8 (1): 49–73.

Meara, P. 1996. The classical research in L2 vocabulary acquisition. In Anderman and Rogers, *Words, words, words: The translator and the language learner,* ed. G. M. Anderman and M. A. Rogers, 27–40. Clevedon, U.K.: Multilingual Matters.

Nord, C. 1997. *Translating as a purposeful activity: Functionalist approaches explained.* Manchester: St. Jerome.

Odlin, T. 1989. *Language transfer: Cross-linguistics influence in language learning.* Cambridge: Cambridge University Press.

Rose, K., and G. Kasper. 2001. *Pragmatics and language teaching.* Cambridge: Cambridge University Press.

Rumelhart, D. 1977. Toward an interactive model of reading. In *Attention and performance,* ed. S. Dornic, 573–603. New York: Academic Press.

———. 1980. Schemata: The building blocks of cognition. In *Theoretical issues in reading comprehension,* ed. R. Spiro, B. Bruce, and W. Brewer, 33–35. Hillsdale, NJ: Lawrence Erlbaum Associates.

Savignon, S. 1972. *Communicative competence: An experiment in foreign language teaching.* Philadelphia: Center for Curriculum Development.

———. 1983. *Communicative competence: Theory and classroom practice.* Reading, MA: Addison-Wesley.

Schäffner, C. 2002. *The role of discourse analysis for translation and in translator training.* Clevedon, UK: Multilingual Matters.

Shreve, G. M. 1997. Cognition and the evolution of translation competence. In *Cognitive Processes in Translation and Interpreting,* ed. J. Danks, G. M. Shreve, S. B. Fountain, and M. K. McBeath, 120–36. Thousand Oaks, CA: Sage.

Tirkkonen-Condit, S. 1986. Text type markers and translation equivalence. In *Interlingual and intercultural communication,* ed. J. House and S. Blum-Kulka, 95–113. Tübingen: Narr.

Tobin, Y. 1986. Discourse variation in the use of selected "contrastive conjunctions" in Modern Hebrew: Theoretical hypotheses and practical applications with regard to translation. In *Interlingual and intercultural communication,* ed. J. House and S. Blum-Kulka, 61–67. Tübingen: Narr.

Toury, G. 1980. *In search of a theory of translation.* Tel Aviv: Porter Institute for Poetics and Semiotics, Tel Aviv University.

———. 1986. Monitoring discourse transfer: A test case for a developmental model of translation. In *Interlingual and intercultural communication,* ed. J. House and S. Blum-Kulka, 79–94. Tübingen: Narr.

———. 1995. *Descriptive translation studies.* Amsterdam: John Benjamins.

van den Broeck, R. 1986. Contrastive discourse analysis as a tool for the interpretation of shifts in translated texts. In *Interlingual and intercultural communication,* ed. J. House and S. Blum-Kulka, 36–47. Tübingen: Narr.

Vygotsky, L. S. 1986. *Thought and language.* Cambridge, MA: MIT Press. Translation of *Myshlenie i rech* (1934) by Alex Kozulin.

———. 1978. *Mind in society: The development of higher psychological processes.* Cambridge: Harvard University Press.

Weizman, E. 1986. An interlingual study of discourse structures: Implications for the theory of translation. In *Interlingual and intercultural communication,* ed. J. House and S. Blum-Kulka, 115–26. Tübingen: Narr.

Wetherby, J. 1998. Teaching translation into L2. In *Translation and language teaching: Language teaching and translation,* ed. K. Malmkjaer, 21–38. Manchester: St. Jerome.

CONTRIBUTORS

Gwendolyn Barnes-Karol (Ph.D., University of Minnesota) is professor of Spanish at St. Olaf College, where she teaches language, literature, and culture as well as courses through St. Olaf's FLAC program. Her recent research in the *ADFL Bulletin* focuses on the curricular and pedagogical implications of how undergraduate readers process book-length literary texts in a foreign language.

Robert Blake (Ph.D., University of Texas at Austin), professor of Spanish at the University of California at Davis and director of the UC Language Consortium, publishes in Spanish linguistics, SLA, and CALL. He has helped author software such as *Nuevos Destinos, Tesoros,* Spanish Without Walls, and Arabic Without Walls. He was recently inducted into the North American Academy for the Spanish Language.

Andrew D. Cohen (Ph.D., Stanford University) is professor of applied linguistics at the University of Minnesota. He has published books and articles on language assessment, learner strategies, pragmatics, and research methods. He is currently coediting *Language Learner Strategies: Thirty Years of Research and Practice* (Oxford University Press).

Sonia Colina (Ph.D., University of Illinois) is associate professor of Spanish linguistics and translation at University of Arizona, where she also directs the Spanish Translation Certificate Program. Her research areas include translation pedagogy and linguistic aspects of translation. She is the author of *Translation Teaching: From Research to the Classroom* (McGraw-Hill, 2003) and of studies in numerous publications, including *Target,* the *Translator,* and *Babel.*

Joseph Collentine (Ph.D., University of Texas at Austin) is associate professor of Spanish and associate dean in the College of Arts and Letters at Northern Arizona University. His research interests include the acquisition of the subjunctive by classroom based learners, developmental issues related to study abroad, and computer-assisted language learning. He is currently the associate editor for applied linguistics for the journal *Hispania.*

Ann Marie Delforge is a doctoral candidate in Spanish linguistics at the University of California at Davis. Her primary research areas are Spanish phonology and phonetics, but she is also very interested in the use of technology in foreign language teaching.

Marta Fairclough (Ph.D., University of Houston) is assistant professor of Spanish linguistics and director of Spanish Undergraduate Studies at the University of Houston. She specializes in heritage language education, language acquisition, and sociolinguistics with an emphasis on U.S. Spanish. She is the author of *Spanish and Heritage Language Education in the United States: Struggling with Hypotheticals* (Iberoamericana, 2005).

Manuel J. Gutiérrez (Ph.D., University of Southern California) is associate professor of Spanish linguistics at the University of Houston. He has conducted research on phenomena of linguistic change in several Spanish dialects and published articles about the subject in numerous journals in the United States, Europe, and Latin America, as well as the book *"Ser" y "estar" en el habla de Michoacán, México* (UNAM, 1994).

Carol A. Klee (Ph.D., University of Texas at Austin) is associate professor of Hispanic linguistics at the University of Minnesota. Her research interests include Spanish sociolinguistics and second language acquisition. She is coauthor of *Lingüística aplicada: La adquisición del español como segunda lengua* (2003) and has published articles on Spanish-Quechua language contact, Spanish in the United States, and second language acquisition.

Barbara Lafford (Ph.D., Cornell University) is professor of Spanish linguistics at Arizona State University. Her research areas include second language acquisition, applied linguistics, sociolinguistics, and the use of technology in foreign language teaching. She has served as the associate editor for applied linguistics for the journal *Hispania* (1996–2002) and is currently the editor of the Monograph/Focus Volume Series of the *Modern Language Journal.*

James P. Lantolf (Ph.D., Pennsylvania State University) is Greer Professor in Language Acquisition, director of the Center for Language Acquisition, and codirector of CALPER at Penn State. He is past president of AAAL and was coeditor of *Applied Linguistics.* His research focuses on sociocultural theory and L2 learning. He recently coauthored (with Steve Thorne) *Sociocultural Theory and the Genesis of Second Language Development* (Oxford University Press, 2006).

Michael Leeser (Ph.D., University of Illinois at Urbana-Champaign) is assistant professor of Spanish and director of the Spanish Basic Language Program at Florida State University. His research interests include input processing during second language reading, classroom interaction, and computer-assisted language learning. His research has appeared in journals such as *Studies in Second Language Acquisition* and *Language Teaching Research.*

Eduardo Negueruela (Ph.D., Pennsylvania State University) is assistant professor of Spanish and applied linguistics at the University of Miami. His research areas include second language pedagogy, Vygotsky's theory of mind and second language learning, gesture and second language communication, and technology-enhanced language learning. His research agenda is grounded on developing a language pedagogy based on concepts as tools of the mind.

Rafael Salaberry (Ph.D., Cornell University) is professor of Spanish linguistics and second language acquisition and director of the language program at the University of Texas at Austin. His main area of research is the development of the semantics and pragmatics of tense and aspect. He coauthored (with Dalila Ayoun) *Tense and Aspect in the Romance Languages* (John Benjamins, 2005). Another area of research is second language teaching, about which he has published articles in journals such as *Applied Linguistics*, the *Modern Language Journal*, and *Language Testing*.

Guadalupe Valdés (Ph.D., Florida State University) is the Bonnie Katz Tenenbaum Professor of Education and professor of Spanish and Portuguese at Stanford University. Much of her work has focused on the English-Spanish bilingualism of Latinos in the United States. Her recent books include *Learning and Not Learning English* (Teachers College Press, 2001) and *Expanding Definitions of Giftedness: Young Interpreters of Immigrant Background* (Lawrence Erlbaum Associates, 2003).

Bill VanPatten (Ph.D., University of Texas at Austin) is professor of Spanish and second language acquisition at University of Illinois at Chicago. He has published widely in the field of second language acquisition but is perhaps best known for his work on input processing, processing instruction, and instructed second language acquisition.

INDEX